Black Women
in America

MACMILLAN
PROFILES

Black Women in America

MACMILLAN LIBRARY REFERENCE USA
New York

RAP 4/1/1953

Macmillan Library Reference USA
1633 Broadway
New York, New York 10019

Manufactured in the United States of America

Printing number
1 2 3 4 5 6 7 8 9 10

Cover design by Berrian Design

Library of Congress Cataloging-in-Publication Data

Black women in America.
      p.   cm. — (Macmillan profiles)
    Includes bibliographical references (p.   ) and index.
    ISBN 0-02-865363-7 (hc. : alk. paper)
    1. Afro-American women—Biography—Dictionaries.   I. Series.
E185.96.B539   1999
920.72'08996073—dc21   98-56447
                                                                          CIP

Front cover clockwise from top: Sojourner Truth (© Corbis-Bettmann);
Billie Holiday (©Bradley Smith / Corbis); Coretta Scott King (©UPI /
Corbis-Bettmann); Florence Griffith-Joyner (©Neal Preston / Corbis)

This paper meets the requirements of ANSI/NISO A39.48-1992
(Permanence of Paper)

Contents

Preface .xi

Alexander, Sadie Tanner Mossell 1
Allen, Debbie 2
Anderson, Marian 4
Angelou, Maya .6
    AFRICAN-AMERICAN AUTOBIOGRAPHY 8
Armstrong, Lillian Hardin "Lil" 9
Ashford, Evelyn .11

Bailey, Pearl .13
Baker, Ella J. 14
Baker, Josephine 18
Bambara, Toni Cade 20
Banks, Tyra .21
Bassett, Angela .23
Battle, Kathleen 25
Belton, Sharon Sayles 27
Berry, Halle 29
Bethune, Mary McLeod 31
    BETHUNE-COOKMAN COLLEGE 32
Blackwell, Unita 34
Bolin, Jane Mathilda 35
Brooks, Gwendolyn Elizabeth 36
    BLACK SCHOLAR 37
Brown, Charlotte Hawkins 39
Browne, Marjorie Lee 41
Burke, Yvonne Brathwaite 43
Burroughs, Nannie Helen 44
Butler, Octavia Estelle 46

Carroll, Diahann 48
Cary, Mary Ann Shadd 49
Catlett, Elizabeth 51
    HOWARD UNIVERSITY 51
Celia 53
Chase-Riboud, Barbara Dewayne 54
Chideya, Farai .56

Childress, Alice 57
    AMERICAN NEGRO THEATRE 58
Chisholm, Shirley 59
Clark, Septima Poinsette 60
    AVERY NORMAL INSTITUTE 61
Cole, Rebecca J. 63
Coleman, Bessie 64
Cooper, Anna Julia Haywood 65
Craft, Ellen 67
Currie, Betty 69

Dandridge, Dorothy 72
Dash, Julie 74
Davis, Angela Yvonne 75
Dawes, Dominique 76
De Passe, Suzanne 78
Dee, Ruby 80
Dickens, Helen Octavia 81
Dove, Rita 82
Dunbar-Nelson, Alice 84
Dunham, Katherine .86

Edelman, Marian Wright 92
Elders, M. Joycelyn Jones 93

Fauset, Crystal Dreda Bird 95
Fitzgerald, Ella 96
Flack, Roberta 98
Franklin, Aretha Louise 99
Fuller, Meta Vaux Warrick 100

Garrison, Zina 104
Gibson, Althea 105
Giovanni, Yolanda Cornelia "Nikki" 107
Goldberg, Whoopi 109
Granville, Evelyn Boyd 110
Griffith-Joyner, Florence Delorez 111
Grimké, Angelina Weld 113
Grimké, Charlotte L. Forten 114
Guinier, Lani 115

Hamer, Fannie Lou (Townsend, Fannie Lou) 118
Hansberry, Lorraine .121

Harper, Frances Ellen Watkins 122
Harris, Barbara Clementine 124
Harris, Patricia Roberts 126
    THE DEPARTMENT OF HOUSING AND
    URBAN DEVELOPMENT 126
Height, Dorothy 128
    NATIONAL COUNCIL OF NEGRO WOMEN 129
Hill, Anita 130
Holiday, Billie 134
Horn, Rosa Artimus 135
Horne, Lena 137
Houston, Whitney 138
Hunter, Clementine Clemence Rubin 140
Hunter-Gault, Charlayne 142
Hurston, Zora Neale 142
    BLACK ENGLISH VERNACULAR 145

Jackson, Janet 147
Jackson, Mahalia 149
Jackson, Rebecca Cox 151
Jackson, Shirley Ann 152
Jacobs, Harriet Ann 153
James, Etta 156
Jamison, Judith 157
Jemison, Mae Carol 159
Jordan, Barbara Charline 161
    SPINGARN MEDAL 162
Jordan, June 163
Joyner-Kersee, Jacqueline 165

Kearse, Amalya Lyle 168
Keckley, Elizabeth 169
Kelly, Sharon Pratt 170
Kincaid, Jamaica 172
King, Coretta Scott 173
Kitt, Eartha Mae 176
Knight, Gladys 177

LaBelle, Patti (Holt, Patricia Louise) 180
Lampkin, Daisy Elizabeth Adams 181
Lee, Rebecca 183
Lewis, Edmonia 183
    THE REDISCOVERY OF *THE DEATH OF CLEOPATRA* . . .184

Lloyd, Ruth Smith 186
Logan, Myra Adele 187
Lorde, Audre Geraldine .188

Mabley, Jackie "Moms" .190
Mahoney, Mary Eliza 191
Malone, Annie Turnbo 192
Marshall, Paule 193
Mason, Biddy Bridget 196
Matthews, Victoria Earle (Smith) 197
McDaniel, Hattie 199
    THE "MAMMY" STEREOTYPE 201
McMillan, Terry 202
McQueen, Thelma "Butterfly" 204
McRae, Carmen 205
Morrison, Toni 206
    TONI MORRISON'S NOBEL PRIZE 207
Moseley-Braun, Carol 209
Motley, Constance Baker 212

Nash, Diane Bevel 214
Naylor, Gloria 215
Norman, Jessye 217
Norton, Eleanor Holmes 218

O'Leary, Hazel Rollins 221
Osborne, Estelle 222

Parks, Rosa Louise McCauley 224
Plato, Ann 226
Price, Mary Violet Leontyne 227

Rainey, Gertrude Pridgett "Ma" 230
Ray, Charlotte E. 231
Remond, Sarah Parker 232
Ringgold, Faith 233
Rolle, Esther 234
Ross, Diana 236
    THE SUPREMES 236
Rudolph, Wilma Glodean 238

Saar, Betye Irene 241
Sanchez, Sonia 243

Savage, Augusta Christine Fells 244
Shange, Ntozake 247
Simone, Nina (Waymon, Eunice Kathleen) 249
Simpson, Coreen 250
Simpson, Lorna 251
Smith, Bessie 253
Smith, Mamie 255
Spencer, Anne (Scales, Annie Bethel) 257
Stewart, Pearl 258
Swoopes, Sheryl 259

Taylor, Susie Baker King .262
Terrell, Mary Eliza Church 263
    NATIONAL ASSOCIATION OF
    COLORED WOMEN'S CLUBS 264
Tharpe, Sister Rosetta 266
Thomas, Alma 267
Thomas, Debra J. "Debi" .268
Thornton, Willie Mae "Big Mama" 269
Truth, Sojourner 270
Tubman, Harriet Ross 274
Turner, Tina 277
Tyson, Cicely 279

Vaughan, Sarah 281
Verrett, Shirley 282

Walker, A'Lelia 284
Walker, Alice 285
Walker, Madame C. J. 287
Walker, Maggie Lena 289
Walker, Margaret 291
Warwick, Dionne 292
Washington, Dinah (Jones, Ruth Lee) 293
Washington, Margaret Murray 294
Waters, Ethel 296
    BLACK SWAN RECORDS .297
Waters, Maxine Moore 298
    CONGRESSIONAL BLACK CAUCUS 299
Wattleton, Faye 300
Weems, Carrie Mae 301
Wells-Barnett, Ida Bell 303
West, Dorothy 307

Wheatley, Phillis 309
Williams, Mary Lou (Scruggs, Mary Elfrieda) 312
Williams, Venus 314
Wilson, Harriet E. Adams 316
Winfrey, Oprah Gail 318
Wright, Jane Cooke 321

Young, Roger Arliner 322

Time Line: The Accomplishments of Black Women
  in the Context of African-American History 325
Article Sources 337
Photo Credits 343
Suggested Reading 345
Glossary 365
Index 375

Preface

Macmillan Profiles: *Black Women in America* is a unique reference featuring 176 profiles of notable African-American women from the eighteenth century to the present. Macmillan Library Reference recognizes the need for reliable, accurate, and accessible biographies of notable figures in American history. The Macmillan Profiles series can help meet that need by providing new collections of biographies that were carefully selected from distinguished Macmillan sources. Macmillan Library Reference has published a wide array of award-winning reference materials for libraries across the world. It is likely that several of the encyclopedias on the shelves in this library were published by Macmillan Reference or Charles Scribner's Sons. All biographies in Macmillan Profiles have been recast and tailored for a younger audience by a team of experienced writers and editors. In some cases, new biographies were commissioned to supplement entries from original sources.

The goal of *Black Women in America* is to present an inspiring introduction to the life and times of woman artists, scientists, journalists, businesswomen, politicians, social activists, educators, and athletes of African-American heritage. The women described in this volume can provide role models for intelligent and ambitious young readers as they look toward their own future. The article list was based on the following criteria: relevance to the curriculum, importance to history, name recognition for students, and representation of as broad a cultural range as possible. The article list was refined and expanded in response to advice from a lively and generous team of librarians from high schools and public schools across the United States. The result is a balanced, curriculum-related work that brings these historical figures to life.

FEATURES

Black Women in America is part of Macmillan's **Profiles Series.** To add visual appeal and enhance the usefulness of the volume, the page format was designed to include the following helpful features:

- Time Lines: Found throughout the text in the margins, time lines provide a quick reference source for dates and important events in the life and times of these important women.

- Notable Quotations: Found throughout the text in the margins, these thought-provoking quotations are drawn from interviews, speeches, and writings of the person covered in the article. Such quotations give readers a special insight into the distinctive personalities of these great women.

- Definitions and Glossary: Brief definitions of important terms in the main text can be found in the margin. A glossary at the end of the book provides students with an even broader list of definitions.

- Sidebars: Appearing in shaded boxes throughout the volume, these provocative asides relate to and amplify topics.

- Pull Quotes: Found throughout the text in the margin, pull quotes highlight essential facts.

- Suggested Reading: An extensive list of books and articles about the women covered in the volume will help students who want to do further research.

- Index: A thorough index provides thousands of additional points of entry into the work.

ACKNOWLEDGMENTS

We thank our colleagues who publish the Merriam Webster's Collegiate Dictionary. Definitions used in the margins and many of the glossary terms come from the distinguished Webster's Collegiate Dictionary, Tenth Edition, 1996.

The biographies herein were written by leading authorities at work in the field of African-American history. *Black Women in America* contains over 75 photographs. Acknowledgments of sources for the illustrations can be found on page 343.

We are also grateful for the contributions of the following inimitable team of librarians who helped compile the article list. Their knowledge of school curriculum and reader interest were invaluable in shaping a volume of optimum usefulness to middle and high school students.

Rosalie Daniels, Mann Magnet Junior High, Little Rock, Arkansas
Dennis Donnelly, Hoover High School, San Diego, California
Bernice Fortini, Resurrection High School, Chicago, Illinois
Kathy Labertew, Clairemon High School, San Diego, California
Dottie Renfro, Madison Middle School Library, Richmond, Kentucky
Merrill Stegal, Whitney Young High School, Chicago, Illinois

This work would not have been possible without the hard work and creativity of our staff. We offer our sincere thanks to all who helped create this marvelous work.

Macmillan Library Reference

Alexander, Sadie Tanner Mossell

JANUARY 2, 1898 – NOVEMBER 1, 1989 ● LAWYER AND ACTIVIST

Sadie T. M. Alexander was a pioneer among African-American women in law and education and a committed civil rights activist. She was born Sadie Tanner Mossell in Philadelphia, to an accomplished family: Bishop Benjamin Tucker Tanner, among the most prominent of nineteenth-century black clergymen, was her grandfather, and the painter Henry Ossawa Tanner was her uncle. Educated in Philadelphia and in Washington, D.C., she graduated from the M Street High School (now Dunbar High School) in Washington. She entered the University of Pennsylvania's School of Education in 1915, receiving a B.S. in education with honors in 1918. (That year, she helped found the Gamma Chapter of the Delta Theta Sorority.) She earned an M.A. (1919) and a Ph.D. in economics (1921) from the University of Pennsylvania, and was one of the first two African-American women to earn a Ph.D. in the United States and the first African American to receive a doctorate in economics.

From 1921 to 1923, Alexander was an assistant **actuary** for the North Carolina Mutual Life Insurance Company, a black-owned company in Durham, North Carolina. On November 29, 1923, she married Raymond Pace Alexander, a graduate of Harvard Law School, who thereafter worked with his wife in numerous Philadelphia-area civil rights cases. Sadie Alexander continued to be a trailblazer for African-American women in the fields of law and education: she entered the University of

actuary: a person who calculates insurance risks, rates, and premiums.

1

1898 Mossell is born in Philadelphia.

1921 Mossell receives Ph.D. in economics from University of Pennsylvania.

1927 Mossell graduates from University of Pennsylvania Law School.

1943 Mossell is elected secretary of National Bar Association.

1946 Mossell is appointed to President's Commission on Civil Rights.

1948 Mossell helps prepare presidential commission report "To Secure These Rights."

1989 Mossell dies in Philadelphia.

Pennsylvania Law School in 1924 (where her father, Aaron Albert Mossell, had graduated in 1888, becoming the first African American to graduate from the law school), worked on the Law Review, and was admitted to the Pennsylvania bar after graduating in 1927. During the late 1920s and 1930s she served as the assistant city solicitor of Philadelphia and as a partner in her husband's law firm. In November 1943 Alexander became the first woman to be elected secretary (or to hold any office) in the National Bar Association, a position she held until 1947.

In addition to her personal achievements and triumphs in overcoming racial barriers, for over half a century Sadie Alexander was at the forefront of the movement for civil rights for African Americans. In the 1920s and 1930s she and her husband successfully challenged discrimination in public accommodations in Pennsylvania. She also worked to integrate the University of Pennsylvania and the U.S. Armed Forces. On December 5, 1946, President Harry S Truman appointed her to the President's Commission on Civil Rights. She helped prepare its report "To Secure These Rights" (1948), which was influential in the formulation of civil rights policy in the years that followed.

Alexander worked with her husband until 1959, when he was appointed judge in the Philadelphia Court of Common Pleas and she began her own law practice. In 1976 she joined the law firm of Atkinson, Myers, Archie & Wallace as counsel, advising the firm on a part-time basis in estate and family law. Alzheimer's disease forced her retirement in 1982. She died in Philadelphia seven years later. ◆

Allen, Debbie

JANUARY 16, 1950 – ● DANCER AND TELEVISION PRODUCER

> *"I pounded pavements and went to every audition. That was my spirit."*
>
> Debbie Allen

Debbie Allen was born in Houston, Texas, where her father, Andrew Allen, was a dentist and her mother, Vivian Ayers Allen, was a Pulitzer Prize-nominated writer. Her sister, Phylicia Rashad, became well known for her role as Claire Huxtable on the television series *The Cosby Show*.

As a child, Allen tried to take ballet classes at the Houston Foundation for Ballet, but she was rejected for reasons her mother thought were discriminatory. Allen began learning dance by studying privately with a former dancer from the Ballet Russes and later by moving with her family to Mexico City where she danced with the Ballet Nacional de Mexico. Allen reauditioned for the Houston Foundation for Ballet in 1964, and this time was admitted on a full scholarship and became the company's first black dancer.

After high school, Allen hoped to attend the North Carolina School of Arts, but when she was rejected she decided to pursue a B.A. at Howard University (1971) with a concentration in classical Greek literature, speech, and theater. During her college years, she continued to dance with students at the university and with choreographer Michael Malone's dance troupe. After graduating in 1971, Allen relocated to New York City where she would develop her talents as a dancer, actress, and singer in her appearances on Broadway, and eventually in television shows and movies.

Allen's Broadway experience began in 1971 when she became a member of the chorus in *Purlie*, the musical version of Ossie Davis's *Purlie Victorious*. The following year, when chorus member George Faison left the show to form the Universal Dance Experience, Allen became his principal dancer and assistant. In 1973 Allen had returned to Broadway and for two years she played the role of Beneatha Younger in *Raisin*, a musical adaptation of Lorraine Hansberry's *A Raisin in the Sun*.

Allen began receiving critical attention in 1980, when she appeared in the role of Anita in the Broadway revival of *West Side Story*, which earned her a Tony Award nomination and a Drama Desk Award. The next year she made her movie debut in the film version of E. L. Doctorow's novel *Ragtime*, and then appeared in the hit movie *Fame*, with a small part as the dance teacher Lydia Grant. When the movie was turned into a television series of the same name, Allen returned as Lydia Grant and developed the role that brought her recognition by international audiences. She remained on the show until it went off the air in 1987, serving as a choreographer, and eventually as a director and producer.

During the 1980s Allen also acted in the television movie *Women of San Quentin* (1983), appeared in Richard Pryor's movie *Jo Jo Dancer, Your Life Is Calling* (1985), and played Charity in the Broadway revival of *Sweet Charity* (1986). In 1988 she became director of *A Different World*, and helped turn it into a Top Twenty television hit. The next year Allen hosted her first

1950 Allen is born in Houston.

1964 Allen becomes the first black dancer with the Houston Foundation for Ballet.

1971 Allen graduates from Howard University; moves to New York City.

1973 Allen begins two-year stint in the cast of *Raisin* on Broadway.

1980 Allen appears as Anita in the Broadway revival of *West Side Story*.

1981 Allen plays dance teacher Lydia Grant in the film *Fame*.

1986 Allen plays Charity in the Broadway revival of *Sweet Charity*.

1988 Allen becomes director of TV's *A Different World*.

1990 Allen directs her first episodes of *Fresh Prince of Bel Air*.

1991 Allen choreographs the Academy Award show for the first time.

television special on ABC, *The Debbie Allen Show*, and later that year she directed the television musical *Polly*, which was followed in 1990 by *Polly: One More Time*. During the 1990–91 season Allen directed episodes of NBC's *Fresh Prince of Bel Air* and *Quantum Leap*. Allen was a choreographer for the Academy Awards show from 1991 to 1994, and in 1992 she produced and directed the television movie *Stompin' at the Savoy*. ◆

Anderson, Marian

FEBRUARY 17, 1897– MAY 19, 1993   ● OPERA AND CONCERT SINGER

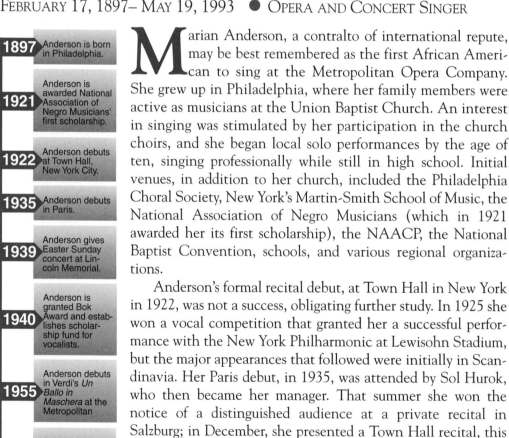

1897 Anderson is born in Philadelphia.

1921 Anderson is awarded National Association of Negro Musicians' first scholarship.

1922 Anderson debuts at Town Hall, New York City.

1935 Anderson debuts in Paris.

1939 Anderson gives Easter Sunday concert at Lincoln Memorial.

1940 Anderson is granted Bok Award and establishes scholarship fund for vocalists.

1955 Anderson debuts in Verdi's *Un Ballo in Maschera* at the Metropolitan

1958 Anderson is appointed to U.S. delegation to U.N.

1965 Anderson gives farewell recital at Carnegie Hall.

Marian Anderson, a contralto of international repute, may be best remembered as the first African American to sing at the Metropolitan Opera Company. She grew up in Philadelphia, where her family members were active as musicians at the Union Baptist Church. An interest in singing was stimulated by her participation in the church choirs, and she began local solo performances by the age of ten, singing professionally while still in high school. Initial venues, in addition to her church, included the Philadelphia Choral Society, New York's Martin-Smith School of Music, the National Association of Negro Musicians (which in 1921 awarded her its first scholarship), the NAACP, the National Baptist Convention, schools, and various regional organizations.

Anderson's formal recital debut, at Town Hall in New York in 1922, was not a success, obligating further study. In 1925 she won a vocal competition that granted her a successful performance with the New York Philharmonic at Lewisohn Stadium, but the major appearances that followed were initially in Scandinavia. Her Paris debut, in 1935, was attended by Sol Hurok, who then became her manager. That summer she won the notice of a distinguished audience at a private recital in Salzburg; in December, she presented a Town Hall recital, this one well received.

Anderson's international acclaim encouraged Howard University in 1939 to seek a recital for her in Washington, D.C. When she was denied access to Constitution Hall by the Daughters of the American Revolution, the public protest

Marian Anderson (at the piano) entertaining a group of soldiers and Women's Army Corps (WAC) members in San Antonio in 1945.

approached that of a scandal. Eleanor Roosevelt resigned her DAR membership and criticism came from opera singer Lawrence Tibbett, New York mayor Fiorello La Guardia, conductor Leopold Stokowski, and other major figures. Secretary of the Interior Harold Ickes granted Anderson use of the Lincoln Memorial for an Easter Sunday concert as an alternative. Seventy-five thousand people heard her program, which began in subtle irony with "My Country 'Tis of Thee" and ended with "Nobody Knows the Trouble I've Seen." The location for this performance was not forgotten nearly a quarter of a century later by the Rev. Dr. Martin Luther King Jr., who arranged for her to sing there again during the 1963 March on Washington.

Anderson's tour schedule intensified, and Metropolitan Opera manager Rudolph Bing determined that she would appear as Ulrica in Verdi's *Un Ballo in Maschera*. She sang the role eight times, starting on January 7, 1955, although she was no longer in her prime. (In 1958 RCA Victor issued a recording of highlights from the opera with Dimitri Mitropoulos conducting and Anderson in the role of Ulrica.) She retired from the stage at Carnegie Hall on Easter 1965, after presenting fifty-one farewell concerts across the country. Her repertory was centered on sacred **arias** by J. S. Bach and Handel, spirituals (especially Harry Burleigh's "Deep River"), **lieder** (Schubert's

"Everyone has a gift for something, even if it is the gift of being a good friend."
Marian Anderson, 1970

aria: a song for a single voice with instrumental accompaniment.

lieder: art songs.

bel canto: a style of operatic singing from 17th- and 18th-century Italy that displays the singer's vocal agility and technical skills.

"Ave Maria" was a favorite), and some opera arias—notably "O Mio Fernando" from Donizetti's *La Favorita*, in which she demonstrated that she could have excelled in **bel canto** roles, given the chance. When granted the Bok Award in 1940, Anderson established a scholarship fund for vocalists whose awards have been granted to McHenry Boatwright, Grace Bumbry, Gloria Davy, Reri Grist, Bonia Hyman, Louise Parker, Rawn Spearman, Camellia Williams, and others.

Her primary voice teacher was Giuseppe Boghetti, although she worked in London with Amanda Aldridge, a daughter of the actor Ira Aldridge. Early in her career, she was accompanied by minstrel pianist William King, then by Kosti Vehanen from Finland, and later by Franz Rupp of Germany. Anderson was appointed in 1958 to the U.S. delegation to the United Nations, where she spoke on behalf of the independence of African nations. Although she denied playing an overt role in the civil rights movement, Anderson's dignity and artistry brought about social change and opened the door for the many concert singers who followed her. In tribute on her seventy-fifth birthday in Carnegie Hall, Leontyne Price paid her respects succinctly: "Dear Marian Anderson, because of you, I am." ◆

Angelou, Maya

APRIL 4, 1928 – ● WRITER

"The ache for home lives in all of us, the safe place where we can go as we are and not be questioned."
Maya Angelou, *All God's Children Need Traveling Shoes*, 1986

Born Marguerite Annie Johnson on April 4, 1928, to Vivian Baxter and Bailey Johnson in St. Louis, Missouri, Angelou was raised in Stamps, Arkansas, by her grandmother, Anne Henderson. She related her experience of growing up in her popular autobiography *I Know Why the Caged Bird Sings* (1970), a title taken from the poetry of Paul Laurence Dunbar. It was nominated for a National Book Award. Like many African-American autobiographers, Angelou saw herself not only as an individual but as a representative of black people.

What *Caged Bird* contributed to the tradition of African-American autobiography was its emphasis on the effects of growing up black and female in the South. Angelou writes of the rape of the protagonist by her mother's boyfriend. Until recently, intragroup rape and incest were taboo subjects in

African-American literature; *Caged Bird* helped to break that silence. Her second autobiography, *Gather Together in My Name* (1974), a title taken from the Bible, focuses on the vulnerable Angelou's entry into the harsh urban world of Los Angeles, while her third autobiography, *Singin' & Swinging & Getting Merry Like Christmas* (1976), relates the experience of her first marriage and of raising her son while pursuing her singing, dancing, and acting career.

The fourth autobiography, *The Heart of a Woman* (1981), a title taken from a poem by Georgia Douglas Johnson, the Harlem Renaissance poet, presents a mature Angelou who works with the Rev. Dr. Martin Luther King Jr. and Malcolm X. Active in the Civil Rights Movement, she served as northern coordinator for the Southern Christian Leadership Conference in 1959–60. In her fifth autobiography, *All God's Children Need Traveling Shoes* (1986), Angelou goes to Ghana, where she experiences the complexity of being an African American in Africa. She has written two more works of autobiographical essays: *Wouldn't Take Nothing for My Journey Now* (1993) and *Even the Stars Look Lonesome* (1997).

Angelou has also published many volumes of poetry: *Just Give Me a Cool Drink of Water 'fore I Diie* (1971), which was nominated for a Pulitzer Prize; *Oh Pray My Wings Are Gonna Fit Me Well* (1975); *And Still I Rise* (1978); *Shaker Why Don't You*

1928 Angelou is born in St. Louis.

1970 *I Know Why the Caged Bird Sings* is published.

1971 Angelou is nominated for Pulitzer Prize.

1977 Angelou receives Emmy nomination for TV miniseries *Roots*.

1981 *The Heart of a Women* is published

1993 Angelou reads a poem at Bill Clinton's inauguration.

1997 *Even the Stars Look Lonesome* is published.

1998 Angelou directs feature film *Down in the Delta*.

African-American Autobiography

Autobiography holds a position of preeminence among the narrative traditions of black America. Perhaps more than any other form in black letters, autobiography has consistently testified to the commitment of people of color to realize the promise of their American birthright and to articulate their achievements as individuals and as persons of African descent. Autobiography has further been recognized by African Americans as a powerful means of addressing and altering social and political realities in the United States. From 1760 to 1865, the form was dominated by autobiographies of ex-slaves. The most widely read of these was *Narrative of the Life of Frederick Douglass,* first published in 1845. In the decades following the Civil War, the autobiographies of Booker T. Washington, Claude McKay, Zora Neale Hurston, and Richard Wright made a more lasting impression on American readers than did any African-American novel of the same era. In 1965 *The Autobiography of Malcolm X* gave voice to the civil rights and black power movements.

The appearance in 1970 of Maya Angelou's *I Know Why the Caged Bird Sings* signaled one of the most remarkable developments in recent African-American autobiography: the unprecedented outpouring of personal, sometimes very intimate, narratives by black women. Although women were longtime contributors to such bedrock African-American traditions as the spiritual autobiography, recent women autobiographers, led by Angelou, Audre Lorde, Alice Walker, and Itabari Njeri, have reenvisioned the ideas of the spirit and salvation, discovering them anew in their experiences as black female artists and activists. Following Angelou's model, many popular entertainers, including Tina Turner, Gladys Knight, and Della Reese, published candid and intimate autobiographies during the 1980s and 1990s.

Sing? (1983); *Now Sheba Sings the Song* (1987); and *I Shall Not Be Moved* (1990). As these titles indicate, Angelou's poetry is deeply rooted in the African-American oral tradition and is uplifting in tone. Angelou says, "All my work is meant to say 'You may encounter many defeats but you *must* not be defeated.'"

A versatile writer, Angelou has written for television: the PBS ten-part series *Black, Blues, Blacks* (1968); a teleplay of *Caged Bird*; and for the screen: *Georgia Georgia* (1971) and *Sister, Sister* (1979). As well as being a prolific writer, Angelou has been a successful actress and received a Tony nomination for best supporting actress in the TV miniseries *Roots*. In 1995 Angelou appeared in the popular film *How to Make an American Quilt*. In 1998 she directed her first feature film, *Down in the Delta*, the story of an African-American family in Chicago. Angelou says of her creative diversity, "I believe all things are possible for a human being and I don't think there's anything in the world I can't do." On January 20, 1993, at the request of President Bill Clinton, Angelou concluded the president's inauguration by reading a poem composed for the occasion, "On the Pulse of Morning," which celebrates a new era of national unity. In 1995 Angelou wrote a poem called "A Brave and Startling Truth" to commemorate the 50th anniversary of the United Nations. ◆

Armstrong, Lillian Hardin "Lil"

FEBRUARY 3, 1898 – AUGUST 27, 1971 ● JAZZ PIANIST

1898 Hardin is born in Memphis.

1921 Hardin joins King Oliver's Creole Jazz Band.

1924 Hardin marries Louis Armstrong.

1925 Lil Armstrong begins performing with Hot Fives and Hot Sevens jazz ensembles.

1928 Lil Armstrong earns a teacher's diploma from Chicago College of Music.

1938 Lil Armstrong is divorced from Louis Armstrong.

1971 Lil Armstrong dies in Chicago at a memorial concert for Louis Armstrong.

Born in Memphis, Tennessee, Lil Hardin studied classical piano and organ as a child. She attended Fisk University in Nashville until around 1917, when her family moved to Chicago. There she studied at the Chicago College of Music and began working as a song demonstrator at Jones's Music Shop. By the early 1920s, Hardin had accompanied the singer Alberta Hunter, played with the Original Creole Jazz Band, and led her own ensemble at the Dreamland Club. She joined King Oliver's Creole Jazz Band in 1921. Oliver's famous band, the first to bring "hot" New Orleans jazz to Chicago, became even more popular after Louis Armstrong joined as second cornet a few months later. The ensemble's recordings, among the first great examples of a jazz ensemble, include "Riverside Blues" (1923), "Dippermouth Blues" (1923), and "Weather Bird Blues" (1923).

In 1924 Hardin and Armstrong were married. That year, at the urging of his wife, Louis Armstrong left Oliver and joined Fletcher Henderson's orchestra, which led to his emergence as the major trumpeter of his era. Starting in 1925, Lil Hardin Armstrong and her husband joined in two ensembles: a quintet known as the Hot Five and a septet called the Hot Seven. Recordings by these groups, including the jazz classics "Cornet Chop Suey" (1926), "Muskrat Ramble" (1926), and "Potato Head Blues" (1927), are usually credited to Louis Armstrong, but Lil Armstrong was the initial force behind organizing the ensembles. Lil Hardin Armstrong gathered the same performers in 1926 to record as Lil's Hot Shots on "Georgia Bo Bo" and "Drop That Sack." She also composed the famous "Struttin' with Some Barbecue" (1927).

Louis Armstrong's 1930s-era "Hot Five" band featured (left to right) Johnny St. Cyr, Edward "Kid" Ory, Louis Armstrong himself, Johnny Dodds, and **Lil Armstrong.**

"Although Louis Armstrong took the spotlight onstage, offstage it was clear that his wife had managed his career."

Although Louis Armstrong took the spotlight onstage, offstage it was clear that his wife had managed his career and even schooled him in musical matters, a situation that led to their separation in 1931 and divorce in 1938. After the late 1920s, Louis Armstrong's career eclipsed that of his wife, but she was nonetheless an accomplished soloist and composer who played a crucial role in the development of the standard jazz ensemble. During the mid to late 1920s, she also performed with the New Orleans Wanderers ("Gate Mouth," 1926) and Johnny Dodds ("San," 1927). In the late 1920s she went back to school, earning a teacher's diploma at the Chicago College of Music in 1928 and a graduate diploma at the New York College of Music in 1929.

In the late 1920s and early '30s, Lil Hardin Armstrong appeared with Ralph Cooper, King Oliver, Freddie Keppard, and an all-female group called the Harlem Harlicans. She recorded "Virginia" (1932), "Just for the Thrill" (1936), "Born to Swing" (1937), "Lindy Hop" (1937), and "You Shall Reap What You Sow" (1938). She also performed in *Hot Chocolates* (1929) and *Shuffle Along* (1933). After a big band tour of the

Midwest in 1935–36, she settled in New York, working as a pianist for Decca Records.

Lil Hardin Armstrong moved to Chicago permanently in 1940. Among her later recordings are "I Did All I Could" (with Lonnie Johnson, 1941), "East Town Boogie" (1947), "Lil's Boogie" (recorded in 1953 in Paris), and "Red Arrow Blues" (1961). She also recorded an album of reminiscences, *Satchmo and Me* (1958–59). Lil Armstrong died in August 1971 after collapsing at a Chicago memorial concert for Louis Armstrong, who had died the month before. ◆

Ashford, Evelyn

APRIL 19, 1957 – ● TRACK AND FIELD ATHLETE

Born in Shreveport, Louisiana, Evelyn Ashford did not run competitively until her senior year of high school, when she ran on the boys' track team because the school had no team for girls. Ashford won a track scholarship to the University of California at Los Angeles in 1975. The following year she finished fifth in the 100-meter dash at the Montreal Olympics, and her 400-meter relay team finished seventh. Although she dropped out of UCLA in 1979, UCLA women's track coach Pat Connolly continued to train her, and Ashford won the 100-meter dash at the 1979 World Cup, becoming the top woman sprinter. Her dream of winning a gold medal in the 1980 Olympics was thwarted, however, when the United States decided to boycott the 1980 Olympics in Moscow.

After this disappointment, Ashford considered dropping out of track and field. But with her husband, Ray Washington, as her coach, she won the women's 100-meter dash at the 1981 World Cup. In the 1984 Los Angeles

> *"Sprinting is a mental thing. You don't want to think about anything else. If I commune with other runners I'll lose my killer instinct. I never want to do that."*
>
> Evelyn Ashford, 1988

Olympics, Ashford won the 100-meter dash and anchored the winning 400-meter relay team. The result of the recognition she finally gained with her Olympic gold medals was promotional work for such large international corporations as American Express and Mazda.

In 1986 Ashford won the 100-meter dash in the 1986 World Cup, ran the fastest 100 meters of the year, and was ranked number one for the year. In 1988 she competed in her third Olympics, and won a silver medal in the 100-meter competition and a gold medal as part of the winning 400-meter relay team. In 1992, at the age of thirty-five, Ashford competed in the Barcelona Olympics, where she won her fourth Olympic gold medal as the lead-off runner in the 400-meter relay. In June 1993 she retired from competition. ◆

Bailey, Pearl

MARCH 29, 1918 – AUGUST 17, 1990 ● SINGER AND ACTOR

Popularly known as Pearlie Mae, Pearl Bailey was born in Newport News, Virginia, to Joseph James Bailey, a revivalist minister, and Ella Mae Bailey. At the age of four, she moved with her family to Washington, D.C., and after her parents divorced she moved to Philadelphia with her mother and her stepfather, Walter Robinson. There Bailey attended school until the age of fifteen, when she began her career as an entertainer after winning an amateur contest at the Pearl Theater. For a while she worked in coal-mining towns in Pennsylvania, then in small clubs in Washington, D.C. Beginning in 1941 she toured with the United Service Organization (USO), and in 1943–44 she performed with bands led by Charles "Cootie" Williams, William "Count" Basie, and Noble Sissle. It was during this period that she began to develop her distinctive trademark, described by one critic as "a warm, lusty singing voice accompanied by an easy smile and elegant gestures that charmed audiences and translated smoothly from the nightclub stage and Broadway to film and television." In the early forties she made solo appearances at the

13

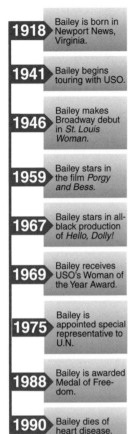

1918 Bailey is born in Newport News, Virginia.

1941 Bailey begins touring with USO.

1946 Bailey makes Broadway debut in *St. Louis Woman*.

1959 Bailey stars in the film *Porgy and Bess*.

1967 Bailey stars in all-black production of *Hello, Dolly!*

1969 Bailey receives USO's Woman of the Year Award.

1975 Bailey is appointed special representative to U.N.

1988 Bailey is awarded Medal of Freedom.

1990 Bailey dies of heart disease.

Village Vanguard and the Blue Angel, before making her Broadway debut in 1946 in the musical comedy *St. Louis Woman*, for which she won the Donaldson Award as the most promising new performer of the year. The following year she appeared in the motion picture *Variety Girl*, in which she sang one of her most popular songs, "Tired." Thereafter, she made numerous stage, screen, and television appearances, including the 1954 Broadway musical *House of Flowers* and such films as *Carmen Jones* (1954), *St. Louis Blues* (1958), and *Porgy and Bess* (1959). Her most acclaimed performance came in 1967, when she appeared with Cab Calloway in the all-black production of *Hello, Dolly!* This brought her a special Tony Award in 1968 for distinguished achievement in the New York theater.

In 1969 Bailey received the USO's Woman of the Year award. The following year President Richard Nixon appointed her "Ambassador of Love," and in 1975 she was appointed special representative to the United Nations. (Despite her popularity, Bailey's association with the Nixon administration was criticized by some African Americans; Harlem congressman Charles Rangel in particular stated that her appointment was an insult to better-qualified blacks.) During this period she returned to school, studying theology at Georgetown University in Washington, D.C., from which she received both an honorary degree in 1978 and a bachelor's degree in 1985, at the age of sixty-seven. An inveterate traveler, frequently accompanied by her husband, jazz drummer Louis Bellson (whom she married in 1952), Bailey also authored several books, including the autobiographical *The Raw Pearl* (1968) and *Talking to Myself* (1971). *Between You and Me: A Heartfelt Memoir on Learning, Loving, and Living* was published in 1989, shortly before she died of heart disease on August 17, 1990. Two years before her death, Bailey was presented with the Medal of Freedom by President Ronald Reagan. ◆

Baker, Ella J.

DECEMBER 13, 1903– DECEMBER 13, 1986 ● ACTIVIST

E lla J. Baker was a leading figure in the struggle of African Americans for equality. In the 1960s she was regarded as the godmother of the Civil Rights Movement, or, as one activist put it, "a Shining Black Beacon." Though she was not accorded recognition by the media, Baker was affiliated with all the major civil rights organizations of her time, and she worked closely with all the better-known leaders of the movement.

Ella Baker was the daughter of a waiter on the Norfolk-Washington ferry, and was a grade-school teacher and the granddaughter of slaves. From the extended family of aunts, uncles, and cousins who lived on land her grandfather had purchased from owners of the plantation on which they had worked as slaves, Baker acquired a sense of community, a profound sense of the need for sharing, and a sense of history and of the continuity of struggle. She also gained a fierce sense of independence and a belief in the necessity of rebellion, which guided her work for the rest of her life.

After leaving Shaw University in Raleigh, North Carolina, from which she graduated as **valedictorian,** Baker immersed herself in the cause of social justice. She moved to New York, where she continued her education on the streets of the city, attending all kinds of political meetings to absorb the intellectual atmosphere. In the 1930s, while earning her living working in restaurants and as a correspondent for several black newspapers, Baker helped to found the Young Negroes Cooperative League, of which she became executive director. She worked for the Works Project (originally Works Progress) Administration (WPA), teaching consumer and labor education. During the depression, Baker learned that, in her words, "a society could break down, a social order could break down, and the individual is the victim of the breakdown, rather than the cause of it."

In 1940 Baker accepted a position as field secretary at the National Association for the Advancement of Colored People (NAACP). She soon established regional leadership-training conferences with the slogan "Give light and the people will find a way." While a national officer, Baker traveled for several months a year throughout the country (concentrating on the segregated South), building NAACP membership and working with the local people who would become the sustaining forces of the civil rights movement. Her organizing strategy was to stress local issues rather than national ones and to take the NAACP to people, wherever they were. She ventured into beer gardens and nightclubs where she would address crowds and secure memberships and campaign workers. Baker was named

"Strong people don't need strong leaders."
Ella Baker, 1981

valedictorian: the highest ranking student in the class.

1903 Baker is born in Virginia.

1940 Baker accepts position as field secretary at the NAACP.

1943 Baker is named NAACP's director of branches.

1946 Baker resigns from the NAACP; begins campaigning to desegregate New York schools.

1951 Baker runs for New York City council.

1957 Baker sets up office of SCLC and organizes voter-registration drive.

1960 Baker begins working as human-relations consultant for YWCA.

1963 Baker joins the staff of SCEF.

1964 Baker helps organize Mississippi Freedom Democratic Party.

1986 Baker dies.

director of branches in 1943, but frustrated by the top-down approach of the NAACP leadership, she resigned in 1946. In this period she married a former classmate, Thomas Roberts, and took on the responsibility of raising her sister's daughter, Jacqueline.

From 1946 to 1957, while working in New York City for the New York Cancer Society and the New York Urban League, Baker participated in campaigns to desegregate New York City schools. She was a founder of In Friendship, a group organized to support school desegregation in the South; a member of the zoning subcommittee of the New York City Board of Education's committee on integration; and president and later education director of the New York City branch of the NAACP.

In 1957 Bayard Rustin and Stanley Levison, advisers to the Rev. Dr. Martin Luther King Jr., asked her to return south to set up the office of the newly organized Southern Christian Leadership Conference (SCLC), headed by King, and to organize the Crusade for Citizenship, a voter-registration drive. Intending to stay six weeks, she remained with the SCLC for two years, serving variously as acting director, associate director, and executive director.

In 1960 Baker mobilized SCLC support for a meeting to bring together the student sit-in protest groups that had sprung up across the South. A battle for control of the sit-in movement ensued. Older civil rights organizations, particularly the SCLC, sought to make the new movement a youth arm of their own operations. Baker, however, advocated an independent role for the student activists.

Baker resigned from the SCLC in 1960 to accept a part-time position as human-relations consultant to the Young Women's Christian Association (YWCA), working with colleges across the South to further integration. In 1963 she joined the staff of the Southern Conference Educational Fund (SCEF), a regionwide interracial organization that put special emphasis on developing white support for racial justice. While affiliated with the YWCA and SCEF, Baker devoted much of her time to the fledgling Student Nonviolent Coordinating Committee (SNCC), in which she found the embodiment of her belief in a "group-centered leadership, rather than a leadership-centered group."

SNCC was for Baker the "new community" she had sought. Her work was an inspiration for other activist movements of the 1960s and '70s: the anti-Vietnam War movement and the feminist movement. But Baker's greatest contribution was her counseling of SNCC. During one crisis she pointed out that both direct action and voter registration would lead to the same result—confrontation and resolution. Her support of confrontation was at variance with the Kennedy administration's policy, which advocated a "cooling-off" period. Baker also counseled the young **mavericks** of SNCC to work with the more conservative southern ministers, who, she advised, had resources that could help them.

maverick: a fiercely independent individual who doesn't follow rules.

In 1964 SNCC was instrumental in organizing the Mississippi Freedom Democratic Party (MFDP), which sent its own **delegation** to Atlantic City to challenge the seating of the segregationist Mississippi delegation at the Democratic National Convention. Baker, in the new party's Washington headquarters and later in Atlantic City, orchestrated the MFDP's fight for the support of other state delegations in its claim to Mississippi's seats. This challenge eventually resulted in the adoption of new Democratic party rules that guaranteed the inclusion of blacks and women in future delegations.

delegation: a group of representatives.

After the convention, Baker moved back to New York, where she remained active in human-rights affairs. Throughout her life she had been a speaker at hundreds of Women's Day church meetings across the country, a participant in tenants' associations, a consultant to the wartime Office of Price Administration, an adviser to the Harlem Youth Council, a founder and administrator of the Fund for Education and Legal Defense. In her later years she worked with such varied groups as the Puerto Rican **Solidarity** Committee, the Episcopal Church Center, and the Third World Women's Coordinating Committee.

solidarity: unity based on common interests.

While never professing a political ideology, Baker consistently held views far to the left of the established civil rights leadership. She was never a member of a political party, but she did run for the New York City Council on the Liberal party ticket in 1951. She acted within the constraints of a radical critique of society and was drawn toward "radical" rather than "safe" solutions to societal problems. Her credo was "a life that is important is a life of service." ◆

Baker, Josephine

JUNE 6, 1906 – APRIL 14, 1975 ● ENTERTAINER

Josephine Baker was born in St. Louis, Missouri, the daughter of Carrie McDonald, an unmarried domestic worker, and Eddie Carson, a jazz drummer. At age eight she was working as a domestic. At age eleven she survived the East St. Louis race riots in which thirty-nine blacks were killed. Before she was fourteen, Baker had run away from a sadistic employer, and married and discarded a husband, Willie Wells. "I was cold, and I danced to keep warm, that's my childhood," she said. After entertaining locally, she joined a traveling show called the Dixie Steppers, where she developed as a dancer and mime.

In 1920 she married a jockey named Willie Baker, but quickly left him to try out for the new black musical, Noble Sissle and composer Eubie Blake's path-breaking *Shuffle Along*. She was turned down as too young, too thin, and too dark. At sixteen she was hired as end girl in a *Shuffle Along* road show chorus line, where she captivated audiences with her mugging. Sissle and Blake wrote her into their next show, *Chocolate Dandies* (1924), and the next year, Caroline Dudley invited her to join a troupe of "authentic" Negro performers she was taking to Paris in *La Revue Nègre*.

Baker was an overnight sensation and became the rage of Paris, a phenomenon whose style and presence outweighed her talents, and a black exotic jungle Venus. Everyone danced her version of the Charleston and Black Bottom. Women copied her hairdo. **Couturiers** saw a new ideal in her body. She took a series of lovers, including Paul Colin, who immortalized her on posters, and Georges Simenon, who worked as her secretary. In 1927 "La Bakair" opened at the *Folies Bergère* in her famous costume of a few rhinestoned bananas.

That same year she met the café-society habitué "Count" Pepito de Abatino (actually a Sicilian stonemason). He became her lover and manager, taught her how to dress and act, trained her voice and body, and sculpted a highly sophisticated and marketable star. They toured Europe and South America. In Vienna, Baker was preached against for being the "impure incarnation of sex." She provoked hostility fueled by economic frustration, moral indignation, **xenophobia,** and racism.

> *"To live is to dance. I would like to die, breathless, spent, at the end of a dance."*
>
> Josephine Baker

couturier: fashion designer.

xenophobia: fear or hatred of foreigners.

Josephine Baker sings the national anthem for U.S. servicemen in Algeria in 1943.

By the time Baker returned to France, Abatino had done what he had promised: turned the diamond-in-the-rough of 1925 into the polished gem of 1930. There followed a ten-year reign of Baker in the music halls of Paris. Henri Varna of the Casino de Paris added to her image a baby leopard in a $20,000 diamond necklace and the song that would become her signature, "J'ai deux amours, mon pays et Paris." Her name was linked with several Frenchmen, including singer Jacques Pills, and in 1934 she made her best motion picture, *Zouzou*, costarring Jean Gabin, followed by *Princess Tam Tam* in 1935.

Baker returned to New York to play in the 1936 *Ziegfeld Follies*, but the show was a fiasco. She learned America would neither welcome her nor look on her with color-blind eyes as France did. Abatino died of cancer before Baker returned to Paris. She married Jean Lion, a wealthy sugar broker, in 1937, and divorced him fourteen months later. By 1939 Baker had become a French citizen. When the Nazis occupied France during World War II, Baker joined the Resistance, recruited by the head of French intelligence. For her activities in counterintelligence, Baker received the Croix de Guerre and the Légion d'Honneur. After operating between Marseilles and Lisbon under cover of a revival of her operetta *La Creole*, she was sent to Casablanca in January of 1940 to continue intelligence activities.

In 1941 Baker delivered a stillborn child, the father unknown. Complications from this birth endangered her life for

1906 Baker is born in St. Louis.

1924 Baker makes Broadway debut in *Chocolate Dandies*.

1925 Baker opens in Paris in *La Revue Nègre*.

1927 Baker opens at the *Folies Bergère* in banana costume.

1934 Baker stars in the film *Zouzou*.

1936 Baker plays in the *Ziegfeld Follies* in New York.

1940 Baker travels to Casablanca as a French government agent.

1951 NAACP organizes Josephine Baker Day in Harlem.

1963 Baker appears at the civil rights March on Washington.

1975 Baker dies during run of farewell performances in Paris.

more than nineteen months, and at one point her obituary was published. She recovered and spent the last years of the war driving an ambulance and entertaining Allied troops in North Africa. After the war, she married orchestra leader Jo Bouillon and adopted four children of different races that she called her "Rainbow Tribe." She turned her **château,** Les Milandes, into her idea of a multiracial community. In 1951 she attracted wide attention in the United States, and was honored by the NAACP, which organized a Josephine Baker Day in Harlem.

She continued to be an outspoken civil rights advocate, refusing to perform before segregated audiences in Las Vegas and Miami, and instigating a notorious *cause célèbre* by accusing the Stork Club of New York of discrimination. Her controversial image hurt her career, and the U.S. State Department hinted they might cancel her **visa.** Baker continued to tour outside America as her Rainbow Tribe grew to twelve. Between 1953 and 1963, she spent more than $1.5 million on Les Milandes, her financial affairs degenerated into chaos, her fees diminished, and she and Bouillon separated.

In 1963 Baker appeared at the March on Washington, and after performing in Denmark, had her first heart attack. In the spring of 1969, she declared bankruptcy and Les Milandes was seized. Baker accepted a villa in Monaco from Princess Grace, began a long series of farewell performances, and begged in the streets when she couldn't work. In 1975 she summoned all her resources and professionalism for a last farewell performance at the Olympia Theatre in Paris. Baker died two days into her performance run on April 14. Her televised state funeral at the Madeleine Church drew thousands of people and included a twenty-one-gun salute. ◆

chateau: a large country house.

cause célèbre: a legal case, person, or incident attracting widespread attention.

visa: a stamp on a passport that authorizes the bearer to enter a foreign country.

Bambara, Toni Cade

MARCH 25, 1939 – ● WRITER

Born Toni Cade in New York City to Helen Brent Henderson Cade, Bambara adopted her last name in 1970. Bambara grew up in various sections of New York (Harlem, Bedford-Stuyvesant, and Queens) as well as in Jersey City, New Jersey. She earned a B.A. in theater arts and English from Queens College in 1959—the year in which she published her first short story, "Sweet Town"—and an M.A. in English from City College of New York in 1965. At the same time, she served as a community organizer and activist as well as occupational therapist for the psychiatric division of Metropolitan Hospital.

Bambara's consciousness was raised early as she watched her mother instruct her grade school teachers about African-American history and culture and as she listened on New York street corners to Garveyites, Father Diviners, Rastafarians, Muslims, Pan-Africanists, and communists. She learned early of the resiliency that would be needed for a poor black female to survive. Bambara's streetwise sensibility informs two collections of writings by black women that she edited, *The Black Woman* (1970) and *Tales and Stories for Black Folks* (1971). The stories that she contributed to these collections portray young black women who weather difficult times and who challenge others to join the struggle for equality.

Between 1959 and 1970 Bambara wrote a series of short stories that were published in 1972 as *Gorilla, My Love*. A collection of fifteen stories, this book focuses on relationships that rejuvenate, and on family, community, and self-love. Her second collection of stories, *The Sea Birds Are Still Alive* (1977), revolves around the theme of community healing. Her characters do not despair; instead, they nurture one another back to spiritual and physical health. The theme of healing is further explored in Bambara's novel *Salt Eaters* (1980), which received the American Book Award that year.

Bambara has taught at several universities, including City College of the City University of New York, Rutgers University, Livingstone College, Duke University, and Spelman College. Her commitment as a writer is to inspire others to continue to fight for improved conditions for the community. ◆

1939	Bambara is born in New York City.
1959	Bambara publishes first short story.
1965	Bambara earns an M.A. from City College of New York.
1970	Bambara edits *The Black Woman*.
1972	Bambara publishes *Gorilla, My Love*.
1980	Bambara's novel *Salt Eaters* receives American Book Award.

"The dream is real, my friends. The failure to make it work is the unreality."
Toni Cade Bambara, *The Salt Eaters*, 1980

Banks, Tyra

DECEMBER 4, 1973 – ● MODEL

Tyra Banks is a fashion model and actress. In the 1990s she quickly became one of the most popular and successful African-American models in the fashion in-

dustry. By the late 1990s Banks ranked among the most highly paid models in the United States, with an estimated fortune of close to $9 million. She has appeared on the cover of magazines, on high-fashion runways, on calendars, on television, in advertisements, in videos, and in film.

Tyra Banks was born on December 4, 1973, in Los Angeles, California, to Carolyn and Don Banks. Her parents divorced when she was six years old. Banks grew up in the L.A. suburb of Inglewood. As a teen, she attended Immaculate Heart High School, a Catholic girls' school in Los Angeles. Like many teens, Banks was shy, a bit awkward, and often teased about her height.

Banks decided to try modeling after graduation. Her mother, who was a medical photographer for NASA's Jet Propulsion Lab, helped her put together a portfolio. Rejected by a number of agencies, Banks decided to pursue her interest in film. She was accepted at Loyola Marymount University in Los Angeles, but weeks before the start of classes, a scout for a French modeling agency saw her and offered her a job in the fall haute couture shows in Paris. Banks accepted and at the age of seventeen she was catapulted into the world of high fashion. She quickly prepped for the runway by watching fashion videos and practicing walks in her mother's high heels and long nightgowns. Once in Paris, designers found her elegance and grace on the runway so alluring that she was immediately booked for twenty-five fashion shows, at that time a record number for a new model.

Her runway work quickly led to lucrative advertising contracts. At the age of twenty she signed with Cover Girl Cosmetics, becoming the third black woman in the world to receive a major cosmetics contract. She has also appeared in ads for McDonald's, Nike, and others. *People* magazine chose her as one of the world's most beautiful people in 1996, and that same year she became the first black woman and model to be featured on the cover of *GQ* magazine. She has also appeared on the

1973 ▶ Banks is born in Los Angeles.

1991 ▶ Banks goes to Paris on her first assignments as a model.

1993 ▶ Banks makes her television debut on *The Fresh Prince of Bel Air.*

1995 ▶ Banks makes her first appearance in the drama *Higher Learning.*

1996 ▶ Banks appears on cover of *Sports Illustrated* swimsuit issue.

1998 ▶ Banks publishes *Tyra's Beauty Inside and Out.*

cover of such magazines as *Vogue, Elle, Cosmopolitan, Seventeen, Harper's Bazaar, Esquire,* and *Sports Illustrated.*

In addition to modeling, Banks has pursued her interest in film and acting. She made her television debut in 1993 as the college student Jackie Ames on the hit television comedy *The Fresh Prince of Bel Air.* Her film debut came in 1995, when Banks appeared as Deja, a young track athlete in the film *Higher Learning.*

Banks manages her many business deals through her corporation, Tygirl, Inc. She contributes to a number of charities and has served as spokesperson for the Center for Children & Families, a New York organization that helps abused and neglected children. Banks also set up a scholarship fund for African-American girls at her high school alma mater, Immaculate Heart.

In 1998 Banks published her first book, *Tyra's Beauty Inside and Out* (HarperCollins). The book provides beauty tips and the author's thoughts on relationships, drug and alcohol abuse, body image, and family dilemmas. Through the book, Banks hopes to help promote self-esteem by including anecdotes of her own struggles with self-image as a youth. ◆

Bassett, Angela

AUGUST 16, 1958 – ● ACTOR

Theater director George C. Wolfe recalls seeing Angela Bassett perform for the first time in an off-off Broadway production of Jean Anouilh's *Antigone* nearly two decades ago: "I remember being rendered powerless by that endless swirl of contradictions that was her performance: Absolutely in control yet the essence of vulnerability; sensual, delicate, provocative . . . fierce!"

That description might just as well sum up the saga of this highly acclaimed African-American actress's trajectory from the housing projects of Saint Petersburg, Florida, to Hollywood stardom.

From her award-winning portrayal of Tina Turner in *What's Love Got to Do With It* (1993) to that of an abandoned wife in *Waiting to Exhale* (1995), from depicting the tranquil dignity of Betty Shabbazz to the personal journey toward love and self-

"You just got to be about your plan. Be about your race and finish it."

Angela Bassett

understanding of a middle-aged stockbroker in *How Stella Got Her Groove Back* (1998), Bassett's most memorable performances are about women who not only endure but prevail.

Those lessons came naturally. Born August 16, 1958, in New York City, Bassett was sent to live with relatives in North Carolina as a baby. At age five, she went to live with her younger sister and mother, by then separated from her husband, in St. Petersburg, Florida. They lived in a housing project, relying on public aid, until Bassett's mother found clerical work while attending night school. Bassett remembers helping her mother drill with flash cards. Her mother's high standards made Bassett push herself: "If you dropped to Cs, no cheerleading, no community theater! I got the message," Bassett told *Time*'s Richard Corliss.

During her junior year at Boca Ciega High School, where she became the first black member of the National Honor Society, she went to Washington, D.C. With her Upward Bound student group, she attended a production of *Of Mice and Men* starring James Earl Jones. That performance sealed Bassett's fate. She returned to St. Petersburg determined to become a professional actor. Her portrayal of Mama in a school presentation of *A Raisin in the Sun* earned her an outstanding ovation. Since then, the plaudits have seldom stopped.

She went to Yale University on scholarship, majoring in African-American and theater studies, and continued on for an M.F.A. in drama under celebrated stage director Lloyd Richards. After a brief stint of fruitless auditions and odd jobs in New York, her **leonine** beauty, Yale credentials, and powerful presence quickly marked her as a dramatic force on stage, where Bassett appeared in productions as varied as Joseph Papp's Shakespearean presentations to August Wilson's *Ma Rainey's Black Bottom*.

leonine: resembling a lion.

She gradually turned toward film, moving to Hollywood for a movie that folded, but snagged the role of "stewardess" in *Kindergarten Cop*. She appeared in John Singleton's highly acclaimed directing debut *Boyz N the Hood* (1991) and in John

Sayles's urban drama *City of Hope* (1991). Next came broad TV recognition with her role as Katherine Jackson, mother of the musical Jackson family, followed in 1992 by her role as Betty Shabbazz in Spike Lee's film *Malcolm.*

Then in 1993 she burst into stardom with her dynamically nuanced portrayal of R&B queen Tina Turner in *What's Love Got to Do With It*, which earned Bassett a Golden Globe Award and an Academy Award nomination. "When the real Tina Turner finally makes an appearance as herself at the end of the movie, it seems perfectly natural, as though she's been on screen throughout," a *Wall Street Journal* critic enthusiastically wrote.

Though few film roles have plumbed her talents, Bassett is among that handful of African-American stars who have helped overturn typecasting of black actors and reshape the way Hollywood—thus Americans—looks at movies about African Americans. *Waiting to Exhale*, adapted from Terry McMillan's best-selling book about the friendships and failed romances of four black women and starring Bassett and Whitney Houston, became a $67-million mainstream box-office hit in 1995. In 1998 Bassett appeared with Whoopi Goldberg in another successful film adaptation of a Terry McMillan novel: *How Stella Got Her Groove Back.*

A daily reader of the Bible, who married fellow actor and Yale classmate Courtney B. Vance in 1997, Bassett has managed to evade tabloid tawdriness, perhaps because she knows how to live by her own words: "You just got to be about your plan. Be about your race and finish it." ◆

1958 Bassett is born in New York City.

1991 Bassett appears in the film *Boyz N the Hood.*

1992 Bassett appears as Betty Shabazz in Spike Lee's *Malcolm.*

1993 Bassett is nominated for Academy Award for *What's Love Got to Do With It?*

1995 Bassett appears in *Waiting to Exhale.*

1998 Bassett stars in *How Stella Got Her Groove Back.*

Battle, Kathleen

AUGUST 13, 1948 – ● OPERA SINGER

Born in Portsmouth, Ohio, Kathleen Battle was the daughter of Ollie Battle, a community and church activist, and Grady Battle, a steelworker who also sang in a gospel quartet. She first sang at the Portsmouth African Methodist Episcopal Church. A National Merit Scholar in mathematics, Battle majored in music education at the University of Cincinnati College-Conservatory (B.M. and M.M.). She taught music for two years in Cincinnati elementary schools

Kathleen Battle and tenor Jose Carreras in 1978, rehearsing a scene from Jules Massanet's opera *Werther*.

1948 Battle is born in Portsmouth, Ohio.

1972 Battle debuts in Brahms's *A German Requiem* in Italy.

1975 Battle debuts on Broadway in Scott Joplin's *Treemonisha*.

1978 Battle debuts at the Metropolitan Opera in Wagner's

1982 Battle debuts in Europe in Mozart's *Così fan Tutte*.

1992 Battle and Jessye Norman give concert of spirituals at Carnegie Hall.

1993 Battle sings a new song cycle by Toni Morrison and Andre Previn.

before embarking on her professional career. A lyric soprano noted for her small, sweet voice, she made her professional singing debut in Brahms's *A German Requiem* with the Cincinnati orchestra at the Spoleto Festival in Italy (1972). Her opera debut came soon after as Rosina in Rossini's *Il Barbiere di Siviglia* with the Michigan Opera Theater. In 1974 she met James Levine, later to become artistic director of the Metropolitan Opera, who became her mentor. The following year, she appeared on Broadway in Scott Joplin's opera *Treemonisha*. In 1976 Battle appeared as Susanna in *The Marriage of Figaro* at the New York City Opera, and made her Metropolitan Opera debut in 1978, singing the shepherd in Wagner's *Tannhäuser*. Since then she has sung several leading roles, among them Mozart's Pamina, Richard Strauss's Sophie in *Der Rosenkavalier*, and Cleopatra in Handel's *Giulio Cesare*. Subsequent to her European debut as Despina in Mozart's *Così Fan Tutte* in Salzburg in 1982, Battle performed there several times as Despina, as Susanna, and as Zerlina in *Don Giovanni*—the last for American national television—as well as in many other places. In 1993 she attracted sellout audiences during a Metropolitan Opera tour of Japan.

Battle, whom *Time* magazine in 1985 called "the best lyric **coloratura** in the world," has shifted effortlessly between the opera stage and the concert hall, where she performs with symphony orchestras and gives several recitals per year. She has won three Grammy awards, including one for her recital album *Kathleen Battle at Carnegie Hall* (1992). Other recordings include a selection of Bach arias, the title role in Handel's *Semele*, pieces by George Gershwin, and two albums of Baroque concert pieces and arias with African-American trumpeter Wynton Marsalis.

In 1991 Battle and soprano Jessye Norman gave a concert of Spirituals at Carnegie Hall that was shown on national television and prompted a best-selling recording. In 1993 Battle sang the premiere of a song cycle she had commissioned from African-American writer Toni Morrison and composer André Previn. ◆

coloratura: an opera singer with an agile voice who specializes in elaborate, ornamented music.

Belton, Sharon Sayles

MAY 13, 1951 – ● POLITICIAN

Sharon Sayles Belton was the first female and the first African American to become the mayor of Minneapolis, Minnesota, in 1993. With a population of nearly 400,000, Minneapolis is the largest city in Minnesota and, with its sister city, St. Paul, forms an economic and cultural powerhouse in one of America's richest agricultural areas. Minnesota's largely Scandinavian population became more diverse in the 1980s and 1990s as African Americans and others were drawn to the state's excellent economy and high standard of living.

Sharon Sayles was born May 13, 1951, in St. Paul, and was raised in the Twin Cities. She was one of four daughters in a family with a tradition of social activism. During high school, Belton volunteered at a local hospital, and in college she helped register voters in Jackson, Mississippi. As a college senior, she became pregnant and quit temporarily. Her daughter, Kilayna, suffered from mental retardation due to complications at birth. Belton raised her daughter alone and earned her bachelor's degree from Macalester College in St. Paul in 1973. Working as a parole officer for the Minnesota Department

"Americans like to say we are strong because we are founded on a tradition of tolerance—that we are nurtured by diversity. Yes, living peacefully and creatively with diversity is the great American experiment."
Sharon Sayles Belton, inaugural address, 1994

of Corrections from 1973 to 1983, Belton gained experience with the criminal justice system.

In 1981 She married Steve Belton, a trial attorney and law firm partner. The couple had two sons in the late 1980s, Coleman and Jordan. From 1983 to 1984, Belton served as associate director of the MN Program for Victims of Sexual Assault, which led her to cofound one of the first shelters for abused women in the United States, the Harriet Tubman Shelter for Battered Women. Belton's community activism led to her election as a Minneapolis city council member in 1984, where she served until 1993. She served as president of the city council from 1989 to 1993.

Responding to the demographic changes in Minneapolis and their resulting problems, Belton sought the mayorship in 1993 based on her support of issues important to minorities and women. She ran against liberal John Derus to replace Mayor Don Fraser, who was retiring after fourteen years. Derus ran on a law-and-order platform, while Belton concentrated on education and employment. She used grassroots strategies to win votes, such as phone banks, public appearances, and door-to-door campaigning. Belton won the election with 58 percent of the vote, considered remarkable in a city that was 78 percent white.

Beginning her service 1994, Belton gained a reputation for working with her city council in a consensus style. A number of her colleagues and advisors were women, including city council president Kathy O'Brien, a close ally of Belton.

In 1997 Belton, at forty-six, was challenged by Barbara Carlson, fifty-nine, a white local radio personality and the former wife of a Minnesota governor. Their campaign was marked by minor racial incidents, including a fight between their supporters at a debate, which led to a police officer firing a shot. No one was injured, and Belton and Carlson tried to downplay race, but it remained a contentious issue. Mayor Sharon Sayles Belton won the election with 55 percent of the vote, and she began her second term in 1998. ◆

1951 Sharon Sayles is born in St. Paul, Minnesota.

1973 Belton graduates from Macalester College.

1984 Belton wins seat on Minneapolis city council.

1994 Belton begins first term as mayor of Minneapolis.

1998 Belton begins second term as mayor.

Berry, Halle

AUGUST 14, 1968 –   ● ACTOR

Screen actress Halle Berry is about overturning stereotypes in quiet—but carefully calculated—ways. This former teen beauty queen has crafted a career studded with proven credentials as a working actor with verve and versatility.

Named one of the 50 Most Beautiful People of 1998 by *People* magazine, the 5' 6½" Revlon spokesmodel and one-time beauty contestant has parlayed her head-turning looks into roles of increasing substance. While embracing her African-American heritage, she has deftly defied Hollywood stereotypes that marginalize black actors, gradually working her way into the movie mainstream.

Berry, named after the Halle (rhymes with Sally) Brothers department store, was born in Cleveland, Ohio, on August 14, 1968—daughter of a white mother, Judith, and black father, Jerome, who left the family when Berry was four. When Berry was seven, Judith moved to a Cleveland suburb, where Berry and her older sister endured the taunts of both black and white schoolmates who called them "zebra."

Early on, Berry decided that no matter how light her skin or soft her hair, she was still a black girl. That understanding was reinforced by her mother, who told Berry: "When you look in the mirror—it doesn't matter who your parents are—that is a black face. You will be treated as a black woman."

In 1984 Berry graduated from Bedford High School, where she had been a cheerleader, editor of the school paper, honor society member and—with a struggle—prom queen. When the "blue-eyed blonde" lost, Berry and her friends were accused of stuffing the ballot box. A

> *"I honestly wouldn't want to be anyone but a black woman in America right now. I feel this is our time to break new ground, to make statements."*
>
> Halle Berry,
> quoted in
> *Essence,* 1994

1968 Berry is born in Cleveland, Ohio.

1983 Berry graduates from high school.

1986 Berry wins first runner-up in the Miss USA pageant.

1990 Berry is cast as a drug addict in Spike Lee's *Jungle Fever*.

1995 Berry plays a young mother in *Losing Isaiah*.

1998 Berry appears with Warren Beatty in *Bulworth*.

coin toss—in Berry's favor—settled the dispute. But her illusions were shattered.

She had worked so hard to be accepted, but when it came to being a standard of beauty for the school, "They didn't want me," she once told *New York Times* interviewer Jill Gerston. "That taught me. No more being a dancing bear." And no stopping her.

At eighteen, Berry won the Miss Teen Ohio pageant and later was named Miss Teen All-American, followed by the Miss Ohio title. In 1986 she was first runner-up in the Miss USA pageant and the first black woman to represent the United States in the Miss World contest in London.

After a brief modeling career in Chicago, Berry moved to New York and within two months landed her first TV role as a teen model on ABC's *Living Dolls*. During filming, she collapsed with diabetes, but she caught the eye of director Spike Lee, who cast her in his 1990 film, *Jungle Fever*. Her harrowing depiction of a crack-addicted girlfriend was a breakout performance, surpassed in the 1995 film *Losing Isaiah* with her wrenching portrayal of the crack addict who abandons her infant son and later sues his white adoptive parents to regain custody.

Her strong showing opposite superstar Jessica Lange in this film gave Berry a credibility that she used to get parts not necessarily scripted for black actresses, including the tough flight attendant in *Executive Decision*, the framed spouse in *The Rich Man's Wife* (both 1996), and even Rosetta, the Stone Age secretarial sexpot in *The Flintstones*, originally scripted for a Sharon Stone lookalike.

"The range she's capable of is phenomenal," *Flintstones* director Brian Levant once said. "She can go from good girl to vamp like you and I shed socks. So few people can do comedy and drama. But that's Halle—beautiful, funny, the entire package."

Despite her successes, Berry contemplated suicide after the bitter breakup of her three-year marriage to Atlanta Braves' outfielder David Justice in 1997. Healing came with therapy and a spate of work that challenged Berry's range, from the comedic *B.A.P.S.* and Warren Beatty's political satire *Bulworth* in 1998, to Oprah Winfrey's acclaimed TV miniseries *The Wedding* and a big-screen rock-and-roll drama, *Why Do Fools Fall in Love?*

A sunflower now covers her tattoo of her ex-husband's name. As Berry explained to an *Ebony* interviewer: "Sunflowers go through the dark times and the bright times and through it all they always reach for the sky. I think that's what my life is going to be about." ◆

Bethune, Mary McLeod

JULY 10, 1875– MAY 18, 1955 ● CIVIL RIGHTS ACTIVIST

" If I have a legacy to leave my people, it is my philosophy of living and serving. As I face tomorrow, I am content, for I think I have spent my life well. I pray now that my philosophy may be helpful to those who share my vision of a world of peace, progress, brotherhood, and love." With these words, Mary McLeod Bethune concluded her last will and testament outlining her legacy to African-Americans. Bethune lived up to her stated philosophy throughout her long career as a gifted institution builder who focused on securing rights and opportunities for African-American women and youth. Her stunning successes as a leader made her one of the most influential women of her day and, for many years, a premier African-American leader.

Mary McLeod was born in 1875, the thirteenth of fifteen children of Sam and Patsy (McIntosh) McLeod. The McLeod

> *"Mine has not been an easy road. Very few of my generation found life easy or wanted it that way. Your road may be somewhat less rugged because of the struggles we have made."*
> Mary McLeod Bethune, 1945

Mary McLeod Bethune (second from left) with Eleanor Roosevelt (center) at the 1943 opening of Midway Hall, a residence facility in Washington, D.C., for black female government workers.

Bethune-Cookman College

On October 3, 1904, Mary McLeod Bethune founded a normal and industrial school for African-American girls in Daytona Beach, Florida. Though she began with only five students in a small rented house, in less than two years Bethune had attracted 250 pupils. After absorbing the Cookman Institute for Boys in 1924, the school was renamed Bethune-Cookman College and established as a high school with junior college courses. Bethune-Cookman became a two-year junior college in 1939 and a four-year institution shortly thereafter, receiving a Grade A accreditation in 1947, the last year of Bethune's presidency. By 1998 Bethune-Cookman College, the only historically black college founded by a woman, had a student body of approximately 2,500, comprised thirty-three buildings on over sixty acres, and offered bachelor's degrees in thirty-nine majors and diplomas in six pre-professional nondegree programs.

family, many of whom had been slaves before the Civil War, owned a farm near Mayesville, South Carolina, when Mary was growing up. Mary McLeod attended the Trinity Presbyterian Mission School near her home from 1885 until 1888, and with the help of her mentor, Emma Jane Wilson, moved on to Scotia Seminary (later Barber-Scotia College), a Presbyterian school in Concord, North Carolina.

McLeod set her sights on serving as a missionary in Africa and so entered the Bible Institute for Home and Foreign Missions (later known as the Moody Bible Institute) in Chicago. She was devastated when she was informed that the Presbyterian Church would not support African-American missionaries to Africa. Instead, McLeod turned her attentions and talents to the field of education at home.

From 1896 through 1897 McLeod taught at the Haines Institute, a Presbyterian-sponsored school in Augusta, Georgia, an experience that proved meaningful for her future. At Haines, McLeod worked with Lucy Craft Laney, the school's founder and a pioneering African-American educator. McLeod took away examples and skills she would put into action throughout her life.

From Haines, McLeod moved on to another Presbyterian school, the Kendall Institute in Sumter, South Carolina, where she met and married Albertus Bethune in 1898. The couple moved to Savannah, Georgia, and in 1899 their only child, Albert Bethune, was born. Although Albertus and Mary McLeod Bethune remained married until Albertus's death in 1918, they were no longer together by 1907. In 1900 Bethune moved to Palatka, Florida, where she founded a Presbyterian school and later an independent school that also offered social services to the community.

In 1904 Bethune settled in Daytona, Florida, in order to establish a school for African-American girls. She opened her Daytona Educational and Industrial Institute in a rented house with little furniture and a tiny group of students. Students at the school learned basic academic subjects, worked on homemaking skills, engaged in religious activities, and worked with Bethune in the fields of a farm she bought in 1910. Through the farm, Bethune and her students were able to feed the members of the school community, as well as sell the surplus to benefit the school. The Daytona Institute also emphasized connections with the community, offering summer school, a playground for children, and other activities. All of this made Bethune an important voice in her local community.

The school's reputation began to grow at the national level through a visit by Booker T. Washington in 1912 and the addition of Frances Reynolds Keyser to the staff in the same year. Keyser had served as superintendent of the White Rose Mission in New York and was a well-known activist. After World War I, the school grew to include a high school and a nurses' training division. In 1923 the school merged with the failing Cookman Institute of Jacksonville, Florida, and embarked on a coeducational program. In 1929 it took the name Bethune-Cookman College. By 1935 Bethune's school, founded on a tiny budget, had become an accredited junior college and, by 1943, a fully accredited college, awarding bachelor's degrees. This success gained Bethune a national reputation and won her the NAACP's prestigious Spingarn Medal in 1935.

In addition to her success as an educator, Bethune also made a major mark on the black women's club movement in America. In 1917 she was elected president of the Florida Association of Colored Women, a post she retained until 1924. Under her leadership, the organization established a home for young women in Ocala. In 1920 Bethune organized the Southeastern Federation of Colored Women and guided this group through 1925. From 1924 to 1928, she served as president of the National Association of Colored Women (NACW), the most powerful organization of African-American women's clubs in the country. During this period, she toured Europe as the NACW's president and established the organization's headquarters in Washington, D.C., in 1928. Bethune's crowning

1875 — McLeod is born in South Carolina.

1896 — McLeod joins faculty of the Haines Institute in Augusta, Georgia.

1898 — McLeod marries Albertus Bethune.

1904 — Bethune founds Daytona Educational and Industrial Institute.

1917 — Bethune becomes president of the Florida Association of Colored Women.

1924 — Bethune becomes president of the National Association of Colored Women.

1935 — Bethune founds National Council of Negro Women.

1936 — Bethune organizes Federal Council on Negro Affairs.

1955 — Bethune dies.

achievement in the club movement was the 1935 founding of the National Council of Negro Women (NCNW). This organization served to coordinate and streamline the cooperative work of a wide variety of black women's organizations. During Bethune's fourteen years as president, the NCNW achieved this goal, began to work closely with the federal government on issues facing African Americans, and developed an international perspective on women's lives.

Bethune's influence with the Franklin D. Roosevelt administration led her to activities that made her an even greater public figure on behalf of African Americans. In 1936 she organized the Federal Council on Negro Affairs, popularly known as the Black Cabinet, a group of black advisers who helped coordinate government programs for African Americans. In this same period, she became deeply involved in the work of the National Youth Administration (NYA), serving on the advisory committee from its founding in 1935. In 1936 Bethune began functioning as director of the NYA's Division of Negro Affairs, a position that became official in 1939 and that she held until 1943. This appointment made her the highest ranking black woman in government up to that point. Bethune's goals in the NYA were to increase the representation of qualified African Americans in leadership in local and state programs and to ensure that NYA benefits distributed to whites and to blacks achieved parity.

In addition to Bethune's many other achievements, she served as the president of the Association for the Study of Negro Life and History from 1936 to 1951, established the Mary McLeod Bethune Foundation, and wrote a column for the Pittsburgh Courier. Bethune's career is testimony to her leadership skills, her commitment to justice and equality for African Americans, her unfailing dedication to the ideals of American democracy, and her philosophy of service. ◆

> *"It seems almost paradoxical, but nevertheless true, that the history of women and the history of Negroes are, in the essential features of their struggle for status, quite parallel."*
>
> Mary McLeod Bethune, 1933

Blackwell, Unita

MARCH 18, 1933 – ● CIVIL RIGHTS ACTIVIST AND POLITICIAN

Born in Lula, Mississippi, Unita Blackwell grew up during the depression and spent her first thirty years migrating from farm to farm in Mississippi, Arkansas, and Tennessee. Blackwell has been an exemplar of grassroots activism and organization within rural African-American communities.

In 1962 Blackwell and her first husband settled in the then-unincorporated town of Meyersville in Issaquena County, Mississippi, where she chopped cotton in the fields for three dollars a day. Inspired by visiting civil rights workers, she registered to vote and began to encourage other laborers to register. Fired by her employers for her activism, Blackwell joined the Student Nonviolent Coordinating Committee full time. In 1964 she helped organize the Mississippi Freedom Democratic Party and traveled to the Democratic convention in Atlantic City with the party in its failed attempt to be seated. In 1968 she would serve as a state delegate at the Democratic convention in Chicago. In 1965 and 1966, she initiated *Blackwell v. Board of Education*, a landmark case that furthered school desegregation in Mississippi.

In 1976, equipped with the political and administrative skills she had developed in the civil rights movement, Blackwell set out to incorporate the 691-acre town of Mayersville, Mississippi, organizing town meetings, filing petitions, and having the land surveyed. The incorporation became official on December 28, 1976. Blackwell was elected mayor, the first African-American woman mayor in Mississippi, a post she held through the mid-1990s. An expert on rural housing and development, Blackwell has campaigned successfully for state and federal funds for public housing and welfare. She has been selected as chairperson of the National Conference of Black Mayors, and she received a MacArthur Fellowship in 1992. ◆

1933 Blackwell is born in Lula, Mississippi.

1962 Blackwell settles in Meyersville, Mississippi.

1964 Blackwell helps organize the Mississippi Freedom Democratic Party.

1965 Blackwell initiates *Blackwell v. Board of Education* case.

1968 Blackwell serves as a delegate at the Democratic convention in Chicago.

1976 Blackwell organizes incorporation of Meyersville and becomes the town's mayor.

1992 Blackwell wins a MacArthur Fellowship.

Bolin, Jane Mathilda

APRIL 11, 1908 – ● JUDGE

Jane Bolin was born in Poughkeepsie, New York. She attended public schools there, then went to Wellesley College, graduating in 1928 as a Wellesley Scholar, an award given to the top twenty students in the class. She then attended Yale Law School and was its first black female graduate in 1931.

Bolin joined the New York **bar** in 1932, becoming the first African-American woman to do so. After working for six

bar: a court of law; a group of practicing lawyers.

1908 Bolin is born in Poughkeepsie, New York.

1928 Bolin graduates from Wellesley College.

1931 Bolin graduates from Yale Law School.

1932 Bolin passes New York bar.

1939 Bolin is named justice of Domestic Relations Court.

1978 Bolin retires from the court.

1993 Bolin receives distinguished service award from New York City.

months at her father's law firm in Poughkeepsie, she looked for employment in New York City law firms but was unable to find a job. She spent the next five years in private practice with her husband, Ralph Mizelle, whom she married in 1933. In 1936 she was an unsuccessful Republican candidate for the state assembly. In April 1937 Bolin was appointed to the Corporation Counsel's office in New York City and assigned to the Domestic Relations Court.

Two years later, Bolin was named justice of the Domestic Relations Court, becoming the first black woman judge in the United States. Mayor Fiorello La Guardia administered the oath of office to her at the 1939 World's Fair in New York. Bolin remained on the court (which was renamed the New York Family Court in 1962) until she reached the mandatory retirement age of seventy in December 1978.

While on the bench, Bolin improved the situation of black children. She worked to increase the number of probation officers assigned to cases in black neighborhoods and made private child-care agencies that receive public funds accept children without regard to their ethnicity.

Bolin also worked in civil rights, serving on the board of the New York Urban League and the national board of the NAACP. She has long been involved with child-care issues, including a stint on the board of the Child Welfare League. After retirement, she returned to private practice as a consultant in family law. In 1993 Bolin received an award for distinguished service from the New York City Corporation Counsel's office. ◆

Brooks, Gwendolyn Elizabeth

JUNE 7, 1917 – ● POET, NOVELIST, AND TEACHER

Taken to Topeka, Kansas, to be born among family, Brooks was reared in Chicago, where she continues to reside. In her autobiography, *Report from Part One* (1972), she describes a happy childhood spent in black neighborhoods with her parents and younger brother, Raymond. "I had always felt that to be black was good," Brooks observes. School awakened her to preferences among blacks, the "black-

and-tan motif" noted in her earlier works by critic Arthur P. Davis. Her father, David Anderson Brooks, was the son of a run-away slave, a janitor with "rich Artistic Abilities" who had spent a year at Fisk University, Nashville, hoping to become a doctor, and who sang, told stories, and responded compassion-ately to the poverty and misfortune around him; her mother, Keziah Wims Brooks, had been a fifth-grade teacher in Topeka and harbored a wish to write. They nurtured their daughter's precocious gifts. When the seven-year-old Gwendolyn began to write poetry, her mother predicted, "You are going to be the *lady* Paul Laurence Dunbar." Years later, Mrs. Brooks took her daughter to meet James Weldon Johnson and then Langston Hughes at church. Hughes became an inspiration, friend, and mentor to the young poet.

Brooks graduated from Wilson Junior College (now Kennedy-King) in 1936. She was employed for a month as a maid in a North Shore home and spent four months as secretary to a spiritual adviser. In 1939 she married Henry Lowington Blakely II, a fellow member of Inez Cunningham Stark's poetry workshop in the South Side Community Art Center and him-self a poet and writer. Motherhood (Henry Jr., 1940; Nora,

> *"Words do won-*
> *derful things.*
> *They sound purr.*
> *They can urge,*
> *they can wheedle,*
> *whip, whine.*
> *They can sing,*
> *sass, singe. They*
> *can churn, check,*
> *channelize."*
> Gwendolyn
> Brooks, *Contending*
> *Forces,* 1968

Black Scholar

Black Scholar is a journal that was established in 1969 by the Black World Foundation. *Black Scholar* actively sought to bridge the gap between black academia and the black community through the promotion and support of black studies programs in colleges and universities. The journal emerged out of the contest of social struggle and black self-realization that characterized the Black Power movement and was planned as a medium through which African-American ideologies could be examined, discussed, and evaluated. Under the editorial leadership of Robert Chrisman, *Black Scholar* provided a forum for black poets such as Maya Angelou and Gwendolyn Brooks. The original list of contributors included such black intellectuals as poet and activist Sonia Sanchez, psychiatrist Prince Cobb, and cultural naturalist Maulana Ron Karenga. In addition, *Black Scholar* contained community service items, such as "The Blackboard," a listing of news, events, confer-ences, and rallies; and the "Prisoner's Fund," which provided free issues of the journal to black prisoners. *Black Scholar* was initially published monthly, but since 1982 it has appeared quarterly. It has remained financially self-sufficient, relying on no outside sources other than subscriptions and selective advertisements. Its zenith of influence was in the mid-seventies; however, it has maintained its visibility into the nineties with a circula-tion base of 10,000.

1951), early publishing (*A Street in Bronzeville*, 1945), warm critical reception, careful supervision of her career by her editor at *Harper's,* and a succession of honors and prizes helped her overcome her reticence about public speaking. The first African American (or "Black," her articulated preference) to win a Pulitzer Prize, for poetry (*Annie Allen*, 1950), Brooks also received two Guggenheim Fellowships. Upon the death of Carl Sandburg (in 1968), she was named the poet **laureate** of Illinois. She was the first black woman to be elected to the National Institute of Arts and Letters (1976); to become consultant in poetry to the Library of Congress (1985–86), just before the title was changed to poet laureate); to become an honorary fellow of the Modern Language Association; and to receive the Poetry Society of America's Shelley Memorial Award and its Frost Medal. She was elected to the National Women's Hall of Fame and given the National Endowment for the Arts Lifetime Achievement Award in 1989. In Illinois, the Junior High School at Harvey, the cultural center at Western Illinois University, and the center and a chair as Distinguished Professor of English at Chicago State University all bear her name. The number of her honorary doctorates already exceeds seventy.

laureate: a person honored for achievement.

Brooks's work is notable for its impeccable craft and its social dimension. It marks a confluence of a dual stream: the black **sermonic** tradition and black music, and white antecedents such as the **ballad,** the **sonnet,** and conventional and free-verse forms. Influenced early by Hughes, T. S. Eliot, Emily Dickinson, and Robert Frost, she was propelled by the Black Arts movement of the 1960s into black nationalist consciousness. Yet her poetry has always been infused with both humanism and heroism, the latter defined as extending the concept of leadership, by both personality and art. In 1969 she moved to Dudley Randall's nascent, historic Broadside Press for the publication of *Riot* and subsequent works.

sermonic: like a sermon (public speech about religion).

ballad: a story poem.

sonnet: a formal 14-line poem.

Brooks's books span six decades of social and political changes. *A Street in Bronzeville* addresses the quotidian realities of segregation for black Americans at home and in World War II military service; *Annie Allen* ironically explores postwar antiromanticism; *Maud Martha,* her novel (1953), sketches a bildungsroman of black womanhood; *Bronzeville Boys and Girls* (1956) presents sturdy, home-oriented black children of the 1950s; *The Bean Eaters* (1960) and new poems in *Selected Poems* (1963) sound the urgencies of the civil rights movement. In 1967, at the second Fisk University Writers' Conference at

Nashville, Brooks was deeply impressed by the activist climate, personified by Amiri Baraka. Though she had always experimented with conventional forms, her work subsequently opened more distinctly to free verse, a feature of the multiform *In the Mecca* (1968), which Haki R. Madhubuti calls "her epic of Black humanity" (*Report from Part One*, p. 22).

Upon returning to Chicago from the conference at Fisk, Brooks conducted a workshop with the Blackstone Rangers, a teenage gang, who were succeeded by young writers such as Carolyn M. Rodgers and Madhubuti (then don l. lee). Broadside published *Riot* (1969), *Family Pictures* (1970), *Aloneness* (1971), and *Beckonings* (1975). Madhubuti's Third World Press published *The Tiger Who Wore White Gloves* (1974) and *To Disembark* (1981). In 1971 Brooks began a literary annual, *The Black Position*, under her own aegis, and made the first of her two trips to Africa. Beginning with *Primer for Blacks* (1980), she published with her own company *The Near-Johannesburg Boy* (1986), the omnibus volume *Blacks* (1987), *Gottschalk and the Grande Tarantelle* (1988), and *Winnie* (1988, a poem honoring Winnie Mandela). Her books are also being reissued by Third World Press. The adult poems of *Children Coming Home* (1991) express the perspective of contemporary children, and may be contrasted with the benign ambience of *Bronzeville Boys and Girls* among her works for children.

Brooks supports and promotes the creativity of other writers. Her annual Poet Laureate Awards distribute considerable sums of her own money, chiefly to the schoolchildren of Illinois. She visits prisons, where her readings have inspired poets such as the late Ethridge Knight. Lauded with affectionate respect in two tribute anthologies, recognized nationally and internationally as a major literary figure, Brooks continues to claim and to vivify our democratic heritage. ◆

1917 Brooks is born in Topeka, Kansas.

1936 Brooks graduates from Wilson Junior College.

1945 Brooks publishes *A Street in Bronzeville*.

1950 Brooks wins Pulitzer Prize for poetry for *Annie Allen*.

1968 Brooks is named poet laureate of Illinois.

1976 Brooks is elected to National Institute of Arts and Letters.

1985 Brooks is named consultant in poetry at Library of Congress.

1989 Brooks receives National Endowment for the Arts Lifetime Achievement Award.

Brown, Charlotte Hawkins

JUNE 11, 1883 – JANUARY 10, 1961 ● EDUCATOR

One of the premier educators of her day, Charlotte Hawkins Brown was also a key figure in the network of southern African-American club women who were active in the late nineteenth and early twentieth centuries.

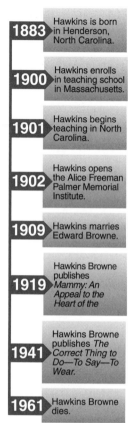

1883 Hawkins is born in Henderson, North Carolina.

1900 Hawkins enrolls in teaching school in Massachusetts.

1901 Hawkins begins teaching in North Carolina.

1902 Hawkins opens the Alice Freeman Palmer Memorial Institute.

1909 Hawkins marries Edward Browne.

1919 Hawkins Browne publishes *Mammy: An Appeal to the Heart of the*

1941 Hawkins Browne publishes *The Correct Thing to Do—To Say—To Wear.*

1961 Hawkins Browne dies.

Brown was born Lottie Hawkins in Henderson, North Carolina. When she was five her family moved to Cambridge, Massachusetts, where her mother and stepfather operated a laundry and boarded Harvard students. During this period the family retained close ties with its Carolina roots.

Hawkins studied hard and was active in church and youth groups in Cambridge. She also developed an interest in art and music that became lifelong. As a high school student, Hawkins met Alice Freeman Palmer, the second president of Wellesley College, who took an immediate interest in her. Palmer was so impressed with Hawkins that she financed her education at the State Normal School in Salem, Massachusetts, where Hawkins enrolled in 1900 to earn a teacher's certificate. She left school in 1901 to take a position with the American Missionary Association at a small school in North Carolina. Although the school soon closed because of inadequate funding, Hawkins determined to dedicate herself to education in her home state.

By October of 1902 Hawkins had secured a donation of land, a building, and funds to open the Alice Freeman Palmer Memorial Institute in Sedalia, North Carolina. In 1909 she married Edward Brown, a graduate of Harvard, who taught at the Palmer Institute briefly before the couple separated and divorced. Over the years, under Charlotte Hawkins Brown's leadership, Palmer developed into a highly respected institution for preparatory training. From its early focus on vocational education, the school moved to a strict academic curriculum. The campus, the student body, and the faculty grew steadily, and Palmer sent many of its graduates to institutions of higher learning. Brown's work as an educator received recognition within her home state and across the country.

Brown was a key figure among black club women, serving as president of the North Carolina State Federation of Negro Women's Clubs. She was also active in interracial work as a member of the national board of the YWCA and also worked with other organizations. She campaigned against lynching and toured widely as a lecturer. Brown also assisted in the founding of other schools in North Carolina, including the Dobbs School for Girls and the Morrison Training School, and she helped to establish scholarship funds for the college education of African-American women.

In addition to her work as an educator and activist, Brown raised her brother's three children and three of her young cousins. She also published two works, *Mammy: An Appeal to the Heart of the South* (1919) and *The Correct Thing to Do—To Say—To Wear* (1940). Brown remained the president of the Palmer Memorial Institute until 1952 and died nine years later. Although the institute ceased operation in 1971, the state of North Carolina has kept the memory of Brown's contributions and achievements alive in a memorial to her and to her institution. ◆

Browne, Marjorie Lee

SEPTEMBER 9, 1914 – OCTOBER 19, 1979 ● MATHEMATICIAN

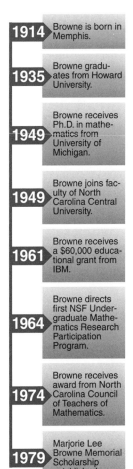

1914 Browne is born in Memphis.

1935 Browne graduates from Howard University.

1949 Browne receives Ph.D. in mathematics from University of Michigan.

1949 Browne joins faculty of North Carolina Central University.

1961 Browne receives a $60,000 educational grant from IBM.

1964 Browne directs first NSF Undergraduate Mathematics Research Participation Program.

1974 Browne receives award from North Carolina Council of Teachers of Mathematics.

1979 Marjorie Lee Browne Memorial Scholarship established.

Marjorie Lee Browne was reared in Memphis, Tennessee, by her father, Lawrence J. Lee, a railroad postal-service worker, and stepmother, Lottie Taylor Lee, a schoolteacher. Her father was an avid reader who shared with her his excitement for travel, visualization, and learning through the written word. Reading—first the classics, then mysteries—became an obsession with her and provided excellent preparation for the development of the analytic reasoning skills she would later employ in her mathematical studies. She was an excellent tennis player, and won many City of Memphis women's singles tennis championships. She was also a singer of some repute and a lover of music, as well as a gifted mathematics student.

Browne was a 1935 cum laude graduate of Howard University and received master of science (1939) and Ph.D. (1949) degrees in mathematics from the University of Michigan. She was one of the first two African-American women to receive a Ph.D. in mathematics (the other was Evelyn Boyd Granville from Yale). Her teaching career at North Carolina Central University in Durham spanned thirty years (1949–79), and under her leadership as mathematics department chairman (1951–70), the university achieved many firsts. In 1961 she received a $60,000 IBM educational grant to establish the first academic computer center at the university; in 1969 she received the first of seven Shell Foundation scholarship grants for outstanding mathematics students. Browne directed the first National Science Foundation (NSF) Undergraduate Mathematics Research

Participation Program (1964–65), and was a principal investigator, coordinator of the mathematics section, and lecturer in thirteen NSF Institutes for Secondary School Teachers of Science and Mathematics (1957–71).

In 1974 the North Carolina Council of Teachers of Mathematics awarded Browne the first W. W. Rankin Memorial Award for Excellence in Mathematics Education in recognition of her efforts in improving the quality of the mathematics preparation of secondary-school teachers in the state. She was one of six African-American women included in the 1981 Smithsonian traveling exhibition "Black Women: Achievements Against the Odds."

Pursuing what she would later call "the life of an academic nomad," she completed four postdoctoral fellowship programs that included studies and research in combinatorial **topology** (her specialty), the applications of mathematics in the behavioral sciences, numerical analysis and computing, **differential** topology, **Lie** groups, and Lie algebras. These activities were undertaken at universities in this country and abroad, including Cambridge University (1952–53), Stanford University (summer 1957), UCLA (1958–59), and Columbia University (1965–66).

Browne's published works include "A Note on the Classical Groups" (*Mathematical Monthly*, August 1955) and four manuscripts: "Sets, Logic and Mathematical Thought," 1957; "Introduction to Linear Algebra," 1959; "Algebraic Structures," 1964; and "Elementary Matrix Algebra," 1969. At the time of her death in 1979, she was pursuing a research project titled "A **Postulational** Approach to the Development of the Real Number System."

During the 1950s, Browne was an ardent advocate for the integration of the previously segregated professional organizations in which she held membership, including the North Carolina Teachers Association, the Mathematical Association of America, and the American Mathematical Society. She also held membership in Beta Kappa Chi, the Society of Sigma Xi, Pi Lambda Theta Honorary Societies, the Woman's Research Society, and Alpha Kappa Alpha Sorority. She was a faculty consultant in mathematics with the Ford Foundation (1968–69) and served three terms as a member of the advisory panel to the NSF Undergraduate Scientific Equipment Program (1966, 1967, and 1973). In 1979, four of her former students established the Marjorie Lee Browne Trust Fund at North Carolina

topology: a branch of geometry.

differential: relating to the product of a mathematical function.

Lie: a system of algebra.

postulational: relating to an unproved assumption used as a basis for reasoning.

Central University to support the Marjorie Lee Browne Memorial Scholarship, awarded annually to a mathematics student who best exemplifies those traits that Browne sought to instill in young people.

Browne was a mathematical **purist** who, like many great mathematicians of the nineteenth century, viewed mathematics as an art form, as an intellectual quest, free from the limitations of the physical universe, in search simply for truth and beauty. ◆

purist: one who adheres strictly to a tradition.

Burke, Yvonne Brathwaite

OCTOBER 5, 1932 – ● LAWYER AND POLITICIAN

Yvonne Brathwaite was born and raised in South Central Los Angeles. She received an associate's degree from Berkeley in 1951, a bachelor's degree in political science from UCLA in 1953, and a law degree from USC in 1956, the year in which she was admitted to the California bar and began a private law practice. In 1965 Burke was appointed by California governor Edmund G. "Pat" Brown as attorney for the McCone Commission, which investigated the Los Angeles Watts riots.

In 1966 Burke was elected to the first of her three two-year terms representing the Sixty-third District in the California State Assembly. California's first black assemblywoman, she focused on prison reform, child care, equality for women, and civil rights. In 1972, she served as vice chairperson of the Democratic National Convention, where she received national attention as a promoter of changes in the party's rules enabling greater participation by minorities. The same year, she was also elected to the first of three terms representing the Thirty-seventh District in the United States House of Representatives, and became the first black congresswoman from California. In Congress, she again focused on social issues, especially housing and urban development. In 1975 she was appointed to the powerful House Committee on Appropriations, and in 1976 she became chair of the Congressional Black Caucus.

Although her early political career made her one of the most prominent black women in American politics, her political

1932 Burke is born in Los Angeles.

1956 Burke earns a law degree from University of Southern California.

1965 Burke is appointed attorney to the commission investigating the Watts riots.

1966 Burke is elected to the California State Assembly.

1972 Burke wins a seat in the U.S. Congress.

1976 Burke becomes chair of the Congressional Black Caucus.

1979 Burke joins the LA County Board of Supervisors.

campaigns in the late 1970s were unsuccessful, and she then concentrated on her career as a lawyer and senior partner at the Los Angeles firm of Jones, Day, Deavis, Bogue. In 1978 she returned to California to run for state attorney general, winning the Democratic nomination, but losing the general election to Republican George Deukmejian. On July 6, 1979, Governor Edmund G. "Jerry" Brown Jr. appointed her to a vacancy in the Los Angeles County Board of Supervisors, a position she held until an election defeat in 1980. She resumed her political career in 1992, when she became the first African American to be elected to the Los Angeles County Board of Supervisors. ◆

Burroughs, Nannie Helen

MAY 2, 1879 – MAY 20, 1961 ● EDUCATOR

Nannie Helen Burroughs was born in Orange, Virginia. Her father, born free, attended the Richmond Institute and became a preacher. Her mother, born a slave in Virginia, left her husband and took her two young daughters to Washington, D.C., to attend school. At the Colored High School (later Dunbar High), where she was deeply interested in domestic science, Burroughs came in contact with Mary Church Terrell and Anna Julia Cooper, two women who became her role models. In 1896, after graduation, she got a job at the Philadelphia office of the *Christian Banner* while also working part-time for the Rev. Lewis Jordan, an official of the National Baptist Convention (NBC). When Jordan moved to Louisville, Kentucky, Burroughs also relocated there. In Louisville she initiated her career of activism by organizing a women's industrial club that offered evening classes in bookkeeping, sewing, cooking, and typing.

"Teach the children pride. Nothing learned is worth anything if you don't know how to be proud of yourself."

Nannie Helen Burroughs, 1927

In 1900, at the annual meeting of the National Baptist Convention in Virginia, Burroughs gave a speech, "How the Sisters Are Hindered from Helping," which gained her national recognition and served as a catalyst for the formation of the largest black women's organization in the United States, the Woman's Convention (WC), an auxiliary to the NBC. The WC was the result of long-standing efforts by women in the Baptist Church to develop an organization to represent them. It

provided a forum for black women to deal with religious, political, and social issues, and took the lead in their religious and
educational training. From 1900 to 1948 Burroughs served as
corresponding secretary to the WC, and from 1948 until her
death in 1961 she served as president. Because of her hard work
and leadership, the membership of the WC grew dramatically,
reaching one million members in 1903 and 1.5 million in 1907.

Burroughs spent nearly her entire adult life in the public
arena challenging racial discrimination and encouraging
African Americans to maintain pride and dignity. An eloquent
public speaker, she toured the country denouncing lynching,
segregation, employment discrimination, and colonialism. She
supported the efforts of the NAACP to attain legal equality for
blacks, and criticized President Woodrow Wilson for his silence
on lynching. She was a staunch feminist who believed women's
suffrage was a route to racial advancement as well as a safeguard
against male domination and sexual abuse. Like many women
of her time, Burroughs believed in the moral superiority of
women and the positive impact they could have on the public
life of African Americans. Referring to the ballot, she wrote,
"The Negro woman needs to get back by the wise use of it what
the Negro man has lost by the misuse of it." She was convinced
that if given political power, black women would take an
uncompromising stand against racial discrimination and political disfranchisement.

In 1896 she joined other women and formed the National
Association of Colored Women (NACW) to promote the
political mobilization of black women. She became deeply
involved in partisan politics, and in 1924 she and other clubwomen founded the National League of Republican Colored
Women. Burroughs became a much sought-after participant by
the Republican party's national speakers bureau. When Herbert
Hoover was elected president in 1928, he chose Burroughs to
head a fact-finding commission on housing. Even after the election of Franklin D. Roosevelt in 1932, when most African
Americans transferred their political loyalty to the Democratic
party, Burroughs continued her steadfast support of the Republicans.

In addition to opposing institutional racism, Burroughs was
also a tireless advocate for black pride and self-help. She
believed that progress was ultimately a question of individual
will and effort, and that with enough self-esteem and self-

1879 Burroughs is born in Orange, Virginia.

1896 Burroughs starts working for the *Christian Banner* and the National Baptist Convention.

1900 Burroughs begins service as corresponding secretary for the Woman's Convention.

1909 Burroughs founds the National Training School for Women and Girls in Washington, DC.

1924 Burroughs helps form the National League of Republican Colored Women.

1928 President Hoover chooses Burroughs to head a fact-finding commission on housing.

1948 Burroughs becomes president of the Woman's Convention.

1961 Burroughs dies in Washington.

confidence people could overcome racial barriers. In 1909 in Washington, D.C., she founded the National Training School for Women and Girls, which was renamed the Nannie Helen Burroughs School in 1964. The core of their training was what Burroughs called the "three B's": Bible, bath, and broom. The school also offered industrial training in a wide variety of occupations, such as printing, bookkeeping, housekeeping, **stenography,** dressmaking, and cooking. Burroughs encouraged black women to work hard and excel, whatever their position in society. Through her religious and educational work, she hoped to imbue black women with moral values, such as thrift and hard work, as well as prepare them to become self-sufficient wage earners. Burroughs died in Washington, D.C., at the age of eighty-two. ◆

stenography: shorthand and typing.

Butler, Octavia Estelle

JUNE 22, 1947 – ● WRITER

Butler is one of a select number of African Americans whose writing deliberately discards the realistic tradition to embrace a specialized genre—science fiction. The only surviving child of Laurice and Octavia M. Guy Butler, she was raised in a racially and culturally diverse neighborhood of Pasadena, California, and educated in the city. College consisted of a two-year program at Pasadena City College and subsequent course work at both California State College and UCLA. Dyslexic, extremely shy, and therefore solitary, Butler began writing as a child, convinced she could write better science fiction stories than those she saw on television.

Respected by the science fiction community of writers, critics, and fans as an important author ever since her first books earned excellent reviews, Butler has produced many novels and several highly regarded short stories. Her first published novel (although plotwise the last in its series), *Patternmaster* (1976), is one of the five books in her past-and-future-history Patternist saga, a series of interrelated stories using genetic breeding and the development of "psionic" powers as a unifying motif. The saga reaches from precolonial Africa to a post-holocaust Earth of the distant future. In the proper reading order, the books in

"My mother read me bedtime stories until I was six years old. It was a sneak attack on her part. As soon as I really got to like the stories, she said, 'Here's the book, now you read.'"

Octavia Butler, quoted in *Essence,* May 1989

the tale are *Wild Seed* (1980), *Mind of My Mind* (1977), *Clay's Ark* (1984), and *Survivor* (1978).

In each of these novels, as in *Kindred* (1979)—her only novel outside a series—Butler conspicuously introduces issues of race and gender to science fiction. Her female protagonists are African, African-American, or mixed-race women operating principally in nontraditional modes. This depiction of women as powerful, self-sustaining, and capable, able either to adapt or to nurture and heal, equally equipped to fight or to compromise, gained Butler the critical approval of two additional audiences—black readers and scholars, and white feminists.

Butler's Xenogenesis series—*Dawn* (1987), *Adulthood Rites* (1988), and *Imago* (1989)—which was deemed "satisfying . . . hard science fiction" by Orson Scott Card, continues an examination of women in differing roles as it explores issues of human survival in another grim post-holocaust future where aliens have landed. Here Butler continues to explore her interest in genetics, anthropology, ecology, and sociobiology. Also central are issues of family, alliances or networks, power, control, and hierarchical structures fueling what Butler designates the "human contradiction," the capacity for self-destruction if humanity refuses to change.

Although she is primarily a novelist, Butler's short stories have won two coveted science fiction awards. "Speech Sounds" (1983) received a Hugo; "Bloodchild" (1984) earned both a Hugo and a Nebula. Each first appeared in *Isaac Asimov's Science Fiction Magazine*. "The Evening and the Morning and the Night" (1987) initially appeared in *Omni*. "Bloodchild" explores a forced human adaptation to change through the metaphor of male pregnancy; "Speech Sounds" examines a violent near-future cityscape whose inhabitants contract a sometimes deadly illness that dramatically affects language. "The Evening . . ." recounts the impact of a terrifying genetically based disease and the efforts of those affected to eradicate or control it.

Butler began a new series with *Parable of the Sower* (1993), a novel about a young **empathic** African-American woman who travels the country during the twenty-first century spreading a new religion called "Earthseed." The Earthseed saga continues in Butler's 1998 *Parable of the Talents: A Novel.* ◆

1947 ▶ Butler is born.

1976 ▶ Butler publishes her first novel, *Patternmaster,* beginning the Patternist saga.

1979 ▶ Butler publishes *Kindred.*

1983 ▶ Butler's story "Speech Sounds" wins a Hugo Award.

1984 ▶ Butler's story "Bloodchild" wins Hugo and Nebula awards.

1987 ▶ Butler publishes *Dawn,* beginning her Xenogenesis series.

1993 ▶ Butler publishes *Parable of the Sower,* beginning the Earthseed series.

empathic: sensitive to the feelings and thoughts of others.

Carroll, Diahann

July 17, 1935 – ● Singer and Actor

In 1968, Diahann Carroll became the first African-American woman to have her own television series when she starred in *Julia*.

Diahann Carroll was born Carol Diahann Johnson in New York, the daughter of John Johnson, a subway conductor, and Mabel (Faulk) Johnson. Her mother had her take voice and piano lessons, and at the recommendation of a guidance counselor she enrolled in the High School of Music and Art. She modeled for *Ebony* and other magazines, and at fourteen, appearing under the name "Diahann Carroll," she won first prize on the popular television show *Arthur Godfrey's Talent Scouts*. Carroll enrolled at New York University, but left during her first year, after winning a talent contest on the television show *Chance of a Lifetime*. Over the following years she toured as a singer in various important hotels and nightclubs. Her light, swinging style was influenced by Frank Sinatra and Ella Fitzgerald. She released several albums, including *Fun Life* (1961).

In 1954 Carroll began an acting career when she was chosen for the role of Ottilie in Harold Arlen and Truman Capote's *House of Flowers*. While small, the role included the song "A Sleepin' Bee," which Carroll popularized. She received a Tony Award nomination for the role. The same year, she made her screen debut in a small role in the film *Carmen Jones*. She went on to perform in such films as *Porgy and Bess* (1959), *Paris Blues* (1961), and *Goodbye Again* (1961). She returned to Broadway in 1962, as the lead in Richard Rodgers's musical *No Strings*, for which she won a Tony Award. Twenty years later she again appeared on Broadway, this time in the drama *Agnes of God*.

In 1968 Carroll became the first African-American woman to have her own television series, when she starred in the series *Julia*. Carroll played a widowed mother who worked as a nurse. The role aroused a storm of opposition among some blacks, who felt that the character was too "white," and represented white liberal images of African Americans rather than being authentically black. Nevertheless the program was a success.

Carroll remained with the program for three seasons; then, tired of the controversy, she asked to be released from her contract. In a reversal of her image, Carroll next played a single ghetto mother in the film *Claudine* (1974), for which she was nominated for an Academy Award and won an NAACP Image Award. In 1976 she was inducted into the Black Filmmakers' Hall of Fame.

Starting in the 1970s, Carroll revived her singing career, starring in nightclubs and in such places as the Kennedy Center for the Performing Arts (1971). Her solo album *Diahann Carroll* (1974) won her a Grammy Award nomination.

During the late 1970s and 1980s Carroll also returned to television. In 1979 she appeared in the miniseries *Roots: The Next Generation*, and in the television film *I Know Why the Caged Bird Sings*. In 1984 she took the role of Dominique Devereaux on the television series *Dynasty*, thus becoming the first African American to star in a nighttime soap opera. Carroll felt that her portrayal of a character as conniving and mean-spirited as her white peers was both her best work and an important step forward for black actors. In the 1990s she appeared frequently on the TV series *A Different World*, as the mother of Whitley Guilbert. ◆

1935	Carroll is born in New York.
1954	Carroll begins her acting career in *House of Flowers*.
1968	Carroll begins her starring role in the TV series *Julia*.
1974	Carroll stars in *Claudine*, for which she earns an Academy Award nomination.
1976	Carroll is inducted into the Black Filmmakers' Hall of Fame.
1984	Carroll begins playing Dominique Devereaux on *Dynasty*.
1990	Carroll begins a recurring role in *A Different World*.

Cary, Mary Ann Shadd

OCTOBER 9, 1823 – JUNE 5, 1893 ● TEACHER AND JOURNALIST

Mary Ann Shadd Cary was born in Wilmington, Delaware, the daughter of free blacks, Abraham and Harriet Parnell Shadd. After attending a Quaker school in West Chester, Pennsylvania, she returned to Wilmington, where at age sixteen she opened a school, the first of several she was to establish during the following decades. After passage of the Fugitive Slave Law of 1850, Mary and her brother Isaac went to Windsor, Canada, where she founded a school for both black and white pupils. In 1856 she married Thomas F. Cary of Toronto. She resumed teaching in Chatham (1859–64) under the **auspices** of the American Missionary Association.

Cary's most noteworthy achievements center on the *Provincial Freeman,* a weekly Canadian newspaper, published with varying regularity between 1853 and 1859. Although men (Samuel Ringgold War and the Rev. William P. Newman) served as **titular** editors, Cary was recognized by her contemporaries as the real editor. She is generally acknowledged to be the first woman publisher of a newspaper in Canada and the first black newspaperwoman in North America. A crusading journalist, Cary became embroiled in particularly bitter quarrels—notably with Henry Bibb—over the issue of integration (the question of whether blacks were exiles or new citizens of Canada) and about the activities of the Refugee Home Society, whose land-purchase scheme, she claimed, offered no advantage over the Canadian government's offers and was sometimes more costly.

During the Civil War, Cary returned to the United States to recruit for the Union army, working in Indiana, Ohio, and Michigan. Between 1869 and 1874, she taught public school in Detroit and in Washington, D.C., where she also served as a principal (1872–74). An activist for women's suffrage, Cary addressed the annual convention of the National Woman Suffrage Association in 1878 and was founder of the Colored Women's Progressive Association (Washington, D.C.). She received her LL.B. degree from Howard University Law School in 1883; she was the first woman to receive the degree from that school and only the second black woman to earn a law degree.

In addition to her work for the *Provincial Freeman,* Cary was the author of an advisory pamphlet, *Hints to the Colored People of the North* (1849), espousing her ideals of self-help; of *A Plea for Emigration, or Notes on Canada West, in Its Moral, Social, and Political Aspect* (1852), a booklet describing opportunities for blacks in Canada; and (with Osborne Anderson, one of the five survivors of John Brown's raid) of *A Voice from Harpers Ferry* (1873). She contributed to Frederick Douglass's *New National Era* and John Wesley Cromwell's *Advocate* as well. ◆

auspices: kindly patronage and guidance.

titular: bearing the title but not the responsibilities.

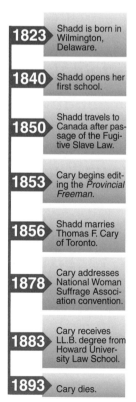

1823 Shadd is born in Wilmington, Delaware.

1840 Shadd opens her first school.

1850 Shadd travels to Canada after passage of the Fugitive Slave Law.

1853 Cary begins editing the *Provincial Freeman.*

1856 Shadd marries Thomas F. Cary of Toronto.

1878 Cary addresses National Woman Suffrage Association convention.

1883 Cary receives LL.B. degree from Howard University Law School.

1893 Cary dies.

Catlett, Elizabeth

APRIL 15, 1919 – ● ARTIST

The youngest of three children, Elizabeth Catlett was educated at Dunbar High School in Washington, D.C. Her father, John Catlett, taught at Tuskeegee Institute and in the D.C. public schools. He died before her birth. Her mother, Mary Carson Catlett, worked as a truant officer.

Catlett graduated cum laude from Howard University School of Art in 1937, studying with James Herring, James Porter (drawing), James Wells (printmaking), and Lois Mailou Jones (design). In 1940 Catlett earned the M.F.A. degree from the University of Iowa. She studied with painter Grant Wood and changed her concentration from painting to sculpture. In

Howard University

Elizabeth Catlett, who graduated from Howard University's School of Art in 1937, is one of numerous distinguished African Americans to graduate from Howard University. Howard was founded in Washington, D.C., in 1867 to train ministers and educators for work among newly freed slaves. The institution was named after Oliver Otis Howard, a Civil War general and head of the Freedmen's Bureau. In the first years of Howard University's operation, very few African Americans were involved in its administration. The first students enrolled at Howard were four white women who graduated from the Normal Department in 1870. In the next several decades, more and more African-American students matriculated at Howard, and African-American membership in the faculty and the board of trustees gradually increased. By the 1920s and 1930s, Howard had become the center of African-American intellectual life and attracted a brilliant faculty committed to finding new directions for black America. In the 1920s, Howard became the first American university to offer comprehensive courses in the civilization and history of Africa. Mordecai W. Johnson, a Baptist minister, became Howard's first African-American president in 1926.

By 1998 Howard had an enrollment of over 10,000, making it the largest predominantly African-American university in the United States. Many distinguished African-American women have served on the Howard faculty, including Martha B. Briggs, Margaret Just Butcher, Hazel Harrison, Anna Arnold Hedgemann, Patricia Harris, and Toni Morrison. Notable African-American women to graduate from Howard include Mary Ann Shadd Cary, Marjorie Lee Browne, Toni Morrison, Jessye Norman, Debbie Allen, Phylicia Rashad, Elaine R. Jones, Sharon Pratt Kelly, and Roberta Flack.

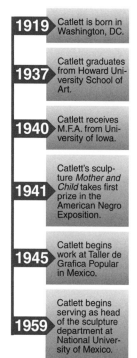

1919 Catlett is born in Washington, DC.

1937 Catlett graduates from Howard University School of Art.

1940 Catlett receives M.F.A. from University of Iowa.

1941 Catlett's sculpture *Mother and Child* takes first prize in the American Negro Exposition.

1945 Catlett begins work at Taller de Grafica Popular in Mexico.

1959 Catlett begins serving as head of the sculpture department at National University of Mexico.

linocut: a print made from a design cut into a piece of linoleum.

collograph: a textured image printed from a collage.

serigraph: a print made using a special silk screen process.

1941, her thesis project, a marble sculpture, *Mother and Child*, took first prize in the American Negro Exposition in Chicago.

From 1940 to 1942, Catlett was head of the art department at Dillard University. Among her students was Samella Sanders (Lewis), who became a lifelong friend and her biographer. In the summer of 1941, Catlett studied ceramics at the Art Institute of Chicago. She met and married Charles White. Over six years they spent time in Chicago, where she worked at the South Side Art Center; New York, where she studied with sculptor Ossip Zadkine (1942 and 1943); and Hampton Institute, where she taught sculpture (1943). She came to believe that graphics was the appropriate medium to reach large, diverse audiences, and in 1944 she took lithography at the Art Students' League in New York.

In 1945 Catlett received a Julius Rosenwald Foundation award to do a series on African-American women. She and Charles White traveled to Mexico to work at the Taller de Grafica Popular. She also studied sculpture at the Escula de Pintura y Ecultura with Francisco Zumiga and wood carving with José L. Ruiz. After a brief period in New York when she divorced, she returned to Mexico. In 1947 she married Mexican artist Francisco Mora. They have three sons, Francisco, Juan, and David. The two artists remained part of the Taller de Grafia Popular until 1966.

In 1958 she became the first woman to teach at the National University of Mexico's School of Fine Arts. From 1959 until her retirement from teaching in 1976, she served as the head of the school's sculpture department.

Catlett's work combines realism and abstract art. Much of her work deals with African-American women: the mother and child theme is strong and recurring. Her art reflects her concern with the needs and aspirations of common people, the poor, and the oppressed. The influence of Mexican as well as African-American culture is evident. Her sculpture ranges from monumental to small. It is in wood, bronze, stone, terra-cotta, or marble. Works on paper are lithographs, **linocuts,** woodcuts, **collographs,** and **serigraphs.** Among the most well known are *Sharecropper* (1968) and *Malcolm X Speaks for Us* (1969).

Beginning in 1940, her work has been shown in numerous solo and group exhibitions. It is included in over two dozen prestigious public collections and in many books, catalogs, periodicals, and film and video productions. She has received awards in several countries. Elizabeth Catlett correctly has been called a pioneer and one of the greatest artists of the twentieth century. She and her husband live in Cuernavaca and New York City. ◆

Celia

? – DECEMBER 23, 1855 ● SLAVE

I n 1855 Celia stood trial in Fulton, Missouri, for the murder of her master, Robert Newsom, a prosperous Callaway County farmer. The events that led to her arrest, her trial, and her ultimate fate provide a fascinating case study of the significance of gender in the slave-holding South and the manner in which the southern legal system was manipulated to ensure the slaveholders' power over their human **chattel** while creating the illusion of a society that extended the protection of the law to its slaves.

chattel: a piece of property that is not land.

Purchased a year after the death of Newsom's wife in 1849, Celia served as his **concubine** for five years, during which time she bore him two children. She lived in a brick cabin he built for her behind the farmhouse, where Newsom lived with two adult daughters, one of whom had two children of her own. By the mid-1850s, Newsom's two sons had established their own farms near that of their father. Sometime in 1854 Celia began a relationship with George, another of Newsom's slaves. When she became pregnant for the third time, George demanded that Celia cease to have sexual relations with her master. Celia appealed to the Newsom women to prevent their father from sexually abusing her. The daughters, however, were in no position to control the actions of their father, who continued to view sexual relations with Celia as his privilege.

concubine: a women with whom a man lives without being married.

On a June night in 1855, Newsom demanded sex of Celia, who responded by beating him to death with a club and disposing of his body by burning it in her fireplace. The family's efforts to find the missing father led George to implicate Celia in his disappearance, and under threat to her children, she confessed and was arrested and tried. Missouri law assigned her public council, led by John Jameson, a noted attorney and democratic politician. Jameson based his defense on the claim that Celia,

The judge presiding over Celia's trial agreed with the prosecution that a female slave had no right to use force to reject her master's sexual demands.

under Missouri law, had the same right to use deadly force to defend her honor as did white women. This defense not only recognized the crime of rape against slave women, something the legal system of no southern state did, it also threatened a slaveholder's control over the reproductive capabilities of female slaves. For precisely these reasons it was disallowed by the presiding judge, who agreed with the prosecution's traditional contention that a female slave had no right to use force to reject her master's sexual demands. A jury of local farmers convicted her, and the Missouri Supreme Court rejected her attorneys' appeal for a new trial. On December 23, 1855, Celia was hanged in Fulton. ◆

Chase-Riboud, Barbara Dewayne

JUNE 26, 1939 – ● SCULPTOR, POET, AND NOVELIST

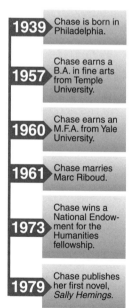

1939 Chase is born in Philadelphia.

1957 Chase earns a B.A. in fine arts from Temple University.

1960 Chase earns an M.F.A. from Yale University.

1961 Chase marries Marc Riboud.

1973 Chase wins a National Endowment for the Humanities fellowship.

1979 Chase publishes her first novel, *Sally Hemings*.

The only child of middle-class parents, Barbara Chase was born in Philadelphia and raised in that city. After earning a B.A. in fine arts from Temple University in 1957, Chase traveled to Rome, Italy, on a John Hay Whitney Foundation fellowship. There she worked for the first time in bronze and entered her sculptures in exhibitions at the Spoleto Festival (1957) and at the American Academy in Rome and the Gallery L'Obeliso (1958). During the winter of 1957, Chase spent three months in Egypt, receiving what she later termed a "blast of Egyptian culture." The visit marked a turning point in her artistic career, as Chase, newly exposed to nonclassical art, was forced to reevaluate the academic training with which her works had previously been infused. "Though I didn't know it at the time," she said, "my own transformation was part of the historical transformation of the blacks that began in the '60s."

After receiving an M.F.A. from Yale University (1960), Chase traveled to London before finally settling in Paris. In 1961, she married the French photographer Marc Riboud; shortly thereafter, the couple journeyed to China, Chase-Riboud being one of the first American women to visit the country after the onset of the Cultural Revolution. Her notes from the trip, which also included visits to Nepal and Inner Mongolia, were later transformed into a collection of poems, issued under the title *From Memphis to Peking* (1974).

Although Chase-Riboud's interest in Asian art can be traced to sculptures dating from as early as 1960, it was not until the latter half of the decade that she began fully to incorporate this and African influences into her own work. She became known for using radically different materials—such as bronze and wool, steel and synthetics, and bronze and silk—in compositions that were both abstract and expressive, elegant and **minimalist.** Hemp, wood, **raffia,** leathers, metals, and feathers were also used in figures reminiscent of African masks. Chase-Riboud exhibited her work internationally at such festivals as the New York Architectural League Show (1965), the Festival of Negro Art in Dakar (1966), and the L'Oeil Ecoute Festival of Avignon (1969).

minimalism: an art form in which the simplest, most basic forms and materials are used.

raffia: fiber from a type of palm tree that grows in Madagascar.

By the early 1970s, Chase-Riboud's work had achieved worldwide renown. She was awarded a National Endowment for the Humanities fellowship in 1973 and an outstanding alumni award from Temple University in 1975. In addition to participating in group shows at the Boston Museum of Fine Arts, the Smithsonian Institution of Washington, D.C. (National Gallery of Art), New York's Whitney Museum, the Centre Pompidou of Paris, and other museums, Chase-Riboud held solo exhibitions at the Betty Parsons Gallery in New York, the Museum of Modern Art in Paris, and the Kunstmuseum in Düsseldorf, among others.

Chase-Riboud came to prominence as an author in 1979 with the publication of her first novel, *Sally Hemings,* a historical work based on Thomas Jefferson's relationship with his slave mistress. She won the Janet Heidinger Kafka Prize for fiction for that volume. Her claim that Jefferson had fathered seven children with Hemings proved extremely controversial, and she was both widely commended and criticized for her endeavor. In 1981 Chase-Riboud divorced Marc Riboud and married Sergio G. Tosi, an Italian art dealer and publisher. Four years later, she published a second volume of poems, *Love Perfecting,* and another novel about slavery, *Valide,* in 1986. Two additional works followed, a collection of poems titled *Study of a Nude Woman as Cleopatra* (1988) and a novel, *Echo of Lions* (1989).

Chase-Riboud, who was awarded an honorary doctorate from Temple University in 1981, continued to exhibit her artwork throughout the 1980s, holding one-woman shows at the Musée Reattu in Arles (France), the Kunstmuseum in Freiburg, the Bronx Museum in New York, the Museum of Modern Art in Sydney (Australia), and the Studio Museum in Harlem. While maintaining permanent residences in Paris and Rome, she has continued to travel widely, to write, and to produce visual art. In the spring of 1990, she was artist-in-residence at Pasadena City College in California.

In 1994 Barbara Chase-Riboud returned to the subject of Thomas Jefferson and Sally Hemings with another novel, *The President's Daughter*, about Harriet Hemings, the slave daughter of Sally Hemings and Jefferson. ◆

Chideya, Farai

JULY 26, 1969 – ● JOURNALIST AND WRITER

Farai Chideya, pronounced "far-EYE shi-DEY-ah," is a journalist and author whose commentaries span politics, African-American issues, and pop culture. She has become one of the most respected young journalists in the nation.

Farai Nduu Chideya-Chihota was born on July 26, 1969, in Baltimore, Maryland, to Lucas and Cynthia Chideya. Her father was a Zimbabwean businessman. Chideya's parents divorced in 1970 and her father returned to Africa. Her mother, a high school teacher, raised the family in Baltimore, teaching the children a love for the written word and the importance of questioning the status quo. Chideya became a voracious reader at an early age. She attended Harvard University, and graduated magna cum laude in 1990. While at Harvard, she received a minority internship at *Newsweek* magazine.

After graduating, Chideya became a reporter at *Newsweek* and worked in the New York, Chicago, and Washington bureaus. There she learned much about news coverage, interview styles, and how editorial decisions are made in the print media.

In 1994 Chideya left *Newsweek* and worked as a news writer for MTV News, a cable TV news program geared at young people. While at MTV News, she began participating as a panelist on the political talk show *Inside Politics* for Cable News Network (CNN). During the 1996 presidential race, she worked as a political analyst for CNN. She also has appeared on other networks as a political reporter and commentator, including ABC's *Nightline*, CBS's *Up to the Minute*, and BET's *Town Hall Meeting on the Black Family*. Chideya became an ABC News correspondent in 1997.

As a freelance journalist, Chideya has covered topics that include African-American issues, music, books, and cultural trends for a variety of publications, including the *Los Angeles Times*, *Mademoiselle*, the *New York Times*, *Spin*, *Time*, and the *Village Voice*. She also has worked as national affairs editor for *Vibe* magazine. Chideya has run her own web site, called Pop & Politics, since 1996. The site features the journalist's personal essays, political commentaries, and music reviews.

Chideya published her first book, *Don't Believe the Hype: Fighting Cultural Disinformation About African-Americans,* in 1995. The book challenges today's pervasive media myths about African Americans, noting that the mass media for the most part fail to portray how the majority of black America lives. Her book *The Color of Our Future* was scheduled for publication in 1999.

Chideya has received a number of awards, including a National Education Reporting Award for her *Newsweek* story "The World's Ten Best Schools," and a fellowship from the Freedom Forum, an international foundation dedicated to free press and free speech. ◆

> *"Most U.S. news outlets post shockingly few reporters in Africa. The ones who are there run from war zone to war zone, never stopping to do the stories on daily life and culture they get to do in European countries."*
> Chideya Farai, in *USA Today*, April 15, 1997

Childress, Alice

OCTOBER 12, 1920 – ● PLAYWRIGHT

Born in Charleston, South Carolina, Childress was reared in Harlem with her grandmother, Eliza Campbell. Childress grew up economically poor but culturally rich

American Negro Theatre

The American Negro Theatre (ANT) was founded in Harlem in New York City in 1940 by writer Abram Hill and actor Frederick O'Neal. Their goal was to establish a community-based theater to provide opportunities for black-theater artists as the Negro Units of the Federal Theatre Project had done before they were discontinued by Congress in 1939. In 1942 Hill and O'Neal established the ANT Studio Theatre, the first black theater institution sanctioned by the New York State Board of Education, to train a new generation of black theater artists. From 1940 through 1949 ANT produced nineteen plays, twelve of which were new. A number of prominent black actors and writers, including Alice Childress, Ruby Dee, Sidney Poitier, and Harry Belafonte, began their careers in ANT productions or in the Studio school. ANT's biggest success was *Anna Lucasta* (1944), based on a play by Philip Yordan about a Polish-American family, which ANT adapted for a black cast. After a five-week run at ANT's theatre in the 135th Street library, the production moved to Broadway, where it played for two years. A national tour and a film followed, but ANT received no royalties from these, and only a small one from the Broadway production. ANT later transferred three more plays to Broadway, but none was financially successful. By the late 1940s, ANT lacked the finances to mount complete productions. It turned instead to producing inexpensive variety shows and by 1949 had ceased production entirely.

1920 Childress is born in Charleston, South Carolina.

1937 Childress publishes her first novel, *Like One of the Family.*

1949 Childress produces first major play, *Florence.*

1956 Childress wins Obie Award for *Trouble in Mind.*

1974 Childress's play *Wedding Band* is broadcast on ABC television.

because her grandmother exposed her to the arts, fostered in her a desire for excellence, and introduced her to testimonials at the Salem Church in Harlem. It was her grandmother who encouraged her to write by creating a game that allowed Childress to develop fictional characters. Childress was forced to drop out of high school when her grandmother died. But she decided to educate herself by reading books borrowed from the public library.

Childress began her writing career in the late 1940s while involved in helping develop and strengthen the American Negro Theatre (ANT), where she studied acting and directing. Her decision to become a playwright was a natural outgrowth of her experiences at ANT. She has written and produced thirteen plays, including *Florence* (1949), *Trouble in Mind* (1955; winner of an Obie Award in 1956 for the best original Off-Broadway play—the first time the award was given to a black woman), *Wedding Band: A Love Hate Story in Black and White* (1966; televised on ABC in 1974), *Wine in the Wilderness* (1969; produced on National Educational Television that year), *Mojo: A Black Love Story* (1970), and *Moms* (1987). Childress's plays treat the plight of the poor and the oppressed. She champions underdogs and shows their dignity and will to survive.

Childress is an equally dynamic novelist, having published five novels, including *Like One of the Family: Conversations from a Domestic's Life* (1937), *A Hero Ain't Nothin' but a Sandwich* (1973), *A Short Walk* (1979), *Rainbow Jordan* (1981), and *Those Other People* (1990). Her novels, like her plays, champion the poor and explore the inspiriting influences of the community.

In addition to the Obie she received in 1956, Childress has received several honors and awards, including a John Golden Fund for Playwrights grant (1957), a Rockefeller grant (1967), and an appointment to Harvard's Radcliffe Institute for Independent Study (1966–68). ◆

Chisholm, Shirley

NOVEMBER 30, 1924 – ● POLITICIAN

Shirley Chisholm's career places her among the most significant black politicians of the twentieth century. Born Shirley St. Hill in Brooklyn, she lived with her family in Barbados for some years before returning to the United States. She graduated cum laude from Brooklyn College in 1946 and then earned a master's degree from Columbia University's Teachers College. After her marriage to Conrad Chisholm in 1949, she taught nursery school and became involved in Democratic party work.

In 1960 Chisholm helped to form the Unity Democratic Club in New York, and in 1965 she ran a successful campaign for a seat in the New York State Assembly. During her tenure there she pressed her interest in education and helped to establish the Search for Education, Equity, and Knowledge (SEEK) program to assist poor students in New York. She also helped win a maternity-leave policy for teachers.

In 1969 Chisholm won a seat in the House of Representatives, becoming the first African-American woman to be elected to Congress. While in the House she served on a number of committees, including Veterans' Affairs, Education and Labor, and House Rules. She was an outspoken opponent of the war in Vietnam, and continued to fight for economic justice and women's rights.

In January of 1972 Chisholm announced her candidacy for the Democratic party nomination for president. She was the

> *"Of my two 'handicaps,' being female put many more obstacles in my path than being Black."*
> Shirley Chisholm,
> *Unbought and Unbossed*, 1970

Shirley Chisholm celebrates in 1968 after winning a seat in the U.S. Congress.

1924 Chisholm is born in Brooklyn, New York.

1960 Chisholm helps form Unity Democratic Club in New York.

1969 Chisholm wins seat in U.S. House of Representatives.

1972 Chisholm seeks Democratic nomination for president.

1982 Chisholm retires from Congress.

first African American ever to do so. While her campaign was unable to gain the support of the Congressional Black Caucus or the major women's groups with which she had long worked, Chisholm's effort was nonetheless groundbreaking.

Shirley Chisholm retired from Congress in 1982. She has since taught at Mount Holyoke and Spelman colleges. She continues to be active in politics as the founder of the National Political Congress of Black Women and as its first president. ◆

Clark, Septima Poinsette

MAY 3, 1898 – DECEMBER 15, 1987 ● EDUCATOR AND CIVIL RIGHTS ACTIVIST

Septima Poinsette was born and reared in Charleston, South Carolina. Her mother, Victoria Warren Anderson, was of Haitian descent and worked as a laundress, and her father, Peter Porcher Poinsette, was a former slave who worked as a cook and a caterer. Her parents deeply influenced Poinsette and instilled in her a willingness to share one's gifts and a belief that there was something redeeming about everyone. In addition, Poinsette's early education, which brought her into contact with demanding black teachers who insisted that students have pride and work hard, left a positive and lasting impression on her. Partly as a result of these influences, Poinsette pursued a career in education. In 1916 she received her teaching certificate from Avery Normal Institute, a private school for black teachers founded after the end of the Civil War by the American Missionary Association in Charleston.

Poinsette's first teaching position was on Johns Island, South Carolina, from 1916 to 1919, because African Americans were barred from teaching in the Charleston public schools. She tried to address the vast educational, political, and economical inequities that faced Johns Island blacks by instituting adult literacy classes and health education and by working with the NAACP. In 1919 she returned to Charleston to work at Avery and spearheaded a campaign against Charleston's exclusionary education system that resulted, one year later, in the overturning of the law barring black teachers from teaching in

"My husband had strong feelings about women and felt they should stay in their place, which was in the house making children or buying groceries. But the civil rights movement would never have taken off if some women hadn't spoken up."
Septima Poinsette Clark, quoted in *Life*, 1988

Avery Normal Institute

Avery Normal Institute was a private college preparatory and teacher training school organized for African Americans by the American Missionary Association, in Charleston, South Carolina, in 1865. During the first two years of its existence, the school was forced to relocate twice because local white authorities opposed its efforts to educate African Americans. In its first years, the school was known by several names, including the Tappan School and the Saxton School. In 1968 northern philanthropist Charles Avery donated money for a permanent location and the school was renamed Avery Institute on May 7, 1868. Under its first principal, Francis L. Cardozo, a leading black Reconstruction politician, Avery began offering a classical curriculum, including Latin, geometry, literature, and philosophy, as well as teacher-training courses. After 1870, when South Carolina began requiring all its children to attend school for a minimum of two years, Avery became the main supplier of black teachers for black students, particularly in rural areas of the state. Some of Avery's most prestigious graduates included artist Edwin A. Harleston, sociologist G. Franklin Edwards, and educator Septima Poinsette Clark. By 1947, financial difficulties forced Avery to become a public school. The school was permanently closed in 1954.

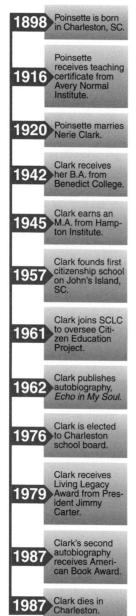

1898 Poinsette is born in Charleston, SC.

1916 Poinsette receives teaching certificate from Avery Normal Institute.

1920 Poinsette marries Nerie Clark.

1942 Clark receives her B.A. from Benedict College.

1945 Clark earns an M.A. from Hampton Institute.

1957 Clark founds first citizenship school on John's Island, SC.

1961 Clark joins SCLC to oversee Citizen Education Project.

1962 Clark publishes autobiography, *Echo in My Soul*.

1976 Clark is elected to Charleston school board.

1979 Clark receives Living Legacy Award from President Jimmy Carter.

1987 Clark's second autobiography receives American Book Award.

1987 Clark dies in Charleston.

public schools. In May 1920 Poinsette married Nerie Clark, a black Navy cook. She had two children, one of whom died at birth. After her husband died in 1924, Clark sent her other child, Nerie Jr., to live with his paternal grandmother because she could not support him financially.

Shortly thereafter, Clark returned to Columbia, South Carolina, became active in various civic organizations, and continued her education, receiving a B.A. from Benedict College (1942) and an M.A. from Hampton Institute (1945). She led the fight for equal pay for black teachers in South Carolina. Her efforts attracted the attention of the NAACP, which initiated litigation and won a 1945 ruling mandating equal pay for black teachers in South Carolina. In 1947 Clark returned to Charleston to teach in public schools and continued her civic activities until she was fired in 1956 because of her membership in the NAACP. Unable to find another position in South Carolina, Clark moved to the Highlander Folk School, in Monteagle, Tennessee, an interracial adult education center founded by Myles Horton in 1932 to foster social activism and promote racial equality. There Clark became director of education. Together with Horton and South Carolina black activists such as Esau Jenkins from Johns Island, she devised educational strategies to challenge black illiteracy and encourage black voter registration. Clark, guided by the belief that literacy was integral to black equality, instituted the citizenship school program, an adult literacy program that focused on promoting voter registration and empowering people to solve their own problems through social activism.

The first citizenship school, founded on John's Island in 1957, was a success, and Clark traveled throughout the deep South, trying to make links with other local activists to foster the expansion of the schools. In 1961 the citizenship school program was transferred to the Southern Christian Leadership Conference (SCLC) after the Tennessee legislature's persistent efforts to disrupt Highlander activities resulted in the school's charter being revoked and its property being confiscated. Clark joined SCLC to oversee the newly renamed Citizen Education Project, and by 1970 over 800 Citizenship schools had been formed that graduated over 100,000 African Americans who served as a key grassroots base for the civil rights movement throughout the deep South. In 1971, however, she retired from SCLC because long-term commitment to the schools had faded.

Clark remained an outspoken spokesperson for racial, as well as gender, equality. She chronicled her life of activism in her autobiography, *Echo in My Soul*, in 1962. In 1966 she spoke at the first national meeting of the National Organization of Women (NOW) about the necessity of women challenging male dominance. In 1976 she was elected to the Charleston, South Carolina, school board. Three years later she was awarded the Living Legacy award from President Jimmy Carter in honor of her continuing dedication to black **empowerment** through education. In 1987 she received an American Book Award for her second autobiography, *Ready from Within: Septima Clark and the Civil Rights Movement*. Later that year, Septima Clark died in Charleston, South Carolina. ◆

empowerment: promotion of a group's political influence and power.

Cole, Rebecca J.

MARCH 16, 1846 – AUGUST 14, 1922 ● PHYSICIAN AND SOCIAL REFORMER

Born in Philadelphia in 1846 (three years before the first American woman, Elizabeth Blackwell, received an M.D.), Rebecca Cole attended the city's prestigious Institute for Colored Youth before pursuing advanced medical studies. The institute had maintained an academic department from its founding by Quakers in 1837 and counted numerous African-American leaders among its alumni. Cole matriculated at the Woman's Medical College of Pennsylvania in 1866 and received an M.D. in 1867 after the submission of her thesis, "The Eye and Its **Appendages**." Upon graduation, Cole became the second black woman to receive an M.D. in the United States and the first to graduate from the Woman's Medical College. She accepted an invitation from Elizabeth Blackwell to be a "sanitary visitor" at Blackwell's New York Infirmary for Women and Children to help spread knowledge of public health among the urban poor. A dedicated advocate for the **disfranchised**, Cole also practiced in Philadelphia, Columbia, South Carolina, and Washington, D.C., where she held her last major appointment as superintendent of the Home for Destitute Colored Women and Children. Throughout her medical career, which spanned over half a century, Cole remained active in the

appendage: a subordinate body part.

disfranchised: those deprived of their legal rights as citizens.

black clubwomen's movement and lectured widely on ways to improve the health status of African Americans. She died in Philadelphia. ◆

Coleman, Bessie

JANUARY 26, 1892 – APRIL 30, 1926 ● AVIATOR

Bessie Coleman was the first African-American female aviator. She was born in Atlanta, Texas, but her family moved to Waxahachie, Texas, when she was still an infant. When she was seven, her parents separated. Her father, who was a Choctaw Indian, returned to the reservation in Oklahoma, and her mother supported the large family by picking cotton and doing laundry, jobs in which she was aided by her children. Because she wanted Coleman to attend college, her mother allowed her to keep her income from her laundry work, but this money only financed one semester at the Colored Agricultural and Normal University in Langston, Oklahoma (now Langston University). After this semester, she returned to Waxahachie briefly; and between 1915 and 1917, she went to Chicago, where she took a course in manicuring and worked at the White Sox barbershop until the early years of World War I. She then managed a small restaurant.

Coleman became interested in the burgeoning field of aviation, which had entered the national consciousness as a consequence of its role in World War I, but all her applications to aviation schools were rejected on the basis of her race and/or gender, until Robert S. Abbott, founder and editor of the *Chicago Defender*, advised her to study aviation abroad. She took a course in French, went to Paris in November 1920, and attended an aviation school in Le Crotoy. She returned to the United States in September 1921 with a pilot's license and went back to Europe in 1922, this time obtaining an international pilot's license, the first African-American woman to obtain these licenses. When she returned to the United States after her second **sojourn** in Europe, Coleman made a name for herself in exhibition flying, performing at shows attended by thousands. She **barnstormed** throughout the United States and became known as "Brave Bessie." She lectured in schools and churches on the opportunities in aviation wherever she performed, and she saved the money she earned from these lectures and performances in the hope of opening an aviation school for African Americans. On April 30, 1926, during a practice run in Jacksonville, Florida, Coleman's plane somersaulted out of a nosedive, and Coleman fell 2,000 feet to her death. ◆

sojourn: a temporary visit.

barnstorm: to fly to various rural districts to perform flying stunts and sell short sightseeing flights.

Cooper, Anna Julia Haywood

AUGUST 10, 1858 – FEBRUARY 27, 1964 ● EDUCATOR AND WRITER

Anna Julia Haywood was born a slave in Raleigh, North Carolina. While still a child, she was hired out as a nursemaid and developed a love for books and learning. In 1867 she entered St. Augustine's Normal and Collegiate Institute in Raleigh, where she soon began to tutor and teach other students. While there, she met George A. C. Cooper, a teacher of Greek. The couple married in 1877, but George Cooper died two years later.

In the fall of 1881 Anna Cooper entered Oberlin College. She received a B.A. in 1884 and an M.A. three years later. She taught for a short while at Wilberforce College in Ohio and at St. Augustine's in Raleigh before going to the M Street (now Paul Laurence Dunbar) High School in Washington, D.C., in 1887. In 1902 Cooper became principal of M Street High School.

Cooper believed that African Americans needed to pursue not only industrial training, but academic education as well. During her tenure as head of M Street, she successfully expanded college prep courses, attracted academically oriented

"Let woman's claim be as broad in the concrete as in the abstract. We take our stand on the solidarity of humanity, the oneness of life, and the unnaturalness and injustice of all special favoritisms, whether of sex, race, country, and condition."

Anna Cooper, *A Voice from the South*, 1892

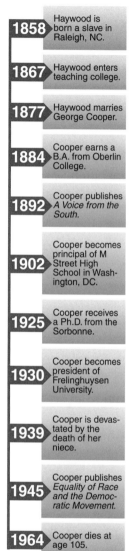

1858 Haywood is born a slave in Raleigh, NC.

1867 Haywood enters teaching college.

1877 Haywood marries George Cooper.

1884 Cooper earns a B.A. from Oberlin College.

1892 Cooper publishes *A Voice from the South.*

1902 Cooper becomes principal of M Street High School in Washington, DC.

1925 Cooper receives a Ph.D. from the Sorbonne.

1930 Cooper becomes president of Frelinghuysen University.

1939 Cooper is devastated by the death of her niece.

1945 Cooper publishes *Equality of Race and the Democratic Movement.*

1964 Cooper dies at age 105.

black students, and increased the proportion of M Street graduates attending Ivy League schools. Cooper's commitment to classical studies for African Americans clashed with Booker T. Washington's philosophies, which dominated black higher education at the time. Her unconventional approach resulted in charges of misconduct and insubordination. Because of the charges leveled against her, the school board decided not to reappoint her as principal in 1906. Cooper then taught for four years at Lincoln University in Missouri before returning to M Street to teach Latin.

At the age of fifty-three, Cooper began doing graduate work. She studied at La Guilde Internationale, Paris (1911–12), and at Columbia University (1913–16), working toward her Ph.D., which she received from the Sorbonne in Paris in 1925. Her dissertation, *L'attitude de la France à l'égard de l'esclavage pendant la révolution* (translated as "The Attitude of France Toward Slavery During the Revolution"), was published in 1925.

Much of the rest of Cooper's career revolved around Frelinghuysen University in Washington, D.C., an institution of adult education offering evening classes in academic, religious, and trade programs. She served as president of Frelinghuysen from 1930 to 1940. Because of financial difficulties, the university lost its charter in 1937, becoming the Frelinghuysen Group of Schools for Colored Working People, and Cooper became its registrar. Cooper continued to be centrally involved with the school, offering her home for classes and meetings, when necessary.

Throughout her career, Cooper was a staunch defender of African-American rights and a relentless proponent of education for females. She believed that race and sex were inseparable and that both racism and sexism affected the social status of black women. She also argued that the struggles of all oppressed people were "indissolubly linked" together. In her book *A Voice from the South*, published in 1892, she asserted that African-American women were a distinct political and social force, and that they could act as spokespersons for their race and as advocates for women.

Cooper believed that the key to achieving social equality for women was education, and she fought for women's collective right to higher education. During her early years at St. Augustine, she protested the exclusion of females from courses for ministerial studies, and argued that boys and girls should have equal access to education. She believed that education would widen women's horizons and make them less dependent on marriage and love. She was one of the earliest advocates for women's rights and one of the most tenacious supporters of women's suffrage. Cooper was also the only woman elected to the American Negro Academy, was a participant in the 1900 Pan African Conference, and was elected to its executive committee.

Although Cooper never had children of her own, she adopted and raised five great-nieces and nephews. The death in 1939 of her niece and namesake, Annie Cooper Haywood Beckwith, who had lived with her since 1915, when she was six months old, devastated Cooper. Shortly after Beckwith's death in 1939, Cooper's public activity diminished. Nevertheless, she continued to write and work at home. She was a prolific writer, publishing on a wide variety of subjects, such as *Le Pélerinage de Charlemagne* (*Charlemagne's Pilgrimage*) (1925), *Equality of Race and the Democratic Movement* (1945), *The Life and Writings of the Grimké Family* (1951), and the essays "College Extension for Working People" and "Modern Education." Cooper died in her sleep in 1964 at the age of 105. ◆

> *"Our only care need be the intrinsic worth of our contributions."*
> Anna Cooper

Craft, Ellen

1826 – 1891 ● FUGITIVE SLAVE

Ellen and William Craft were fugitive slaves known for their dramatic escape to freedom. Ellen Smith was born in Clinton, Georgia, the daughter of a mulatto slave, Maria, and her owner, Major James Smith. At age eleven, Ellen was given as a wedding gift to one of Smith's daughters living in Macon, Georgia. Ellen soon met William Craft, a fellow slave and cabinetmaker, and within a few years they began to plot their escape from bondage.

Escape from the deep South was a rare and dangerous undertaking. The Crafts' plan was indeed bold, creative, and worked out in detail. They first procured passes to visit friends during the Christmas season, when discipline was known to be lax. Their pass was good for several days, so they had time to travel some distance before they were noticed. Ellen, of fair

> *"I had much rather starve in England, a free woman, than be a slave for the best man that ever breathed upon the American continent."*
> Ellen Craft, *Running a Thousand Miles for Freedom*, 1860

1826 Craft is born a slave in Clinton, Georgia.

1848 Craft and her husband escape to Philadelphia in disguise.

1850 Crafts flees to England after Fugitive Slave Act is passed.

1851 Crafts begin teaching at the Ockham School.

1860 Crafts publish *Running a Thousand Miles for Freedom*.

1868 Crafts return to America and open a school in Georgia.

1871 Crafts buy a Georgia plantation.

1874 William Craft runs for Georgia State Senate.

1890 Crafts move to Charleston.

1891 Ellen Craft dies.

complexion, posed as a white male slave owner, an invalid traveling north to consult doctors; William impersonated her black slave. She cut her hair, wrapped her head in a bandage, and practiced imitating a man's gait. As a final touch, she wore eyeglasses to disguise her appearance, and because she was illiterate, she held her writing arm in a cast to avoid having to sign her name. The final part of the disguise would be crucial when they were forced to sign hotel registers.

The couple left for freedom on December 21, 1848, and traveled by train, steamer, and ferry through Georgia, South Carolina, North Carolina, Virginia, and Maryland, in a journey that involved several near discoveries. Finally, they arrived in free territory in Philadelphia on Christmas day, 1848.

In Philadelphia, Ellen and William Craft stayed with free blacks and Quakers. They were befriended by abolitionist luminaries such as William Wells Brown and William Lloyd Garrison, and the Crafts frequently lectured on their dramatic escape on the antislavery circuit.

In 1850, however, national events changed their lives dramatically. In that year the Fugitive Slave Law was passed and the Crafts were literally hunted down in Boston by southern slave hunters and driven into exile in England. Their plight became a national issue when President Millard Fillmore insisted that if the laws of the land were not obeyed in Boston and the Crafts were not shipped back to the South, he would use the United States Army to force the issue.

While in England, the Crafts remained active in the abolitionist movement. They went on a speaking tour with abolitionist William Wells Brown, and in 1851 they took a post teaching at the Ockham School, a pioneering trade school that combined classroom work in traditional subjects with farming, carpentry, and other crafts. William Craft also gained a reputation as a public spokesman against slavery and made several return trips to the United States to speak out against the Confederacy during the Civil War. Ellen was active in the British and Foreign Freedmen's Aid Society, a missionary organization that organized "civilizing" work in British colonies in Africa and the Caribbean. The Crafts published the story of their escape from slavery, *Running a Thousand Miles for Freedom*, while in London in 1860. Between 1863 and 1867, William was in Dahomey in West Africa with the Company of African-American Merchants, where he started a school and established commercial ties.

In 1868 the Crafts returned to the United States with two of their five children and settled in Bryan County, Georgia, where they opened an industrial school for black youths. They purchased a plantation in Woodville in 1871, where they continued their school and hired tenant farmers to grow rice, cotton, corn, and peas, which they sold in the Savannah area. By 1877 they had seventy-five pupils, but were suffering from the financial burden of keeping up the school.

William became a leader in the local Republican Party, ran for State Senate in 1874, and in 1876 represented his district at the state and national Republican conventions. He also spent a good part of his time in the North, raising funds for the school and lecturing to church groups on the conditions in the South. Ellen managed the plantation while he was away, negotiated the annual contracts with tenants, and drove their crops to market. But the plantation never prospered, and Northerners, in the mood for reconciliation with the South, were less forthcoming with donations to the experimental school. Rumors spread by the Crafts' enemies suggesting that they were living off the largess of naive northern philanthropists did not help their project, and they eventually gave up the school. Around 1890 they left the Woodville plantation and moved to Charleston, South Carolina, where they remained for the rest of their lives. ◆

When the Fugitive Slave Law was passed in 1850, the Crafts were literally hunted down in Boston by southern slave hunters and driven into exile.

Currie, Betty

1939 – ● EXECUTIVE ASSISTANT TO THE PRESIDENT

Betty Currie is the executive assistant of President Bill Clinton. She joined Clinton's White House staff in 1993, and quickly became known as a friendly, humble, loyal, and efficient aide to the president. Currie, a private person who thrived behind the scenes of the nation's government for over two decades, was thrust before the public eye in early 1998, when Independent Counsel Kenneth W. Starr subpoenaed Currie to appear before a grand jury. Her subpoena was part of an investigation by Starr into charges that Clinton obstructed justice in attempts to cover up a relationship between himself and White House intern Monica Lewinsky. Starr was appointed in 1994 to investigate charges against

subpoena: a legal paper commanding a person to appear in court.

1939 Currie is born in Waukegan, Illinois.

1957 Currie graduates from Waukegan Community High School.

1959 Currie moves to Washington and begins a career in government.

1984 Currie works as a volunteer office manager for Geraldine Ferraro.

1988 Currie works for the Michael Dukakis presidential campaign.

1988 Currie marries Robert Currie.

1992 Currie joins Bill Clinton's presidential campaign as an office manager.

1993 Currie becomes Clinton's executive assistant.

1998 Currie is subpoenaed by Independent Counsel Kenneth Starr.

Clinton's possible financial misconduct with Whitewater Development Corporation, a small real estate company.

In five grand jury sessions, from January to July 1998, Currie testified to what she knew of Clinton's relationship with Lewinsky. After the testimony, in a report released in September 1998, Starr accused Currie of facilitating the affair by allowing Lewinsky's visits and gifts to the president to go unlogged, and by phoning Lewinsky for the president without going through the official operator. In the end, however, Currie did not prove to be the incriminating witness against the president that some prosecutors had hoped for.

Currie was born in 1939 in Waukegan, Illinois, a town on the shore of Lake Michigan about 50 miles north of Chicago. Her maiden name was Williams. Her mother, a housekeeper, raised her in Waukegan, where Currie attended Waukegan Community High School. After her graduation in 1957, Currie worked as a typist at the Great Lakes Naval Training Center in Waukegan. Two years later, she moved to Washington and worked as a secretary in the Navy Department. She later became an executive secretary at the Agency for International Development.

In 1969 Currie became secretary to Joseph Blatchford, who headed the Peace Corps. She then followed Blatchford to ACTION, the federal agency that ran the Peace Corps. Currie remained at ACTION through three directors. During her tenure at ACTION, Currie became part of an influential network of executive assistants who work at the top levels of government.

Currie took an early retirement in 1984, but was beckoned into the world of campaign politics. In 1984 she worked as a volunteer office manager for vice presidential candidate Geraldine Ferraro. In 1988 she worked for the Michael Dukakis presidential campaign, and in 1992 she joined Bill Clinton's campaign as an office manager in Clinton's Little Rock, Arkansas, campaign "war room." There, political strategists plotted the course of the campaign. During that time, she became known for her ability to remain calm during political chaos. When Clinton was elected president in 1992, she landed a job as secretary to the transition team led by Warren Christopher.

Nancy Hernreich, the director of Oval Office operations, recommended Currie as personal secretary to the president, and Currie began her position as executive assistant in 1993. As

Clinton's assistant, Currie sits outside the Oval Office, handling all the president's mail, faxes, and memos, screening calls, and scheduling visits. She typically works twelve-hour days, six days a week.

In 1988 she married Robert Currie, an official from ACTION. She now lives in Arlington, Virginia, where she also cares for her ailing mother. ◆

Dandridge, Dorothy

c. NOVEMBER 1923 – SEPTEMBER 8, 1965 ● SINGER AND ACTOR

1923 Dandridge is born in Cleveland, Ohio.

1937 Dandridge appears in the Marx Brothers' *A Day at the Races*

1952 Dandridge sings at New York's La Vie En Rose nightclub.

1954 Dandridge receives Oscar nomination for *Carmen Jones.*

1957 Dandridge stars in *Island in the Sun.*

1959 Dandridge stars in Otto Preminger's *Porgy and Bess.*

1965 Dandridge dies in Los Angeles from a drug overdose.

The daughter of a minister and a stage entertainer, Dorothy Dandridge was born in Cleveland, Ohio, and was groomed for a stage career by her mother, Ruby Dandridge, who separated from her husband and began touring the country as a performer shortly after her second daughter was born. While still a child, Dandridge sang, danced, and did comedy skits as part of her mother's show. When their mother settled in Los Angeles, she and her older sister, Vivian—together they had been billed as "The Wonder Kids"—attended school and appeared in bit parts in films, including the Marx Brothers comedy *A Day at the Races* (1937). During the 1940s, Dorothy and Vivian joined with another young African-American woman, Etta Jones, to form an act called "The Dandridge Sisters," and embarked on a tour with the Jimmie Lunceford band. Dandridge met her first husband, Harold Nicholas (of the Nicholas Brothers dancing team), while she was performing at the Cotton Club in Harlem. A brain-damaged daughter, Harolyn, was born to the couple before they divorced.

During this time, Dandridge managed to secure a few minor Hollywood roles, and appeared in such films as *Drums of the Congo* (1942), *The Hit Parade of 1943, Moo Cow Boogie* (1943), *Atlantic City* (1944), *Pillow to Post* (1946), and *Flamingo* (1947). The early 1950s witnessed the flowering of her movie career, as she acquired leading roles in the low-budget films *Tarzan's Perils, The Harlem Globe-Trotters*, and *Jungle Queen* (all made in 1951). Dandridge, who was exceptionally beautiful, worked actively at cultivating a cosmopolitan, transracial persona, brimming with sexual allure. She also became increasingly well known as a nightclub singer. Indeed, Dandridge's performances at New York's La Vie En Rose (1952) were in such demand that the club—then on the brink of bankruptcy—was saved from financial collapse. She was one of the first African Americans to perform at the Waldorf-Astoria's Empire Room, and appeared at such prestigious clubs as Ciro's (Los Angeles), the Cafe de Paris (London), the Copacabana (Rio de Janeiro), and the Chi Chi (Palm Springs).

Dandridge's big break as a motion picture actress came in 1954, when she secured the title role in Otto Preminger's all-black production *Carmen Jones*. That year, she became the first black actor to be nominated for an Oscar for a leading role. That she had achieved celebrity stature was evidenced by her appearances on the cover of *Life*, as well as in feature articles in national and international magazines. However, three years were to pass before Dandridge made another film, largely because, in racist Hollywood, she was not offered roles commensurate with her talent and beauty, and she could no longer settle for less. Her next film, *Island in the Sun* (1957), was the first to feature an interracial romance (between Dandridge and white actor John Justin); the film was poorly received, as were *The Decks Ran Red* (1958), *Tamango* (1959), and *Malaga* (1962), all of which touched on interracial themes. Although Dandridge won acclaim in 1959 for her portrayal of Bess (opposite Sidney Poitier) in Otto Preminger's film of *Porgy and Bess*, she received fewer and fewer film and nightclub offers as time passed. After divorcing her second husband, white restaurant-owner Jack Dennison, she was forced to file for bankruptcy and lost her Hollywood mansion. Her sudden death in 1965 was attributed to an overdose of antidepressants; she was forty-one years old. Dandridge's autobiography, *Everything and Nothing*, was published posthumously in 1970; in 1977 she was inducted into the Black Filmmakers' Hall of Fame. ◆

Dash, Julie

OCTOBER 22, 1952 – ● FILMMAKER

Born and raised in New York City, Julie Dash began studying film as a teenager in 1969 at the Studio Museum of Harlem. After receiving a B.A. in film production from the City College of New York, Dash moved to Los Angeles to attend the Center for Advanced Film Studies at the American Film Institute, the youngest fellow ever to attend this institution. Later, she did graduate work at the University of California at Los Angeles.

Dash's films are sensitive, complex portrayals of the dilemmas confronting a diverse group of black women. While at the American Film Institute, she directed *Four Women*, an experimental dance film inspired by the Nina Simone song of the same title (1977 winner of the Golden Medal for Women in Film at the Miami International Film Festival); and *Diary of an African Nun*, based on a short story by Alice Walker (1977 winner of the Director's Guild Award). Her 1983 black-and-white short *Illusions*, the story of a fair-skinned black woman film executive set in 1942, was nominated for a Cable ACE Award in art direction and is permanently archived at Indiana University and at Clark College in Atlanta.

In 1986 Dash relocated to Atlanta from Los Angeles and began work on *Daughters of the Dust*.

Generally regarded as the first feature-length film by an African-American woman, *Daughters of the Dust* opened in 1992 to critical acclaim. "Its **nonlinear** narrative, focusing on the Gullah culture of the South Carolina Sea Islands, centers on the lives of African-American women. They are the bearers of the culture, tellers of the tales, and most important, spectators for whom she created the film." Dash's approach to filmmaking has been "to show black women at pivotal moments in their lives . . . [to] focus on and depict experiences that have never been shown on screen before."

> *"With the educational system here in the United States, you grow up assuming we had no input. But we've had so much input into this society, and it's not just music and athletes. It's the language, motor habits, how we move."*
> Julie Dash, quoted in the *Washington Post*, Feb. 28, 1992

nonlinear: concerning a story not told in traditional or chronological sequence.

After *Daughters*, Dash moved to London to collaborate on a screenplay with Maureen Blackwood of Sankofa. She made several films for television and directed music videos for Tracy Chapman; Tony, Toni, Tone; and others. She also began work on a series of films depicting black women in the United States from the turn of the twentieth century to the year 2000. ◆

Davis, Angela Yvonne

JANUARY 26, 1944 – ● POLITICAL ACTIVIST

Angela Davis lived in a section of Birmingham, Alabama, known as "Dynamite Hill" because of the violent attacks by white nightriders intent on maintaining the residential demarcation line between blacks and whites. Both of her parents were educators, worked actively for the NAACP, and taught their children not to accept the socially segregated society that existed at the time. She attended Brandeis University, where she was influenced by the teachings of Marxist philosopher Herbert Marcuse. After graduating in 1961, she spent two years in Europe, where she was exposed to student political radicals. Her own radicalism, however, came into focus with the murder in 1963 of four young black Sunday school children in a Birmingham, Alabama, church bombing. In California, where she went to pursue graduate study with Marcuse (who was now at the University of California, San Diego), Davis began working with the Student Nonviolent Coordinating Committee (SNCC), the Black Panthers, and the Communist party, which she joined in 1968.

Hired in 1969 by UCLA to teach philosophy, Davis not long after was fired by the Board of Regents and then-governor Ronald Reagan because of her Communist party affiliation. Ultimately, her case went to the Supreme Court, which overturned the dismissal. By that time, however, Davis herself was in hiding as a result of an incident at the Soledad state prison. In August 1970, George Jackson, a prisoner and member of the Black Panthers, assisted by his brother Jonathan, attempted to escape using smuggled guns. Both brothers were killed, and some of the guns were traced to Davis. Fearful for her safety and distrustful of the judicial system, Davis went underground. For

> *"We, the black women of today, must accept the full weight of a legacy wrought in blood by our mothers in chains."*
> Angela Davis,
> *Women, Race, and Class*, 1981

two months she was on the FBI's Ten Most Wanted list before being apprehended and incarcerated. She remained in jail for sixteen months before being tried for murder and conspiracy. In June 1972 she was acquitted of all charges against her. Davis resumed her academic career at San Francisco State University and again became politically active, running as the Communist party candidate for vice president in 1980 and 1984. In 1991 she joined the faculty of the University of California, Santa Cruz, as professor of the history of consciousness. She is the author of several books, including *If They Come in the Morning* (1971), *Women, Race, and Class* (1983), and *Women, Culture, and Politics* (1989). Her autobiography, *Angela Davis: An Autobiography*, originally published in 1974, was reissued in 1988. In 1998, Davis published *Blues Legacies and Black Feminism: Gertrude 'Ma' Rainey, Bessie Smith, Billie Holiday*. ◆

> *"Racism cannot be separated from capitalism."*
> Angela Davis, letter from prison, 1971

Dawes, Dominique

NOVEMBER 20, 1976 – ● GYMNAST

Dominique Dawes became the first African-American woman to win a national gymnastics championship. She also was one of the first black American women to make the United States Olympic gymnastics team.

Dominique Margaux Dawes was born in a suburb of Washington, D.C.—Silver Spring, Maryland—on November 20, 1976. She has an older sister and a younger brother. Dawes bounced around the house so much that her parents, Don and Loretta, enrolled her in a nearby gymnastics school when she was six years old. There she came under the long-term guidance of coach Kelli Hill, who immediately recognized Dawes's potential and encouraged her family to give her as much training as they could.

Dawes saw her gymnastics activities as fun and did not take them too seriously. This may have helped her maintain a positive attitude in a sport that has been extremely demanding on some girls. Dawes entered her first competition at age ten and won each event. She became more serious about the sport after that and began to observe the techniques of other gymnasts. Dawes also took dance classes, which she credited with giving her more grace in her routines. When Hill's gym moved to

> *"My most thrilling moment was pulling together as a team and just working so hard at practicing all day. Then we all stood together on the awards stand, getting our medals. I knew is was all worth it."*
> Dominique Dawes

Dominique Dawes
performs on the balance
beam at the 1996
Olympic games.

Gaithersburg, Maryland, Dawes rose each morning at 4:30 to ride to a 6 A.M. workout. After school, she would spend five more hours at the gym. Her family let Dawes move in with her coach so she could work our more easily and prepare for the 1992 Olympics.

By 1991 Dawes ranked thirteenth nationally in compulsories, third in optionals, and ninth overall. Her accomplishments were especially impressive as she did not have an Olympic coach or train at an Olympic training center. By 1992 Dawes easily qualified for the 1992 Olympic Summer Games in Barcelona, Spain. At age fifteen, she was one of the youngest members of the team. Dawes performance was disappointing, finishing twenty-sixth overall. However, she did help her team win the bronze medal.

At the 1993 World Championships in Birmingham, England, Dawes began to shine. She scored fourth in the all-around and won two silver medals, for the uneven parallel bars and the balance beam. At the 1993 U.S. National Championships in Salt Lake City, she placed first in the vault and the balance beam. She also placed second in the individual all-around and the floor exercise competitions and third in the uneven bars.

In 1994 Dawes excelled in many areas of her life. She reigned as queen of the senior prom, graduated with honors, and outdid herself athletically. She won the gold in the all-around, the vault, the uneven bars, and the balance beam at the American Cup in Orlando, Florida. Later in 1994 Dawes did something that had not been done in twenty-five years—she took first place in all five individual women's events: vault, uneven

1976 Dawes is born in Silver Spring, Maryland.

1986 Dawes enters her first competition and wins each event.

1992 Dawes wins team bronze medal at Olympic Games in Barcelona.

1994 Dawes takes first place in all five individual events at U.S. National Championships.

1996 Dawes wins bronze at Summer Olympics and helps team win gold medal.

bars, balance beam, all-around, and floor exercises at the U.S. National Championships in Nashville, Tennessee. This accomplishment made Dawes famous and she found herself suddenly the object of attention for journalists and fans, who picked up on her nickname, "Awesome Dawesome." Looking toward the 1996 Olympics, Dawes told journalists, "I'm really excited right now, but I don't like to get overexcited about competitions. You know there will be good days and bad days. And I know I still will have some bad days."

After graduating from Gaithersburg High School in 1994, Dawes received an athletic scholarship to Stanford University but she deferred her enrollment until after the summer of 1996. In 1995 bad days did come for Dawes. She suffered stress fractures in her foot and one in her wrist. But she soon rebounded and made the commitment to train for the 1996 Summer Olympic Games. She worked out each day from 6 to 9 A.M. and then from 3 to 8 P.M. She said, "This year I decided I wanted to make something of my life. I wanted people to remember me, so I wanted to give it all I have."

By the 1996 Summer Olympics in Atlanta, Dawes was twenty years old, nearly ancient in the sport of gymnastics. But she won a bronze medal for her floor exercise. Her team became famous as the "Magnificent Seven" and included Shannon Miller, the most decorated gymnast in United States history. Delivering one of the Olympics' most impressive performances and thrilling world viewers with their flawless routines, the team won the gold medal.

Still making public gymnastics appearances in 1998, Dawes also had some acting and modeling jobs. ◆

> Dawes found herself suddenly the object of attention for journalists and fans, who picked up on her nickname, "Awesome Dawesome."

De Passe, Suzanne

1946? – ● ENTERTAINMENT EXECUTIVE

Suzanne de Passe grew up in Harlem. She guards her private life carefully, and as a result little is known about her early life and career. De Passe apparently was working as a booking agent at the Cheetah Disco in New York when she met Berry Gordy, then the head of Motown Records. Her strong criticisms of Motown's business operations, delivered directly to Gordy, earned her a position as his creative assistant. Until 1972 she served as road manager, costume designer, and choreographer for the Jackson Five, then Motown's newest sensation. She was also responsible for signing the Commodores, who went on to become one of Motown's biggest sellers during the 1970s.

In the 1970s de Passe became increasingly involved with Motown's theater, television, and film productions. In 1971 she helped write *Diana,* the first production by Motown's television and theatrical division. That project was so successful that the next year Gordy named de Passe corporate director of Motown's Creative Production division, and vice president of Motown's parent corporation, positions that allowed her to work almost exclusively in television and film. De Passe was nominated for an Academy Award for cowriting the Motown-produced film *Lady Sings the Blues* (1972).

In the late 1970s Gordy began to entrust de Passe with the fastest-growing, most profitable divisions of Motown. In 1977 she was promoted to vice president of Motown Industries, another television and film subsidiary, and in 1981 she was named president of Motown Productions. Under de Passe, the budget for the company grew from $12 million in 1980 to $65 million in 1989. She won Emmy awards for *Motown 25: Yesterday, Today, Forever* (1982–83) and *Motown Returns to the Apollo* (1984–85).

By the early 1980s de Passe was considered one of the rising black female Hollywood executives. In 1985 her reputation soared further after she paid $50,000 for the rights to *Lonesome Dove,* the Larry McMurtry novel about a nineteenth-century western cattle drive that had been rejected by every major Hollywood studio. De Passe sold telecast rights to CBS for $16 million, and by 1989 she had produced an eight-hour program that won seven Emmy awards and drew one of the largest audiences ever for a miniseries. In 1990 de Passe produced *Motown 30: What's Goin' On.*

In the early 1990s de Passe started a new company, de Passe Entertainment, and produced the five-hour miniseries *The Jacksons: An American Dream* (1992). In that year she also was co-executive producer of the film *Class Act.* Considered one of the most powerful female black executives in Hollywood, de Passe won a 1989 Essence award, and the next year was inducted into the Black Filmmakers' Hall of Fame. In 1990 de Passe received a Micheaux award for her contribution to the entertainment industry. ◆

1971 De Passe helps write *Diana* for television.

1972 De Passe becomes corporate director for Motown's Creative Production division.

1972 De Passe receives Oscar nomination for cowriting *Lady Sings the Blues.*

1977 De Passe becomes vice president of Motown Industries.

1981 De Passe is named president of Motown Productions.

1989 De Passe produces *Motown 30: What's Goin' On* and *Lonesome Dove.*

1990 De Passe is inducted into Black Filmmakers' Hall of Fame.

1992 De Passe produces *The Jacksons: An American Dream* for television.

Dee, Ruby

OCTOBER 27, 1924 – ● ACTOR

> *"The first function of art is to effect change. Nothing really exists in isolation, and artists are providers of direction for change."*
> Ruby Dee, quoted in the *Washington Post*, 1989

Born Ruby Ann Wallace in Cleveland, Ohio, Dee and her family soon moved to New York City and settled in Harlem. After graduating from high school, Dee attended Hunter College, and from 1941 to 1944 prepared for a stage career at the American Negro Theater. In 1943 she made her Broadway debut with Canada Lee in Harry Rigsby and Dorothy Heyward's *South Pacific* (not to be confused with the later Rodgers and Hammerstein musical of the same name). She had her first starring role on Broadway in *Jeb*, alongside Ossie Davis. Two years later she married Davis, who subsequently appeared with her in several productions. Her notable New York theater performances include *A Raisin in the Sun* (1959); *Purlie Victorious* (1961); *Boseman and Lena* (1971), for which she won a 1971 Obie Award; and *Wedding Band* (1972–73), for which she won a Drama Desk Award (1974).

Dee's film debut was in the role of Rachel Robinson in *The Jackie Robinson Story* (1950). She went on to perform in *St. Louis Blues* (1957), *A Raisin in the Sun* (1961), *Gone Are the Days* (1963), and *Buck and the Preacher* (1971). In 1965 she joined the American Shakespeare Festival in Stratford, Connecticut, and was the first black actress to play major roles in the company. In 1975 Dee and Ossie Davis received a special award from Actor's Equity for "outstanding creative contributions both in the performing arts and in society at large." Dee collaborated on the screenplay for *Uptight* in 1968, and wrote the Off-Broadway musical *Twin-Bit Gardens* (1979).

Together with Ossie Davis, Dee has long been a participant in civil rights efforts. She has served on national committees of the National Association for the Advancement of Colored People (NAACP) and the Southern Christian Leadership Conference, and has performed in numerous fundraising benefits. In the late 1960s she hosted benefits for the Black Panther Party and the Young Lords. In 1970 Dee and Ossie Davis were presented with the Frederick Douglass Award by the New York Urban League. Her other activities include reading for the blind, raising money to fight drug addiction, and helping black women study drama through the Ruby Dee Scholarship in Dramatic Art, established in the late 1960s. A frequent reader of poetry and drama in national tours, she has also written several

1924 Dee is born in Cleveland, Ohio.

1943 Dee makes Broadway debut in *South Pacific.*

1950 Dee makes film debut in *The Jackie Robinson Story.*

1961 Dee appears in *A Raisin in the*

1975 Dee and Ossie Davis receive a special Actor's Equity award.

1989 Dee appears in Spike Lee's *Do the Right Thing.*

1991 Dee wins Emmy Award for *Decoration Day.*

Ruby Dee (foreground) and Claudia McNeil in a scene from the 1961 film version of Lorraine Hansberry's play *A Raisin in the Sun.*

books of poetry and short stories, including *Glowchild* (1972), *My One Good Nerve* (1987), *Two Ways to Count to Ten* (1988), and *Tower to Heaven* (1991). Dee has contributed columns to the *New York Amsterdam News,* and she was the assistant editor of the magazine *Freedomways* in the early 1960s.

In recent years, Dee has been seen in *Cat People* (1982) and the Spike Lee films *Do the Right Thing* (1989) and *Jungle Fever* (1991). Television appearances include her Public Television Series *With Ossie and Ruby* (1981), the Negro Ensemble Company's production of *Long Day's Journey into Night* (1983), and the Hallmark Hall of Fame production *Decoration Day* (1991), for which she was awarded an Emmy. In 1990 Dee wrote the script and starred in the American Playhouse production *Zora Is My Name,* a one-woman show based on the life and work of Zora Neale Hurston. ◆

> *"The greatest gift is not being afraid to question."*
> Ruby Dee, *Tower to Heaven,* 1974

Dickens, Helen Octavia

FEBRUARY 21, 1909 – ● PHYSICIAN AND MEDICAL EDUCATOR

Helen Octavia Dickens, the first black woman admitted to the American College of Surgeons, was born in Dayton, Ohio, to Charles and Daisy Jane Dickens. Her

1909 — Dickens is born in Dayton, Ohio.

1921 — Dickens graduates from the University of Illinois.

1934 — Dickens receives M.D. from the University of Illinois.

1935 — Dickens completes her residency and internship in Chicago.

1946 — Dickens is certified by the American Board of Obstetrics and Gynecology.

1950 — Dickens is admitted to the American College of Surgeons.

1965 — Dickens joins faculty of University of Pennsylvania School of Medicine.

emerita: a woman retired from professional life but permitted to retain as an honorary title the last rank held.

father, a former slave, worked as a janitor and her mother as a domestic. After attending public schools in Dayton, Dickens enrolled at Crane Junior College in Chicago and later at the University of Illinois, where she earned a B.S. in 1921 and an M.D. in 1934. She was the only black woman in her graduating class of 175. In 1935, after completing her internship and residency at Chicago's Provident Hospital, she moved to Philadelphia to share the family practice established by another African-American woman physician, Virginia Alexander. Dickens left the practice seven years later to obtain additional training in obstetrics and gynecology at Provident Hospital, Harlem Hospital, and the University of Pennsylvania, from which she received the degree of Master of Medical Science in 1945.

Dickens married Purvis S. Henderson, a pediatric neurosurgeon, in 1943. The couple remained together until Henderson's death in 1961 and raised two children, Jayne and Norman. Marriage and children did not impede the progression of Dickens's career: she became certified by the American Board of Obstetrics and Gynecology in 1946. Her admission to the American College of Surgeons came four years later. She served as director of obstetrics and gynecology at Mercy-Douglass Hospital in Philadelphia from 1948 to 1967. In 1965 Dickens joined the faculty of the University of Pennsylvania School of Medicine. Her major achievements there include the creation of one of the nation's first teen-pregnancy clinics and the establishment of a successful program to recruit minority students. Dickens remained an active member of Pennsylvania's faculty as **emerita** professor of obstetrics and gynecology and associate dean for minority affairs. ◆

Dove, Rita

August 28, 1952 – ● Poet

Rita Dove was born in Akron, Ohio. She graduated *summa cum laude* from Miami University in Oxford, Ohio, in 1973, then spent the following year in Tubingen, Germany, as a Fulbright scholar. In 1975 she enrolled in the Writers' Workshop at the University of Iowa, where she

received her Master's in Fine Arts degree two years later. In 1981 Dove joined the English department at Arizona State University, where she continued to teach creative writing until 1989. In that year she accepted a position at the University of Virginia, which named her Commonwealth Professor of English in 1992.

Dove's first volume of poems, *Yellow House on the Corner,* was published in 1980. It was followed in 1983 by *Museum,* which displays a more conscious awareness of the conventions of artistic and historical practice. Three years later, Dove published *Thomas and Beulah* (1986), two versions of the story of two ordinary African Americans. The volume, which loosely narrates the lives of Dove's grandparents, was awarded the Pulitzer Prize in Poetry in 1987. *Thomas and Beulah* was a turning point in Dove's career for more reasons than its award-winning status. Not coincidentally, its narrative style emerged just after Dove's first published foray into fiction, *First Sunday* (1985), a collection of stories. Dove had also published one novel, *Through the Ivory Gate* (1992), the story of a black woman whose work as a puppeteer evokes painful childhood memories of disturbing cultural significance. What *First Sunday* and *Through the Ivory Gate* may lack in believable dialogue and depth of characterization is made up for in the echoes of *Grace*

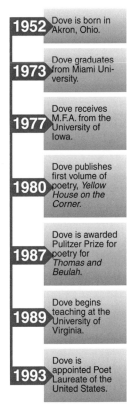

1952 Dove is born in Akron, Ohio.

1973 Dove graduates from Miami University.

1977 Dove receives M.F.A. from the University of Iowa.

1980 Dove publishes first volume of poetry, *Yellow House on the Corner.*

1987 Dove is awarded Pulitzer Prize for poetry for *Thomas and Beulah.*

1989 Dove begins teaching at the University of Virginia.

1993 Dove is appointed Poet Laureate of the United States.

Notes (1989). In these poems, each moment is filled by the persistent ringing of carefully culled metaphor.

More public attention has fallen on Dove's career than on that of any other contemporary African-American poet. Recognized for her virtuoso technical ability, Dove represents a generation of poets trained in university writers' workshops who are sometimes chastised for their formal competence at the expense of emotional depth. Dove has distinguished herself in her capacity to filter complex historical and personal information through precise selections of poetic form. In this, she is most closely allied to black poets such as Gwendolyn Brooks, Michael S. Harper, and Robert Hayden. Her unusual range of subject matter, thematically and geographically, has earned her a reputation as as black writer unafraid to set African-American culture within a global context. Dove's gifts as a poet were most fully acknowledged in 1993 when she was appointed Poet Laureate of the United States, the first black writer and the youngest poet ever to have been so honored.

During her two-year tenure as Poet Laureate, Dove published *Mother Love: Poems* (1995), which examines mother-daughter relationships, and a collection of essays entitled *The Poet's World* (1995). She also wrote *The Darker Face of Earth* (1994), a verse play based on the ancient Greek story of Oedipus, and set on a nineteenth-century plantation in South Carolina. ◆

> *"Not that I'd want to forget being black, but I would love to walk through life without the anxiety of being prejudged and pigeon-holed on the basis of my race."*
>
> Rita Dove, quoted in *Callaloo*, 1991

Dunbar-Nelson, Alice

JULY 19, 1875 – SEPTEMBER 18, 1935 ● WRITER

Alice Dunbar-Nelson was born Alice Ruth Moore in New Orleans, Louisiana. From her father, Joseph Moore, a sailor who never lived with the family, she inherited the light-colored skin and hair that enabled her to pass as white when she wished. Her mother, Patricia Wright Moore, an ex-slave who was part black and part Native American, supported the family as a seamstress. After attending public schools, Dunbar-Nelson graduated from the teachers' training program at Straight College (now Dillard University) in her hometown in 1892. In addition to her teaching, she worked as a stenographer and bookkeeper for a black printing firm. She was interested in theater, played the piano and cello, and presided over a literary society. In 1895, *Violets and Other Tales*, her first collection of stories, essays, and poetry, was published.

In 1896 she moved with her family to West Medford, Massachusetts. The following year she moved to New York, where she taught public school in Brooklyn while she helped her friend Victoria Earle Matthews found the White Rose Mission (later the White Rose Home for Girls in Harlem), where she also taught. On March 8, 1898, she married the poet Paul Laurence Dunbar, and moved to Washington, D.C., where he lived. Their romance had been conducted through letters. He first wrote to her after seeing her picture alongside one of her poems in a poetry review. At their first meeting they agreed to marry.

Although it was a stormy marriage, it significantly aided Dunbar-Nelson's literary career. In 1899 her husband's agent had her second collection, *The Goodness of St. Roque*, published as a companion book to Dunbar's *Poems of Cabin and Field*. The couple separated in 1902 and Dunbar-Nelson moved to Wilmington, Delaware, where she taught English at the Howard High School. Paul Dunbar died in 1906. In 1910 Dunbar-Nelson married a fellow teacher, Henry Arthur Callis, but that union soon dissolved. In 1916 she married Robert J. Nelson, a journalist with whom she remained until her death in 1935.

Dunbar-Nelson's writings, published continually throughout her life, displayed a wide variety of interests. After studying English literature as a special student at Cornell University, she published "Wordsworth's Use of Milton's Description of Pandemonium" in the April 1909 issue of *Modern Language Notes*. She also published several pedagogical articles, including "Is It Time for the Negro Colleges in the South to Be Put into the Hands of Negro Teachers?" (*Twentieth Century Negro Literature*, 1902) and "Negro Literature for Negro Pupils" (*The Southern Workman*, February 1922). The *Journal of Negro History* published her historical essay "People of Color in Louisiana" in two parts; the first appeared in October 1916 and the second in January 1917. From 1920 to 1922 she and Nelson published and edited the *Wilmington Advocate*. In addition, she wrote columns for the Pittsburgh *Courier* (1926, 1930) and the Washington *Eagle* (1926–30) in which she reviewed contemporary literature and delivered political analyses.

1875 Alice Moore is born in New Orleans.

1892 Moore graduates from teachers college.

1895 Moore publishes her first book, *Violets and Other Tales*.

1898 Moore marries poet Paul Laurence Dunbar.

1916 Moore marries Robert Nelson.

1920 Dunbar-Nelson founds the Industrial School for Colored Girls in Delaware.

1926 Dunbar-Nelson begins working for the American Inter-Racial Peace Committee.

1929 Dunbar-Nelson organizes the National Negro Music Festival.

1935 Dunbar-Nelson dies.

1984 Dunbar-Nelson's diary is published.

> *"I have come to the center of a stagnant pool where I drift aimlessly around a slow oozy backwash of putrid nothingness."*
>
> Alice
> Dunbar-Nelson,
> diary

In 1920 Dunbar-Nelson lost her job at Howard High School due to her political activity on behalf of women's and civil rights. That year she founded the Industrial School for Colored Girls in Marshalltown, Delaware, which she directed from 1924 to 1928. From 1929 to 1931 she served as Executive Secretary of the American Inter-Racial Peace Committee, a subsidiary of the American Friends (Quakers) Service Committee. She used this position to organize the National Negro Music Festival in 1929, and to engage in a ten-week cross-country speaking tour in 1930. In 1932 she moved to Philadelphia, where her husband was a governor appointee to the Pennsylvania Athletic Commission. Her lifelong interest in the African-American oral tradition prompted her to publish *Masterpieces of Negro Eloquence* in 1914 and *The Dunbar Speaker and Entertainer* in 1920. She was a member of the Delta Sigma Theta sorority and the Daughter Elks. Dunbar-Nelson is often considered a poet of the Harlem Renaissance. Her two most anthologized poems are "Sonnet" (often called "Violets"), and "I Sit and Sew." Her diary, published in 1984, is an invaluable source of information about her life. ◆

Dunham, Katherine

JUNE 22, 1909 – ● CHOREOGRAPHER AND DANCER

> *"I wasn't concerned about the hardships, because I always felt I was doing what I had to do, what I wanted to do and what I was destined to do."*
>
> Katherine Dunham, quoted in *American Vision*, 1987

Born in Chicago, and raised in Joliet, Illinois, Katherine Dunham did not begin formal dance training until her late teens. In Chicago she studied with Ludmilla Speranzeva and Mark Turbyfill, and danced her first leading role in Ruth Page's ballet *La Guiablesse* in 1933. She attended the University of Chicago on scholarship (B.A., social anthropology, 1936), where she was inspired by the work of anthropologists Robert Redfield and Melville Herskovits, who stressed the importance of the survival of African culture and ritual in understanding African-American culture. While in college she taught youngsters' dance classes and gave recitals in a Chicago storefront, calling her student company, founded in 1931, "Ballet Nègre." Awarded a Rosenwald Travel Fellowship in 1936 for her combined expertise in dance and anthropology, she departed after graduation for the West Indies (Jamaica, Trinidad, Cuba,

Katherine Dunham
dancing in the 1950s.

Haiti, Martinique) to do field research in anthropology and dance. Combining her two interests, she linked the function and form of Caribbean dance and ritual to their African **progenitors.**

progenitors: ancestors in the direct line.

The West Indian experience changed forever the focus of Dunham's life (eventually she would live in Haiti half of the time and become a priestess in the *vodoun* religion), and caused a profound shift in her career. This initial fieldwork provided the nucleus for future researches and began a lifelong involvement with the people and dance of Haiti. From this Dunham generated her master's thesis (Northwestern University, 1947) and more fieldwork. She lectured widely, published numerous articles, and wrote three books about her observations: *Journey to Accompong* (1946), *The Dances of Haiti* (her master's thesis, published in 1947), and *Island Possessed* (1969), underscoring how African religions and rituals adapted to the New World.

vodoun: voodoo, a religion derived from African polythesism and ancestor worship that is practiced chiefly in Haiti.

And, importantly for the development of modern dance, her fieldwork began her investigations into a vocabulary of movement that would form the core of the Katherine Dunham

articulated: clearly defined movement with sharp turns at the joints.

polyrhythm: simultaneous combination of contrasting rhythms in music.

seminal: original, contributing new ideas that others will develop later.

Technique. What Dunham gave modern dance was a coherent lexicon of African and Caribbean styles of movement—a flexible torso and spine, **articulated** pelvis and isolation of the limbs, a **polyrhythmic** strategy of moving—which she integrated with techniques of ballet and modern dance.

When she returned to Chicago in late 1937, Dunham founded the Negro Dance Group, a company of black artists dedicated to presenting aspects of African-American and African-Caribbean dance. Immediately she began incorporating the dances she had learned into her choreography. Invited in 1937 to be part of a notable New York City concert, *Negro Dance Evening,* she premiered "Haitian Suite," excerpted from choreography she was developing for the longer *L'Ag'Ya.* In 1937–38 as dance director of the Negro Unit of the Federal Theater Project in Chicago, she made dances for *Emperor Jones* and *Run Lil' Chillun,* and presented her first version of *L'Ag'Ya* on January 27, 1938. Based on a Martinique folktale (ag'ya is a Martinique fighting dance), *L'Ag'Ya* is a **seminal** work, displaying Dunham's blend of exciting dance-drama and authentic African-Caribbean material.

Dunham moved her company to New York City in 1939, where she became dance director of the New York Labor Stage, choreographing the labor union musical *Pins and Needles.* Simultaneously she was preparing a new production, *Tropics and Le Jazz Hot: From Haiti to Harlem.* It opened February 18, 1939, in what was intended to be a single weekend's concert at the Windsor Theatre in New York City. Its instantaneous success, however, extended the run for ten consecutive weekends and catapulted Dunham into the limelight. In 1940 Dunham and her company appeared in the black Broadway musical *Cabin in the Sky,* staged by George Balanchine, in which Dunham played the sultry siren Georgia Brown—a character related to Dunham's other seductress, "Woman with a Cigar," from her solo "Shore Excursion" in *Tropics.* That same year Dunham married John Pratt, a theatrical designer who worked with her in 1938 at the Chicago Federal Theater Project, and for the next forty-seven years, until his death in 1986, Pratt was Dunham's husband and her artistic collaborator.

With *L'Ag'Ya* and *Tropics and le Jazz Hot: From Haiti to Harlem,* Dunham revealed her magical mix of dance and theater—the essence of "the Dunham touch"—a savvy combination of authentic Caribbean dance and rhythms with the heady spice of American showbiz. Genuine folk material was presented with lavish costumes, plush settings, and the orchestral arrangements based on Caribbean rhythms and folk music. Dancers moved through fantastical tropical paradises or artistically designed juke-joints, while a loose storyline held together a succession of diverse dances. Dunham aptly called her spectacles "revues." She choreographed more than ninety individual dances, and produced five revues, four of which played on Broadway and toured worldwide. Her most critically acclaimed revue was her 1946 *Bal Nègre*, containing another Dunham dance favorite, *Shango*, based directly on *vodoun* ritual.

If her repertory was diverse, it was also coherent. *Tropics and le Jazz Hot: From Haiti to Harlem* incorporated dances from the West Indies as well as from Cuba and Mexico, while the "Le Jazz Hot" section featured early black American social dances, such as the Juba, Cake Walk, Ballin' the Jack, and Strut. The sequencing of dances, the theatrical journey from the tropics to urban black America implied—in the most entertaining terms—the **ethnographic** realities of cultural connections. In her 1943 *Tropical Revue*, she recycled material from the 1939 revue and added new dances, such as the balletic "Choros" (based on formal Brazilian **quadrilles**), and "Rites de Passage," which depicted puberty rituals so explicitly sexual that the dance was banned in Boston.

ethnographic: describing the study and recording of human societies and cultures.

quadrille: a square dance for four couples.

Beginning in the 1940s, the Katherine Dunham Dance Company appeared on Broadway and toured throughout the United States, Mexico, Latin America, and especially Europe, to enthusiastic reviews. In Europe Dunham was praised as a dancer and choreographer, recognized as a serious anthropologist and scholar, and admired as a glamorous beauty. Among her achievements was her resourcefulness in keeping her company going without any government funding. When short of money between engagements, Dunham and her troupe played in elegant nightclubs, such as Ciro's in Los Angeles. She also supplemented her income through film. Alone, or with her company, she appeared in nine Hollywood movies and in several foreign films between 1941 and 1959, among them *Carnival of Rhythm* (1939), *Star Spangled Rhythm* (1942), *Stormy Weather* (1943), *Casbah* (1948), *Boote e Risposta* (1950), and *Mambo* (1954).

In 1945 Dunham opened the Dunham School of Dance and Theater (sometimes called the Dunham School of Arts and Research) in Manhattan. Although technique classes were the

1909 Dunham is born in Chicago.

1931 Dunham forms Ballet Negre, a student dance company.

1933 Dunham dances her first leading role in Ruth Page's *La Guiablesse.*

1936 Dunham graduates from the University of Chicago; travels to the West Indies.

1937 Dunham founds Negro Dance Group in Chicago.

1938 Dunham presents first version on *L'Ag'Ya.*

1939 Dunham opens *Tropics and le Jazz Hot* in New York.

1940 Dunham and company star on Broadway in *Cabin in the Sky.*

1945 Dunham opens Dunham School of Dance and Theater.

1947 Dunham earns an M.A. from Northwestern University.

1963 Dunham choreographs *Aida* for the Metropolitan Opera.

1967 Dunham opens the Performing Arts Training Center.

1992 Dunham fasts to protest deportation of Haitian refugees.

heart of the school, they were supplemented by courses in humanities, philosophy, languages, aesthetics, drama, and speech. For the next ten years many African-American dancers of the next generation studied at her school, then passed on Dunham's technique to their students, situating it in dance mainstream (teachers such as Syvilla Fort, Talley Beatty, Lavinia Williams, Walter Nicks, Hope Clark, Vanoye Aikens, and Carmencita Romero; the Dunham technique has always been taught at the Alvin Ailey studios).

During the 1940s and '50s Dunham kept up her brand of political activism. Fighting segregation in hotels, restaurants and theaters, she filed lawsuits and made public condemnations. In Hollywood, she refused to sign a lucrative studio contract when the producer said she would have to replace some of her darker skinned company members. To an enthusiastic but all-white audience in the South, she made an after-performance speech, saying she could never play there again until it was integrated. In São Paulo, Brazil, she brought a discrimination suit against a hotel, eventually prompting the president of Brazil to apologize to her and to pass a law that forbade discrimination in public places. In 1951 Dunham premiered *Southland,* an hour-long ballet about lynching, though it was only performed in Chile and Paris.

Toward the end of the 1950s Dunham was forced to regroup, disband, and reform her company, according to the exigencies of her financial and physical health (she suffered from crippling knee problems). Yet she remained undeterred. In 1962 she opened a Broadway production, *Bambouche,* featuring fourteen dancers, singers, and musicians of the Royal Troupe of Morocco, along with the Dunham company. The next year she choreographed the Metropolitan Opera's new production of *Aida*—thereby becoming the Met's first black choreographer. In 1965–66 she was cultural adviser to the president of Senegal. She attended Senegal's First World Festival of Negro Arts as a representative from the United States.

Moved by the civil rights struggle and outraged by deprivations in the ghettos of East St. Louis, an area she knew from her visiting professorships at Southern Illinois University in the 1960s, Dunham decided to take action. In 1967 she opened the Performing Arts Training Center, a cultural program and school for the neighborhood children and youth, with programs in dance, drama, martial arts, and humanities. Soon thereafter she expanded the programs to include senior citizens. Then in 1977 she opened the Katherine Dunham Museum and Children's Workshop to house her collections of artifacts from her travels and research, as well as archival material from her personal life and professional career.

During the 1980s Dunham received numerous awards acknowledging her contributions. These include the Albert Schweitzer Music Award for a life devoted to performing arts and service to humanity (1979); a Kennedy Center Honor's Award (1983); the Samuel H. Scripps American Dance Festival Award (1987); induction into the Hall of Fame of the National Museum of Dance in Saratoga Springs, New York (1987). That same year Dunham directed the reconstruction of several of her works by the Alvin Ailey American Dance Theater and *The Magic of Katherine Dunham* opened Ailey's 1987–88 season.

In February 1992, at the age of eighty-two, Dunham again became the subject of international attention when she began a forty-seven-day fast at her East St. Louis home. Because of her age, her involvement with Haiti, and the respect accorded her as an activist and artist, Dunham became the center of a movement that coalesced to protest the United States's deportations of Haitian boat-refugees fleeing to the United States after the military overthrow of Haiti's democratically elected president Jean-Bertrand Aristide. She agreed to end her fast only after Aristide visited her and personally requested her to stop.

Boldness has characterized Dunham's life and career. And although she was not alone, Dunham is perhaps the best known and most influential pioneer of black dance. Her synthesis of scholarship and theatricality demonstrated, incontrovertibly and joyously, that African-American and African-Caribbean styles are related and powerful components of dance in America. ◆

"Go within everyday and find the inner strength so that the world will not blow your candle out."

Katherine Dunham, quoted in *American Visions*, 1987

Edelman, Marian Wright

JUNE 6, 1939 – ● ATTORNEY AND FOUNDER OF
THE CHILDREN'S DEFENSE FUND

The daughter of Arthur Jerome Wright, minister of Shiloh Baptist Church, and Maggie Leola Wright, a community activist, Marian Edelman was born and raised in Bennetsville, South Carolina. She attended Spelman College, from which she graduated as valedictorian in 1960. During her senior year, Edelman participated in a sit-in at City Hall in Atlanta. Responding to the need for civil rights lawyers, Edelman entered Yale Law School as a John Hay Whitney Fellow in 1960. After graduating from law school in 1963, she became the first black woman to pass the bar in Mississippi. From 1964 to 1968 she headed the NAACP Legal Defense and Education Fund in Mississippi, where she met her husband, Peter Edelman, a Harvard Law School graduate and political activist. In 1971 she became director of the Harvard University Center for Law and Education. She was also the first black woman elected to the Yale University Corporation, where she served from 1971 to 1977.

Edelman is best known for her work with the Children's Defense

Fund (CDF), a nonprofit child advocacy organization that she founded in 1973. The CDF offers programs to prevent adolescent pregnancy, to provide health care, education, and employment for youth, and to promote family planning. In 1980 Edelman became the first black and the second woman to chair the Board of Trustees of Spelman College. She has been the recipient of numerous honors and awards for her contributions to child advocacy, women's rights, and civil rights, including the MacArthur Foundation Prize Fellowship (1985) and the Albert Schweitzer Humanitarian Prize from Johns Hopkins University (1988). Edelman has published numerous books and articles on the condition of black and white children in America, including *Children Out of School in America* (1974), *School Suspensions: Are They Helping Children?* (1975), *Portrait of Inequality: Black and White Children in America* (1980), *Families in Peril: An Agenda for Social Change* (1987), and *The Measure of Our Success: A Letter to My Children and Yours* (1992). ◆

"People who do not vote have no line of credit with people who are elected and thus pose no threat to those who act against our interests."
Marian Wright Edelman, 1987

Elders, M. Joycelyn Jones

AUGUST 13, 1933 – ● U.S. SURGEON GENERAL

Born in Schaal, Arkansas, Joycelyn Jones was the eldest daughter of Haller and Curtis Jones. She attended Philander Smith College in Little Rock, Arkansas, where she received her B.A. in 1952. Wishing to become a doctor, she joined the U.S. Army and trained in physical therapy at the Brooke Army Medical Center at Fort Sam Houston, Texas. In 1956 she left the Army and enrolled at the University of Arkansas Medical School, one of the first African Americans to attend, and received her M.D. degree in 1960, the same year she married Oliver Elders. Joycelyn Elders did an internship in pediatrics at the University of Minnesota, then returned to the University of Arkansas in 1961 for her residency period. Elders was ultimately named chief resident, and also received an M.S. in biochemistry in 1967. In 1971 Elders was hired by the University of Arkansas Medical School as an assistant professor in pediatrics, and five years later was named a full professor. Over the succeeding years, she published 138 articles, mostly on child growth problems and diabetes.

"Picture with me for a moment a room full of preschoolers, each with a cigarette in their mouths. In essence, this is what we are doing to our children every time we expose them to secondhand smoke."
Joycelyn Elders, 1994

1933 Elders is born in Schaal, Arkansas.

1952 Elders graduates from Philander Smith College.

1960 Elders receives M.D. from the University of Arkansas.

1971 Elders becomes a professor at the University of Arkansas.

1987 Elders is named Arkansas Health Commissioner.

1993 Elders is appointed U.S. Surgeon General.

1994 Elders is dismissed from the post of U.S. Surgeon General.

In 1987, Arkansas governor Bill Clinton named Elders as the Arkansas Health Commissioner. Elders's advocacy of making birth control information and condoms available in schools as ways of fighting teenage pregnancy and AIDS caused a storm of controversy. Conservative critics decried her supposedly permissive attitudes toward sex, and her implementation of a kindergarten-to-college health education program that included sex education as well as the usual information about hygiene, substance abuse, and other matters.

In 1993 Clinton, by then president of the United States, appointed Elders U.S. surgeon general. Despite conservative opposition in Congress over her advocacy of abortion rights and sex education, she was confirmed, and was sworn in on September 10, 1993. During Elders's first year as surgeon general, she faced continued opposition by conservatives to her advocacy of condom distribution and sex education in schools and stirred debate through several controversial stands, such as her support of the medical and compassionate use of marijuana, her warnings to parents against purchasing toy guns for children, and most notably her proposal that the question of legalizing drugs in order to "markedly reduce" the nationwide crime rate be studied. Her supporters claimed that Elders was simply being used as a target by opponents of the administration, and her courageous, forthright style made her a hero to thousands of African Americans and whites throughout the United States. In the wake of continuing controversy, however, President Clinton asked for her resignation; she left the surgeon general's office on December 30, 1994. Elders returned to the University of Arkansas Medical School to teach pediatrics. In 1996 she published an autobiography, *Joycelyn Elders, M.D.: From Sharecropper's Daughter to Surgeon General of the United States of America.* ◆

Fauset, Crystal Dreda Bird

JUNE 27, 1893 – MARCH 27, 1965 ● PUBLIC OFFICIAL

Born in Princess Anne, Maryland, the daughter of Benjamin O. and Portia E. Bird, Crystal Bird was orphaned at age six and moved to Boston to be raised by her aunt, Lucy Groves. She attended Boston Normal School, and in 1914 began to teach in Boston. In 1918 she became the national secretary for younger Negro girls of the Young Women's Christian Association (YWCA), and traveled the country studying the condition of blacks. Already an experienced public speaker, she received further public visibility in 1927 when the American Friends Service Committee (AFSC) asked her to tour and give lectures on black aspirations. She went on to study at Teachers College, Columbia University, where she earned a B.S. degree in 1931. That year, she was made a social worker and administrator of Negro affairs of the New York and Philadelphia YWCAs. Two years later she helped found the Swarthmore College summer Institute of Race Relations, and became the executive secretary. Catalyzed by the Great Depression and passionate about the need to redress economic inequality,

1893 ▸ Bird is born in Princess Anne, Maryland.

1918 ▸ Bird becomes national secretary for Negro girls of the YWCA.

1927 ▸ Bird lectures for American Friends Service Committee.

1935 ▸ Bird marries Arthur Huff Fauset.

1938 ▸ Fauset is elected to Pennsylvania House of Representatives.

1941 ▸ Fauset is appointed special consultant in the Office of Civilian Defense.

1945 ▸ Fauset helps establish the UN Council.

1953 ▸ Fauset founds the Korean-American foundation.

1965 ▸ Fauset dies in Philadelphia.

she became active in the Democratic party. In 1935 the same year she married Arthur Huff Fauset, she became director of Negro women's activities for the Democratic National Committee and became assistant personnel director for the Philadelphia office of the Works Project Administration (WPA).

In 1938 Democratic leaders persuaded Fauset to run for the Pennysylvania House of Representatives, from a heavily white district. There had been few, if any, African-American female elected officials. Minnie Harper had briefly sat in the West Virginia Legislature in 1927, but only as a replacement for her deceased husband. In November 1938 Fauset was elected, becoming the first African-American woman elected to a state legislature. She only served for a year, however, before resigning her seat. Hoping to improve economic conditions for both blacks and whites, she became assistant director of education and recreation programs for the Pennsylvania WPA. In October 1941, with the aid of her friend Eleanor Roosevelt, she was appointed special consultant on Negro affairs in the Office of Civilian Defense in Washington, D.C.

During World War II, Fauset broke with the Democratic party over their treatment of blacks and joined the Republican party. She spent the postwar years concentrating on world affairs. In 1945 she helped establish the United Nations Council (now the World Affairs Council) of Philadelphia and traveled to San Francisco to attend the founding of the United Nations. In 1953 she founded the Korean-American Foundation, for which she was awarded a Meritorious Service Medal by Pennsylvania's governor John S. Fine. Fauset died in Philadelphia in 1965, following a heart attack. ◆

Fitzgerald, Ella

APRIL 25, 1918 – JUNE 15, 1996 ● JAZZ VOCALIST

I n a career lasting half a century, Ella Fitzgerald's superb pitch and diction, infallible sense of rhythm, and masterful scat singing have all become part of the fabric of American music, and she was recognized as "First Lady of Song." While her background and technique were rooted in jazz, she was always a popular singer, with a soothing yet crystalline sound that brought wide acclaim. Born in Newport News, Virginia, she came north as a child to Yonkers, New York, with her mother. In 1934, on a dare, she entered a Harlem amateur-night contest as a dancer, but became immobile with stage fright when called on to perform. Instead, she sang two songs popularized by the Boswell Sisters, "Judy" and "The Object of My Affection," and won first prize.

After she had won several more amateur competitions, an opportunity came in February 1935, when she appeared at the Apollo and was spotted by Bardu ali, the master of ceremonies for Chick Webb's band, who persuaded Webb to hire her. Fitzgerald began performing with Webb's band at the Savoy Club, and cut her first record, "Love and Kisses," with them in June 1935. Inspired by a nursery rhyme, Fitzgerald cowrote and recorded "A-Tisket, A-Tasket" with Webb's group in 1938; it became one of the most successful records of the swing era and transformed the young singer into a national celebrity.

When Webb died suddenly in 1939, Fitzgerald assumed nominal leadership of his band, which broke up two years later. During the 1940s she gained prominence as a solo performer through hit records that showcased her versatility. Influenced by Dizzy Gillespie and **bebop,** in 1947 Fitzgerald recorded, "Oh, Lady Be Good" and "How High the Moon," two songs that utilized her scat singing, the wordless vocal improvising that became her signature style. By the early 1950s she had appeared around the world with the star-studded Jazz and the Philharmonic tours organized by Norman Granz, a record producer and **impresario** who became her manager in 1954. Under his supervision and on his Verve label, she recorded *The Cole Porter Songbook* in 1956, followed by anthologies devoted to George and Ira Gershwin, Duke Ellington, Irving Berlin, and other popular composers. Heavily arranged and cannily designed to promote both songwriter and performer, Fitzgerald's "songbooks" extended her appeal.

bebop: jazz with complex harmonies, often played very fast.

impresario: the promoter, manager, or sponsor of an entertainment such as a concert.

> *"I always thank God. I'm here because this is what I love to do. When they say come and sing, that's the medicine."*
>
> Ella Fitzgerald, quoted in *Jet*, 1988

By the 1960s she was one of the world's most respected and successful singers. In the following years, she became something of an institution, regularly honored. She was named "Best Female Vocalist" by *Down Beat* magazine several times, and she won more Grammy Awards than any other female jazz singer. Following heart bypass surgery in 1986, she suffered from erratic health, but she intermittently recorded and gave concerts. Fitzgerald died in 1996 of complications related to diabetes. ◆

Flack, Roberta

1939 – ● POPULAR SINGER

> *"You have to give your own announcement, and then you roll out your own red carpet, and then you go back and put your crown on. And then you say, 'The Queen, the Queen!'"*
>
> Roberta Flack, quoted in *Essence*, 1989

Born in Black Mountain, North Carolina, but raised in Arlington, Virginia, Roberta Flack learned to play piano on an upright salvaged from a junkyard. At fifteen she won a full scholarship to Howard University. She graduated in 1958 with a degree in music education. After teaching for several years she began performing in 1967 at a Washington, D.C., nightclub and was spotted by jazz artist Les McCann, who helped arrange a contract for her at Atlantic Records. She was signed in 1969 and later that year released her debut album, *First Take*, distinguished by its broad range of material and plaintive folk-song style alongside up-tempo jazz. Included was a song that would become her breakthrough recording three years later, "The First Time Ever I Saw Your Face" (1972). That same year the song was featured in the film *Play Misty for Me*, propelling the single to the Number-One place on the *Billboard* charts for six weeks, capturing Grammy Awards for Song and Record of the Year and for Best Pop Vocal—Female. In 1973 Flack recorded another number-one single, "Killing Me Softly with His Song," which topped the charts for five weeks. She won a Grammy for Song of the Year in 1973 and a trophy for Best Pop Vocal Performance—Female.

Besides doing solo work, Flack also recorded several hit duets with longtime collaborator Donny Hathaway, who died in 1979, including "Where Is the Love," from 1972, and "The Closer I Get to You" from 1978. In the early 1980s, Flack teamed up with Peabo Bryson for a number of recording duets, producing in 1983 a Top-Twenty single, "Tonight I Celebrate My Love." Flack continues to release meticulously crafted albums such as *Oasis* (1988) and *Set the Night to Music* (1991), both full of ethereal, romantic vocals that characterize her work and win her a devoted listening audience. ◆

Franklin, Aretha Louise

MARCH 25, 1942 – ●   SINGER

Known as "Lady Soul" and "The Queen of Soul," Aretha Franklin brought the undiluted power of black gospel singing to American popular music beginning in the late 1960s. Born March 25, 1942, in Memphis, Tennessee, and raised in Detroit, Michigan, she was the fourth of five children of Barbara Siggers Franklin and the well-known gospel preacher and singer, the Rev. C. L. Franklin of Detroit's New Bethel Baptist Church. Her mother, also a gospel singer, left her husband and children in 1948 when Aretha was six, and died shortly thereafter.

> *"Soul is something creative, something active. Soul is honesty."*
> Aretha Franklin, 1991

Aretha's formative years were spent singing in her father's church choir and traveling with him on the gospel circuit. Numerous jazz and gospel figures visited the Franklins' home, and James Cleveland boarded with the family and worked with Aretha as she practiced playing the piano and singing. Clara Ward sang at an aunt's funeral, and Franklin was so moved she decided to become a professional singer herself. At fourteen she recorded a selection of gospel songs including Thomas A. Dorsey's "Precious Lord, Take My Hand." She became pregnant at fifteen and dropped out of school.

At eighteen Franklin was brought to the attention of John Hammond, the producer at Columbia Records who had "discovered" Bessie Smith, Billie Holiday, and other African-American musicians. Hammond praised Franklin's voice as

1942 Franklin is born in Memphis.

1948 Franklin's mother abandons the family.

1966 Franklins signs with Atlantic Records.

1966 Franklin records "I Never Loved a Man."

1980 Franklin switches to Arista label.

1984 Franklin's father dies after five years in a coma.

the best he had heard in twenty years. Franklin signed with Columbia and moved to New York but achieved only marginal success as a pop singer because of Columbia's material and arrangements, a confused hodgepodge of jazz, pop, and standards.

Her breakthrough came in 1966 when her Columbia contract expired and she signed with Atlantic Records, where she was teamed with veteran producer Jerry Wexler. He constructed simple, gospel-influenced arrangements for her, often based on her own piano playing. In these comfortable musical settings her true voice emerged with intensity and emotion. Wexler said, "I took her to church, sat her down at the piano, and let her be herself." Franklin's first record with Wexler was "I Never Loved a Man (The Way I Love You)" in February 1967. It was an immediate success and topped *Billboard*'s charts. Her second hit, "Respect," was sung with such conviction it became a call for black and feminist pride and empowerment.

Often compared to Ray Charles for her fusion of sacred and secular styles, Franklin came to personify African-American "soul" music. She produced a series of top records including "Chain of Fools," "Think," and "Don't Play That Song." She has won fifteen Grammy Awards, three American Music Awards, and a Grammy Living Legend Award. With thirty-five albums, she has had seventeen Number One rhythm-and-blues singles, and more million-selling singles than any other woman singer. In 1980 she switched to the Arista label.

Throughout her career, her dominant public voice has been contrasted with her private, even reclusive, personality, although she carefully monitors her career and the music industry. Her personal life has at times been difficult, with her mother's abandonment, her own pregnancy at age fifteen, several unsuccessful marriages, and, particularly, the fact that her father, to whom she was very close, spent five years in a coma from a gunshot wound in 1979 until his death in 1984. ◆

Fuller, Meta Vaux Warrick

JUNE 9, 1877 – MARCH 18, 1968 ● SCULPTOR

Named for one of her mother's clients (Meta, daughter of Pennsylvania senator Richard Vaux), Meta Vaux Warrick Fuller was born in Philadelphia, the youngest

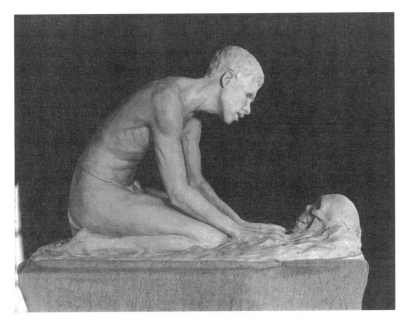

The Talking Skull (1937) by **Meta Warrick Vaux Fuller.**

of three children of William and Emma (Jones) Warrick, prosperous hairstylists. She enjoyed a privileged childhood, with dancing and horseback-riding lessons. While attending Philadelphia public schools, Fuller took weekly courses at J. Liberty Tadd, an industrial arts school. At eighteen, she won a three-year scholarship to the Pennsylvania Museum and School for Industrial Art. In 1898 she graduated with honors, a prize in metalwork for her *Crucifix of Christ in Anguish*, and a one-year graduate scholarship. The following year, she was awarded the Crozer (first) Prize in sculpture for *Procession of the Arts and Crafts*, a terra-cotta **bas-relief** of thirty-seven medieval costumed figures.

> **bas-relief**: sculpture in which the image stands out only slightly from the background.

From 1899 to 1903 Fuller studied in Paris, at first privately with Raphael Collin, and then at the Colarossi Academy. Among her supporters in France were **expatriate** painter Henry O. Tanner and philosopher W. E. B. Du Bois, who encouraged her to depict her racial heritage. Fuller produced clay, painted-plaster, and bronze **figurative** works based on Egyptian history, Greek myths, French literature, and the Bible.

> **expatriate:** a person living in a foreign land.

> **figurative:** depicting human figures and other recognizable forms.

In 1901 sculptor Auguste Rodin praised Fuller's clay piece *Secret Sorrow* (or *Man Eating His Heart*). With his sponsorship, Fuller began to receive wider notice. Art dealer Samuel Bing exhibited twenty-two of her sculptures at his L'Art Nouveau Gallery in June 1902. *The Wretched*, a bronze group of seven figures suffering physical and mental disabilities (as well as other macabre pieces such as *Carrying the Dead Body* and *Oedipus*, in the latter of which the figure is blinding himself) earned Fuller the title "delicate sculptor of horrors" from the French press. She later enlarged a plaster model of *The Impenitent Thief*, which she had shown at Bing's gallery. Although she never finished the piece, Rodin saw that it was exhibited at the prestigious Société National des Beaux Arts Salon in April 1903.

Upon Fuller's return to Philadelphia, she established a studio on South Camac Street in a flourishing artistic neighborhood. Her sculptures were exhibited at the Pennsylvania Academy of Fine Arts in 1906, 1908, 1920, and 1928. In 1907 the Jamestown **Tercentennial** Exposition commissioned Fuller to create fifteen **tableaux** of 24-inch-high plaster figures depicting African-American progress since the Jamestown settlement in 1607. She received a gold medal for *The Warrick Tableaux*, a 10-foot-by-10-foot **diorama.**

The artist's career slowed considerably after her marriage in 1909 to the Liberian neurologist Solomon C. Fuller and a fire in 1910 that destroyed the bulk of her work in storage. By 1911 Fuller was the devoted mother of two sons (the last was born in 1916), an active member of Saint Andrew's Episcopal Church, and host to prominent guests who frequently visited the family in the quiet town of Framingham, Massachusetts.

Fuller began to sculpt again in 1913, when Du Bois commissioned a piece for New York state's celebration of the fiftieth anniversary of the Emancipation Proclamation. *The Spirit of Emancipation* represented Humanity weeping for her freed children (a man and woman) as Fate tried to hold them back. Positive public response promoted Fuller to continue working. In 1914 the Boston Public Library exhibited twenty-two of her recent works. Among the numerous requests and awards that followed from African-American and women's groups were a plaster medallion commissioned by the Framingham Equal Suffrage League (1915); a plaster group, *Peace Halting the Ruthlessness of War* (for which she received second prize from the Massachusetts branch of the Women's Peace Party in 1917); and a portrait relief of the NAACP's first president, Moorfield Storey, commissioned by Du Bois in 1922. The same year, the New York Making of America Exposition displayed Fuller's *Ethiopia Awakening*, a one-foot-high bronze sculpture of a woman shedding mummy cloths. This **Pan-Africanist** work symbolized the strength of womanhood, the emergence of

tercentennial: 300th anniversary.

tableaux: motionless representations of scenes using costumed figures.

diorama: a life-size exhibit of a scene with realistic natural surroundings and artificial background.

Pan-African: including all of Africa.

nationhood, and the birth of what Alain Locke would call three years later the "New Negro." One of Fuller's most poignant works, *Mary Turner: A Silent Protest Against Mob Violence* (1919), commemorates both the silent parade of ten thousand black New Yorkers against lynching in 1917 and the lynching of a Georgian woman and her unborn child in 1918. Fuller never finished the piece because she believed Northerners would find it too inflammatory and Southerners would not accept it. She created numerous other works that depicted symbolic and actual African and African-American culture, including her celebrated *Talking Skull* (1937), based on an African fable. She also produced portrait busts of friends, family members, and African-American abolitionists and other black leaders, such as educator Charlotte Hawkins Brown, composer Samuel Coleridge Taylor, and Menelik II of Abyssinia. The Harmon Foundation exhibited Fuller's work in 1931 and 1933. She later served as a Harmon juror.

Fuller participated in numerous local organizations; she was a member of the Boston Art Club, an honorary member of the Business and Professional Women's Club, chair of the Framingham Women's Club art committee, and the only African-American president of Zonta, a women's service club. Additionally, she designed costumes for theatrical groups and produced "living pictures": re-creations of artistic masterpieces with actors, costumes, sets, and lighting.

In the 1940s Fuller's husband went blind and became increasingly ill. She nursed him until his death in 1953, then contracted tuberculosis herself and stayed at the Middlesex County Sanatorium for two years. She wrote poetry there, too frail to create more than a few small sculptures.

By 1957 Fuller was strong enough to continue her work. She produced models of ten notable African-American women for the Afro-American Women's Council in Washington, D.C. She also created a number of sculptures for her community, including several religious pieces for Saint Andrew's Church, a plaque for the Framingham Union Hospital, and the bronze *Storytime* for the Framingham Public Library. For her achievements, Livingstone College (her husband's alma mater) awarded her an honorary doctorate of letters in 1962, and Framingham posthumously dedicated a public park in the honor of Meta and Solomon Fuller in 1973. Since then, Fuller's sculptures have been included in numerous exhibitions. ◆

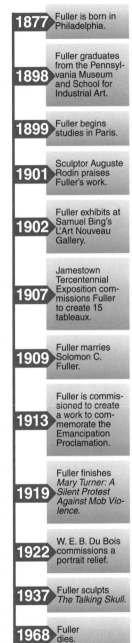

1877 ▸ Fuller is born in Philadelphia.

1898 ▸ Fuller graduates from the Pennsylvania Museum and School for Industrial Art.

1899 ▸ Fuller begins studies in Paris.

1901 ▸ Sculptor Auguste Rodin praises Fuller's work.

1902 ▸ Fuller exhibits at Samuel Bing's L'Art Nouveau Gallery.

1907 ▸ Jamestown Tercentennial Exposition commissions Fuller to create 15 tableaux.

1909 ▸ Fuller marries Solomon C. Fuller.

1913 ▸ Fuller is commissioned to create a work to commemorate the Emancipation Proclamation.

1919 ▸ Fuller finishes *Mary Turner: A Silent Protest Against Mob Violence.*

1922 ▸ W. E. B. Du Bois commissions a portrait relief.

1937 ▸ Fuller sculpts *The Talking Skull.*

1968 ▸ Fuller dies.

G

Garrison, Zina

NOVEMBER 6, 1963 – ● TENNIS PLAYER

Zina Garrison was born in Houston, Texas, in 1963. At the age of seventeen she won the junior women's singles titles at Wimbledon and the U.S. Open. In 1982 she turned professional and by the end of the year was ranked the sixteenth best woman tennis player in the world. Over the next decade Garrison remained one of the world's top twenty women players, reaching as high as number four in May 1990.

Although Garrison has not won a grand slam tournament, in 1985 she reached the semifinals at Wimbledon and the quarterfinals at both the Australian and U.S. Opens. In 1988 Garrison beat Martina Navratilova in the U.S. Open quarterfinals and stopped Chris Evert's attempt at a comeback in the quarters the following year. At the 1988 Seoul Olympics Garrison earned a bronze medal in women's singles and, with her partner, Pam Shriver, a gold in women's doubles. In 1988 she also won the mixed doubles at Wimbledon with Sherwood Stewart (who became her coach in 1990). Garrison's greatest success as a player came at Wimbledon in 1990: she defeated Monica Seles and

Steffi Graf in the quarters and semis to face Navratilova in the final. Though she lost, the tennis world took notice, as did equivalent sponsors, and the top-ranked U.S. woman player received a clothing and shoe contract with Reebok. In 1993 Garrison and her husband, Houston businessman Willard Jackson, founded the All Court Tennis Academy for Houston's inner-city children. ◆

Gibson, Althea

AUGUST 25, 1927 – ● TENNIS PLAYER

Althea Gibson was the first black tennis player to win the sport's major titles. Born in Silver, South Carolina, to a garage hand and a housewife, she came to New York City at age three to live with an aunt. The oldest of five children, she was a standout athlete at Public School 136 and began playing paddleball under Police Athletic League auspices on West 143rd Street in Harlem. In 1940 she was introduced to tennis by Fred Johnson, a one-armed instructor, at the courts (now named after him) on 152nd Street. She was an immediate sensation.

Gibson became an honorary member of Harlem's socially prominent Cosmopolitan Tennis Club (now defunct) and won her first tournament—the American Tennis Association (ATA) junior girls title—in 1945. (The ATA is the oldest continuously operated black noncollegiate sports organization in America). Though Gibson lost in the finals of the ATA women's singles in 1946, she attracted the attention of two black physicians: Dr. Hubert Eaton of Wilmington, North Carolina, and Dr. R. Walter Johnson of Lynchburg, Virginia, who tried to advance her career.

1927 — Gibson is born in Silver, SC.

1945 — Gibson wins American Tennis Association junior girls title.

1947 — Gibson wins the first of ten consecutive ATA singles titles.

1950 — Gibson plays at USLTA Nationals at Forest Hills.

1955 — Gibson begins tour of Southeast Asia.

1956 — Gibson wins French singles.

1957 — Gibson wins women's singles at Wimbledon.

1958 — Gibson sings on the *Ed Sullivan Show*.

1971 — Gibson is elected to International Tennis Hall of Fame.

1986 — Gibson is appointed to New Jersey State Athletic Commission.

In September 1946 Gibson entered high school in Wilmington while living with the Eatons, and she graduated in 1949. She won the ATA women's single title ten years in a row, from 1947 to 1956. As the best black female tennis player ever, she was encouraged to enter the U.S. Lawn Tennis Association (the white governing body of tennis) events. Jackie Robinson had just completed his third year in major league baseball, and pressure was being applied on other sports to integrate. Though she was a reluctant crusader, Gibson was finally admitted to play in the USLTA Nationals at Forest Hills, New York, on August 28, 1950.

Alice Marble, the former USLTA singles champion, wrote a letter, published in the July 1950 issue of *American Lawn Tennis* magazine, admonishing the USLTA for its reluctance to admit Gibson when she was clearly more than qualified. Gibson's entry was then accepted at two major events in the summer of 1950 before her Forest Hills debut. She was warmly received at the Nationals, where she lost a two-day, rain-delayed match to the number-two-seeded Louise Brough in the second round.

Gibson's breakthrough heralded more to come. The ATA began a serious junior development program to provide opportunities for promising black children. (Out of that program came Arthur Ashe, who became the first black male winner of the sport's major titles.) Sydney Llewelyn became Gibson's coach, and her rise was meteoric. Her first grand slam title was the French singles in Paris in 1956. Before she turned professional, she added the Wimbledon and the U.S. singles in both 1957 and 1958, and the French women's doubles and the U.S. mixed doubles. She was a Wightman Cup team member in 1957 and 1958. After her Wimbledon victory, she was presented her trophy by Queen Elizabeth II, she danced with the queen's husband, Prince Philip, at the Wimbledon Ball, and New York City accorded her a ticker-tape parade.

The poise Gibson showed at Wimbledon and at other private clubs where USLTA-sanctioned events were played was instilled by Dr. Eaton's wife and by her time spent as an undergraduate at Florida A&M University in Tallahassee, Florida. Jake Gaither, FAMU's famed athletic director, helped secure a teaching position for her in physical education at Lincoln University in Jefferson City, Missouri. In the winter of 1955–56 the State Department asked her to tour Southeast Asia with Ham Richardson, Bob Perry, and Karol Fageros.

In 1957 Gibson won the Babe Didrickson Zaharias Trophy as Female Athlete of the Year, the first black female athlete to win the award. She also began an attempt at a career as a singer, taking voice lessons three times a week. While singing at New York City's Waldorf-Astoria Hotel for a tribute to famed songwriter W. C. Handy, she landed an appearance on the *Ed Sullivan Show* in May 1958. Moderately successful as a singer, she considered a professional tour with tennis player Jack Kramer, the American champion of the 1940s. She also became an avid golfer, encouraged by Joe Louis, the former world heavyweight champion, who was a golf enthusiast. Louis had also paid her way to her first Wimbledon championships.

> *"Most of us who aspire to be tops in our fields don't really consider the amount of work required to stay tops."*
> Althea Gibson, *So Much to Live For*, 1968

The Ladies Professional Golfers Association (LPGA) was in its infancy and purses were small. But Gibson was a quick learner and was soon nearly a "scratch" player. She received tips from Ann Gregory, who had been the best black female golfer ever. Gibson, a naturally gifted athlete, could handle the pressure of professional sports. But the purses offered on the LPGA tour were too small to maintain her interest.

In 1986 New Jersey governor Tom Kean appointed Gibson to the state's athletic commission. She became a sought-after teaching professional at several private clubs in central and northern New Jersey and devoted much of her time to counseling young black players. The first black female athlete to enjoy true international fame, Gibson was elected to the International Tennis Hall of Fame in 1971. ◆

Giovanni, Yolanda Cornelia "Nikki"

JUNE 7, 1943 –   ● POET

Nikki Giovanni was born in Knoxville, Tennessee. Her father, Jones Giovanni, was a probation officer; her mother, Yolanda Cornelia Watson Giovanni, was a social worker. The Giovannis were a close-knit family, and Nikki felt a special bond with her younger sister, Gary, and her maternal grandmother, Louvenia Terrell Watson. Watson

1943 Giovanni is born in Knoxville, Tennessee.

1967 Giovanni graduates from Fisk University.

1968 Giovanni publishes first book of poetry, *Black Judgment.*

1971 Giovanni publishes her first book of children's poetry, *Spin a Soft Black Song.*

1971 Giovanni produces her first album of spoken poetry, *Truth Is on Its Way.*

"Humans have a great and profound need to debate the heat while ignoring the sun; to need the rain while decrying the clouds."

Nikki Giovanni, quoted in *Catalyst,* 1988

instilled in Giovanni a fierce pride in her African-American heritage.

After graduating from Fisk University in 1967, Giovanni was swept up by the Black Power and Black Arts movements. Between 1968 and 1970 she published three books of poetry reflecting her preoccupation with revolutionary politics: *Black Judgment* (1968), *Black Feeling, Black Talk* (1970), and *Re: Creation* (1970).

But *Re: Creation* also introduced more personal concerns. In the spring of 1969, Giovanni gave birth to a son, Tom. The experience, she said, caused her to reconsider her priorities. Her work through the middle 1970s concentrated less overtly on politics and confrontation and more on personal issues such as love and loneliness. Yet Giovanni would always deny any real separation between her "personal" and her "political" concerns. During this time she began writing poetry for children. *Spin a Soft Black Song: Poems for Children* appeared in 1971, *Ego-Tripping and Other Poems for Young People* in 1973, and *Vacation Time: Poems for Children* in 1980.

In the 1970s Giovanni expanded her horizons in other ways. Between 1971 and 1978 she made a series of six records, speaking her poetry to an accompaniment of gospel music (the first in the series, *Truth Is on Its Way,* was the best-selling spoken-word album of 1971). She published essays and two books of conversations with major literary forebears: *A Dialogue: James Baldwin and Nikki Giovanni* (1973) and *A Poetic Equation: Conversations Between Nikki Giovanni and Margaret Walker* (1974). She was also a sought-after reader and lecturer.

Critical reaction to Giovanni's work has often been mixed. While some have praised her work for its vitality and immediacy, some have felt that her early popularity and high degree of visibility worked against her development as a poet. Others have criticized her work as politically naive, uneven, and erratic. Some of these reactions were due in part to Giovanni's very public growing up as a poet and the diversity of her interests. These criticisms have never bothered Giovanni, who believes that life is "inherently incoherent."

Other works of Giovanni's include *My House* (1972), *The Women and the Men* (1972), *Cotton Candy on a Rainy Day* (1978), *Those Who Ride the Night Winds* (1983), and a collection of essays, *Sacred Cows and Other Edibles* (1988). ◆

Goldberg, Whoopi

NOVEMBER 13, 1950 – ● ACTOR

Whoopi Goldberg was born Caryn Johnson in New York City and raised in a housing project by her mother. She received her earliest education at a parish school, the Congregation of Notre Dame. She gained her first stage experience at the Helena Rubinstein Children's Theatre at the Hudson Guild, where she acted in plays from the age of eight to ten.

In the mid-1960s Goldberg dropped out of high school and worked on Broadway as a chorus member in the musicals *Hair*, *Jesus Christ Superstar*, and *Pippin*. She was married briefly in the early 1970s and has a daughter from the marriage, Alexandrea Martin.

In 1974 Goldberg moved to Los Angeles and has since maintained California residence. She became a founding member of the San Diego Repertory Theatre and later joined Spontaneous Combustion, an improvisation group. It was about this time that she adopted the name Whoopi Goldberg.

In 1981 Goldberg, with David Schein, wrote the extended comedy sketch *The Last Word*. The eclectic ensemble of characters in her sketches include a self-aborting surfer girl, a panhandling ex-vaudevillian, a junkie, and a Jamaican maid. Goldberg's style, a blend of social commentary, humor, and improvisation, earned her both critical acclaim and a large audience. In 1983 she developed an hourlong piece entitled *The Spook Show*, which played in London and New York to great acclaim. After appearing in Berkeley, California, in a one-woman show called *Moms*, based on the life of comedian Moms Mabley, Goldberg opened on Broadway in 1984 in a new version of her comedy sketches, *Whoopi Goldberg*, produced by Mike Nichols.

> *"If there wasn't something called acting they would probably hospitalize people like me. The giddiness and the joy of life is the moving and grooving, the exploration."*
>
> Whoopi Goldberg, quoted in *Ebony*, 1991

1950 — Goldberg is born in New York City.

1983 — Goldberg writes and appears in *The Spook Show*.

1984 — Goldberg stars on Broadway in a new version of her comedy sketches.

1985 — Goldberg receives Oscar nomination for *The Color Purple*

1988 — Goldberg begins appearing on *Star Trek*.

1990 — Goldberg receives Oscar for *Ghost*.

1992 — Goldberg and friends found comedy benefit "Comic Relief."

1998 — Goldberg produces new *Hollywood Squares*.

The following year Goldberg starred as Celie in Steven Spielberg's film of Alice Walker's *The Color Purple*. She received an Academy Award nomination for her performance, which propelled her into the Hollywood mainstream. She subsequently starred in such films as *Jumping Jack Flash* (1986), *Burglar* (1987), *Fatal Beauty* (1987), *Clara's Heart* (1988), and *The Long Walk Home* (1990). She appeared in a continuing role on the television series *Star Trek: The Next Generation* from 1988 through 1993. In 1990 she received an Academy Award for best supporting actress for her role as a psychic in *Ghost*. Goldberg became only the second black woman—the first since Hattie McDaniel in 1939—to win an Oscar in a major category. Subsequently she appeared in *Soapdish* (1991), *Sister Act* (1992), and *Sarafina!* (1992), becoming the first African American to star in a film shot on location in South Africa.

In 1992 Goldberg cofounded the annual comedy benefit "Comic Relief" on the cable television network Home Box Office to raise money for the homeless. In 1993 she appeared in the films *Sister Act 2* and *Made in America*, a comedy about an interracial relationship. Since then, Goldberg has appeared in numerous feature films, including *Corrina, Corrina* (1994), *Boys on the Side* (1995), *Ghosts of Mississippi* (1996), and *How Stella Got Her Groove Back* (1998). Her television projects included an appearance as the queen mother in Disney's *Cinderella* (1997). Beginning in 1998, Goldberg coproduced and appeared in the new version of the classic game show *Hollywood Squares*. She also published a volume of personal observances, entitled simply *Book* (1997). ◆

Granville, Evelyn Boyd

MAY 1, 1924 – ● MATHEMATICIAN, EDUCATOR, AND AUTHOR

Evelyn Boyd was born in Washington, D.C., the second of two daughters of Julia Walker Boyd, a U.S. government employee, and William Boyd, an apartment building superintendent. William Boyd did not remain with the family; Evelyn Boyd was reared primarily by her mother and aunt. Boyd attended Dunbar High School and won a partial scholarship to study at Smith College in Northampton, Massachusetts.

Boyd excelled in mathematics, and in 1945 she graduated summa cum laude from Smith, where she was elected to Phi Beta Kappa. She won several grants that allowed her to enter a graduate program at Yale University, from which she earned a Ph.D. with a specialty in **functional** analysis in 1949. She was one of the first two black female recipients of a doctorate in mathematics. She had a postgraduate fellowship at New York University and, in 1950, was appointed to the mathematics faculty of Fisk University in Nashville. She remained on the faculty for two years and inspired at least two young women to pursue a Ph.D. in mathematics. She left Fisk and spent sixteen years working in government and private industry. Some of her employers included the National Bureau of Standards, IBM, the Computation and Data Reduction Center of the Space Technology Laboratories, the Diamond Ordinance Fuze Laboratories, and the North American Aviation Company. Her work involved primarily **celestial** mechanics, **trajectory** and orbit computation, and associated numerical and digital computer techniques.

functional: relating to a mathematical correspondence that assigns exactly one element of one set to each element of the same or another set.

celestial: relating to the sky or the visible heavens.

In 1967 Boyd was appointed to the faculty at California State University in Los Angeles. While there, she cowrote a book with Jason Frand, *Theory and Application of Mathematics for Teachers* (1975). She accepted a position in 1985 at Texas College in Tyler, where she had purchased a farm with her husband, Edward V. Granville. Boyd Granville left Texas College in 1988 and, in 1990, was appointed to the Sam A. Lindsey Chair at the University of Texas in Tyler. In addition to teaching at the university level, Boyd Granville has taught in secondary school programs in the California and Texas public-school systems. ◆

trajectory: the curve that an object moving in space represents.

Griffith-Joyner, Florence Delorez

DECEMBER 21, 1959 – SEPTEMBER 21, 1998 ● ATHLETE

Florence Griffith was born in Los Angeles, the seventh of eleven children of an electronics technician and a garment worker. When she was four, her parents separated and she moved with her mother and siblings to the Jordan Downs housing project in the Watts section of Los Angeles. Griffith began running at age seven in competitions sponsored

1959 — Griffith is born in Los Angeles.

1984 — Griffith wins Olympic silver medal.

1987 — Griffith marries Al Joyner.

1988 — Griffith-Joyner wins three gold and one silver Olympic medals.

1993 — Griffith-Joyner cochairs President's Council on Physical Fitness and Sports.

1998 — Griffith-Joyner dies at age 38.

by the Jesse Owens National Youth Games for underprivileged youth and won races at ages fourteen and fifteen. She became a member of the track team at Jordan High School, where she set two school records before graduating in 1978.

In 1979 Griffith enrolled at California State University at Northridge, where she met assistant track coach Bob Kersee. However, she was forced to drop out of college the next year due to lack of funds. With the help of Kersee, who had moved to the University of California at Los Angeles (UCLA), Griffith won an athletic scholarship to UCLA and returned to college in 1981. Griffith competed on the track team, and in 1982 she won the NCAA championships in the 200 meters. In 1983 she won the NCAA championships in the 400 meters and graduated from UCLA with a major in psychology. In the 1984 Olympics in Los Angeles, she finished second to fellow American Valerie Brisco-Hooks in the 200 meters.

After the Olympics Griffith worked as a customer-service representative for a bank during the day and as a beautician at night. In early 1987, however, she decided to train full-time for the 1988 Olympics. In October 1987 she married Al Joyner, brother of athlete Jackie Joyner-Kersee.

After strong showings in the world championships and the U.S. trials, Griffith-Joyner was a favorite for the 1988 Olympics in Seoul, Korea. Flo-Jo, as she was dubbed by the media, did not disappoint, winning three gold medals and one silver medal. Griffith-Joyner set an Olympic record in the 100 meters and a world record in the 200 meters. She ran the third leg for the American winning team in the 4 × 100-meter relay and the anchor leg for the American silver-medal winners in the 4 × 400-meter relay. Griffith-Joyner's outstanding performance and striking appearance (including long, extravagantly decorated fingernails and brightly colored one-legged running outfits) earned her worldwide media attention. She won the 1988 Jesse

Owens Award and the 1988 Sullivan Award, given annually to the best amateur athlete.

Griffith-Joyner settled comfortably into post-Olympic life with numerous endorsements and projects, including designing her own sportswear line and a brief acting stint on the television soap opera *Santa Barbara* (1992). In 1993 President Bill Clinton named her cochairwoman of the President's Council on Physical Fitness and Sports.

Griffith-Joyner died suddenly in September 1998 at the age of thirty-eight. An autopsy revealed that she suffocated during an epileptic seizure caused by a congenital blood flow abnormality. ◆

> *"People don't pay much attention to you when you are second best. I wanted to see what it felt like to be number one."*
> Florence Griffith-Joyner, quoted in *Essence*, 1989

Grimké, Angelina Weld

FEBRUARY 27, 1880 – JUNE 10, 1958 ● WRITER

Born in Boston, Grimké was the daughter of Archibald Grimké and Sarah Stanley Grimké. She attended integrated schools in Hyde Park, Massachusetts, and graduated in 1902 from Boston Normal School of Gymnastics, later part of Wellesley College. Grimké worked as a teacher in Washington, D.C., from that time until her retirement in 1926. In 1930 she moved to Brooklyn, where she lived for the rest of her life.

Grimké's best-known work was a short play entitled *Rachel*, first presented in 1916 and published in book form in 1920. The play portrays a young African-American woman who is filled with despair and, despite her love of children, despondently resolves not to bring any of her own into the world. With its tragic view of race relations, *Rachel* was staged several times by the National Association for the Advancement of Colored People (NAACP) as a response to D. W. Griffith's racist 1915 film *Birth of a Nation*.

But Grimké's most influential work was her poetry. Publishing first as a teenager, she initially wrote in the sentimental style of late-nineteenth-century popular poetry. In the early years of the twentieth century, however, she began to display an interest in experimentation, both formal and thematic. She openly took

1880 Grimké is born in Boston.

1902 Grimké graduates from Boston Normal School of Gymnastics.

1916 Grimké first play, *Rachel*, is produced.

1930 Grimké moves to Brooklyn.

1958 Grimké dies.

up sexual themes, with a frankness that was not common among African-American poets of her time. Only occasionally addressing racial issues, she nevertheless did so with a militance and subjectivity that looked toward the Harlem Renaissance. Although she was not to be a major figure in that movement, such work did much to contribute its foundations.

(Angelina Weld Grimké should not be confused with the nineteenth-century abolitionist Angelina Grimké Weld, though they were related. The former's father was the nephew of the latter.) ◆

Grimké, Charlotte L. Forten

AUGUST 17, 1837 – JULY 22, 1914 ● ABOLITIONIST,
TEACHER, AND WRITER

C harlotte Forten was born into one of Philadelphia's leading African-American families. Her grandfather, James Forten, was a well-to-do sailmaker and abolitionist. Her father, Robert Bridges Forten, maintained both the business and the abolitionism.

Charlotte Forten continued her family's traditions. As a teenager, having been sent to Salem, Massachusetts, for her education, she actively joined that community of radical abolitionists identified with William Lloyd Garrison. She also entered enthusiastically into the literary and intellectual life of nearby Boston, and even embarked on a literary career of her own. Some of her earliest poetry was published in antislavery journals during her student years. And she began to keep a diary, published almost a century later, which remains one of the most valuable accounts of that era.

Completing her education, Forten became a teacher, initially in Salem, and later in Philadelphia. Unfortunately, she soon began to suffer from ill health, which would plague her for the rest of her life. Nevertheless, while unable to sustain her efforts in the classroom for any length of time, she did continue to write and to engage in antislavery activity. With the outbreak of the Civil War, she put both her convictions and her training to use, joining other abolitionists on the liberated islands off the South Carolina coast to teach and work with the newly emancipated slaves.

"Let us labor to acquire knowledge, to break down the barriers of prejudice and oppression believing, that if not for us, for another generation there is a brighter day in store."

Charlotte Forten Grimké, journal, 1854

On the Sea Islands, she also kept a diary, later published. This second diary, and two essays she wrote at the time for the *Atlantic Monthly*, are among the most vivid accounts of the abolitionist experiment. Like many teachers, Forten felt a cultural distance from the freedpeople but worked with dedication to teach and to prove the value of emancipation. After the war, she continued her work for the freedpeople, accepting a position in Massachusetts with the Freedmen's Union Commission.

She also continued her literary efforts, which included a translation of the French novel *Madame Thérèse*, published by Scribner in 1869. In 1872, after a year spent teaching in South Carolina, Forten moved to Washington, D.C., where she worked first as a teacher and then in the Treasury Department. There she met the Rev. Francis Grimké, thirteen years her junior, and pastor of the elite Fifteenth Street Presbyterian Church. At the end of 1878, they married.

The marriage was long and happy, despite the death in infancy of their only child. Apart from a brief residence in Jacksonville, Florida, from 1885 to 1889, the Grimkés lived in Washington, D.C., and made their Washington home a center for the capital's social and intellectual life. Although Charlotte Grimké continued to suffer from poor health, she maintained something of her former activism, serving briefly as a member of the Washington school board and participating in such organizations as the National Association of Colored Women. She did a small amount of writing, although little was published. Finally, after about 1909, her failing health led to her virtual retirement from active life. ◆

1837 Forten is born in Philadelphia.

1869 Forten publishes a translation of the French novel *Madame Therese*.

1870 Forten moves to Washington, DC.

1878 Forten marries Francis Grimké.

1909 Failing health forces Forten Grimké's retirement from public life.

1914 Forten Grimké dies.

Guinier, Lani

APRIL 9, 1950 – ● LAWYER AND COLLEGE PROFESSOR

Lani Guinier appeared briefly on the stage of history when the president of the United States nominated her to the nation's top civil rights post, that of Assistant Attorney General, in 1993 and critics of the administration shot the nomination down. But the experience merely gave momentum to Guinier's outstanding career.

It is difficult to imagine someone closer to ideal for a major civil rights role than Carol Lani Guinier, born April 19, 1950,

1950 Guinier is born in New York City.

1971 Guinier graduates from Radcliffe College.

1974 Guinier receives a law degree from Yale University Law School.

1977 Guinier begins working for the Civil Rights Division of the U.S. Department of Justice.

1981 Guinier wins first of 32 civil rights cases she argues for the NAACP.

1988 Guinier becomes a law professor at the University of Pennsylvania.

1993 President Clinton nominates Guinier for Assistant Attorney General.

1995 Guinier publishes *The Tyranny of the Majority.*

1998 Guinier joins the faculty of Harvard Law School, becoming its first tenured black woman.

"Democracy in a heterogeneous society is incompatible with rule by a racial monopoly of any color."
Lani Guinier, *The Tyranny of the Majority,* 1995

in New York City, the daughter of a white Jewish mother and a black West Indian father. Guinier's father, Ewart, had lost a scholarship to Harvard University when school officials discovered his race. He then worked his way through New York's City College and through New York University Law School, eventually teaching history at Columbia and Harvard universities. Guinier's mother, Genii, raised Lani and her sisters to have a strong pride in their African-American roots.

Guinier developed a strong social conscience and commitment to civil rights. She graduated third in a high school class of over 1,000, and then graduated from Radcliffe College in 1971. She received a law degree from Yale University Law School in 1974. Guinier then clerked for the U.S. Court of Appeals in Detroit until 1976, when she served briefly in Detroit's Wayne County Juvenile Court.

In 1977 Guinier arrived in Washington, D.C., to work in the Civil Rights Division of the U.S. Department of Justice, helping enforce the Voting Rights Act of 1965. In 1981 Guinier joined the National Association for the Advancement of Colored People (NAACP), a leading civil rights group. She won 31 out of 32 civil rights cases she argued in court for the NAACP.

Guinier married Nolan A. Bowie in 1986, and they had a son, Niklas. She became a professor at the University of Pennsylvania Law School in 1988, and wrote scholarly papers that generated respect among her legal and academic peers.

On April 29, 1993, President Bill Clinton nominated Guinier for the post of Assistant Attorney General, to preside over the Civil Rights Division of the Department of Justice, the same office she had worked in fifteen years earlier. Guinier had been a friend of Clinton and Hillary Rodham since their days at Yale, and the Clintons had attended Guinier's wedding.

The day after her nomination, though, a *Wall Street Journal* editorial attacked Guinier, condemning papers Guinier had written about making the vote more meaningful for disadvantaged groups. Guinier had argued that, although the Voting Rights Act of 1965 had removed many hurdles, blacks were still unable to elect many of their own into office. The reason for this, she wrote, lay in a voting system based on districts, the borders of which could be drawn to give whites a majority in each district. If each district, for example, in a city with 10 districts, elected a white city council member, the city council could be 100 percent white even if the city were 20 percent black. Guinier advocated a system called cumulative voting which gives each voter as many votes as there are seats to fill. Thus, voters in the city with 10 districts would each have 10 votes. The resulting city council could achieve a racial proportion equal to that of the city.

Many news media ran with the criticism of Guinier without investigating her work. They accused her of wanting to create a "complex racial spoils system," and called her "quota queen," "radical," and "black separatist." One newspaper called her a "madwoman" with "cockamamie ideas," and a prominent newsmagazine said she had a "strange name, strange hair, strange ideas." In fact, Guinier's writings promoted "cross-racial coalitions" that would "reduce racial polarization." The public debate ignored Guinier's vast civil rights qualifications.

As the furor grew, Guinier could not defend herself because Clinton had ordered her to remain silent until hearings. Guinier met with Clinton on the night of June 3 and urged him to press for a hearing. But later that night she watched the president on television say that some of her ideas were antidemocratic, and he withdrew her nomination without holding hearings.

Disappointed in Clinton, but undaunted, Guinier went on to make public speaking appearances. She kept her teaching position and wrote several books. In *The Tyranny of the Majority: Fundamental Fairness in Representative Democracy* (1995) Guinier discussed the news articles that caused the controversy over her nomination. In her book *Lift Every Voice: Turning a Civil Rights Setback into a New Vision of Social Justice* (1998), Guinier explains her writings and offers her perspective on the nomination episode.

In the fall of 1998, Guinier, forty-seven, became the first tenured black woman to join the faculty of Harvard Law School. Guinier's husband began a senior fellowship at the John F. Kennedy School of Government at Harvard at the same time. ◆

> *"I am a democratic idealist who believes that politics need not be forever seen as 'I win, you lose,' a dynamic in which some people are permanent monopoly winners and others are permanent excluded losers."*
> Lani Guinier, 1994

Hamer, Fannie Lou
(Townsend, Fannie Lou)

OCTOBER 6, 1917 – MARCH 14, 1977 ● CIVIL RIGHTS ACTIVIST

F annie Lou Townsend was born to Ella Bramlett and James Lee Townsend in Montgomery County, Mississippi, in 1917. Her parents were sharecroppers, and the family moved to Sunflower County, Mississippi, when she was two. Forced to spend most of her childhood and teenage years toiling in cotton fields for white landowners, Townsend was able to complete only six years of schooling. Despite wrenching rural poverty and the harsh economic conditions of the Mississippi Delta, she maintained an enduring optimism. She learned the value of self-respect and outspokenness through her close relationship with her mother. In 1944 she married Perry Hamer, moved with him to Ruleville, and worked as a sharecropper on a plantation owned by W. D. Marlowe.

> "Whether you have a Ph.D., a D.D., or no D, we're in this together. Whether you're from Morehouse or No house, we're in this bag together."
> Fannie Lou
> Hamer, 1954

During her years on the Marlowe plantation, Hamer rose to the position of time- and recordkeeper. In this position she acquired a reputation for a sense of fairness and a willingness to speak to the landowner on behalf of aggrieved sharecroppers. She began to take steps directly to challenge the racial and economic inequality that had so circumscribed her life after meeting civil rights workers from the Student Nonviolent Co-

Fannie Lou Hamer at the 1954 Democratic National Convention.

ordinating Committee (SNCC) in 1962. In Mississippi, SNCC was mounting a massive voter registration and desegregation campaign aimed at empowering African Americans to change their own lives.

Inspired by the organization's commitment to challenging the racial status quo, Hamer and seventeen other black volunteers attempted to register to vote in Indianola, Mississippi, on August 31, 1962, but were unable to pass the necessary literacy test, which was designed to prevent blacks from voting. As a result of this action, she and her family were dismissed from the plantation, she was threatened with physical harm by Ruleville whites, and she was constantly harassed by local police. Eventually, she was forced to flee Ruleville and spent three months in Tallahatchie County, Mississippi, before returning in December.

In January 1963 Hamer passed the literacy test and became a registered voter. Despite the persistent hostility of local whites, she continued her commitment to civil rights activities and became a SNCC field secretary. By 1964 Hamer had fully

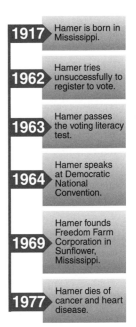

1917 Hamer is born in Mississippi.

1962 Hamer tries unsuccessfully to register to vote.

1963 Hamer passes the voting literacy test.

1964 Hamer speaks at Democratic National Convention.

1969 Hamer founds Freedom Farm Corporation in Sunflower, Mississippi.

1977 Hamer dies of cancer and heart disease.

tenuous: doubtful, weak, shaky, or flimsy.

immersed herself in a wide range of local civil rights activities, including SNCC-sponsored voter registration campaigns and clothing- and food-distribution drives. At that time she was a central organizer and vice-chairperson of the Mississippi Freedom Democratic Party (MFDP), a parallel political party formed under the auspices of SNCC in response to black exclusion from the state Democratic Party. Hamer was one of the sixty-eight MFDP delegates elected at a state convention of the party to attend the Democratic National Convention in Atlantic City in the summer of 1964. At the convention the MFDP delegates demanded to be seated and argued that they were the only legitimate political representatives of the Mississippi Democratic Party because unlike the regular party that formed and operated at the exclusion of blacks, their party was open to all Mississippians of voting age.

Hamer's televised testimony to the convention on behalf of the MFDP propelled her into the national spotlight. A national audience watched as she described the economic reprisals that faced African Americans who attempted to register to vote and recounted the beating that she and five other activists had received in June 1963 in a Winona County, Mississippi, jail. Hamer's proud and unwavering commitment to American democracy and equality inspired hundreds of Americans to send telegrams supporting the MFDP's challenge to the southern political status quo. Although the MFDP delegates were not seated by the convention, Hamer and the party succeeded in mobilizing a massive black voter turnout and publicizing the racist exclusionary tactics of the state Democratic Party.

By the mid-sixties SNCC had become ideologically divided and Hamer's ties to the organization became more **tenuous.** However, she continued to focus her political work on black political empowerment and community development. Under her leadership, the MFDP continued to challenge the all-white state Democratic party. In 1964 Hamer unsuccessfully ran for Congress on the MFDP ticket, and one year later spearheaded an intense lobbying effort to challenge the seating of Mississippi's five congressmen in the House of Representatives. She played an integral role in bringing the Head Start Program for children to Ruleville, and organized the Freedom Farm Cooperative for displaced agricultural workers. In 1969 she founded the Freedom Farm Corporation in Sunflower, a cooperative farming and landowning venture to help poor blacks become more self-sufficient. It fed well over 5,000 families before collapsing in 1974. Three years later, after over a decade of activism, she died from breast cancer and heart disease.

Fannie Lou Hamer was a symbol of defiance and indomitable black womanhood that inspired many in the civil rights movement. Morehouse College and Howard University, among others, have honored her devotion to African-American civil rights with honorary doctoral degrees. Her words "I'm sick and tired of being sick and tired" bear testament to her lifelong struggle to challenge racial injustice and economic exploitation. ◆

Hansberry, Lorraine

MAY 19, 1930 – JANUARY 12, 1965 ● PLAYWRIGHT

Lorraine Hansberry was the youngest child of a nationally prominent African-American family. Houseguests during her childhood included Paul Robeson and Duke Ellington. Hansberry became interested in theater while in high school, and in 1948 she went on to study drama and stage design at the University of Wisconsin. Instead of completing her degree, however, she moved to New York, worked at odd jobs, and wrote. In 1959 her first play, *A Raisin in the Sun*, was produced and was both a critical and commercial success. It broke the record for longest-running play by a black author and won the New York Drama Critics Circle Award. Hansberry was the first African American and the youngest person ever to win that award. The play, based on an incident in the author's own life, tells the story of a black family that attempts to move into a white neighborhood in Chicago. Critics praised Hansberry's ability to deal

> *"It is difficult for the American mind to adjust to the realization that the Rhetts and Scarletts were as much monsters as the keepers of Buchenwald— they just dressed more attractively."*
>
> Lorraine Hansberry, 1964

with a racial issue and at the same time explore the American dream of freedom and the search for a better life. The play was turned into a film in 1961, and then was adapted as a musical, *Raisin*, which won a Tony Award in 1974.

Hansberry's second play, *The Sign in Sidney Brustein's Window*, focuses on white intellectual political involvement. Less successful than *A Raisin in the Sun*, it closed after a brief run at the time of Hansberry's death from cancer in 1965. After her death, Hansberry's former husband, Robert B. Nemiroff, whom she had married in 1953, edited her writings and plays, and produced two volumes: *To Be Young, Gifted and Black* (1969) and *Les Blancs: The Collected Last Plays of Lorraine Hansberry* (1972). *To Be Young, Gifted and Black* was presented as a play and became the longest-running off-Broadway play of the 1968–69 season. ◆

Harper, Frances Ellen Watkins

SEPTEMBER 24, 1825 – FEBRUARY 20, 1911 ● WRITER AND ACTIVIST

O ne of the most prominent activist women of her time in the areas of abolition, temperance, and women's rights, Frances Ellen Watkins Harper also left an indelible mark on African-American literature. Frances Watkins was born in Baltimore and raised among the city's free black community. She was orphaned at an early age and her uncle, the Rev. William Watkins, took responsibility for her care and education, enrolling her in his prestigious school for free blacks, the Academy for Negro Youth. Here Watkins received a strict, classical education, studying the Bible, Greek, and Latin. Although she left school while in her early teens in order to take employment as a domestic, she never ceased her quest for additional education. She remained a voracious reader; her love of books contributed to her beginnings as a writer.

> *"The respect that is only bought by gold is not worth much. It is no honor to shake hands politically with men who whip women and steal babies."*
>
> Frances Harper, 1859

Frances Watkins published her first of several volumes of poetry in 1845. This early work, *Forest Leaves*, has been lost, however. From 1850 until 1852, Watkins taught embroidery and sewing at Union Seminary, an African Methodist Episcopal Church school near Columbus, Ohio. She then moved on to teach in Pennsylvania. Both teaching situations were difficult, since the schools were poor and the facilities overtaxed. During this period, she was moved by the increasing number of strictures placed on free people of color, especially in her home state of Maryland, a slave state. From this point, she became active in the antislavery movement .

In 1854 Watkins moved to Philadelphia and became associated with an influential circle of black and white abolitionists. Among her friends there were William Still and his daughter Mary, who operated the key Underground Railroad station in the city. The same year another collection of Watkins's verse, *Poems on Miscellaneous Subjects*, was published. Many of the pieces in this volume dealt with the horrors of slavery. The work received popular acclaim and was republished in numerous revised, enlarged editions. Watkins also published poems in prominent abolitionist papers such as *Frederick Douglass' Paper* and the *Liberator*. Later would come other collections—*Sketches of Southern Life* (1872), the narrative poem *Moses: A Story of the Nile* (1889), *Atlanta Offering: Poems* (1895), and *Martyr of Alabama and Other Poems* (1895).

1825 ▸ Watkins is born in Baltimore.

1845 ▸ Watkins publishes *Forest Leaves*, her first book of poetry.

1854 ▸ Watkins publishes *Poems on Miscellaneous Subjects*.

1860 ▸ Watkins marries Fenton Harper.

1872 ▸ Harper publishes *Sketches of Southern Life*.

1892 ▸ Harper's novel *Iola Leroy; or, Shadows Uplifted* is pub-

1911 ▸ Harper dies in Philadelphia.

With her literary career already on course, Watkins moved to Boston and joined the antislavery lecture circuit, securing a position with the Maine Anti-Slavery Society. She later toured with the Pennsylvania Anti-Slavery Society. Watkins immediately distinguished herself, making a reputation as a forceful and effective speaker, a difficult task for any woman at this time, especially an African American. Public speaking remained an important part of her career for the rest of her life, as she moved from antislavery work to other aspects of reform in the late nineteenth century.

In 1860 Frances Watkins married Fenton Harper and the two settled on a farm near Columbus, Ohio. Their daughter, Mary, was born there. Fenton Harper died four years later, and Frances Harper resumed her public career. With the close of the Civil War, she became increasingly involved in the struggle for suffrage, working with the American Equal Rights Association, the American Woman Suffrage Association, and the National Council of Women. Harper also became an active member of the Women's Christian **Temperance** Union. Despite her disagreements with many of the white women in these organizations and the racism she encountered, Harper remained steadfast in her commitment to the battle for women's rights. She refused to sacrifice any aspect of her commitment to

temperance: abstinence from the use of intoxicating liquor.

"A man landless, ignorant, and poor may use the vote against his interests, but with intelligence and land he holds in his hand the basis of power and the element of strength."

Frances Harper, 1871

African-American rights in seeking the rights of women, however. She was also a key member of the National Federation of Afro-American Women and the National Association of Colored Women.

In addition to the many poems, speeches, and essays she wrote, Frances Ellen Watkins Harper is probably best known for her novel, *Iola Leroy; or, Shadows Uplifted*, published in 1892. The work tells the story of a young octoroon woman who is sold into slavery when her African-American heritage is revealed. It is a story about the quest for family and for one's people. Through Iola Leroy and the characters around her, Harper addresses the issues of slavery, relations between African Americans and whites, feminist concerns, labor in freedom, and the development of black intellectual communities. In this book, she combined many of her lifelong interests and passions.

Harper's public career ended around the turn of the century. She died in Philadelphia in 1911, leaving an enduring legacy of literary and activist achievement. ◆

Harris, Barbara Clementine

JUNE 12, 1930 – ● EPISCOPAL BISHOP

"I am not used to quiet. I am used to boom boxes and people talking in the street."

Barbara C. Harris, quoted in *Episcopalian*, 1990

Barbara Harris was the first female bishop of the Protestant Episcopal Church. She was born in Philadelphia, where her father, Walter Harris, was a steelworker and her mother, Beatrice, was a church organist. A third generation episcopalian, Harris was very active in the St. Barnabas Episcopal Church. While in high school, she played piano for the church school and later started a young adults group.

After graduating from high school, Harris went to work for Joseph V. Baker Associates, a black-owned public relations firm. She also attended and graduated from the Charles Morris Price School of Advertising and Journalism in Philadelphia. In 1968 she went to work for Sun Oil Company and became community relations manager in 1973.

During the 1960s, Harris participated in several civil rights events. She was part of the 1965 Freedom March from Selma, Alabama, to Montgomery, Alabama, with the Rev. Dr. Martin Luther King Jr., and was also a member of a church-sponsored team of people who went to Mississippi to register black voters. Harris began attending North Philadelphia Church of the Advocate in 1968. That same year, the Union of Black Clergy was established by a group of black Episcopalian ministers. Harris and several other women lobbied for membership. Eventually, they were admitted and the word **laity** was added to the organization's name. Later it became the Union of Black Episcopalians.

laity: religious people who are not members of the clergy.

Once the Episcopal Church began to ordain women in 1976, Harris began to study for the ministry. From 1977 to 1979 she took several courses at Villanova University in Philadelphia, and spent three months in informal residency at the Episcopal Divinity School in Cambridge, Massachusetts. She was named **deacon** in 1979, served as a deacon-in-training in 1979–80, and was ordained to the priesthood in 1980. She left Sun Oil Company to pursue her new career full-time.

deacon: a subordinate officer in a Christian church.

The first four years of Harris's ministry were spent at St. Augustine-of-Hippo in Norristown, Pennsylvania. She also worked as a chaplain in the Philadelphia County Prison System, an area in which she had already spent many years as a volunteer. In 1984 she became the executive director of the Episcopal Church Publishing Company. Her writings were critical of church policies, which she believed to be in contrast to social, political, and economic fairness.

In 1988 the Episcopal Church approved the consecration of women as bishops. Harris was elected to become bishop to the Massachusetts diocese in the fall of 1988. Her election was ratified in January 1989 and she was ordained in a ceremony in Boston on February 11, 1989, with over 7,000 in attendance.

As the first female Episcopal bishop, Harris was surrounded by controversy centered on three issues: her gender, her lack of traditional seminary education and training, and her liberal viewpoints. Policies toward women, black Americans, the poor, and other minorities were always at the forefront of Harris's challenges to the church and its doctrines. Harris overcame the objections and focused her attention on her duties as a bishop. She has served the diocese of Massachusetts, where she has been extremely active in local communities and prison work. Greatly concerned with the prison ministry, she represents the Episcopal Church on the board of the Prisoners Visitation and Support Committee. ◆

1930 Harris is born in Philadelphia.

1965 Harris takes part in the Freedom March in Alabama.

1968 Harris goes to work for Sun Oil Company.

1973 Harris becomes Sun Oil's community relations manager.

1977 Harris begins studying for the Episcopalian ministry.

1979 Harris is named a deacon.

1980 Harris is ordained a priest.

1988 Harris is elected a bishop.

Harris, Patricia Roberts

MAY 31, 1924 – MARCH 23, 1985 ● EDUCATOR, LAWYER, AND POLITICIAN

"We defeat oppression with liberty. We cure indifference with compassion. We remedy social injustices with justice. And if our journey embodies these lasting principles, we find peace."

Patricia Harris,
1985

Patricia Roberts was born in the blue-collar town of Mattoon, Illinois, where her father was a Pullman porter. She attended high school in Chicago and then enrolled at Howard University in Washington, D.C. She became active in civil rights causes at Howard, participating in one of the nation's first student sit-ins at a segregated Washington cafeteria and by serving as the vice chairman of a student chapter of the National Association for the Advancement of Colored People (NAACP).

After graduating in 1945, Roberts returned to Chicago where she briefly attended graduate school at the University of Chicago and worked as program director of the Chicago Young Women's Christian Association. In 1949 she returned to Washington and accepted a position as the assistant director of the American Council on Human Rights. In 1953 she became executive director of Delta Sigma Theta, a black sorority, and two years later, she married Washington lawyer William Beasley Harris.

The Department of Housing and Urban Development

Patricia Harris became the first black woman member of a presidential cabinet when she was nominated by President Jimmy Carter to head the Department of Housing and Urban Development (HUD) in 1976. HUD was created in 1965 to provide a cabinet-level spokesperson for the problems of American cities, which had become acute in the 1950s and 1960s. Housing was an especially important problem, for there were large numbers of housing units (apartments or homes) that did not meet modern standards of health or comfort, and many new units were needed. Since its formation, HUD has helped city and state governments build thousands of new housing units. HUD provides subsidies and insures mortgages for low- and middle-income homeowners, and helps low-income families pay for cooperative and rental housing. HUD also helps individuals and local governments finance rehabilitation of old, but structurally sound, houses and apartment buildings. HUD's community development initiatives have embraced urban renewal, offering grants to build parks, playgrounds, hospitals, and sewerage. HUD is also responsible under law for enforcing the parts of the Civil Rights Act of 1968 that prohibit discrimination in housing based on race, color, religion, or national origins.

Patricia Harris during her tenure as secretary of HUD, with Jimmy Carter and New York mayor Abraham Beame in the South Bronx in 1977.

1924 Roberts is born in Mattoon, Illinois.

1945 Roberts graduates from Howard University.

1949 Roberts becomes assistant director of the American Council on Human Rights.

1953 Roberts becomes executive director of Delta Sigma Theta.

1955 Roberts marries William Harris.

1960 Harris becomes an attorney for the Department of Justice.

1961 Harris joins Howard faculty.

1963 Harris cochairs National Women's Committee for Civil Rights.

1965 Harris is appointed envoy to Luxembourg.

1976 Harris is appointed Secretary of Housing and Urban Development.

1979 Harris is appointed Secretary of Health, Education and Welfare.

1985 Harris dies.

Patricia Roberts Harris entered George Washington Law School in 1957. Upon graduation in 1960, she accepted a position as an attorney at the U.S. Department of Justice. In the following year, Harris joined the Howard University Law School faculty where she also served as the associate dean of students. In 1963, with the support of the Kennedy administration, Harris was chosen to cochair the National Women's Committee for Civil Rights, a clearing house and coordinating committee for a wide range of national women's organizations. She also served on the District of Columbia advisory committee to the United States Commission on Civil Rights.

In 1965 Harris became the first African-American woman to hold an ambassadorship when she was appointed envoy to Luxembourg. She held the post until September 1967, when she rejoined the faculty at Howard University. In 1969 she was appointed Dean of Howard Law School, becoming the first black woman to head a law school, but her tenure lasted only thirty days. Caught between disputes with the faculty and the president of the university over student protests, Harris resigned.

She accepted a position with a private law firm—Fried, Frank, Harris, Shriver, Kampelman—and also held a number of positions in the Democratic party during the 1970s, such as the temporary chairmanship of the credentials committee. Harris became the first black woman cabinet member when she was nominated by President Jimmy Carter to head the Department of Housing and Urban Development in 1976. She held the job for two years, and in 1979 she became Secretary of Health, Education, and Welfare (renamed the Department of Health and Human Services in 1980), serving until 1981.

In 1982 Harris ran for mayor of Washington, D.C. Running against Marion S. Barry in the Democratic primary, she lost a bitter contest in which she was depicted as an **elitist** who could not identify with the city's poorer blacks. She spent her remaining years as a professor at George Washington National Law Center before her death in 1985. ◆

elitist: someone who considers him- or herself better than others.

Height, Dorothy

MARCH 24, 1912 –   ● CLUBWOMAN AND ACTIVIST

Dorothy Height's career as an activist and reformer has been dedicated to working for African Americans through women's organizations, ranging from girls' clubs and sororities to the YWCA and the National Council of Negro Women (NCNW). Height was born in Richmond, Virginia; her family moved to Rankin, Pennsylvania, when she was four. In this mining town, she and her family were active in the life of their church and community groups. As a young woman, Height participated in local girls' clubs and the YWCA, moving into leadership at a young age. This was the beginning of her successful combination of religious and community work, part of a long African-American tradition.

Height graduated from New York University in 1932. She was able to complete the degree in three years through her hard work and the support of an Elks scholarship. During this period she also took on a number of part-time jobs in restaurants, in a factory, in laundries, writing newspaper obituaries, and doing proofreading for Marcus Garvey's paper, *Negro World*. Height then spent an additional year at the university to earn a master's degree in educational psychology. From here she took a position as assistant director of the Brownsville Community Center in Brooklyn and became involved with the United Christian Youth Movement. She traveled to England and Holland to represent her group at Christian youth conferences in 1937; she

"History reminds us that our life traditions were wholly encompassed by our kinships and tribes. No children and mothers were ever unsheltered and unprotected."
Dorothy Height, 1982

was also introduced to Eleanor Roosevelt, and helped Roosevelt to plan the 1938 World Youth Congress, held at Vassar College.

From 1935 until 1937 Height was a caseworker for the New York City Department of Welfare. In the wake of the 1935 Harlem riots, she became the first black personnel supervisor in her department. Seeking a position that would give her a broader range of work experience, she left the Department of Welfare in 1937 to work for the Harlem YWCA as the assistant director of its residence, the Emma Ransom House. In this position, Height gained expertise in issues facing many African-American women in domestic labor and learned to administer a community-based organization. She also became involved with the NCNW through her friendship with Mary McLeod Bethune.

In 1939 Height accepted the position of executive secretary of the Washington, D.C., Phillis Wheatley YWCA. She also began to work with the Delta Sigma Theta sorority,

National Council of Negro Women

The National Council of Negro Women (NCNW) has been among the most influential African-American women's organizations of the twentieth century. Mary McLeod Bethune founded the NCNW in 1935 as an umbrella organization to bring together the skills and experience of black women in a variety of organizations. Bethune hoped this national organization would provide leadership and guidance in order to make African-American women's voices heard in every arena of social and political life. The effectiveness of the council and its leadership was immediately apparent. With Bethune's influence in the federal government, the NCNW pressed for federal jobs for African Americans, and was one of the forces behind the founding of the Fair Employment Practices Committee. The NCNW also established an important journal, the *Aframerican Woman's Journal*, which in 1949 became *Women United*. Bethune retired from the presidency in 1949 and was succeeded by Dorothy Boulding Ferebee, who was followed by Vivian Carter Mason. Under the tenure of Ferebee and Mason, the council continued to press issues of concern to black women, primarily civil rights, education, jobs, and health care. In 1957 the NCNW elected Dorothy Height to be the organization's fourth president. Among Height's many accomplishments as president was the construction of the Bethune Memorial Statue, unveiled in Lincoln Park, Washington, D.C., in 1974. Height also oversaw the founding in 1979 of the National Archives for Black Women's History, which has become an important force in preserving the records and achievements of black women in the twentieth century. After more than forty years as president of the NCNW, Height was succeeded by Jane Smith in 1998.

1912 Height is born in Richmond, Virginia.

1932 Height graduates from New York University.

1935 Height becomes a caseworker for the New York City welfare department.

1937 Height becomes assistant director of Harlem YWCA residence.

1939 Height becomes secretary of Washington, DC, YWCA.

1944 Height joins the YWCA national board.

1946 Height helps organize YWCA conference on racial integration.

1947 Height becomes president of Delta Sigma Theta.

1957 Height becomes president of National Council of Negro Women.

encouraging both organizations to improve the lives of working African-American women. Her outstanding efforts led Height to a position with the national board of the YWCA in 1944. She was involved in organizing the YWCA's watershed conference in 1946 at which the organization took a stand for the racial integration of its programs. From 1947 until 1956 Height served as president of Delta Sigma Theta, moving it to become an international organization in addition to expanding its work at home.

Height became president of the National Council of Negro Women in 1957. Under her leadership the NCNW, an umbrella group for a wide variety of black women's organizations, became an active participant in the civil rights struggles in the United States. She also involved the YWCA in civil rights issues through her position as secretary of the organization's Department of Racial Justice, a job she assumed in 1963.

Although she was moderate in her approach to the question of civil rights, Height has never ceased her activities in search of equality. Her commitment has been to a struggle carried on through the widest possible range of organizations, and so she has served as a consultant to many private foundations and government agencies. Height was a major force in moving the YWCA to be true to its 1946 declaration on interracial work. At the group's 1970 convention, she helped to write a new statement of purpose for the YWCA, declaring its one imperative to be the elimination of racism.

Through Dorothy Height's involvement, the YWCA has taken many steps forward in its attitudes and actions concerning African-American women. The organization's full commitment to integration and parity in its operation owes much to her work. She continues to work with the NCNW, and has made it an important voice in articulating the needs and aspirations of women of African descent around the world. ◆

Hill, Anita

July 30, 1956 – ● Lawyer and Professor

In October 1991 Anita Hill, lawyer and professor, suddenly became famous in a way she never planned. Her name became nationally known during Senate hearings on the

Anita Hill with Clarence Thomas (center) and a colleague during the early 1980s when they worked together at the EEOC.

nomination of African-American U.S. District Judge Clarence Thomas to the Supreme Court. Denounced as a liar by many and praised as a feminist champion by many others, the background of Anita Hill suggested neither of these designations.

Anita Faye Hill was born on July 30, 1956, in Morris, Oklahoma, fifty-five miles south of Tulsa. Her parents, Albert and Irma, farmed and Anita was their thirteenth and youngest child. The Hill family all worked the land, breaking only for school and Sunday services at the Lone Pine Baptist Church. Encouraged in her studies, Anita earned As in the integrated schools of Okmulgee County and graduated from high school as valedictorian and a National Honor Society student. Hill recalled her youth as one of strong family ties, a caring church community, and a tranquil rural life-style. Money could be tight for the Hills, but Anita felt secure and well cared for.

Hill attended Oklahoma State University, in nearby Stillwater, graduating in 1977 with honors and a degree in psychology. An internship with a local judge interested Hill in law. She gained admission to Yale University's School of Law, becoming one of eleven black students in a class of 160. The quiet, studious Hill found the East Coast world much different from that of the rural South, but she worked hard at Yale and formed several lasting friendships.

After graduation, Hill began working for the law firm of Wald, Harkrader, & Ross in Washington, D.C., in 1980. She

> Denounced as a liar by many and praised as a feminist champion by others, the background of Anita Hill suggested neither of these designations.

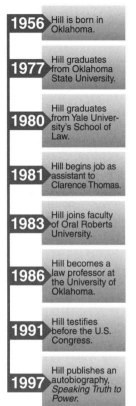

1956 Hill is born in Oklahoma.

1977 Hill graduates from Oklahoma State University.

1980 Hill graduates from Yale University's School of Law.

1981 Hill begins job as assistant to Clarence Thomas.

1983 Hill joins faculty of Oral Roberts University.

1986 Hill becomes a law professor at the University of Oklahoma.

1991 Hill testifies before the U.S. Congress.

1997 Hill publishes an autobiography, *Speaking Truth to Power.*

did not find the large law firm environment best suited to her, and after a year she accepted a position as the personal assistant to Clarence Thomas, who headed the Office of Civil Rights at the Education Department in Washington.

At this job, Hill later testified, Thomas made repeated unwanted overtures toward her. In addition to pressuring her for dates, Hill said, Thomas made sexually suggestive remarks to her. When Thomas began dating someone, according to Hill, he stopped harassing her, and she hoped the problem had resolved itself. Hill even accepted a new job as his assistant when Thomas became chairman of the Equal Employment Opportunity Commission (EEOC). However, according to Hill, the harassment began again. Hill recalled her response to Thomas as one of dismay, perhaps even naivete. At the time, she felt strongly disturbed by Thomas's behavior. She hoped he would leave her alone, as she did not want to lose the opportunities her job could open up in the competitive world of Washington. She began to develop stomach problems.

Hill decided to return to the world she knew best. She accepted a position teaching civil rights law at Oral Roberts University in Tulsa in 1983. In 1986 the law school moved to Virginia, so Hill became a professor at the University of Oklahoma, in Normal, specializing in contract law. Hill earned early tenure—after four years instead of the school's usual requirement of six—and in addition to her teaching duties, Hill sat on key university boards and committees.

Out of this comfortable academic niche, events suddenly plucked Hill and placed her on the world stage in September 1991. President George Bush had nominated Clarence Thomas to replace the retiring Justice Thurgood Marshall, the first black Supreme Court justice. The Senate Judiciary Committee had held the confirmation hearing, and on September 27 sent the vote to the floor of the Senate. It seemed likely the Senate would confirm Thomas. However, on October 6, the press ran a story about Anita Hill telling FBI investigators of Thomas's alleged harassment of her. The press story came from a leak of a confidential affidavit Hill had provided the committee on September 23. Once her story became public, Hill, who had not intended to speak out about the issue, spoke publicly. She expressed her concern that the all-male judiciary committee had ignored her affidavit and had not questioned Thomas about the harassment. Under national scrutiny, the Senate decided to delay the vote on Thomas's confirmation and scheduled further hearings in order to allow Hill and Thomas to testify.

On October 11 the televised hearings began, and the nation watched as Hill described Thomas's behavior toward her. The senators asked Hill why she had continued to work under Thomas, even moving to a new job with him, if he had treated her so badly. Hill explained that the harassment had stopped for a while and that she feared she would be unable to get another job without a good recommendation from Thomas.

Thomas testified that Hill was lying, and he denied any wrongdoing. He refused to discuss his personal life and became increasingly angry, denouncing the committee's process as "un-American." He assailed the senators' racial intentions by calling the hearing a "high-tech lynching" of him. In the following days, Senate Republicans attempted to discredit Hill's character and honesty, some suggesting that Hill was in collusion with liberal groups or that she harbored erotic fantasies about Thomas.

Throughout the country, controversy developed over whether Hill or Thomas was telling the truth and over the relevance of his alleged sexual actions to his ability to serve on the Supreme Court. The black community split along many lines in the debate. Many blacks found the accusations against Thomas to be reminiscent of old stereotypes of black males. Some thought Hill had told the truth but saw Thomas's overtures as harmless courting. Many blacks blamed Hill for speaking out against one of their own and complained that her testimony could block the rise of a black man to the Supreme Court. Other blacks praised Hill's courage. Many black women denounced the sexism that Thomas's alleged actions displayed. Among blacks and whites nationwide, the topic of sexual harassment dominated conversations.

On October 15 the Senate confirmed Thomas by 52–48, the second narrowest margin of any Supreme Court confirmation. Many women became incensed that the male-dominated Senate had sided with Thomas and sent him to the nation's highest court. Women mobilized politically and voted a number of men out of office in the next election. Female candidates ran for Senate and House seats in record numbers, including Carol Moseley-Braun, who became the nation's first female African-American senator.

Many women became emboldened by Hill's example to act on incidents of harassment. In the year after the hearings, complaints

"It would have been more comfortable to remain silent. I took no initiative to inform anyone. But when I was asked by a representative of this committee to report my experience, I felt that I had to tell the truth. I could not keep silent."
Anita Hill, statement to the Senate Judiciary Committee, 1991

of sexual harassment registered to the EEOC, the agency responsible for action on such complaints, increased by 50 percent.

Hill returned to her life as a professor, turning down requests for interviews and finding support among family and friends. Hill wrote her autobiography, *Speaking Truth to Power* (1997), to give her version of events. She taught at the University of Oklahoma until 1997, after which she spent her time lecturing nationally and writing about civil rights and sexual harassment. ◆

Holiday, Billie

APRIL 7, 1915 – JULY 17, 1959 ● JAZZ SINGER

Born Eleanora Fagan in Philadelphia, the daughter of Sadie Fagan and jazz guitarist Clarence Holiday, Billie Holiday grew up in Baltimore and endured a traumatic childhood of poverty and abuse. As a teenager, she changed her name (after screen star Billie Dove) and came to New York, where she began singing in speakeasies, influenced, she said, by Louis Armstrong and Bessie Smith. In 1933 she was spotted performing in Harlem by critic-producer John Hammond, who brought her to Columbia Records, where she recorded classic sessions with such jazz greats as pianist Teddy Wilson and tenor saxophonist Lester Young.

Following grueling tours with the big bands of Count Basie and Artie Shaw, Holiday became a solo act in 1938, achieving success with appearances at Cafe Society in Greenwich Village, and with her 1939 recording of the dramatic antilynching song "Strange Fruit." Performing regularly at intimate clubs along New York's Fifty-second Street, she gained a sizable income and a reputation as a peerless singer of torch songs. A heroin addict, she was arrested for narcotics possession in 1947 and spent ten months in prison, which subsequently made it illegal for her to work in New York clubs. Yet despite such hardships and her deteriorating health and voice, she continued to perform and make memorable, sometimes challenging recordings on Decca, Verve, and Columbia until her death in 1959.

Although riddled with inaccuracies, Holiday's 1956 autobiography, *Lady Sings the Blues*, remains a fascinating account of her mercurial personality. A 1972 film of the same title, starring pop singer Diana Ross, further distorted her life but introduced her to a new generation of listeners. Holiday was one of America's finest and most influential jazz singers. Her voice was light, with a limited range, but her phrasing, in the manner of a jazz instrumentalist, places her among the most consummate of jazz musicians. She was distinguished by her impeccable timing, her ability to transform song melodies through **improvisation,** and her ability to render lyrics with absolute conviction. While she was not a blues singer, her performances were infused with the same stark depth of feeling that characterizes the blues. ◆

> *"You've got to have something to eat and a little love in your life. Everything goes smack back to that."*
> Billie Holiday, interview with Ted Wallace, 1955

improvisation: creating new music while performing.

Horn, Rosa Artimus

1880 – 1976 ● MINISTER

Affectionately called "Mother," Rosa Artimus Horn was best known for her radio program, the *You, Pray for Me Church of the Air*, which reached listeners as far as one thousand miles away from her Harlem-based congregation. Mother Horn began her ministry in Evanston, Illinois, where she was also a clothing designer. She moved to New York City in 1926, believing that God had sent her there to "establish true holiness." She began her work in Brooklyn, holding revivals and faith-healing meetings, with many reports of conversions and miracles.

Her following was interracial and intercultural, attracting members of the Italian and Jewish communities as well as African Americans and people from the Caribbean. In 1929 she became the founder and first bishop of the Pentecostal Faith Church for All Nations, also known as the Mount Calvary Pentecostal Faith Church. The following year, after a summer-long

> Mother Horn's following was interracial and intercultural, attracting members of the Italian and Jewish communities, as well as African Americans and people from the Caribbean.

1880 Horn is born in Sumter, SC.

1926 Horn moves to New York City to begin her ministry.

1929 Horn forms the Pentecostal Faith Church of All Nations.

1934 Horn begins a radio broadcast.

1962 Horn's church buys a farm in the Catskills.

1976 Horn dies and her daughter, Jessie, becomes church leader.

1981 Gladys Brandhagen becomes church leader.

preaching and healing crusade in Harlem, she established a church at 392–400 Lenox Avenue, fondly referred to by long-standing members as "Old 400."

In 1934 Horn began her radio broadcasting. The *You, Pray for Me Church of the Air* reached audiences as far away as Tennessee, Massachusetts, and the Caribbean. In the New York metropolitan area, many joined Mother Horn's church after having heard the broadcasts of her services from "Old 400." She did not confine her outreach to the masses of poor during the depression to radio messages. With personal funds, she leased a house at the corner of 132nd Street and Madison Avenue and had it renovated as a shelter and soup kitchen for the hungry and homeless. Called the Gleaners' Aid Home, Mother Horn's facility provided breakfast and dinner for thousands, and housed many women and children. She also took great interest in the adolescent and young-adult populations, offering them alternatives to street life through religion and hard work.

During World War II Mother Horn's church, consistent with the majority of African-American Pentecostal groups of the time, encouraged young men to register as conscientious objectors. She went to local draft boards to ensure that her young ministers were not drafted. Burdened by their plight, she decided to create work for them that would be approved by the federal government as an alternative to military service. She secured farmland near her birthplace of Sumter, South Carolina, and there personally trained young men in farming. The produce was sold to local supermarkets and hospitals.

During the 1950s and 1960s Mount Calvary sponsored a mission home for the poor in Los Angeles. Mother Horn's ministry also included foreign missions in the Dominican Republic and the Bahamas. She expanded her youth work in 1962 when the church purchased a camp in the Catskills. Named the Bethel Sunshine Camp, the forty-acre facility provided summer recreation and religious instruction for youth from poor communities.

She was assisted in the development of these ministries by her natural daughter, Jessie Artimus Horn, who succeeded Mother Horn as presiding bishop upon her death in 1976, and by an adopted daughter, Gladys Brandhagen, who succeeded her adopted sister in 1981. Bishop Brandhagen, a woman of Norwegian ancestry, had become part of Mother Horn's movement in Evanston, after her father's conversion under Mother Horn's ministry. The Pentecostal Faith Church reports some twenty-two churches with an estimated membership of 1,200. ◆

Horne, Lena

JUNE 30, 1917 – ● SINGER AND ACTOR

Born in New York, Lena Horne accompanied her mother on a tour of the Lafayette Stock Players as a child and appeared in a production of *Madame X* when she was six years old. She received her musical education in the preparatory school of Fort Valley College, Georgia, and in the public schools of Brooklyn. Horne began her career at the age of sixteen as a dancer in the chorus line at the Cotton Club in Harlem. She also became a favorite at Harlem's Apollo Theatre, and was among the first African-American entertainers to perform in "high-class" nightclubs. Appearing on stages and ballrooms from the Fairmont in San Francisco to the Empire Room at the Waldorf-Astoria in New York, Horne was among the group of black stars— including Sammy Davis Jr., Eartha Kitt, and Diahann Carroll—who had musicals especially fashioned for them on Broadway.

Horne made her first recording in 1936 with Noble Sissle and recorded extensively as a soloist and with others. She toured widely in the United States and Europe. In 1941 she became the first black performer to sign a contract with a major studio (MGM). Her first film role was in *Panama Hattie* (1942), which led to roles in *Cabin in the Sky* (1942), *Stormy Weather* (1943), *I Dood It* (1943), *Thousands Cheer* (1943), *Broadway Rhythm* (1944), *Two Girls and a Sailor* (1944), *Ziegfeld Follies of 1945* and 1946, *The Duchess of Idaho* (1950), and *The Wiz* (1978). Horne was blacklisted during the McCarthy era of the early 1950s, when her friendship with Paul Robeson, her interracial marriage, and

her interest in African freedom movements made her politically suspect. Her Broadway musicals include *Blackbirds of 1939*, *Jamaica* (1957), and the successful one-woman Broadway show *Lena Horne: The Lady and Her Music* (1981). The record album of the latter musical won her a Grammy Award as best female pop vocalist in 1981.

Horne's spectacular beauty and sultry voice helped to make her the first nationally celebrated black female vocalist. Her powerful and expressive voice is perhaps captured best in the title song of *Stormy Weather*. In 1984 she was a recipient of the Kennedy Center Honors for lifetime achievement in the arts. She published two autobiographies: *In Person: Lena Horne* (1950) and *Lena* (1965). ◆

> *"I never thought I'd be working at my age, but you get caught up in the gratification of feeling you're a worker—you get into the habit of surviving."*
> Lena Horne, *Day by Day*, 1989

Houston, Whitney

AUGUST 9, 1963 – ● SINGER AND ACTOR

Whitney Houston is an American singer and actor known for her powerful voice. Her tremendous success in the world of music and film has made her an international star, performing to sellout concerts and breaking box-office records around the world.

Houston was born on August 9, 1963, in Newark, New Jersey, to the musical family of John R. Houston and Emily "Cissy" Houston. Her mother was an acclaimed gospel singer and her cousin Dionne Warwick is a successful pop singer. Gospel, soul, and R&B music were a part of everyday life in the Houston household, and this environment helped shape the vocal talent of the young Whitney. Houston began singing in the church choir when she was a child. She gave her first public performance when she was eight years old, singing for the congregation at the New Hope Baptist Church in Newark. In her mid-teens, she went on to sing backup vocals for such stars as Lou Rawls and Chaka Khan.

At the age of seventeen, Houston capitalized on her tall, willowy figure and good looks, and began modeling. She appeared in several fashion magazines, including *Glamour* and *Seventeen*. Houston also made her acting debut as a teenager, appearing in episodes of the television programs *Silver Spoons* and *Gimme a Break*.

> *"I guess it's flattering to know that I can sing it all. My mother always said if you can sing you can sing. Having a church background has allowed me to be able to sing every note, every lyric."*
> Whitney Houston, quoted in *Newsweek*, 1998

Discontented with the modeling life, Houston returned to music. In 1983, she caught the attention of Arista Records' president, Clive Davis, at a showcase performance in a Manhattan nightclub. Over the next two years, Davis groomed Houston for her record debut and put together a group of star songwriters and producers to work on Houston's first album. Houston signed with Arista in 1985 and released her debut album, *Whitney Houston*, that year. It became one of the biggest selling albums by a solo artist and led to soldout concert performances for Houston throughout the United States and Europe. In 1986 Houston received a Grammy Award for her hit song "Saving All My Love for You." Her second album, *Whitney* (1987), became the first album by a female artist ever to debut at Number One on the *Billboard* chart, and it earned her a second Grammy Award in 1988. In 1990 Houston released her funky and versatile third album, *I'm Your Baby Tonight*, complete with soulful ballads and upbeat dance tunes.

Over the years, Houston has appeared on several television programs and has performed in several distinguished settings, notably a birthday gala for South African leader Nelson Mandela at Wembley Arena in London. In 1991 she sang the National Anthem at the Super Bowl, creating a hit single out of the song. Proceeds from the song went to the American Red Cross Gulf Crisis Fund.

Houston's film career was launched in 1995, when she costarred with Kevin Costner in the feature film *The Bodyguard*.

1963 Houston is born in Newark, NJ.

1985 Houston signs with Arista Records and releases her debut album, *Whitney Houston*.

1986 Houston receives her first Grammy for best pop vocal performance.

1987 Houston's second album, *Whitney*, debuts at Number One.

1990 Houston's third album, *I'm Your Baby Tonight*, hits the stores.

1992 Houston marries singer Bobby Brown.

1992 Houston stars in her first film, *The Bodyguard*.

1993 Houston has her first child.

1995 Houston stars in *Waiting to Exhale*.

1996 Houston stars in *The Preacher's Wife*.

> *"Being a wife and a mother kind of teaches you a little more about life and what you can endure—things you didn't think you could. I know more today than I did yesterday, so I can sing about it."*
>
> Whitney Houston, quoted in *New York Daily News*, 1998

The film tells the story of a singer (Houston) who needs a body-guard (Costner) to fend off an obsessed fan, and the romance that develops between the singer and her bodyguard. Though not a critical success, *The Bodyguard* became a box-office hit around the world. Houston sang on the movie sound track and garnered three Grammy Awards in 1994 for her performances on the sound track album.

Her next film, *Waiting to Exhale*, was released in 1995. It tells the story of four friends and their search for Mr. Right. Houston also starred in the 1996 film *The Preacher's Wife*, an update of the classic comedy *The Bishop's Wife*. Houston performed on the sound track of both films.

In addition to Grammys, Houston has received a number of other awards throughout her career, including several American Music Awards, MTV's Best Female Video Award, NAACP Image Awards, Soul Train Music Awards, Billboard Music Awards, Emmy Awards, and the key to the city of Newark, New Jersey.

Houston married singer Bobby Brown in 1992. Their child, Bobbi Kristina Houston Brown, was born in 1993. Houston established the Whitney Houston Foundation for Children, Inc. in 1989. This nonprofit group is dedicated to improving the lives of children. She also has shown generous support for other causes, particularly the United Negro College Fund and AIDS research. ◆

Hunter, Clementine Clemence Rubin

C. 1885 – 1988 ● PAINTER AND QUILT ARTIST

Born on Hidden Hill Plantation in northern Louisiana near Natchitoches, Hunter moved during her early teens to nearby Melrose Plantation, where she worked as a cotton picker and then for almost sixty years as a plantation cook. She produced her first painting in 1946 on a windowshade, using paints and brushes that had been discarded by a New Orleans artist visiting Melrose. During the course of her career, Hunter completed more than 4,000 paintings. She worked in oils on cardboard and canvas panels, using a thick **impasto** technique.

impasto: thick application of color to a canvas or panel in painting

Hunter's paintings usually depict scenes of the rural Cane River settlement on Isle Breville, Louisiana. Those subjects include cotton and pecan harvesting, cotton gins, weddings, funerals, birthday parties, revivals, still-lifes, and religious scenes. Her paintings possess the salient characteristics of folk art: flat bold primary colors, no attempts at modeling of form, and scale and perspective that defy logical interpretation. She painted the same subjects repeatedly, yet no two subjects are identical. Using her lap as an easel, she supported her panels in one hand while painting with the other. She did not date her paintings. They may be broadly classified, however, as early or late by the forward or reverse position of the "C" in the artist's signature.

Hunter's masterpiece is a series of nine four-by-ten-foot panels depicting a panorama of life in Cane River country that she painted in 1955. These murals are located on the second floor of the African House at Melrose Plantation, and represent the artist at the height of her creative powers. She also made quilts, both geometric and pictorial, that depict buildings at Melrose Plantation including the Big House, African House, and Yucca House. In 1956 Hunter and Francois Mignon (1899–1980), writer-in-residence at Melrose, published *Melrose Plantation Cookbook*, which recorded Hunter's legendary culinary talents. Mignon recorded the recipes, which were dictated to him by Hunter, including such original delicacies as Madame Gobar Game Soup, Calinda Cabbage, Parrain Pie, and Riz Isle Breville.

In 1955 Hunter was the first African-American artist to have a one-person exhibition at the Delgado Museum in New Orleans (now the New Orleans Museum of Art). In 1973 her works were included in a three-person exhibition at the Museum of American Folk Art in New York, and one of her paintings, *Threshing Pecans*, was used in 1976 as a UNICEF calendar selection. She is represented in numerous public and private collections, and had been the subject of many magazine and newspaper articles, two television documentaries, and a book published in 1988.

In 1985 Hunter was honored with numerous celebrations during the anniversary of her one hundredth birthday, and on May 16 of that year she was awarded an honorary Doctor of Fine Arts degree by Northwestern University in Natchitoches, Louisiana. Unable to read or write, she never traveled more than fifty miles from her birthplace. Married twice, she was the mother of seven children, all but one of whom she outlived. At

1885 ▸ Hunter is born near Natchitoches, Louisiana.

1946 ▸ Hunter produces her first painting on a window shade.

1955 ▸ Hunter paints murals of Cane River County.

1956 ▸ *Melrose Plantation Cookbook* records Hunter's recipes.

1973 ▸ Hunter exhibits at Museum of American Folk Art in New York.

1976 ▸ Hunter's *Threshing Pecans* appears in a UNICEF calendar.

1988 ▸ Hunter dies in Louisiana.

"The Lord puts pictures in my head and he means me to paint them."

Clementine Hunter

the time of her death on New Year's Day in 1988, Hunter was the most celebrated contemporary African-American folk artist. ◆

Hunter-Gault, Charlayne

FEBRUARY 27, 1942 – ● JOURNALIST

"When people at the top exercise aggressive leadership and will, even when they don't work miracles, they set a tone and create an atmosphere that makes things happen."

Charlayne Hunter-Gault, *In Our Place*, 1992

As the creator and chief of the Harlem bureau of the *New York Times* in the late 1960s, Charlayne Hunter-Gault sought to move media coverage of African Americans away from stereotypes to in-depth, realistic, and accurate stories. Born in Due West, South Carolina, Hunter-Gault became the first black woman admitted to the University of Georgia. She graduated in 1963 with a degree in journalism. Her career has included work with the *New Yorker* magazine, NBC News in Washington, D.C., and PBS's *MacNeil/Lehrer Newshour*. Hunter-Gault has also taught at the Columbia University School of Journalism. Her distinguished career has brought her a number of important honors: she has won two Emmy awards, for national news and documentary film; was named the Journalist of the Year in 1986 by the National Association of Black Journalists; and was the 1986 recipient of the George Foster Peabody award. In 1992 she published her autobiography, *In My Place*. ◆

Hurston, Zora Neale

C. 1891 – JANUARY 28, 1960 ● FOLKLORIST AND WRITER

"There are years that ask questions and years that answer."

Zora Neale Hurston, *Their Eyes Were Watching God*, 1937

Zora Neale Hurston was born and grew up in Eatonville, Florida, the first black incorporated town in America. (Her exact date of birth is uncertain. She claimed to be born in either 1901 or 1910, but a brother thinks it was as early as 1891.) Her father, a carpenter and Baptist preacher and a signer of the town's charter, was elected mayor three terms in succession. Her mother, formerly a country schoolteacher, taught Sunday school but spent most of her time raising her eight children. In Eatonville, unlike most of the South at the turn of the century, African Americans were not demoralized by the constant bombardment of poverty and racial hatred, and Hurston grew up surrounded by a vibrant and creative secular and religious black culture. It was here she learned the dialect, songs, folktales, and superstitions that are at the center of her works. Her stories focus on the lives and relationships among black people within their communities.

The untimely death of Hurston's mother in 1904 disrupted her economically and emotionally stable home life, and a year later, at age fourteen, she left home for a job as a maid and wardrobe assistant in a traveling Gilbert and Sullivan company. She left the company in Baltimore, found other work, and attended high school there. In 1918 she graduated from Morgan Academy, the high school division of Morgan State University, and entered Howard University in Washington, D.C., where she took courses intermittently until 1924. She studied there with poet Georgia Douglas Johnson and philosopher Alain Locke. Her first story, "John Redding Goes to Sea" (1921), appeared in *Stylus*, Howard's literary magazine.

Hurston arrived in New York in 1925, at the height of the Harlem Renaissance. She soon became active among the group of painters, musicians, sculptors, entertainers, and writers who came from across the country to be there. She also studied at Barnard College under the anthropologist Franz Boas and graduated with a B.A. in 1928. Between 1929 and 1931, with support from a wealthy white patron, Mrs. Osgood Mason, Hurston returned south and began collecting folklore in Florida and Alabama. In 1934 she received a Rosenwald fellowship and in 1936 and 1937 Guggenheim fellowships that enabled her to study folk religions in Haiti and Jamaica. She was a member of the American Folklore Society, the Anthropological Society, the Ethnological Society, the New York Academy of Sciences, and the American Association for the Advancement of Science. From her extensive research Hurston published *Mules and Men* (1935), the first collection (seventy folktales) of black folklore

"She knew things that nobody ever told her. For instance, the words of the trees and the wind."
Zora Neale Hurston, *Their Eyes Were Watching God*, 1937

1891 Hurston is born in Eatonville, Florida.

1904 Hurston leaves home after her mother's death.

1918 Hurston enters Howard Univer-

1925 Hurston moves to New York.

1928 Hurston gradu- ates from Barnard College.

1929 Hurston begins collecting folklore in Florida and Alabama.

1934 Hurston begins researching Hait- ian and Jamaican folk religions.

1935 Hurston pub- lishes *Mules and Men*.

1937 Hurston pub- lishes *Their Eyes Were Watching God*.

1938 Hurston pub- lishes *Tell My Horse*.

1942 Hurston publishes *Dust Tracks on a Road*.

1960 Hurston dies in Fort Pierce, Florida.

1973 Alice Walker works to revive interest in Hurston's work.

to appear by a black American. *Tell My Horse* (1938), a second folklore volume, came after her travels to the Caribbean. Her most academic study, *The Florida Negro* (1938), written for the Florida Federal Workers Project, was never published.

While Franz Boas and Mrs. Mason stimulated Hurston's anthropological interests that gave her an analytical perspec- tive on black culture that was unique among black writers of her time, she was fully vested in the creative life of the cultural movement as well. Her close friends included Carl Van Vechten, Alain Locke, Langston Hughes, and Wallace Thur- man, with whom she coedited and published the only issue of the journal *Fire!!* Appearing in November 1926, its supporters saw it as a forum for younger writers who wanted to break with traditional black ideas. Ironically, *Fire!!* was destroyed by a fire in Thurman's apartment.

Hurston's first novel, *Jonah's Gourd Vine* (1934), reveals the lyric quality of her writing, her skillfulness with and mastery of dialect. The story is about a Baptist preacher with a personal weakness that leads him to an unfortunate end. But Hurston's protagonist, modeled on her father, is a gifted poet/philosopher with an enviable imagination and speech filled with the imagery of black folk culture. He is also a vulnerable person who lacks the self-awareness to comprehend his dilemma; thus, his tragedy.

For its beauty and richness of language, *Their Eyes Were Watching God* (1937), the first novel by a black woman to explore the inner life of a black woman, is Hurston's art at its best. Her most popular work, it traces the development of the heroine from innocence to her realization that she has the power to control her own life. An acknowledged classic since its recovery in the 1970s, it has been applauded by both black and white women scholars as the first black feminist novel. *Moses, Man of the Mountain* (1939), Hurston's third and most ambitious novel, makes of the biblical Israelite deliverance from Egypt an exploration of the black transition from slavery to freedom. Taking advantage of the pervasiveness of the Moses mythology in African and diaspora folklore and culture, Hurston removes Moses from Scripture, demystifies him, and relocates him in African-American culture, where he is a con- jure man possessed with magical powers and folk wisdom. The novel tells the story of a people struggling to liberate themselves from the heritage of bondage. In *Seraph on the Suwanee* (1948), Hurston's last and least successful work, she turns away from

Black English Vernacular

Black English Vernacular (BEV), also known as Black English or Ebonics, is the term used to describe the dialect of Standard American English (SAE) spoken by many African Americans and used as a literary language by some American writers. The existence of some form of BEV dates to the arrival of the first African people on the North American continent and the dialect has been historically recorded in court records, travelers' diaries, and slave narratives. Linguists who study BEV have outlined numerous distinctive phonetic and grammatical characteristics of the dialect. For example, in BEV the sound "R" is often omitted, producing identical pronunciations for "fort" and "fought." Final "TH" and "F" sounds are merged, creating identical pronunciations for "Ruth" and "roof." The verb forms of "to be" are frequently omitted: "He is nice" in SAE becomes "He nice" in BEV. The "S" endings are absent from the third person singular tense: "She knows" in SAE becomes "She know" in BEV.

Ongoing research has demonstrated the validity of BEV as a chosen in-group form of communication that reflects racial and cultural pride. Educators, however, continue to debate the use of BEV in the classroom. American writers have long used BEV as a device to convey class distinctions and race, as well as African-American culture and experience. Fiction writers like Mark Twain, William Faulkner, Richard Wright, Terry McMillan, and Alice Walker have used BEV to represent specific African-American characters in their stories and novels. Other writers, like Zora Neale Hurston, Ralph Ellison, and Toni Morrison, have relied more heavily on BEV, using the dialect to both narrate their texts and characterize African-American people, settings, and situations.

black folk culture to explore the lives of poor white southerners. This story focuses on a husband and wife trapped in conventional sexual roles in a marriage that dooms to failure the wife's search for herself.

Dust Tracks on a Road (1942), Hurston's autobiography, is the most controversial of her books; some of her staunchest admirers consider it a failure. Critics who complain about this work focus on its lack of self-revelation, the inaccurate personal information Hurston gives about herself, and the significant roles that whites play in the text. Other critics praise it as Hurston's attempt to invent an alternative narrative self to the black identity inherited from the slave narrative tradition. Poised between the black and white worlds, not as victim of either but participant-observer in both, her narrative self in *Dust Tracks* presents positive and negative qualities of each. From this perspective, *Dust Tracks* is a **revisionary** text, a revolutionary alternative women's narrative inscribed into the **discourse** of black autobiography.

revisionary: alteration of a traditional view or attitude.

discourse: spoken or written interchange of ideas.

Reviews of Hurston's books in her time were mixed. White reviewers, often ignorant of black culture, praised the richness of her language but misunderstood the works and characterized them as simple and unpretentious. Black critics in the 1930s and 1940s, in journals like *The Crisis*, objected most to her focus on black folklife. Their most frequent criticism was the absence from her works of racial terror, exploitation, and misery. Richard Wright expressed anger at the "minstrel image" he claimed Hurston promoted in *Their Eyes Were Watching God*. None of her books sold well enough while she was alive to relieve her lifetime of financial stress.

Hurston and her writings disappeared from public view from the late 1940s until the early 1970s. Interest in her revived after writer Alice Walker went to Florida "in search of Zora" in 1973, and reassembled the puzzle of Hurston's later life. Walker discovered that Hurston returned to the South in the 1950s and, still trying to write, supported herself with menial jobs. Without resources and suffering a stroke, in 1959 she entered a welfare home in Fort Pierce, Florida, where she died in 1960 and was buried in an unmarked grave. On her pilgrimage, Walker marked a site where Hurston might be buried with a headstone that pays tribute to "a genius of the South." Following her rediscovery, a once-neglected Hurston rose into literary prominence and enjoys acclaim as the essential forerunner of black women writers who came after her. ◆

> *"You who play the zigzag lightning of power over the world, with the grumbling thunder in your wake, think kindly of those who walk in the dust."*
>
> Zora Neale Hurston, *Dust Tracks on the Road*, 1942

J

Jackson, Janet

MAY 16, 1966 – ● SINGER AND ACTOR

Janet Jackson is an American pop singer and actor. She is best known for her charismatic and highly produced vocal recordings and for her spirited music videos, complete with dynamic choreography and pounding dance beats.

Janet Damita Jackson was born on May 16, 1966, in Gary, Indiana, to Joseph and Katherine Jackson. Her father was a crane operator and a guitarist in an R&B band. Her mother played piano and sang. Janet was the youngest of nine children in the Jackson family, five of whom—Jackie, Tito, Jermaine, Marlon, and Michael— later became the superstar pop group the Jackson Five in the 1970s. The family moved to an affluent part of California after the group signed a record contract with Motown Records in 1969.

As a youth, Jackson attended both public and private schools. She had her first stage performance at the age of seven, when she appeared with the Jackson Five in a Las Vegas revue. When she was eleven she began acting in the popular television series *Good Times*. She later appeared in such programs as *Diff'rent Strokes* and *Fame*.

1966 Jackson is born in Gary, Indiana.

1982 Jackson releases her first solo album, *Janet Jackson.*

1984 Jackson's *Dream Street* hits the stores.

1986 Jackson releases *Control.*

1989 *Janet Jackson's Rhythm Nation 1814* is released.

1991 Virgin Records signs Jackson for a reported $50 million.

1993 Jackson appears in her first feature film, *Poetic Justice.*

1993 Jackson releases her fifth album, *janet.*

1996 Jackson signs an $80 million contract with Virgin Records.

1997 *The Velvet Rope* is released.

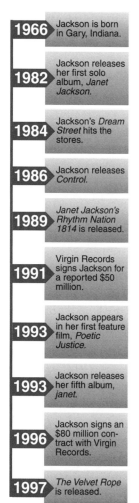

"I don't believe in luck. It's hard work and not forgetting your dream—and going after it. It's about still having hunger in your heart."

Janet Jackson, quoted in *Ebony*, 1993

Despite her interest in acting, Jackson entered the world of music at the behest of her father, who became her manager. She signed with A&M Records and released *Janet Jackson*, her first solo record, in 1982. The album, which featured teen ballads and upbeat dance tracks, fared only moderately well on the national charts. Sales on her second album, *Dream Street* (1984), were similar.

In 1984 Jackson eloped with singer James DeBarge. However, her marriage was annulled the following year.

Fueled by a strong desire for independence and the ability to direct her own career, Jackson told her father she did not want him to manage her any longer. She then turned to A&M Records producers James "Jimmy Jam" Harris and Terry Lewis to help her with the production and writing on her next project. Jackson's funky next album, *Control* (1986), soared to the top of the R&B chart and quickly went platinum, eventually selling about eight million copies worldwide. Her dynamic music videos, which were choreographed by pop singer and dancer Paula Abdul, became favorites among many MTV viewers and helped launch sales of her record.

Working again with Jimmy Jam and Lewis, Jackson released *Janet Jackson's Rhythm Nation 1814* in 1989 and promoted it with a world tour in 1990. Both the album and the tour garnered rave reviews and were a tremendous financial success. In 1991 Virgin Records rewarded Jackson's success with a contract worth a reported $50 million.

In 1993 Jackson appeared in her first feature film, *Poetic Justice*, as a hairdresser poet in Los Angeles. The movie received poor reviews, but Jackson tackled her next project full on. Her 1993 album, *janet*, became a smash hit. Its music spans a variety of musical styles, including funk, hip-hop, jazz, rock, and rap. And its lyrics and accompanying video introduce Jackson as a bolder, more exciting persona.

Jackson's next recording success came in 1995 on her brother Michael's single "Scream" and its video, which won a Grammy Award in 1996. In late 1995 her greatest hits compilation, *Design of a Decade 1986/1996*, which included two new singles, debuted near the top of the charts.

In 1996 Jackson made headlines when she signed a contract with Virgin Records worth an estimated $80 million. She released *The Velvet Rope* in 1997.

Throughout her career, Jackson has won many awards, most notably several American Music Awards, Soul Train Music Awards, and MTV Video Music Awards. She has also been recognized for her generosity to a number of social causes, including the United Negro College Fund; Cities in Schools, a dropout prevention program; and the Make-a-Wish Program for terminally ill children. ◆

Jackson, Mahalia

OCTOBER 26, 1911 – JANUARY 27, 1972 ● GOSPEL SINGER

When sixteen-year-old Mahala Jackson (as she was named at birth) arrived in Chicago in 1927, she had already developed the vocal style that was to win her the title of "world's greatest gospel singer." Though born into an extremely religious New Orleans family, she spent hours listening to the recordings of blues singers Bessie Smith and Ma Rainey, and could be found at every parade that passed her neighborhood of Pinching Town in New Orleans.

In later life she would admit that though she was a thoroughgoing Baptist, the Sanctified church next door to her house had had a powerful influence on her singing, for though the members had neither choir nor organ, they sang accompanied by a drum, tambourine, and steel triangle. They clapped and stomped their feet and sang with their whole bodies. She recalled that they had a powerful beat she believed was retained from slavery, and once stated, "I believe blues and jazz and even rock 'n' roll stuff got their beat from the Sanctified church."

Jackson's style was set early on: from Bessie Smith and Ma Rainey she borrowed a deep and dark resonance that complemented her own timbre; from the Baptist church she inherited the moaning and bending of final notes in phrases; and from the Sanctified church she adopted a full-throated tone, delivered with a holy beat. Surprisingly, though gospel in its early stages was being sung in New Orleans, none of her vocal influences came from gospel singers.

Upon arriving in Chicago with her Aunt Hannah, Jackson joined the Johnson Singers, an **a cappella** quartet. The group quickly established a reputation as one of Chicago's better gospel groups, appearing regularly in concerts and gospel-song plays with Jackson in the lead. In time, Mahalia, as she now chose to call herself, became exclusively a soloist. In 1935 Thomas A. Dorsey persuaded her to become his official song demonstrator, a position she held until 1945. Dorsey later stated that Jackson "had a lot of soul in her singing: she meant what she sang."

Though she made her first recordings in 1937 for Decca, it was not until 1946, when she switched to the small Apollo label, that Jackson established a national reputation in the African-American community. Her 1947 recording of "Move On Up a Little Higher" catapulted her to the rank of superstar and won her one of the first two Gold Records for record sales in gospel music. (Clara Ward won the other.) Accompanied on this recording by her longtime pianist, Mildred Falls, Jackson demonstrated her wide range and ability to improvise on melody and rhythm. As a result of this recording, she became the official soloist for the National Baptist Convention and began touring throughout the United States. She was the first gospel singer to be given a network radio show when, in 1954, CBS signed her for a weekly show on which she was the host and star. In the same year she moved to the Columbia label, becoming a crossover gospel singer through her first recording on that label, "Rusty Old Halo." Several triumphs followed in rapid succession. She appeared on the Ed Sullivan and Dinah Shore television shows, at Carnegie Hall, and in 1958 for the first time at the Newport Jazz Festival. Tours throughout the world began, with Jackson garnering accolades in France, Germany, and Italy.

A crowning achievement of Jackson's was the invitation to sing at one of the inaugural parties of President John F. Kennedy

a cappella: sung without instrumental accompaniment.

1911	Jackson is born in New Orleans.
1927	Jackson moves to Chicago and joins Johnson Singers.
1935	Jackson becomes song demonstrator for Thomas Dorsey.
1937	Jackson makes her first recording for Decca.
1947	Jackson records "Move On Up a Little Higher."
1954	Jackson is signed for weekly CBS radio program.
1958	Jackson appears at Newport Jazz Festival.
1961	Jackson sings at inauguration of John F. Kennedy.
1963	Jackson sings at March on Washington.
1972	Jackson dies in Chicago.

in 1961. In 1963 she was asked to sing just before Rev. Dr. Martin Luther King Jr. was to deliver his famous "I Have a Dream" speech at the March on Washington. Her rendition of "I've Been Buked and I've Been Scorned" contributed to the success of King's speech. During her career, she appeared in such films as *Imitation of Life* (1959) and *Jazz on a Summer's Day* (1958), sang "Precious Lord, Take My Hand" at the funeral of Dr. King, and recorded with Duke Ellington. Toward the end of her life, she suffered from heart trouble but continued to sing. She died in Chicago on January 27, 1972. ◆

> *"It's easy to be independent when you've got money. But to be independent when you haven't got a thing—that's the Lord's test."*
> Mahalia Jackson,
> *Movin' On Up,*
> 1966

Jackson, Rebecca Cox

FEBRUARY 15, 1795 – MAY 24, 1871 ● PREACHER

Rebecca Cox Jackson was born into a free family in Horntown, Pennsylvania, and lived at different times with her maternal grandmother and with her mother, Jane Cox (who died when Rebecca was thirteen). In 1830, when her religious autobiography begins, she was living in the household of her older brother, Joseph Cox, a **tanner** and local preacher of the Bethel African Methodist Episcopal (AME) Church in Philadelphia. Married to Samuel S. Jackson, and childless herself, Jackson cared for her brother's four children while earning her own living as a seamstress.

tanner: a person who converts hides into leather.

As the result of a powerful religious awakening during a thunderstorm, Jackson became active in the early Holiness Movement. She moved from leadership of praying bands to public preaching, stirring up controversy within AME circles not only as a woman preacher but also because she had received the revelation that **celibacy** was necessary for a holy life, and she criticized the churches roundly for "**carnality**." Jackson's insistence on being guided entirely by the dictates of an inner voice ultimately led to her separation from husband, brother, and church.

celibacy: a vow to abstain from sex and marriage.

carnality: crude bodily appetites and desires.

After a period of **itinerant** preaching in the late 1830s and early 1840s, Jackson joined the United Society of Believers in Christ's Second Appearance (Shakers), at Watervliet, New York, attracted by their religious celibacy, emphasis on spiritualistic experience, and dual-gender concept of deity. With her

itinerant: traveling from place to place.

1795 Jackson is born in Horntown, Pennsylvania.

1847 Jackson joins Shakers at Watervliet, NY.

1851 Jackson leaves Watervliet on an unauthorized mission to Philadelphia.

1857 Jackson returns to Watervliet; soon forms Shaker "outfamily" in Philadelphia.

1871 Jackson dies in Philadelphia.

younger disciple and lifelong companion, Rebecca Perot, Rebecca Jackson lived there from June 1847 until July 1851.

Disappointed in the predominantly white Shaker community's failure to take the gospel of their founder, Ann Lee, to the African-American community, Jackson left Watervliet in 1851, on an unauthorized mission to Philadelphia. In 1857 she and Perot returned to Watervliet, and after a brief second residence Jackson won the right from Shaker leadership to found and head a new Shaker "outfamily" in Philadelphia. This predominantly African-American and female Shaker family survived her death in 1871 by at least a quarter of a century.

Rebecca Jackson's major legacy is her remarkable spiritual autobiography, *Gifts of Power*. Here Jackson records her receipt of a wide variety of visionary experiences, dreams, and supernatural gifts, and her spiritual journey as a woman with a divine calling. Her visionary writing has received growing recognition both as source material for African-American history and theology and as spiritual literature of great power. Alice Walker has described Jackson's autobiography as "an extraordinary document" that "tells us much about the spirituality of human beings, especially of the interior spiritual resources of our mothers." ◆

Jackson, Shirley Ann

AUGUST 5, 1946 – ● THEORETICAL PHYSICIST

"Technical experts, not just in the nuclear field, need to guard against the attitude that people lacking technical expertise are unnecessary, or even a hindrance, when it comes to resolving issues."

Shirley Jackson, 1996

Born, raised, and educated in Washington, D.C., Shirley Jackson was one of only thirty or so women who entered MIT in 1964. She was awarded a B.S. in physics in 1968 and a Ph.D. in 1973 for her work in elementary particle physics. Jackson's was the first female African-American doctorate from M.I.T. After earning her degree, she was a research associate (1973–74, 1975–76) at the Fermi National Accelerator Laboratory in Batavia, Illinois, and a visiting scientist (1974–75) at the European Center for Nuclear Research (CERN), where she worked on theories of strongly interacting elementary particles.

In 1975 Jackson moved to the Stanford Linear Accelerator Center and Aspen Center for Physics before leaving the following year to work for the Bell Laboratories of American Telephone and Telegraph in Murray Hill, New Jersey. During her early years at Bell Laboratories, Jackson's research was in the areas of theoretical physics, scattered- and low-energy physics, and solid-state quantum physics. She studied the electrical and optical properties of semiconductors.

Jackson was elected in 1975 as a member of the Massachusetts Institute of Technology Corporation, the institute's board of trustees. She was made a lifetime trustee in 1992. In 1985 New Jersey governor Thomas Kean appointed her to the state's Commission on Science and Technology. Specializing in optical physics research, she was named a distinguished member of the technical staff of Bell Laboratories in 1990. In 1991 she received an appointment as professor of physics at Rutgers

University. Jackson's achievements in science have been recognized by other scientists through her election as a fellow of the American Physical Society and the American Academy of Arts and Sciences.

In May 1995 President Bill Clinton nominated Jackson as a commissioner to the United States Nuclear Regulatory Commission (NRC), which monitors commercial, industrial, academic, and medical uses of nuclear energy. Jackson became chairperson of the NRC two months later. When the International Nuclear Regulatory Commission was formed in 1997, Jackson was elected as the INRC's first chairperson. ◆

Jacobs, Harriet Ann

1813 – MARCH 7, 1897 ● WRITER AND REFORMER

Born a slave in Edenton, North Carolina, Jacobs's major contribution is her narrative, *Incidents in the Life of a Slave Girl: Written by Herself* (1861). The most compre-

pseudonymous: using a fictitious name.

taboo: social custom that prohibits doing certain things or discussing certain subjects.

licentious: disregarding sexual or moral discipline.

hensive antebellum autobiography by an African-American woman, *Incidents* is the first-person account of Jacobs's **pseudonymous** narrator "Linda Brent," who writes of her sexual oppression and her struggle for freedom. After publishing her book, Jacobs devoted her life to providing relief for black Civil War refugees in Alexandria, Virginia; Savannah, Georgia; and Washington, D.C.

Writing as "Linda Brent," Jacobs tells the story of her life in the South as slave and as fugitive, and of her life as a fugitive slave in the North. Breaking the **taboos** forbidding women to discuss their sexuality, she writes of the abuse she suffered from her **licentious** master, Dr. James Norcom, whom she calls "Dr. Flint." She confesses that to prevent him from making her his concubine, at sixteen she became sexually involved with a white neighbor. Their alliance produced two children, Joseph (c. 1829–?), whom she calls "Benny," and Louisa Matilda (1833–1917), called "Ellen." Jacobs describes her 1835 flight from Norcom and the almost seven years she spent in hiding, in a tiny crawl space above a porch in her grandmother's Edenton home.

She further recounts her 1842 escape to New York City; her reunion with her children, who had been sent north; and her subsequent move to Rochester, New York, where she became part of the circle of abolitionists around Frederick Douglass's newspaper, the *North Star.* Condemning the compliance of the North in the slave system, she describes her North Carolina master's attempts to catch her in New York after passage of the 1850 Fugitive Slave Law. Jacobs explains that despite her principled decision not to bow to the slave system by being purchased, in 1853 her New York employer, Nathaniel Parker Willis (called "Mr. Bruce"), bought her from Norcom's family. Like other slave narrators, she ends her book with her freedom and the freedom of her children.

Most of the extraordinary events that "Linda Brent" narrates have been documented as having occurred in Jacobs's life. In addition, a group of letters that Jacobs wrote while composing her book presents a unique glimpse of its inception, composition, and publication, and recounts her complex relationships with black abolitionist William C. Nell and white abolitionists Amy Post and Lydia Maria Child. They also make an interesting commentary on Jacobs's northern employer, the litterateur

Nathaniel Parker Willis, and on Harriet Beecher Stowe, the author of *Uncle Tom's Cabin*, whom Jacobs tried to interest in her narrative.

Although *Incidents* was published anonymously, Jacobs's name was connected with her book from the first; only in the twentieth century were its authorship and its autobiographical status disputed. *Incidents* made Jacobs known to the northern abolitionists, and with the outbreak of the Civil War she used this newfound celebrity to establish a new career for herself. She collected money and supplies for the "contrabands"—black refugees crowding behind the lines of the Union Army in Washington, D.C., and in occupied Alexandria, Virginia—and returned south.

Supported by Quaker groups and the newly formed New England Freedmen's Aid Society, in 1863 Jacobs and her daughter moved to Alexandria, where they provided emergency relief supplies, organized primary medical care, and established the Jacobs Free School—a black-led institution providing black teachers for the refugees. In 1865 mother and daughter moved to Savannah, where they continued their relief work. Throughout the war years, Harriet and Louisa Jacobs reported on their southern relief efforts in the northern press and in newspapers in England, where Jacobs's book had appeared as *The Deeper Wrong: Incidents in the Life of a Slave Girl: Written by Herself* (1862). In 1868 they sailed to England, and successfully raised money for Savannah's black orphans and aged.

But in the face of increasing violence in the South, Jacobs and her daughter then retreated to Massachusetts. In Boston, they were connected with the newly formed New England Women's Club, then moved to Cambridge, where for several years Jacobs ran a boardinghouse for Harvard faculty and students. She and Louisa later moved to Washington, D.C., where the mother continued to work among the destitute freedpeople and the daughter was employed in the new "colored schools" and at Howard University. In 1896, when the National Association of Colored Women held its organizing meetings in Washington, Harriet Jacobs was confined to a wheelchair, but it seems likely that Louisa was in attendance. The following spring, Harriet Jacobs died at her Washington home. She is buried in Mount Auburn Cemetery, Cambridge, Massachusetts. ◆

1813 Jacobs is born in Edenton, NC.

1835 Jacobs flees her slave master and lives seven years in hiding.

1842 Jacobs escapes to New York.

1850 Fugitive Slave Law is passed.

1853 Jacobs's New York employer "buys" her from her southern slave owner.

1861 Jacobs publishes *Incidents in the Life of a Slave Girl.*

1863 Jacobs establishes a school in Alexandria to train black teachers.

1865 Jacobs begins relief work in Savannah, Georgia.

1868 Jacobs travels to England.

1897 Jacobs dies in Washington, DC.

James, Etta

JANUARY 5, 1938 – ● RHYTHM AND BLUES SINGER

Etta James, born Jamesetta Hawkins in Los Angeles, sang during her childhood in the choir of Saint Paul's Baptist Church. She began to sing professionally at the age of fourteen, when she worked with a rhythm and blues ensemble led by Johnny Otis. Her first recording, "Roll With Me Henry" (1954), was originally banned by radio stations because of its **salacious** content. However, the record became a hit, and it was rereleased in 1955 under the title "Wallflower."

In the mid-to-late 1950s, James was one of the most popular singers in rhythm and blues, behind only Dinah Washington and Ruth Brown in her number of hit rhythm and blues records. Nominally a blues shouter, her gospel-influenced voice was also by turns sweet, pouting, or gruff. Among her hit records, many of which were recorded for Chicago's Chess Records, were "Good Rockin' Daddy" (1955), "W-O-M-A-N" (1955), "How Big a Fool" (1958), "All I Could Do Was Cry" (1960), "Stop the Wedding" (1962), "Pushover" (1963), and "Something's Got a Hold on Me" (1964). James toured with Little Richard, James Brown, Little Willie John, and Johnny "Guitar" Watson.

Heroin addiction forced James to quit recording in the mid-to-late 1960s. She eventually entered a rehabilitation program that culminated in her return to the music industry in 1973

salacious: obscene, indecent.

1938 James is born in Los Angeles.

1954 James records "Roll With Me Henry."

1973 James wins Grammy Award for album *Etta James.*

1990 James win an NAADP image award.

1993 James is inducted into Rock and Roll Hall of Fame.

with the album *Etta James*, which won a Grammy Award. James then recorded numerous albums, including *Come a Little Closer* (1974), *Etta Is Betta than Evvah* (1976), *Deep in the Night* (1978), *Blues in the Night* with Eddie "Cleanhead" Vinson (1986), *Seven Year Itch* (1988), and *Stickin' to My Guns* (1990). Nonetheless, her pioneering role as a rhythm and blues singer was often overlooked until the 1990s. In 1990 she won an NAACP Image Award, and in 1993 she was inducted into the Rock and Roll Hall of Fame. She published a memoir, *Rage to Survive*, in 1995. ◆

Jamison, Judith

MAY 10, 1943 – ● DANCER

Born the younger of two children in Philadelphia, Pennsylvania, Jamison studied piano and violin as a child. Tall by the age of six, Jamison was enrolled in dance classes by her parents in an effort to complement her exceptional height with grace. She received most of her early dance training in classical ballet with master teachers Marion Cuyjet, Delores Brown, and John Jones at the Judimar School of Dance. Jamison decided on a career in dance only after three semesters of coursework in psychology at Fisk University, and she completed her education at the Philadelphia Dance Academy. In 1964 she was spotted by choreographer Agnes de Mille and invited to appear in de Mille's *The Four Marys* at the New York–based American Ballet Theatre. Jamison moved to New York in 1965 and that same year joined the Alvin Ailey American Dance Theater (AAADT).

Jamison performed with AAADT on tours of Europe and Africa in 1966. When financial pressures forced Ailey to briefly disband his company later that year, Jamison joined the Harkness Ballet for several months and then returned to the reformed AAADT in 1967. She quickly became a principal dancer with that company, dancing a variety of roles that showcased her pliant technique, stunning beauty, and exceptional stature of five feet, ten inches. Jamison excelled as the goddess Erzulie in Geoffrey Holder's *The Prodigal Prince* (1967), as the Mother in a revised version of Ailey's *Knoxville: Summer of 1915* (1968), and as the Sun in the 1968 AAADT revival of

"The black issue is one thing that I don't want to take up because it forces people into pigeonholes. I like the idea of responding to all ethnic backgrounds—not focusing on a single one."

Judith Jamison, quoted in the *Los Angeles Times*, 1989

Lucas Hoving's *Icarus*. These larger-than-life roles fit neatly with Jamison's regal bearing and highly responsive emotional center, and critics praised her finely drawn dance interpretations that were imbued with power and grace. Jamison's and Ailey's collaboration deepened, and she created a brilliant solo in his *Masekela Language* (1969). Set to music of South African trumpeter Hugh Masekela, Jamison portrayed a frustrated and solitary woman dancing in a seedy saloon. Her electrifying performances of Ailey's fifteen-minute solo *Cry* (1971) propelled her to an international stardom unprecedented among modern dance artists. Dedicated by Ailey "to all black women everywhere—especially our mothers," the three sections of *Cry* successfully captured a broad range of movements, emotions, and images associated with black womanhood as mother, sister, lover, goddess, **supplicant,** confessor, and dancer.

In 1976 Jamison danced with ballet star Mikhail Baryshnikov in Ailey's *Pas de Duke* set to music by Duke Ellington. This duet emphasized the classical line behind Jamison's compelling modern dance technique and garnered her scores of new fans. Jamison's celebrity advanced, and she appeared as a guest artist with the San Francisco Ballet, the Swedish Royal Ballet, the Cullberg Ballet, and the Vienna State Ballet. In 1977 she created the role of Potiphar's Wife in John Neumeier's *Josephslegende* for the Vienna State Opera, and in 1978 she appeared in Maurice Béjart's updated version of *Le Spectre de la Rose* with the Ballet of the Twentieth Century. Several choreographers sought to work with Jamison as a solo artist, and important collaborations included John Parks's *Nubian Lady* (1972), John Butler's *Facets* (1976), and Ulysses Dove's *Inside* (1980).

In 1980 Jamison left the Ailey company to star in the Broadway musical *Sophisticated Ladies,* set to the music of Duke Ellington. She later turned her formidable talent to choreography, where her work has been marked by a detached sensuality and intensive responses to rhythm. Jamison founded her own dance company, the Jamison Project, "to explore the opportunities of getting a group of dancers together, for both my choreography [and] to commission works from others." Alvin Ailey's failing health caused Jamison to rejoin the AAADT as artistic associate for the 1988–89 season. In December 1989 Ailey died, and Jamison was named artistic director of the company. She has continued to choreograph, and her ballets include

supplicant: someone who asks humbly and earnestly, especially in praying to God.

1943 Jamison is born in Philadelphia.

1964 Jamison is discovered by Agnes de Mille.

1965 Jamison joins Alvin Ailey American Dance Theater.

1966 Jamison tours Europe with Alvin Ailey.

1969 Jamison dances solo in Ailey's *Masekela Language.*

1971 Jamison appears in *Cry.*

1976 Jamison appears with Mikhail Baryshnikov in *Pas de Duke.*

1980 Jamison stars on Broadway in *Sophisticated Ladies.*

1989 Jamison is named artistic director of Alvin Ailey company.

Divining (1984), *Forgotten Time* (1989), and *Hymn* (1993), all performed by the AAADT.

Jamison has received numerous awards and honors, including a Presidential Appointment to the National Council of the Arts, the 1972 Dance Magazine Award, and the Candace Award from the National Coalition of One Hundred Black Women. Her greatest achievement as a dancer has been an inspiring ability to seem supremely human and emotive within an elastic and powerful dance technique. ◆

> *"Women are blessed with a jewel of strength that glows all the time."*
>
> Judith Jamison, quoted in *Essence*, 1990

Jemison, Mae Carol

OCTOBER 17, 1956 – ● ASTRONAUT

Mae Jemison, a computer engineer and physician, was a mission specialist aboard STS-47, the eight-day Spacelab J (Japan) flown in September 1992, becoming the first African-American woman in space. The STS-47 crew conducted over 40 experiments in space manufacturing and life sciences. In order to test human responses to the stress of spaceflight, Jemison served as a test subject.

Jemison was born October 17, 1956, in Decatur, Alabama, and grew up in Chicago, where she graduated from Morgan Park High School in 1973. She attended Stanford University, receiving a B.S. in chemical engineering in 1977 while also fulfilling requirements for a B.A. in African and Afro-American Studies. She received her M.D. from Cornell University in 1981.

Following completion of her internship at Los Angeles County/USC Medical Center in July 1982 Jemison worked as a general practitioner with the Ross Loos Medical Group in Los Angeles until December of that year. In January 1983 she became a Peace Corps area medical officer in Sierra Leone, and later Liberia, in West Africa. (As a graduate student Jemison had visited Cuba, Kenya, and Thailand doing medical studies and relief work.) While in Africa she managed health care for the Peace Corps and U.S. embassy personnel in those areas. She also took part in hepatitis research projects for the National Institutes of Health and the Center for Disease Control.

Returning to the United States in October 1985, Jemison joined the CIGNA Health Plan of California, and was working

> *"It's important not only for a little black girl growing up to know, yes, you can become an astronaut because there's Mae Jemison. But it's important for older white males who sometimes make decisions on those careers of those little black girls."*
>
> Mae Jemison, quoted in the *New York Times*, 1992

Mae Jemison (second from right, back row) with the crew of space shuttle *Endeavour* during training in Houston, Texas, in 1992.

1956 Jemison is born in Decatur, Alabama.

1977 Jemison graduates from Stanford University.

1981 Jemison earns an M.D. from Cornell University Medical College.

1983 Jemison travels to Africa with the Peace Corps.

1985 Jemison begins working as a physician in Los Angeles.

1987 Jemison is accepted into NASA's astronaut training program.

1988 Jemison qualifies as a shuttle mission specialist.

1992 Jemison flies into space aboard shuttle *Endeavour.*

1993 Jemison forms the Jemison Group.

as a CIGNA general practitioner in Los Angeles when she became one of the seventeen astronaut candidates selected by NASA in June 1987.

After qualifying as a shuttle mission specialist in August 1988 Jemison worked with the astronaut support group at the Kennedy Space Center, and in the Shuttle Avionics Integration Laboratory. In September 1992 Jemison became the first black woman in space when she flew as a mission specialist aboard the space shuttle *Endeavour*. During the seven-day flight, Jemison conducted experiments to determine the effects of zero gravity on humans and animals.

Reportedly frustrated by her experiences with NASA, Jemison declined a second fight assignment and resigned from the astronaut office in March 1993 to pursue other interests. After her resignation Jemison formed her own company, the Jemison Group, which specializes in adapting technology for use in underdeveloped nations. Jemison's historic spaceflight brought her much adulation. In Detroit a school was named after her. And in the spring of 1993, a PBS special, *The New Explorers,* focused on her life story, while *People* magazine named her one of the year's "50 Most Beautiful People in the World." Also in 1993, Jemison made a guest appearance as a transport operator named Lieutenant Palmer on the television series *Star Trek:*

The Next Generation. This was fitting, as Jemison said she was inspired to become an astronaut by the actress Nichelle Nichols, who portrayed the black Lieutenant Uhura on the original *Star Trek*. ◆

Jordan, Barbara Charline

FEBRUARY 21, 1936 – JANUARY 17, 1996 ● CONGRESSWOMAN AND PROFESSOR

B arbara Jordan was born in Houston, Texas, the daughter of Arlyne Jordan and Benjamin M. Jordan, a Baptist minister. She spent her childhood in Houston, and graduated from Texas Southern University in Houston in 1956. Jordan received a law degree from Boston University in 1959. She was engaged briefly in private practice in Houston before becoming the administrative assistant for the county judge of Harris County, Texas, a post she held until 1966.

In 1962, and again in 1964, Jordan ran unsuccessfully for the Texas State Senate. In 1966, helped by the marked increase in registered African-American voters, she became the first black since 1883 elected to the Texas State Senate. The following year she became the first woman president of the Texas Senate. That year, redistricting opened a new district in Houston with a black majority. Jordan ran a strong campaign, and in 1972 she was elected to the House of Representatives from the

"What the people want is very simple. They want an America as good as its promise."
Barbara Jordan, 1977

Spingarn Medal

In 1992 the National Association for the Advancement of Colored People (NAACP) presented the prestigious Spingarn Medal to Barbara Jordan. The Spingarn Medal is awarded annually by the NAACP for "the highest or noblest achievement by an American Negro." The medal was named for Joel E. Spingarn (1874–1939), who originated the idea of it. Spingarn, who was white, was professor and chair of the Department of Comparative Literature at Columbia University from 1909 until 1911, when he resigned over free-speech issues. He became involved in the NAACP because of civil rights abuses in the South and joined the NAACP's board of directors in 1913. While traveling throughout the country, organizing the association and speaking for the rights of black people, Spingarn noticed that newspaper coverage of African Americans tended to be negative, focusing on black murderers and other criminals. A close collaborator of W. E. B. Du Bois, Spingarn was sensitive to media portrayals of blacks. Independently wealthy, he endowed an award that would pinpoint black achievement, strengthen racial pride, and publicize the NAACP. The first medal was awarded in 1915 to biologist Ernest E. Just. Beginning with Mary B. Talbert in 1922, ten women have won the Spingarn Medal, including Jordan, Mary McLeod Bethune, Marian Anderson, Daisy Bates, Rosa Parks, Lena Horne, Dorothy Height, Maya Angelou, and Myrlie Evers-Williams.

district, becoming the first African-American woman elected to Congress from the South.

Jordan's short career as a high-profile congresswoman took her to a leadership role on the national level. In her first term, she received an appointment to the House Judiciary Committee, where she achieved national recognition during the Watergate scandal, when in 1974 she voted for articles of impeachment against President Richard M. Nixon. A powerful public speaker, Jordan eloquently conveyed to the country the serious constitutional nature of the charges and the gravity with which the Judiciary Committee was duty-bound to address the issues. "My faith in the Constitution is whole, it is complete, it is total," she declared. "I am not going to sit here and be an idle spectator to the **diminution,** the **subversion,** the destruction of the Constitution."

Jordan spent six years in Congress, where she spoke out against the Vietnam War and high military expenditures, particularly those earmarked for support of the war. She supported environmental reform as well as measures to aid blacks, the poor, the elderly, and other groups on the margins of society. Jordan was a passionate campaigner for the Equal Rights Amendment, and for grassroots citizen political action. Central

diminunition: the act of decreasing or reducing.

subversion: systematic attempt to undermine or overthrow from within.

to all of her concerns was a commitment to realizing the ideals of the Constitution.

Public recognition of her integrity, her legislative ability, and her oratorical excellence came from several quarters. Beginning in 1974, and for ten consecutive years, the *World Almanac* named her one of the twenty-five most influential women in America. *Time* magazine named Jordan one of the Women of the Year in 1976. Her electrifying keynote address at the Democratic National Convention that year helped to solidify her stature as a national figure.

In 1978, feeling she needed a wider forum for her views than her congressional district, Jordan chose not to seek reelection. Returning to her native Texas, Jordan accepted a professorship in the School of Public Affairs at the University of Texas at Austin in 1979, and from 1982 to 1993 she held the Lyndon B. Johnson Centennial Chair in Public Policy. Reflecting her interest in minority rights, in 1985 Jordan was appointed by the secretary-general of the United Nations to serve on an eleven-member commission charged with investigating the role of transnational corporations in South Africa and Namibia. In 1991 Texas governor Ann Richards appointed her "ethics guru," charged with monitoring ethics in the state's government. In 1992, although confined to a wheelchair by a degenerative disease, Jordan gave a keynote speech at the Democratic National Convention, again displaying the passion, eloquence, and integrity that had first brought her to public attention nearly two decades earlier.

In 1993 President Bill Clinton appointed Jordan to chair the U.S. Commission on Immigration Reform. She received the Presidential Medal of Freedom in 1994. Jordan died in 1996 from pneumonia and complications related to leukemia. ◆

> *"The majority of the American people still believe that every single individual in this country is entitled to just as much respect, just as much dignity, as every other individual."*
> Barbara Jordan, 1990

Jordan, June

JULY 9, 1936 – ● WRITER

Born in Harlem to Jamaican immigrants Granville and Mildred Jordan, June Jordan grew up in Brooklyn's Bedford Stuyvesant, where poverty and racism were rampant. She absorbed quite early, as she records in the introduction to her first collection of essays, *Civil Wars* (1981), her community's belief in the power of the word. In her family, literature was important, so that by age seven she was writing poetry. She attended an exclusive white New England high school and went to Barnard College in 1953, both of which she found alienating experiences.

In college she met Michael Meyer, a student at Columbia, whom she married in 1955. They had a son, Christopher David, in 1958 and were divorced by 1965, experiences she explores in later essays. In the 1960s Jordan, now a single working mother, actively participated in and wrote about African-American political movements in New York City. Her first book-length publication, *Who Look at Me* (1969); her poems collected in *Some Changes* (1971); and her essays in *Civil Wars* exemplify her illumination of the political as intimate, the personal as political change, poetry as action—concepts central to all Jordan's work.

Jordan's writing workshop for Brooklyn children in 1965 resulted in the anthology *Voice of the Children* (1970), and anticipated her many books for children: *His Own Where* (1971), written in black English; *Dry Victories* (1972); *Fannie Lou Hamer* (1972); *New Life: New Room*; and *Kimako's Story* (1981), while her organizing of poets in the 1960s resulted in the poetry anthology *SoulScript*. Her collaboration with Buckminster Fuller in 1964 to create an architectural design for Harlem indicates her concern with black urban environments, a theme evident in *His Own Where* and *New Life: New Room*. Her work as an architect won Jordan a Prix de Rome in 1970, a year she spent in Rome and Greece, geographical points for many poems in *New Days: Poems of Exile & Return* (1974).

Jordan's teaching at City College, New York City, and the State University of New York at Stony Brook is a starting point for theoretical essays on black English, of which she is a major analyst. Her reflections on her mother's suicide in 1966 are the genesis for black feminist poems such as "Getting Down to Get Over," in *Things That I Do in the Dark: Selected Poems* (1977). In the 1970s, Jordan contributed to black feminism with major essays and poems. Her "Poem about My Rights" in *Passion: New Poems, 1977–80* also indicates her growing internationalism, as she relates the rape of women to the rape of Third World countries by developed nations.

1936 Jordan is born in New York City.

1964 Jordan collaborates with Buckminster Fuller.

1965 Jordan conducts children's writing workshop in Brooklyn.

1969 Jordan publishes *Who Look at Me.*

1970 Jordan publishes *Voice of the Children.*

1981 Jordan publishes *Civil Wars.*

In the 1980s, through poetry in *Living Room* (1985) and *Naming Our Destiny* (1989), as well as in *On Call: Political Essays*, Jordan writes about oppression in South Africa, Lebanon, Palestine, and Nicaragua as she widens her personal vision as an African-American woman to include more of the struggling world. The growth of her international audience is indicated by the translation of her work into many languages (including Arabic and Japanese), by British publications of *Lyrical Campaigns: Poems* (1985) and *Moving towards Home: Political Essays* (1989), and by recordings of her poems as sung by Sweet Honey in the Rock.

In 1978 and 1980 Jordan recorded her own poems, and in the 1980s she began writing plays, a genre she calls "a living forum." Her play *The Issue* was produced in 1981; *Bang Bang über Alles*, in 1986, and *All These Blessings*, in 1990, had staged readings. Jordan has also widened her audience by being a regular columnist for the *Progressive* magazine. In her poetry, prose, and plays, Jordan continues to dramatize how life seems to be an increasing revelation of the "intimate face of universal struggle," a truth she offers to those who would hear her. ◆

> *"I do not believe that we can restore and expand the freedoms that our lives require until we embrace the justice of our rage."*
>
> June Jordan, quoted in *Progressive*, 1989

Joyner-Kersee, Jacqueline

MARCH 3, 1962 – ● TRACK AND FIELD ATHLETE

Born and raised in East St. Louis, Illinois, Jacqueline Joyner entered her first track and field competition at age nine. Five years later, she won the first four Amateur Athletic Union Junior Pentathlon championships. At Lincoln High School, she received All-American selections in basketball and track. Joyner graduated in the top 10 percent of her high school class and accepted a basketball scholarship to the University of California at Los Angeles (UCLA). A four-year starter for the Lady Bruins basketball team, she continued her track and field career, winning the National Collegiate Athletic Association (NCAA) heptathlon title in 1982 and 1983. After winning the heptathlon at the 1984 U.S. Olympic Trials, Joyner won a silver medal at the Olympic Games in Los Angeles.

> *"I will never forget what it took to get where I am. I see the struggle. I see the hard times. I would not abuse it by getting big-headed and cocky."*
>
> Jackie Joyner-Kersee, quoted in *Jet*, 1989

Jackie Joyner-Kersee during high jump competition.

1962 ▸ Joyner is born in East St. Louis, Illinois.

1984 ▸ Joyner wins Olympic silver medal for heptathlon.

1986 ▸ Joyner marries Bob Kersee; sets world record for heptathlon at Goodwill Games.

1987 ▸ Joyner-Kersee wins two gold medals at World Championships.

1988 ▸ Joyner-Kersee wins two Olympic gold medals.

1990 ▸ Joyner-Kersee wins heptathlon gold at Goodwill Games.

1992 ▸ Joyner-Kersee wins Olympic gold and bronze medals.

1994 ▸ Joyner-Kersee wins heptathlon gold at Goodwill Games.

1996 ▸ Joyner-Kersee wins Olympic bronze medal.

In 1986 Joyner married her coach, Bob Kersee. Later that year, at the Goodwill Games in Moscow, she set a world record in the heptathlon when she led all competitors with 7,148 points. Breaking the old mark by 200 points, Joyner-Kersee became the first American woman since 1936 to establish a multievent world record. That same year, she broke her own world record at the U.S. Olympic Sports Festival in Houston and won the Sullivan Memorial Trophy, awarded to America's top amateur athlete. At the 1987 World Track and Field Championships in Rome, Joyner-Kersee won the gold medal in both the long jump and heptathlon competitions and became the first woman to win gold medals in multisport and individual events at the same Olympic-level competition. She repeated this feat at the 1988 Olympics in Seoul, winning the long jump with an Olympic record leap of 24′ 3$^1/_2$″ and the heptathlon with a new world record of 7,291 points.

Joyner-Kersee continued to dominate the heptathlon into the 1990s; she won at the 1990 Goodwill Games, the 1992 Olympics in Barcelona (where she also earned a bronze medal in the long jump), the 1993 World Championships, and, once again, at the Goodwill Games in 1994. At the 1994 USA/ Mobil Outdoor Track and Field Championships, she won gold medals in the long jump and the 100-meter hurdles. Eager to provide inspiration and support for young people and women interested in athletics, she established the Jackie Joyner-Kersee Community Foundation in her home town of East St. Louis. In

1992 she was named Amateur Sports Woman of the Year by the Women's Sports Foundation.

Joyner-Kersee qualified for the 1996 Olympic team at age 34. She won a bronze medal in the individual long jump, but was forced to withdraw from the heptathlon after pulling a muscle. In 1997 Joyner-Kersee published her autobiography, *A Kind of Grace: The Autobiography of the World's Greatest Female Athlete*. ◆

Kearse, Amalya Lyle

JUNE 11, 1937 – ● JUDGE AND BRIDGE EXPERT

1959 — Kearse graduates from Wellesley College.

1962 — Kearse receives a law degree from the University of Michigan.

1969 — Kearse is named partner at Hughes, Hubbard & Reed.

1979 — Kearse is appointed U.S. Appeals Court judge.

1986 — Kearse wins world-class championship in contract bridge.

expropriation: government seizure of private property for public use.

Born and raised in Vauxhall, New Jersey, Amalya L. Kearse graduated from Wellesley College in Massachusetts in 1959 and received her law degree from the University of Michigan in 1962. Upon graduating, she went to work for the law firm of Hughes, Hubbard & Reed in New York City, where, in 1969, she became the firm's first African-American partner.

In 1979 Kearse was appointed by President Jimmy Carter to serve as a judge on the United States Court of Appeals, Second District, in New York City. She became the first woman and the second African American to sit on the federal appeals court in Manhattan. Among her notable decisions was her 1981 ruling that Banco Para el Comercio Exterior, the Cuban state bank, could not be held liable on a United States bank's claim for losses resulting from the Cuban government's **expropriation** of the U.S. bank's assets. The Cuban bank, she held, had a status independent from the government. Her decision, however, was later overturned by the U.S. Supreme Court. In 1987 Kearse wrote an opinion upholding a lower court ruling against the city of Yonkers, in which she ruled that Yonkers had intentionally segregated schools for decades by creating segregated public housing projects.

During the 1991 Senate Judiciary Committee hearings on the nomination of Clarence Thomas to the U.S. Supreme Court, Kearse was named a possible alternative choice to Thomas in an article in the *American Lawyer*, which listed her among fifteen "first-rate centrists." She was considered as a serious candidate by the Clinton administration in 1992 for the position of U.S. Attorney General and, later in the year, as a candidate for another opening on the U.S. Supreme Court. In 1994 Kearse ruled in a Second Circuit decision that the Bush administration's 1990 census had vastly undercounted African Americans and Latinos in major cities in a way that diminished the flow of federal monies and the distribution of congressional seats.

Generally considered a social liberal and fiscal conservative, Kearse is highly respected by her peers for having a keen intellect, for being well prepared for each case that has come before her, and for being evenhanded and thoughtful. Her written opinions are regarded as both scholarly and thorough.

Kearse is also an avid bridge player. In 1972 she won the National Women's Pairs Bridge Championship in the American Contract Bridge League. She wrote a book on the subject in 1980, *Bridge at Your Fingertips*. She won her first world-class championship in contract bridge in 1986. ◆

Amalya Kearse won her first world-class championship in contract bridge in 1986.

Keckley, Elizabeth

1818 – MAY 26, 1907 ● DRESSMAKER

Elizabeth Keckley was born Elizabeth Hobbs to a slave family in Dinwiddie Court House, Virginia. While in her teens she was sold to a North Carolina slave owner. In North Carolina she was raped, probably by her owner, and gave birth to a son. At the age of eighteen she was repurchased, along with her son, by the daughter of her original owner and taken to St. Louis. There she began her career as a dressmaker, supporting her owners and their five children as well as her own son. In St. Louis she married James Keckley—a slave who convinced her to marry him by claiming to be free—but soon separated from him.

In 1855 Elizabeth Keckley was loaned $1,200 by her dressmaking customers to purchase her own freedom. She then established a successful dressmaking business. In 1860 she moved first to Baltimore and then to Washington, D.C., where she established herself as one of the capital's elite dressmakers. One of her customers was the wife of Jefferson Davis.

Mary Todd Lincoln, the wife of Abraham Lincoln, became one of Keckley's most loyal customers. Keckley soon made all of the First Lady's clothes, and the two struck up a close friendship. From 1861 to 1865 Keckley worked in the White House as Mary Todd Lincoln's dressmaker and personal maid.

Mary Todd Lincoln, the wife of Abraham Lincoln, became one of Elizabeth Keckley's most loyal customers.

1818	Keckley is born a slave in Virginia.
1855	Keckley buys her freedom.
1860	Keckley establishes herself as a dressmaker in Washington, DC.
1861	Keckley is retained as Mary Todd Lincoln's dressmaker and personal maid.
1868	Keckley publishes her diaries.
1890	Keckley becomes teacher of domestic science.
1907	Keckley dies in Washington, DC.

During the Civil War Keckley became active in the abolitionist movement, helping to found an organization of black women to assist former slaves seeking refuge in Washington, D.C. The Contraband Relief Association received a $200 donation from Mary Todd Lincoln, and Keckley successfully solicited several prominent abolitionists for financial support, including Wendell Phillips and Frederick Douglass.

After the assassination of President Lincoln, Mary Todd Lincoln and Keckley remained close friends until 1868, when Keckley's diaries were published as a book, *Behind the Scenes; or, Thirty Years a Slave, and Four Years in the White House.* Mary Todd Lincoln considered the book a betrayal and broke off her relationship with Keckley. Even several noted African Americans criticized Keckley for what they believed to be a dishonorable attack on "the Great Emancipator." Nonetheless, the book has long been considered an invaluable resource for scholars of the Lincoln presidency. It reveals much about the personalities of Abraham and Mary Todd Lincoln, their family life, and their opinions about government officials. The memoir also offers an intimate depiction of Keckley's life in slavery, particularly of the sexual violence she endured as a teenager. While its accuracy has not been questioned, the book's true authorship has been the subject of considerable debate, since its polished prose seems to be at odds with Keckley's lack of formal education.

Keckley's dressmaking business declined as a result of the controversy surrounding the book. In the 1890s she was briefly a teacher of domestic science, but for most of her later years lived in obscurity, supported by a pension paid to her because her son had been killed fighting for the Union Army. Keckley died on May 26, 1907, in a Washington rest home she had helped found. ◆

Kelly, Sharon Pratt

JANUARY 30, 1944 – ● POLITICIAN

Sharon Pratt Kelly became America's first black woman mayor of a major city when she was elected to the post in Washington, D.C., in 1990. She began her term as Sharon Pratt Dixon, but changed her name when she married during her first year in office. Kelly faced unique challenges as leader of the nation's capital, a city that depends on the United States Congress as its final authority on legislation and finances. She took office at a time when the city's crime problems, especially drug-related murders, fell under the national spotlight.

Kelly was born Sharon Pratt in Washington, D.C., on January 30, 1944. Her father, Carlisle E. Pratt, became a District of Columbia Superior Court judge. Kelly's mother, Mildred (Petticord) Pratt, died of breast cancer when Sharon was four years old, after which she and her sister lived with their aunt and grandmother. Kelly studied political science at Howard University and earned a bachelor's degree in 1965. She received a law degree from Howard in 1968. At age twenty-two, Kelly married fellow student Arrington L. Dixon, who became a District of Columbia Council chairman. The couple have two daughters, Aimee and Drew.

Kelly entered her father's law firm in 1971. In 1976 she accepted a position at the Potomac Electric Power Company (PEPCO). Within thirteen years, Kelly rose to become PEPCO's first black female vice president. Kelly also represented Washington on the Democratic National Committee from 1977 to 1990 and served as the committee's treasurer from 1985 to 1989.

In 1982 Kelly and Dixon divorced. Also that year, Kelly campaigned for the candidate who opposed Mayor Marion Barry Jr. Barry won the race and a second term in office. However, although he had achieved some successes during his first term, reports of official and personal misconduct emerged in his second term.

Responding to the problems plaguing her city and its leader, Kelly quit her high-paying position at PEPCO and declared her candidacy for the 1990 mayoral election. As she told the *Washington Post*, she couldn't watch and do nothing. "I don't have a lot of patience with people who sit on the sidelines," Kelly said.

Kelly's first run for office met with substantial opposition. However, circumstances changed swiftly when police arrested Barry on charges of cocaine possession in January. Kelly called for Barry's resignation, and she also blasted the other candidates—three city council members—for allowing Barry's corruption. Kelly promised voters she would "clean house" in city government. Barry dropped out of the race when he went to trial, and Kelly won the election with a record 86 percent of the vote.

Kelly had many ups and downs in her term. First, both her grandmother and a close friend died. Then in December 1991,

> *"Well, I guess it's best to own up to it at the outset. I am a recovering politician."*
> Sharon Pratt Kelly, 1997

1944 Kelly is born in Washington, DC.

1965 Kelly earns a B.A. from Howard University.

1968 Kelly receives a law degree from Howard University.

1971 Kelly enters her father's law firm.

1976 Kelly begins at PEPCO, rising to become the company's first black female vice president.

1977 Kelly begins representing Washington, DC, on the Democratic National Committee.

1991 Kelly begins term as mayor of Washington, DC.

1994 Marion Berry defeats Kelly in her bid for reelection.

Kelly surprised people by marrying businessman James R. Kelly III and changing her name. Politically, the new mayor had trouble winning over government officials loyal to Barry and seemed unable to build an effective team around her. She did succeed in persuading Congress to grant $100 million in emergency aid to reduce the city's budget problems. However, Kelly later clashed with Congress on several matters. The city's crime problems did not diminish. Critics attributed Kelly's inexperience for helping Barry make a comeback. After serving six months in prison, Barry won a city council seat in 1992. When Kelly ran for reelection in 1994, Barry ran against her and won.

After the spotlight of Washington, Kelly relished returning to normal life and did not plan to seek further office. In 1996 she lectured nationally and began writing a book about the changing political system. ◆

Kincaid, Jamaica

MAY 25, 1949 – ● WRITER

Born Elaine Potter Richardson in St. Johns, Antigua, Jamaica. Kincaid moved to New York at the age of sixteen, ostensibly to become a nurse. Working first as an au pair and then at other odd jobs, she spent brief periods studying photography at New York's School for Social Research and at Franconia College in New Hampshire. She began her career as a writer by conducting a series of interviews for *Ingénue*. Between 1974 and 1976 she contributed vignettes about African-American and Caribbean life to the *New Yorker*. In 1976 she became a staff writer for the *New Yorker*, which two years later published "Girl," her first piece of fiction. Most of Kincaid's fiction has first appeared in the magazine, for which she also began to write a gardening column in 1992.

Kincaid's first volume of stories, *At the Bottom of the River* (1983), has a dreamlike, poetic character. Her early interest in photography, evident here, also undergirds the rest of her work with its emphasis on condensed images. The choice of the short-story form allows her to isolate moments of heightened emotion. Published separately, the stories that make up the novel *Annie John* (1985) string such brief glimpses together to explore a defiant Annie's growing up in Antigua and especially her relationship to her mother. Themes of mother-daughter conflict are central to Kincaid's work and can be extended into metaphorical relations, such as that between the Caribbean island and those who leave it. For those who visit it, *A Small Place* (1988) is an extended essay on contemporary Antigua, an essay directed toward the tourist. Its tone is alternately cynical and wise, its information painful to accept, but its characteristically careful wording entices the reader as much as any poster of island beauty. *Lucy* (1990) combines the vigor of this Antiguan commentary and the embryonic artistic sensibility of *Annie John* into an extended allegory of the colonial relation set in the contemporary period. Lucy Josephine Potter, a young woman from the Caribbean entrusted with caring for four blond children, brazenly charges through her new world until the blank page confronts her with the fragility of her own identity.

Kincaid's 1996 novel, *The Autobiography of My Mother*, is narrated by an elderly West Indian woman as she looks back over the course of her life. In 1997 Kincaid published *My Brother*, a nonfiction account of her younger brother Devon's 1996 death in Antigua from AIDS.

Kincaid's colorful personality and life history, perhaps best exemplified in the selection of her assumed name, propel critical interest in her biography. Like many black writers, especially women, she is burdened both with the expectation that she will represent not merely herself but her community and with the assumption that her stories will be true and factual. The insistent presence of the first person in Kincaid's work is a challenge to that combined requirement. Filtering every perception through an individual, even selfish, lens, her stories are not autobiography; only the depth of feeling is. Kincaid has maintained that she is uninterested in literary realism. Borne by her plainspoken prose, her audacious girl/woman protagonists gain an audience they might never have gotten in life. ◆

> *"I can't part with a book once I've read it. It's just an obsession I have. I can't go into a bookstore without spending money. When I look at somebody's library, I wish I could put my head to it and just absorb it."*
>
> Jamaica Kincaid, quoted in *Salon*, 1996

King, Coretta Scott

APRIL 27, 1927 – ● CIVIL RIGHTS ACTIVIST

Born in Marion, Alabama, a rural farming community, Coretta Scott attended Lincoln High School, a local private school for black students run by the American

Missionary Association. After graduating in 1945, she received a scholarship to study music and education at Antioch College in Yellow Springs, Ohio. Trained in voice and piano, she made her concert debut in 1948 in Springfield, Ohio, as a soloist at the Second Baptist Church. Scott officially withdrew from Antioch in 1952 after entering the New England Conservatory of Music in 1951 to continue her music studies.

During her first year at the conservatory, she met the Rev. Dr. Martin Luther King Jr., who was a doctoral candidate at Boston University's school of theology. The two were married on June 18, 1953, despite Martin Luther King Sr.'s opposition to the match because of his disapproval of the Scott family's rural background and his hope that his son would marry into one of Atlanta's elite black families. The couple returned to Boston to continue their studies. The following year, Coretta Scott King received a bachelor's degree in music (Mus.B.) from the New England Conservatory of Music, and in September the two moved to Montgomery, Alabama, despite Coretta King's misgivings about returning to the racial hostility of Alabama.

Although Coretta King aspired to become a professional singer, she devoted most of her time to raising her children and working closely with her husband after he had assumed the presidency of the Montgomery Improvement Association in 1955. She participated in many major events of the Civil Rights Movement along with her husband, both in the United States and overseas, as well as having to endure the hardships resulting from her husband's position, including his frequent arrests and the bombing of their Montgomery home in 1956.

Early in 1960 the King family moved to Atlanta when King became copastor of Ebenezer Baptist Church with his father. Later that year, Coretta King aided in her husband's release from a Georgia prison by appealing to presidential candidate

"Woman, if the soul of the nation is to be saved, I believe that you must become its soul."

Coretta Scott King, My *Life With Martin Luther King,* 1969

John F. Kennedy to intervene on his behalf. In 1962, Coretta King became a voice instructor at Morris Brown College in Atlanta, but she remained primarily involved in sharing the helm of the civil rights struggle with her husband. She led marches, directed fund-raising for the Southern Christian Leadership Conference and gave a series of "freedom concerts" that combined singing, lecturing, and poetry reading. A strong proponent of disarmament, King served as a delegate to the Disarmament Conference in Geneva, Switzerland, in 1962, and in 1966 and 1967 she was a cosponsor of the Mobilization to End the War in Vietnam. In 1967, after an extended leave of absence, she received her bachelor of arts degree in music and elementary education from Antioch College.

On April 8, 1968, only four days after the Rev. Dr. Martin Luther King Jr. was assassinated in Memphis, Coretta King substituted for her deceased husband in a march on behalf of sanitation workers that he had been scheduled to lead. Focusing her energies on preserving her husband's memory and continuing his struggle, Coretta King also took part in the Poor People's Washington Campaign in the nation's capital during June 1968, serving as the keynote speaker at the main rally at the Lincoln Memorial. In 1969 she helped found and served as president of the Atlanta-based Martin Luther King, Jr. Center for Nonviolent Social Change, a center devoted to teaching young people the importance of nonviolence and to preserving the memory of her husband. In 1969 she also published her autobiography, *My Life with Martin Luther King, Jr.,* and in 1971 she received an honorary doctorate in music from the New England Conservatory.

In 1983 Coretta King led the twentieth-anniversary march on Washington and the following year was elected chairperson of the commission to declare King's birthday a national holiday, which was observed for the first time in 1986. She was active in the struggle to end apartheid, touring South Africa and meeting with Winnie Mandela in 1986 and returning there in 1990 to meet the recently released African National Congress leader Nelson Mandela.

Coretta King has received numerous awards for her participation in the struggle for civil rights, including the outstanding citizenship award from the Montgomery Improvement Association in 1959 and the Distinguished Achievement Award from the National Organization of Colored Women's Clubs in 1962.

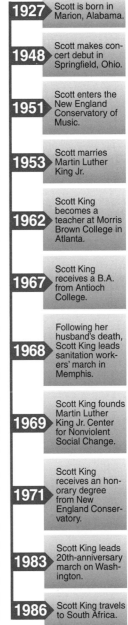

1927 Scott is born in Marion, Alabama.

1948 Scott makes concert debut in Springfield, Ohio.

1951 Scott enters the New England Conservatory of Music.

1953 Scott marries Martin Luther King Jr.

1962 Scott King becomes a teacher at Morris Brown College in Atlanta.

1967 Scott King receives a B.A. from Antioch College.

1968 Following her husband's death, Scott King leads sanitation workers' march in Memphis.

1969 Scott King founds Martin Luther King Jr. Center for Nonviolent Social Change.

1971 Scott King receives an honorary degree from New England Conservatory.

1983 Scott King leads 20th-anniversary march on Washington.

1986 Scott King travels to South Africa.

As of 1993, she has retained her position as chief executive officer of the Martin Luther King, Jr. Center for Nonviolent Change, having resigned the presidency to her son Dexter Scott King in 1989. As she has done for many years, Coretta Scott King continues to press for the worldwide recognition of civil rights and human rights. ◆

Kitt, Eartha Mae

JANUARY 26, 1928 – ● SINGER AND ACTOR

B orn on a farm in the town of North, South Carolina, Eartha Kitt and her sister, Pearl, were abandoned as small children by their mother. They were raised in a foster family until 1936, when Eartha moved to New York City to live with her aunt.

In New York Kitt attended the Metropolitan High School (which later became the High School of Performing Arts), and at sixteen she met Katherine Dunham, who granted her a scholarship with Dunham's dance troupe. Kitt toured Europe and Mexico with the troupe, developing a sexually provocative stage presence and a throaty, sensual singing style. When the troupe arrived in Paris, Kitt was offered a job singing at a top nightclub. Orson Welles saw her perform and cast her as "Girl Number Three" in his 1951 stage production of Marlowe's *Doctor Faustus*. After touring Germany with the production and a brief singing engagement in Turkey, Kitt returned to New York. She performed at La Vie en Rose and at the Village Vanguard, where Leonard Sillman saw her and decided to cast her in his Broadway show *New Faces of 1952*. Kitt also appeared in the 1954 film version of *New Faces*. In both versions she sang "C'est Si Bon," "Monotonous," and "Uska Dara," which were recorded for her 1955 album, *The Bad Eartha*.

Kitt performed from the mid-1950s through the '60s in theaters, nightclubs, and cabarets in the United States and abroad, honing her reputation as a "sex kitten." Her stage appearances included *Mrs. Patterson* (1954), a musical produced by Sillman, for which she received a Tony Award nomination, and *Shinbone Alley* (1957). Kitt also appeared in the films *St. Louis Blues* (1958), *The Accused* (1957), and *Anna Lucasta* (1959), which

> *"My birth was never recorded. I have no birth certificate, therefore I do not exist, that is why I am a legend."*
>
> Eartha Kitt, 1988

earned her an Oscar nomination. During this period she recorded two notable albums, *Bad but Beautiful* in 1961 and *At the Plaza* in 1965. Kitt also made numerous television appearances, including a stint on the 1960s *Batman* series, in which she played "Catwoman."

In 1968 Kitt's career took a dramatic turn when she criticized the war in Vietnam at a White House luncheon hosted by the First Lady Lady Bird Johnson. As a result Kitt lost bookings and was vilified by conservatives and much of the mainstream press and was investigated by the Central Intelligence Agency and the Federal Bureau of Investigation. Although Kitt's subsequent appearances in Europe were commonly believed to be the result of her being blacklisted in the United States, in fact she maintained a significant presence in American clubs, film, and television. In 1972 her political reputation took a sharp turn when she performed in South Africa and publicly complimented her white hosts for their hospitality.

In the late 1970s and '80s Kitt continued her career as a cabaret singer and occasional actor. Her return to Broadway in the 1978 show *Timbuktu* earned her a second Tony nomination. She recorded the album *I Love Men* in 1984 and published two autobiographies during this period, *I'm Still Here* in 1989 and *Confessions of a Sex Kitten* in 1991. Kitt also appeared in a variety of marginal Hollywood films, including *Erik the Viking* in 1989, *Ernest Scared Stupid* in 1991, *Boomerang* in 1992, and *Fatal Instinct* in 1993. A five-compact disc retrospective of her work, entitled *Eartha Quake*, was released in 1993. ◆

1928	Kitt is born in South Carolina.
1936	Kitt moves to New York City.
1951	Orson Welles casts Kitt in *Doctor Faustus*.
1952	Kitt appears on Broadway in *New Faces*.
1959	Kitt earns an Academy Award nomination for *Anna Lucasta*.
1968	Kitt criticizes the Vietnam War during luncheon at the White House.
1972	Kitt performs in South Africa.
1978	Kitt earns a Tony nomination for *Timbuktu*.
1993	A retrospective of Kitt's recordings is released on a five-CD set.

Knight, Gladys

MAY 28, 1944 – ● SINGER

Gladys Knight, who was born and raised in Atlanta, Georgia, made her public singing debut at the age of four at Mount Mariah Baptist Church, where her parents were members of the choir. By the time she was five, Knight had performed in numerous Atlanta churches and toured through Florida and Alabama with the Morris Brown Choir. At the age of seven Knight won the Grand Prize on Ted Mack's nationally televised *Original Amateur Hour*.

Gladys **Knight** and the Pips (Merald "Bubba" Knight, William Guest, Edward Patten) in 1975.

1944 ▶ Knight is born in Atlanta.

1951 ▶ Knight wins the Grand Prize on *Original Amateur Hour.*

1952 ▶ Knight forms the Pips.

1961 ▶ The group makes their first recording.

1965 ▶ Knight and the Pips sign with Motown Records.

1967 ▶ Knight and the Pips record "I Heard It Through the Grapevine."

1973 ▶ Knight and the Pips record "Midnight Train to Georgia."

1974 ▶ Knight and the Pips win two Grammy Awards.

1980 ▶ The group reunites after brief separation.

1989 ▶ Knight leaves the Pips to pursue solo career.

In 1952 Knight formed a quartet with her brother Merald "Bubba" Knight and cousins William Guest and Edward Patten. The group, named "The Pips" after James "Pip" Woods, another cousin and the group's first manager, quickly established itself in Atlanta nightclubs. By the late 1950s the group was a popular fixture on the national rhythm and blues circuit. Their first recording came in 1961, when Vee Jay Records released the single "Every Beat of My Heart," which became a Top Ten pop and Number-One R&B hit. The following year Fury Records signed the group, changed its name to Gladys Knight and the Pips, and released their Top Ten R&B single "Letter Full of Tears."

Though well known in R&B circles, Gladys Knight and the Pips did not become a major crossover act until 1965, when they signed with Motown Records and were featured on the label's touring reviews. Their 1967 Motown single "I Heard It Through the Grapevine" reached Number Two on the *Billboard* pop chart. The late 1960s brought the group mass acclaim for its polished, call-and-response singing style and slick, synchronized dance routines. The next big hit came in 1970 with the top-selling single "You Need Love Like I Do." Six of the group's albums made the R&B charts: *Nitty Gritty* (1970); *Greatest Hits* (1970); *If I Were Your Woman* (1971); *Standing Ovation* (1972); *Neither One of Us*; and *All I Need Is Time* (1972).

In 1972 Gladys Knight and the Pips had another big hit with "Neither One of Us (Wants to Be the First to Say Goodbye)." In 1973 the group switched to the Buddah label for its Top-Forty album *Imagination*, which included two of the group's most enduring successes, "Midnight Train to Georgia," a Number-One pop single in 1973, and "I've Got to Use My Imagination." The group won two 1974 Grammy Awards for "Neither One of Us" and "Midnight Train to Georgia."

In the late 1970s the group's popularity began to wane. Legal conflicts with Motown forced Knight to record separately for a brief period in the late 1970s. The group reunited in 1980 and continued touring, but was not able to record another chart-topping record until 1988, when "Love Overboard" reached the Top Twenty on the *Billboard* pop chart. The following year Knight once again left the group, this time voluntarily, to establish a solo career. The following year she released *Good Woman*, a solo LP that was moderately successful on black radio. ◆

The Pips, named after the group's first manager James "Pip" Woods, was a popular fixture on the national rhythm and blues circuit.

LaBelle, Patti
(Holt, Patricia Louise)

OCTOBER 4, 1944 – ● SINGER

Born and raised in Philadelphia, Pennsylvania, Patti LaBelle grew up singing in the choir of the Beaulah Baptist Church. She was sixteen years old when she joined a vocal group called the Ordettes; a year later LaBelle, Cindy Birdsong (who joined the Supremes as Florence Ballard's replacement in 1967), Nona Hendrix, and Sarah Dash signed on with Newton Records, and named their group the Blue-Belles after Newton's subsidiary label Bluebelle Records. After their song "I Sold My Heart to the Junkman" reached the Top Twenty in 1962, the group was rechristened Patti LaBelle and the BlueBelles.

LaBelle, who is known for her fiery stage presence and outrageous attire—a mixture of leather, feathers, glitter, and enormous fanlike coiffures—received her first big break in 1968, when she and the BlueBelles opened for the Who during their U.S. tour. The following year, she married Armstead Edwards, an educator who enrolled in business courses in order to become her personal manager. In 1971 LaBelle and the BlueBelles became known as simply "LaBelle." Their album *Nightbirds*, with its Number One single "Lady Marmalade," made the Top Ten in 1973. In 1974 LaBelle became the first black band to perform in New York's Metropolitan Opera House; as the lead singer, Patti LaBelle caused a sensation when she began the show by descending from the ceiling, where she hung suspended, to the stage.

LaBelle went solo in 1977, after personal and artistic differences between the singers caused the band's dissolution the previous year. By the end of the 1970s, she had recorded two LPs for Epic Records, and she continued to appear live and record albums throughout the '80s and early '90s. In 1985 LaBelle appeared in Pennsylvania to perform in the Live Aid Benefit Rock Concert; her album *Burnin'* earned her a Grammy Award for best rhythm and blues performance by a female vocalist in 1991.

LaBelle is well known for her support of numerous charitable and social organizations, including Big Sisters and the United Negro College Fund, as well as various urban renewal and homelessness projects in Philadelphia, where she lives. In addition to giving concert performances, she costarred with singer Al Green in a revival of *Your Arms Too Short to Box with God* on Broadway in 1982, and appeared in the films *A Soldier's Story* and *Beverly Hills Cop,* in her own television special, and in the television series *A Different World* and *Out All Night.* ◆

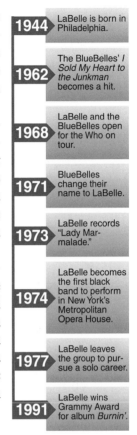

1944 LaBelle is born in Philadelphia.

1962 The BlueBelles' *I Sold My Heart to the Junkman* becomes a hit.

1968 LaBelle and the BlueBelles open for the Who on tour.

1971 BlueBelles change their name to LaBelle.

1973 LaBelle records "Lady Marmalade."

1974 LaBelle becomes the first black band to perform in New York's Metropolitan Opera House.

1977 LaBelle leaves the group to pursue a solo career.

1991 LaBelle wins Grammy Award for album *Burnin'.*

Lampkin, Daisy Elizabeth Adams

MARCH 1884 – MARCH 10, 1965 ● CIVIL RIGHTS LEADER

The date and place of Daisy Elizabeth Adams Lampkin's birth is not certain. Some records list her as being born in March 1884 in the District of Columbia (the stepdaughter of John and Rosa Temple), while others list her as born on August 9, 1888, in Reading, Pennsylvania, to George and Rosa Anne (Proctor) Adams. Records become more reliable for her late adolescent years: she finished high school in Reading, moved to Pittsburgh in 1909, and married William Lampkin in 1912.

Daisy Lampkin met *Pittsburgh Courier* publisher Robert L. Vann in 1913, after she had won a cash prize for selling the most

1912 Daisy Adams marries William Lampkin.

1913 Lampkin meets publisher Robert Vann.

1915 Lampkin becomes president of Negro Women's Franchise League.

1924 Lampkin is delegate-at-large to Republican National Convention.

1929 Lampkin becomes vice president of *Pittsburgh Courier*.

1935 Lampkin is named national field secretary for NAACP.

1947 Lampkin resigns as NAACP field secretary due to fatigue.

1965 Lampkin dies in Pittsburgh.

1983 Lampkin becomes the first black women honored by Pennsylvania with a historical marker.

copies of the newspaper; with the prize, she purchased stock in the *Courier* corporation. She continued to invest in the *Courier* corporation until 1929, when she began a lifelong tenure as the corporation's vice president.

In 1915 Lampkin became president of the Negro Women's Franchise League, and became involved in the National Suffrage League and the women's division of the Republican party. In July 1924, as president of the National Negro Republican Convention in Atlantic City, she helped pass a strong resolution against lynching. She also took part that year in a black delegation to the White House, led by James Weldon Johnson, to vindicate black soldiers involved in the Houston Riot of 1917. She also became a delegate-at-large to the 1924 Republican National Convention in Cleveland, Ohio.

In 1929 National Association for the Advancement of Colored People (NAACP) acting executive secretary Walter White had Lampkin appointed regional field secretary for the organization. She used her positions in the NAACP and the powerful *Courier* corporation to attract new funds and members to both organizations. In 1930 her grassroots political influence helped defeat Roscoe McCullough's reelection bid as senator from Ohio. McCullough had supported the nomination of Judge John J. Parker (who had once opposed black suffrage) to the U.S. Supreme Court.

In 1935 Lampkin was named national field secretary of the NAACP, a post she held until 1947. In this capacity, Lampkin displayed a great skill for raising funds while keeping operating expenses to a minimum. She and White campaigned strongly, although unsuccessfully, for the passage of the 1935 Costigan-Wagner federal antilynching bill. During Franklin Roosevelt's administration, she encouraged blacks to change their voting preferences from the Democratic party to the Republican party. However, she supported the Democrats selectively. Under Roosevelt, she supported the party despite the NAACP directives against partisan activity; under Truman, she cited those same directives as a reason to withhold her official support.

Although physical fatigue forced her to resign as national field secretary in 1947, Lampkin continued her fund-raising activities as a member of the NAACP board of directors. She continued to challenge any symbolic or substantive threats to African-American progress, but at the increasing cost of her physical stamina. She supported the Republicans in 1952 when the Democrats ran a segregationist vice presidential candidate,

Alabama's John J. Sparkman. She also led a major fund-raising effort for the Delta Sigma Theta sorority's purchase of a $50,000 building that year.

Lampkin remained active in NAACP activities through the early 1960s, receiving the National Council of Negro Women's first Eleanor Roosevelt-Mary McLeod Bethune award in December 1964. Lampkin died at her home in Pittsburgh on March 10, 1965. In 1983 she became the first black woman honored by the state of Pennsylvania with a historical marker, located at the site of her Webster Avenue home. ◆

Lee, Rebecca

1833 – ? ● PHYSICIAN

Rebecca Lee was born in Richmond, Virginia, but grew up in Pennsylvania where she lived with her aunt, who worked as a health care provider. From 1852 to 1860 Lee was a nurse in Massachusetts. In 1860 she decided to go to medical school and was accepted by the New England Female Medical College in Boston. When she received her M.D. in 1864, she became the first black female physician in the United States, as well as the first and only black woman to graduate from the New England Female Medical College. For many years Lee maintained a private practice in Richmond, Virginia, catering to the needs of freed black people. In 1883, after having moved back to Boston, she published *A Book of Medical Discourses in Two Parts*. The book focused primarily on the health care concerns of women and children. Little is known about her life after this point; the year of her death also is unknown. ◆

1833 ▸ Lee is born in Richmond, Virginia.

1864 ▸ Lee receives M.D. from New England Female Medical College.

1883 ▸ Lee publishes *A Book of Medical Discourses in Two Parts.*

Lewis, Edmonia

1844 – ? ● SCULPTOR

Information on Edmonia Lewis's life is sparse and difficult to verify. She was often inconsistent in her own accounts of her early days. Born in upstate New York in 1844, the daughter of a Chippewa mother and a black father, Lewis, who

The Rediscovery of *The Death of Cleopatra*

Edmonia Lewis sculpted her masterpiece, *The Death of Cleopatra*, in Rome in the mid 1870s, then sent it to Philadelphia for the Centennial Exposition of 1876, where it was greatly admired and widely discussed. Two years later, Lewis's work was exhibited in Chicago, where it was again a major attraction. When Lewis returned to Rome after the Chicago exhibition, she was apparently unable to carry the two-ton work with her and left it in storage. Somehow Lewis's sculpture ended up on display in a Chicago saloon during the early 1890s. After several years the sculpture was sold to "Blind John" Cordon, who owned a horse-racing track in Forest Park, north of Chicago. Cordon placed the sculpture on top of the grave of his favorite horse, Cleopatra, and it remained in that spot after the race track was converted into a golf course and after a munitions factory was built on the site during World War II. Meanwhile, Lewis and her work were largely forgotten, and no one knew where the sculpture had come from or who had created it. When a U.S. Postal Service facility was built on the site of the munitions factory in the early 1970s, *Cleopatra* was removed to a nearby salvage yard. The sculpture remained there until a local fire inspector happened upon it during the 1980s and brought it to the attention of the Historical Society of Forest Park. The society investigated the work and eventually identified it as the lost *Death of Cleopatra* by Edmonia Lewis, whose work art historians had recently rediscovered. Realizing its value, the society gave *Cleopatra* to the National Museum of American Art in Washington, D.C., where it was cleaned and restored, and where it is now on display with several other works by Lewis.

idyll: a time of carefree, peaceful contentment in simple, rustic surroundings.

was given the Indian name Wildfire, Lewis and her older brother, Sunrise, were orphaned when she was five years old. Raised by maternal aunts, she described her youth as something of an **idyll** in which she lived in the wild, fished for food, and made moccasins to sell. She was able, as well, to study at a school near Albany.

With financial help from her older brother, Lewis attended Oberlin College, where her studies included drawing and painting. In a dramatic incident, she was accused of the attempted murder, by poisoning, of two classmates who were stricken shortly after enjoying a hot drink she had prepared. While the young women lay ill, Lewis was abducted by a mob and severely beaten. After her recovery and subsequent **vindication** in the courts, she ended her studies and moved to Boston, Massachusetts, in order to pursue a career in the arts.

vindication: declaration of innocence.

There, she found encouragement and support from William Lloyd Garrison, Lydia Maria Child, the sculptor Edward Brackett, with whom she studied, and a community of friends and patrons of the arts, many of whom were active in the Abolitionist Movement. Her *Bust of Robert Gould Shaw* (1864), the Boston Brahmin and Civil War hero who died leading black troops into battle, was a great success. Sales of copies of that work enabled her to finance a trip to Europe, where, following travels in England, France, and Italy, she settled in a studio once occupied by Antonio Canova on the Via Della Frezza in Rome.

A friend of sculptors Anne Whitney and Harriet Hosmer, and the actress Charlotte Cushman, Lewis was a member of the group of British and American expatriate women artists dubbed by Henry James the "white, **marmorean** flock." About Lewis, he wrote: "One of the sisterhood . . . was a Negress, whose color, picturesquely contrasting with that of her plastic material, was the pleading agent of her fame."

marmorean: suggesting marble or a marble statue.

James's opinion notwithstanding, Lewis's work was much in demand during the heyday of the "literary" sculptors. Her studio, listed in the best guidebooks, was a fashionable stop for Americans and others on the grand tour, many of whom ordered busts of family members or of literary and historical figures to adorn their mantels and front parlors.

The first African American to gain an international reputation as a sculptor, Lewis was a prolific artist. The catalog of her work runs to over sixty items, not all of which have been located. Her early work in Boston included portrait medallions and busts of major abolitionists such as John Brown, Maria Weston Chapman, and Garrison. There was also a small statue, now lost, showing the black hero Sgt. William H. Carney holding aloft the flag at the battle of Fort Wagner.

In Rome, she executed such major works as *Forever Free* (1867), a depiction of a slave couple hearing the news of emancipation, and *Hagar* (1868–75) about which she said, "I have a strong feeling for all women who have struggled and suffered." Henry Wadsworth Longfellow's poem *Song of Hiawatha* made him a literary folk hero and inspired numerous artists. Lewis drew on that familiar resource with groups such as *The Marriage of Hiawatha* (1867) and *The Old Arrow-Maker and His Daughter* (1867). These works seemed to patrons all the more authentic coming from the hand of a young woman, part Indian, reputed to have grown up in the wild.

Lewis's considerable celebrity reached its height with the unveiling of her *Death of Cleopatra* (1876) at the Philadelphia Centennial Exhibition. That monumental work, a life-sized depiction of Cleopatra on her throne, was praised for the

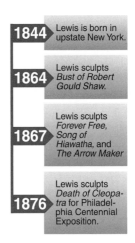

1844 Lewis is born in upstate New York.

1864 Lewis sculpts *Bust of Robert Gould Shaw.*

1867 Lewis sculpts *Forever Free, Song of Hiawatha,* and *The Arrow Maker*

1876 Lewis sculpts *Death of Cleopatra* for Philadelphia Centennial Exposition.

verisimilitude: the quality of appearing to be true or realistic.

horrifying **verisimilitude** of the moment when the snake's poison takes hold, and for Lewis's attempt to depict the "authentic" Egyptian queen from the study of historic coins, medals, and other records.

In the 1880s, as the vogue for late neoclassical sculpture declined, references to Lewis dwindled as well. While it is known that she was living in Rome as late as 1909, it is not certain where and when she died. ◆

Lloyd, Ruth Smith

JANUARY 25, 1917 – ● ANATOMIST

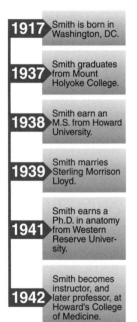

1917 Smith is born in Washington, DC.

1937 Smith graduates from Mount Holyoke College.

1938 Smith earn an M.S. from Howard University.

1939 Smith marries Sterling Morrison Lloyd.

1941 Smith earns a Ph.D. in anatomy from Western Reserve University.

1942 Smith becomes instructor, and later professor, at Howard's College of Medicine.

Ruth Smith Lloyd was born in Washington, D.C., the daughter of Bradley Donald and Mary Elizabeth Morris Smith. A 1933 graduate of Dunbar High School, she attended Mount Holyoke College, where she earned an A.B. in zoology (magna cum laude) in 1937. On the urging of her zoology professors, she went on for graduate work at Howard University under the eminent black zoologist Ernest Everett Just. In 1938 she earned an M.S. in zoology, and Just motivated her to pursue doctoral studies. With the support of a Rosenwald Fellowship, she earned a Ph.D. in anatomy at Western Reserve University in 1941. Her thesis focused on adolescent development in macaques, a type of monkey. She was the first African-American woman to receive a doctorate in anatomy.

Lloyd began her professional career in physiology at Howard (1940–41, 1942) and in zoology at Hampton Institute (1941–42). In 1942 she was appointed instructor in anatomy at Howard's college of medicine. She became assistant professor of anatomy in 1947 and associate professor in 1955, the position she held until her retirement in 1977. Lloyd's primary research interest was ovarian anatomy. She also assisted William Montague Cobb, head of the anatomy department at Howard, on a bibliography of physical anthropology, published in the December 1944 issue of *American Journal of Physical Anthropology*. Among her numerous educational activities, she was a director of Howard's academic reinforcement program for medical students during the mid-1970s.

Lloyd was a member of the American Association of Anatomists, American Association of Medical Colleges, and New York Academy of Sciences. Her husband, Sterling Morrison Lloyd (whom she married in 1939), was a physician. The couple had three children. ◆

Logan, Myra Adele

1908 – JANUARY 13, 1977 ● PHYSICIAN AND SURGEON

Myra Logan was born in Tuskegee, Alabama, where her father was treasurer of the Tuskegee Institute. She attended Tuskegee's laboratory school, the Children's House. A 1923 honors graduate of Tuskegee High School, she was the valedictorian of her graduating class at Atlanta University in 1927. She then moved to New York City where her sister, Ruth Logan Roberts, a nurse involved in public health issues, was already living. Logan received an M.S. in psychology from Columbia University in New York, and an M.D. from New York Medical College in 1933. (She went to medical school on a $10,000 four-year scholarship established by Walter Gray Crump, a white surgeon committed to helping blacks advance in the medical profession.)

Logan did her internship at Harlem Hospital, and continued to practice there as a surgeon. She is generally regarded as the first woman successfully to operate on the heart, and was the first black woman elected a Fellow of the American College of Surgeons. She did extensive research on the use of aureomycin and other antibiotics, publishing many articles on the subject in such medical journals as *The Archives of Surgery* and *The Journal of American Medical Surgery*. Along with her brother, the physician Arthur C. Logan, she was a founding member of an early health maintenance organization, the Upper Manhattan Medical Group of the Health Insurance Plan. She left the group in 1970 to join the Physical Disability Program of the New York State Workmen's Compensation Board. Logan was a member of many organizations, including the Planned Parenthood Association and the National Medical Association of the NAACP. She had been a member of the New York State Committee on Discrimination, but resigned in

1908 ▶ Logan is born in Tuskegee, Alabama.

1927 ▶ Logan graduates as valedictorian from Atlanta University.

1933 ▶ Logan is awarded M.D. from New York Medical College.

1944 ▶ Logan resigns in protest from the New York State Committee on Discrimination.

1970 ▶ Logan joins the New York State Workman's Compensation Board.

1977 ▶ Logan dies in New York City.

1944 to protest Governor Thomas E. Dewey's disregard of the antidiscrimination legislation the committee had proposed. She died in New York City in 1977. ◆

Lorde, Audre Geraldine

FEBRUARY 18, 1934 – NOVEMBER 17, 1992   ● POET, NOVELIST, AND TEACHER

> *"Change did not begin with you, and it will not end with you, but what you do with your life is an absolutely vital piece of that chain. The testimony of each of our daily lives is a vital missing remnant in the fabric of the future."*
>
> Audre Lorde, commencement address at Oberlin College, 1989

Born in Harlem to West Indian parents, Audre Lorde described herself as "a black lesbian feminist mother lover poet." The exploration of pain, rage, and love in personal and political realms pervades her writing. Perhaps because Lorde did not speak until she was nearly five years old and also suffered from impaired vision, her passions were equally divided between a love of words and imagery and a devotion to speaking the truth, no matter how painful. Her objective, she stated, was to empower and encourage toward speech and action those in society who are often silenced and disfranchised.

Lorde published her first poem while in high school, in *Seventeen* magazine. She studied for a year (1954) at the National University of Mexico, before returning to the United States to earn a bachelor of arts degree in literature and philosophy from Hunter College in 1959. She went on to receive a master's degree from the Columbia School of Library Science in 1960. During this time she married attorney Edward Ashley Rollins and had two children, Elizabeth and Jonathan. Lorde and Rollins divorced in 1970. Juggling her roles as black woman, lesbian, mother, and poet, she was actively involved in causes for social justice. Throughout this period she was a member of the Harlem Writers Guild.

An important juncture in Lorde's life occurred in 1968. She published her first collection of poetry, *The First Cities*, and also received a National Endowment for the Arts Residency Grant, which took her to Tougaloo College in Mississippi. This appointment represented the beginning of Lorde's career as a full-time writer and teacher. Returning to New York, she continued to teach and publish. In 1973, her third book, *From a Land Where Other People Live*, was nominated for the National Book Award for Poetry. It was praised for its attention to racial oppression and injustice around the world. She spent ten years on the faculty of John Jay College of Criminal Justice and then became professor of English at her alma mater, Hunter College, in 1980. She wrote three more books of poetry before the appearance of *The Black Unicorn* (1978), for which she received the widest acclaim and recognition. It fuses themes of motherhood and feminism while placing African spiritual awakening and black pride at its center.

Lorde's devotion to honesty and outspokenness is evident in the works she produced in the 1980s. She published her first nonpoetry work, *The Cancer Journals* (1980), so she could share the experience of her cancer diagnosis, partial mastectomy, and apparent triumph over the disease with as wide an audience as possible. *Zami: A New Spelling of My Name* (1982) was enthusiastically received as her first prose fiction work. Self-described as a "biomythography," it is considered a lyrical and evocative autobiographical novel. She was a founding member of Women of Color Press and Sisters in Support of Sisters in South Africa.

Sister Outsider (1984), a collection of speeches and essays spanning the years 1976 to 1984, details Lorde's evolution as a black feminist thinker and writer. In 1986 she returned to poetry with *Our Dead behind Us. Burst of Light* (1988), which won an American Book Award, chronicles the spread of Lorde's cancer to her liver, and presents a less hopeful vision of the future than *The Cancer Journals*. Lorde's work appeared regularly in magazines and journals and has been widely anthologized. In 1991 she became the poet laureate of New York State. She died in St. Croix, U.S. Virgin Islands. ◆

1934 Lorde is born in Harlem.

1954 Lorde studies at the National University in Mexico.

1959 Lorde graduates from Hunter College.

1960 Lorde earns an M.A. from Columbia University.

1968 Lorde publishes *The First Cities.*

1973 *From a Land Where People Live* is nominated for the National Book Award.

1978 Lorde publishes *The Black Unicorn.*

1980 Lorde becomes English professor at Hunter College.

1991 Lorde is named poet laureate of New York State.

1992 Lorde dies in the Virgin Islands.

Mabley, Jackie "Moms"

MARCH 19, 1897 – MAY 23, 1975 ● COMEDIENNE

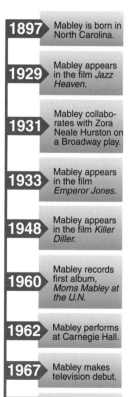

1897 — Mabley is born in North Carolina.

1929 — Mabley appears in the film *Jazz Heaven*.

1931 — Mabley collaborates with Zora Neale Hurston on a Broadway play.

1933 — Mabley appears in the film *Emperor Jones*.

1948 — Mabley appears in the film *Killer Diller*.

1960 — Mabley records first album, *Moms Mabley at the U.N.*

1962 — Mabley performs at Carnegie Hall.

1967 — Mabley makes television debut.

1975 — Mabley dies.

Born Loretta Mary Aiken in Brevard, North Carolina, Jackie "Moms" Mabley was one of twelve children, of mixed African-American, Cherokee, and Irish ancestry. During childhood and adolescence, she spent time in Anacostia (in Washington, D.C.) and Cleveland, Ohio. Mabley—who borrowed her name from Jack Mabley, an early boyfriend—began performing as a teenager, when she joined the black vaudeville circuit as a comedienne, singer, and dancer, appearing with such well-known performers as Dewey "Pigmeat" Markham, Cootie Williams, Peg Leg Bates, and Bill "Bojangles" Robinson. In the mid-1920s, she was brought to New York by the dance team of Butterbeans and Suzie. After making her debut at Connie's Inn, Mabley became a favorite at Harlem's Cotton Club and at the Club Harlem in Atlantic City, where she played with Louis Armstrong, Cab Calloway, Duke Ellington, and Count Basie, among others. It was during this time that she began cultivating the frumpily dressed, granny-like stage personality for which she became famous. Trundling on stage in a tacky housedress with a frilly nightcap, sagging stockings, and outsized shoes, "Moms"—as she was later known—would begin her ad-lib stand-up comedy routine, consisting of bawdy jokes ("The only thing an old man can do for me is bring a message from a young one") and songs, belted out in a gravelly "bullfrog" voice.

Mabley appeared in small parts in two motion pictures, *Jazz Heaven* (also distributed as *Boarding House Blues*, 1929) and *Emperor Jones* (1933), and collaborated with Zora Neale

Hurston in the Broadway play *Fast and Furious: A Colored Revue in 37 Scenes* (1931) before she started performing regularly at the Apollo Theater in Harlem. By the time she made the film *Killer Diller* (1948), she had cultivated a considerable following among black audiences, as well as among fellow performers; however, it was not until 1960, when she cut her first album for Chess Records, that she became known to white audiences. *Moms Mabley at the U.N.*, which sold over a million copies, was followed by several others, including *Moms Mabley at the Geneva Conference, Moms Mabley—The Funniest Woman in the World, Moms Live at Sing Sing,* and *Now Hear This.* In 1962 Mabley performed at Carnegie Hall in a program featuring Cannonball Adderley and Nancy Wilson. She made her television debut five years later in an all-black comedy special, *A Time for Laughter,* produced by Harry Belafonte. Throughout the late 1960s and early 1970s she was featured in frequent guest spots on television comedy and variety shows, hosted by Merv Griffin, the Smothers Brothers, Mike Douglas, Bill Cosby, Flip Wilson, and others. Mabley had a heart attack while starring in *Amazing Grace* (1974), a successful feature film, and died the following year. ◆

> "Moms" Mabley would begin her nightclub routine by trundling on stage in a tacky housedress with a frilly nightcap, sagging stockings, and outsized shoes.

Mahoney, Mary Eliza

MAY 7, 1845 – JANUARY 4, 1926 ● NURSE

Mary Eliza Mahoney was born in Dorchester, Massachusetts. Little is known about her life before 1878, when she was accepted into the professional nursing program at the New England Hospital for Women and Children in Boston. After completing the highly competitive sixteen-month program in 1879, Mahoney graduated and began a forty-year career as a professional nurse. Mahoney seems to have spent her career as a nurse in private homes in Boston, probably because of the general unwillingness of hospitals to hire black nurses.

At the turn of the century Mahoney became one of the first African-American members of the newly organized American Nurses Association (ANA), most of whose state and local organizations excluded black nurses. In 1908 Mahoney supported

1845 ▶ Mahoney is born in Dorchester, Massachusetts.

1879 ▶ Mahoney graduates from New England Hospital for Women and Children.

1909 ▶ Mahoney addresses National Association of Colored Graduate Nurses.

1922 ▶ Mahoney retires from nursing.

1936 ▶ Mary Mahoney Medal is established.

the creation of the National Association of Colored Graduate Nurses (NACGN), which was established in order to integrate the profession and serve as a black alternative to the ANA. The following year she gave the opening address to the NACGN's first annual meeting in Boston where she was elected national chaplain, responsible for the induction of new officers. Mahoney was also active in the women's suffrage movement and publicly supported the ratification of the Nineteenth Amendment in 1920.

Mahoney retired in 1922 and died four years later in Boston. In 1936 the NACGN established in her honor the Mary Mahoney Medal in recognition of significant contributions to integration in nursing. The award continued to be awarded annually by the ANA, which officially desegregated in 1948, after the NACGN was dissolved in 1951. ◆

Malone, Annie Turnbo

AUGUST 9, 1869 – MAY 10, 1957 ● ENTREPRENEUR AND PHILANTHROPIST

Annie Turnbo Malone was born to Robert and Isabell Turnbo in Metropolis, Illinois, and attended high school in nearby Peoria. Orphaned at a young age, she was raised by her older brothers and sisters. In her twenties she began experimenting with chemicals to develop a hair straightener for African-American women. Living in Lovejoy, Illinois, Turnbo invented and sold a hot pressing-iron as well as several lotions and creams, one for restoring lost hair. In 1902 she moved her business to 223 Market Street, in St. Louis, Missouri. She and her trained assistants began selling her "Wonderful Hair Grower" and other products door-to-door. One of her agents was Madame C. J. Walker, who went on to found her own hair-care company. Turnbo copyrighted the name "Poro" for her products in 1906. On April 28, 1914, she married Aaron E. Malone, who became the chief manager and president of the Poro company.

Attaining success, Annie Malone built Poro College, a beauty school, in St. Louis in 1917. The college became a social center for the black community, housing for a time the National Negro Business League as well as other organizations.

After a tornado hit the city in 1927, Poro College served as a principal relief facility for the Red Cross. Poro also trained women to be agents, teaching them the rudiments of salesmanship and beauty culture. The company enjoyed tremendous expansion in the early 1920s, employing thousands of agents. Toward the end of the decade, however, the company ran into trouble and began its decline. In 1927 Malone and her husband had a bitter divorce and struggled for control of the company. With the support of Mary McLeod Bethune and others, Annie Malone kept control of the enterprise and settled with her husband for $200,000. In 1930, Annie Malone relocated the business and the college to Chicago. She ran into further difficulties because of her refusal to pay excise taxes. Between 1943 and 1951 she was the subject of government suits. In the latter year the government seized control of the company and sold off most of Poro's property to pay taxes and fines.

Throughout her leadership of the Poro company, Malone distinguished herself as a philanthropist. In the 1920s she gave over $25,000 to the Howard University Medical School Fund. Malone also gave substantial sums to Tuskegee University, the Citywide YMCA of St. Louis, and the St. Louis Colored Orphans' Home. The Annie Malone Crisis Center and the Annie Malone Children and Family Service Center, both in St. Louis, are named in her honor. She died in Chicago in 1957. ◆

1869	Turnbo is born in Illinois.
1902	Turnbo establishes hair-care product company in St. Louis.
1914	Turnbo marries Aaron E. Malone.
1917	Malone opens Poro College beauty school in St. Louis.
1930	Malone relocates business and college to Chicago.
1957	Malone dies in Chicago.

Marshall, Paule

APRIL 9, 1929 – ● WRITER

Paule Marshall was born in Brooklyn, New York, the daughter of Samuel and Ada (Clement) Burke, who had emigrated from Barbados shortly after World War I. Marshall lived in a richly ethnic *"Bajan"* neighborhood in Brooklyn, and visited Barbados for the first time when she was only nine years old. She graduated from Brooklyn College, cum laude and Phi Beta Kappa, in 1953; while attending New York's Hunter College in the mid-1950s, she began her first novel—*Brown Girl, Brownstones*. Its publication in 1959 was followed by a Guggenheim Fellowship (1960). Later awards include the Rosenthal award of the National Institute for Arts and Letters

> *"Words were living things bestriding the air and charging the room with strong colors."*
>
> Paule Marshall, *Brown Girl, Brownstones*, 1959

(1962) for *Soul Clap Hands and Sing,* a Ford Foundation grant (1964–65), a National Endowment for the Arts grant (1967–68), and the American Book Award of the Before Columbus Foundation for *Praisesong for the Widow* (1983).

During the 1950s Marshall was a staff writer for a small magazine, *Our World,* which sent her on assignments to Brazil and the Caribbean. Since the publication of *Brown Girl, Brownstones* in 1959, Marshall has been a full-time writer and a part-time teacher. She has taught African-American literature and creative writing at Yale, Columbia, Iowa, and, since 1987, at Virginia Commonwealth University in Richmond, Virginia.

Marshall's writing explores the interaction between the materialist and individualistic values of white America and the spiritual and communal values of the African **diaspora.** With the exception of *Soul Clap Hands and Sing* (1961), a collection of four long stories about aging men, Marshall's work is focused on African-American and Caribbean women. Each of her novels presents a black woman in search of an identity that is threatened or compromised by modern society. Marshall's narratives locate that search within black communities that are still connected to ancient spiritual traditions, sharpening the contrast between Americanized Africans and various diasporic modes of Africanizing the New World.

In her essays and interviews, Marshall has explained the influence of the Bajan community of her childhood on her work. Listening to the "poets in the kitchen," as she called her mother's women friends and neighbors in a *New York Times Book Review* essay, she learned the basic skills that characterize her writing—**trenchant** imagery and idiom, relentless character analysis, and a strong sense of ritual. In "Shaping the World of My Art," Marshall speculates that the verbal power of the women gathered around her mother's kitchen table so intimidated her that she may have conceived of writing "to see if, on paper, I couldn't have some of that power." Marshall's development of her poetic relationship to the community of storytelling Bajan women has made her an intensely ethnic writer, one whose themes and manner measure the difference between the homeland (the West Indies and Africa) and the new land (the United States).

Marshall's fiction explores the divided immigrant or colonized self. In *Brown Girl, Brownstones* (1959), her protagonist, Selina Boyce, is an adolescent girl torn between the assimila-

diaspora: people settled far from their ancestral homelands.

trenchant: sharply penetrating and clear-cut.

tionist materialism of her mother, Silla, and the dreamy resistance to Americanization of her father, Deighton. As she matures, Selina learns from both the Bajan community and the world at large how to be her own woman. Each of the four stories in *Soul Clap Hands and Sing* explores a man in old age who reaches out toward a woman in the hope of transforming a failed and empty life. The stories contrast men defeated by materialism, colonialism, and internal compromise with young women full of vitality and hope. Like the men in numerous stories by Henry James, Marshall's old men cannot connect, and the young women serve as the painful instruments of their self-realization.

Marshall's second novel, *The Chosen Place, The Timeless People* (1969), is her largest literary conception. The major figure is Merle Kinbona, a middle-aged West Indian woman educated in Britain and psychologically divided in a number of ways. The struggle to resolve the divided self is very fully elaborated, here again seen as inextricably related to a community and its history. The rituals of recovery are more broadly drawn here, for they are more self-consciously communal in nature. Merle wants to be a leader in the development of her community, but she is almost literally **catatonic** with impotence until she comes to terms with her personal past and its relationship to the colonial order that is her communal past. As Merle is both the product and emblem of her divided community, her self-healing and newly found clarity of purpose prefigure the possibilities for the community as well. Her third novel, *Praisesong for the Widow* (1983), presents a middle-class black American woman who, like the old men of the four long stories, realizes the depth of her spiritual emptiness. Unlike the old men, Avatara is able, through dream and ritual, to recover her spiritual past. *Daughters* (1991) is the complex story of how Ursa McKenzie, the only child of a Caribbean politician father and an African-American mother, comes to grips with her ambivalent feelings about her father's emotional domination. Ursa's liberation involves every aspect of her life—her past in her island homeland, her professional life in New York City, her love life and friendships, and her understanding of political and economic relations between the United States and the island nations of the Caribbean.

In all her works, Marshall develops a rich psychological analysis, making use of powerful scenes of confrontation, revela-

1929 Marshall is born in Brooklyn.

1953 Marshall graduates from Brooklyn College.

1959 Marshall publishes her first novel, *Brown Girl, Brown-*

1960 Marshall is awarded a Guggenheim fellowship.

1969 Marshall publishes *The Chosen Place, The Timeless People.*

1983 Marshall is awarded American Book Award for *Praisesong for the Widow.*

1987 Marshall begins teaching at Virginia Commonwealth University.

catatonic: unable to move.

tion, and self-realization. Her style, while essentially realistic, is always capable of expressionist and surrealist scenes and descriptions, which are seamlessly integrated in the fabric of the narrative. Marshall's originality—her **prototypical** black feminism, her exploration of "the international theme" arising from the African diaspora, her control of a wide range of narrative techniques—places her in the first rank of twentieth-century African-American writers. ◆

prototypical: forming an original model.

Mason, Biddy Bridget

AUGUST 5, 1818 – JANUARY 15, 1891 ● PHILANTHROPIST

1818 · Mason is born a slave in Mississippi.

1836 · Mason is given as a wedding gift to Robert Smith.

1847 · Mason moves to Utah with Smith's family.

1851 · Smith and his slaves move to California.

1856 · Mason is freed from slavery.

1866 · Mason purchases property in downtown Los Angeles.

1872 · Mason founds First AME Church in Los Angeles.

1891 · Mason dies in Los Angeles.

Biddy Mason was born and raised on the slave plantation of John Smithson in Hancock County, Mississippi, and was given as a wedding present to Robert Marion Smith and Rebecca Crosby Smith in 1836. When her owner converted to Mormonism in 1847, she moved along with him and his other slaves to Utah, where they lived for four years. In 1851 Smith and his slaves moved west by caravan to San Bernadino, California. When Smith learned that California had been declared a free state in 1850, he made plans to move to Texas with his fourteen slaves. Meanwhile, with the aid of local free blacks, Mason escaped from captivity and arranged to have Smith put on trial for owning slaves. Smith failed to appear in court, and Mason and her family were freed from slavery on January 1, 1856.

Biddy Mason settled in Los Angeles, where she worked as a midwife and nurse, using skills she had learned on the plantation and perfected on her journey westward. By 1866 she had saved enough money to be one of the first African-American women to purchase her own property in downtown Los Angeles. She established a house at 331 South Spring Street, where poor people and minorities could find a safe haven. She later sold part of her land at great profit and built a commercial building from which she collected rent. She eventually bought large sections of downtown property, and died wealthy.

Mason's primary renown comes from her achievements as the first black philanthropist in Los Angeles. In 1872 she helped found Los Angeles's First African Methodist Episcopal Church, the city's oldest black church. From this church came other community organizations. Mason also operated a day nursery for orphans and poor children, and supplied needy families with food.

Mason died in 1891 and was buried in an unmarked grave. In 1988 a tombstone was erected by Los Angeles mayor Tom Bradley and members of the First AME Church. Mason was further honored by the declaration of Biddy Mason Day in Los Angeles on November 16, 1989. ◆

Matthews, Victoria Earle (Smith)

MAY 27, 1861 – MARCH 10, 1907 ● WRITER, JOURNALIST, SOCIAL REFORMER

Victoria Smith was born a slave in Fort Valley, Georgia. During the Civil War, her mother, Caroline Smith, fled to New York, but she returned to Georgia after Emancipation to reestablish contact with her nine children. She regained custody of four of her children and moved with them to Richmond and then Norfolk, Virginia. The family lived there for four years before going to New York City in 1873. Smith attended Grammar School 48 in New York, but was forced to begin working as a domestic to help support her family. She developed a deep interest in learning and borrowed books to read from the library of one of her employers. In 1879 she married William Matthews, a coachman, and they had a son.

Shortly after her marriage, Matthews began to write stories that were published in the *Waverly, New York Weekly,* and other literary journals. In 1893, under the pen name Victoria Earle, she published *Aunt Lindy,* a novel about a former slave in Georgia after the Civil War. She thereafter used the name Victoria Earle Matthews in most of her writings and public engagements. She wrote articles for a variety of black and white newspapers, including the *Boston Advocate* and the *New York Times,* before becoming a journalist for the *New York Age.* In 1898, with the support of T. Thomas Fortune, Matthews compiled and edited *Black Belt Diamonds,* a collection of quotations by Booker T. Washington.

Like most club-women of her time, Matthews was motivated by deep religious convictions and advocated both self-improvement and social reform to assist the less fortunate.

1861 — Smith is born a slave in Georgia.

1873 — Smith's family moves to New York City.

1879 — Smith marries William Matthews.

1892 — Matthews organizes a testimonial for Ida B. Wells.

1893 — Matthews publishes *Aunt Lindy* under a pen name.

1895 — Matthews attends First National Conference of Black Women.

1897 — Matthews founds the White Rose Mission.

1898 — Matthews compiles and edits *Black Belt Diamonds.*

1905 — Matthews forms the White Rose Traveler's Aid Society.

1907 — Smith dies of tuberculosis.

nonsectarian: unconnected to a particular religious denomination.

Matthews was a dedicated social reformer and played a leading role in the club movement. She helped organize a testimonial for the antilynching crusader Ida B. Wells in 1892. The event brought together 250 women from Boston, Philadelphia, and New York, and inspired the founding of black women's clubs in these cities. In New York Matthews helped found the Woman's Loyal Union Club and became its first president. The club was committed to social and political improvement of the African-American community, including better schools and employment opportunities.

In 1895 Matthews attended the First National Conference of Black Women, which led to creation of the National Federation of Afro-American Women (NFAAW). She spoke on "The Value of Race Literature," praising the creative abilities of black women and men. Matthews was the first chair of NFAAW and was on the editorial staff of its journal, *The Woman's Era*. In 1896 she helped consolidate the NFAAW and the Colored Women's League into the National Association of Colored Women, a coalition of women's clubs across the country, and served as national organizer from 1897 to 1899.

In 1897, after the death of her sixteen-year-old son, Matthews's interest in social welfare increased. During that year she founded the White Rose Mission, which provided food, shelter, and employment for migrants from the South, and served as a social space for young black women and children. The goals of the White Rose Mission included "establishing and maintaining a Christian, **nonsectarian** Home for Colored Girls and Women, where they may be trained in the principles of practical self-help and right living." Women were trained in such domestic activities as cooking and sewing, while boys were trained in vocational activities. Matthews taught black history at the White Rose Mission and helped create a library there of books by and about African Americans.

Like most clubwomen of her time, Matthews was motivated by deep religious convictions and advocated both self-improvement and social reform to assist the less fortunate. She was an active member of the Episcopal Church and lectured on uplift and the political and social responsibilities of African Americans. At the same time, she and other clubwomen provided services and support to young women to prevent them from becoming victims of a "white slave" traffic.

Matthews continued to work at the White Rose Mission until her health began to fail. Although she was only in her forties when this happened, she left behind an important legacy. Her idea of service centers spread, and travelers' aid societies were formed all along the eastern seaboard. In 1905 Matthews formed the White Rose Travelers' Aid Society, a chain of service centers from Virginia to New York, designed to support and protect young women. Two years later, Matthews died of tuberculosis at the age of forty-five. ◆

McDaniel, Hattie

JUNE 10, 1895 – OCTOBER 26, 1952 ● SINGER AND ACTOR

Hattie McDaniel was born in Wichita, Kansas. Her father, Henry McDaniel, was a Baptist preacher and an entertainer, and her mother, Susan (Holbert) McDaniel, was a choir singer. McDaniel was one of thirteen children. Soon after her birth the family moved to Colorado, and in 1901 they settled in Denver. In 1910, at the age of fifteen, she was awarded a gold medal by the Women's Christian **Temperance** Union for excellence in "the dramatic art" for her recital of "Convict Joe," which reportedly "moved the house to tears." On the strength of this success, McDaniel persuaded her family to allow her to leave school and to join her brothers in her father's newly formed traveling company, the Henry McDaniel Minstrel Show. Over the next decade she traveled and performed on the West Coast, mostly with her father's company, and she began at this time to develop her abilities as a songwriter and singer.

temperance: abstention from drinking alcohol.

Around 1920 McDaniel came to the notice of George Morrison, one of Denver's notable popular musicians. Taken on as a singer with Morrison's orchestra, McDaniel became increasingly well known throughout the West Coast **vaudeville** circuit. She also appeared with the orchestra on Denver radio during this time, and she is reputed to be the first black woman soloist to sing on the radio. In 1929 she secured a place with a traveling production of *Show Boat*, but the stock market crash of October 1929 eliminated the show's financing.

vaudeville: theatrical shows featuring a variety of acts, including dancers, singers, and comedians.

Hattie McDaniel (center) and a group of entertainers before a performance for soldiers at Minter Field during World War II.

1895 McDaniel is born in Wichita, Kansas.

1910 Women's Christian Temperance Union awards McDaniel a medal.

1920 George Morrison discovers McDaniel.

1929 McDaniel is cast in touring company of *Show Boat*.

1931 McDaniel moves to Hollywood.

1932 McDaniel receives first screen credit in *Blonde Venus*.

1939 McDaniel wins Academy Award for *Gone with the Wind*.

1947 McDaniel stars in radio series *Beulah*.

1952 McDaniel dies in Los Angeles.

After the crash, McDaniel moved to Milwaukee, where she worked in the coatroom of the Club Madrid and eventually got an opportunity to perform. Encouraged by her success, McDaniel moved to Hollywood in 1931 and soon began working regularly in radio and film. Over the course of the next two decades she appeared in more than three hundred films, though mostly in minor, uncredited roles. Her debut was in *The Golden West* (1932). The first film for which she received screen credit was *Blonde Venus* (1932), in which she played the affectionate, loyal, but willful domestic, a type of character that was virtually the only role available at the time to large black women in Hollywood. Over the course of the next two decades McDaniel successfully established herself in this role, gaining substantial, credited parts in over fifty films, including *Alice Adams* (1935), *The Mad Miss Manton* (1935), *Show Boat* (1936, with Paul Robeson), *Affectionately Yours* (1941), *Since You Went Away* (1944), and Walt Disney's animated *Song of the South* (1946).

McDaniel's career reached its high point in 1939 when she won an Academy Award, the first ever given to a black performer, for her portrayal of Mammy in *Gone with the Wind*. Praised by some and maligned by others for the image she portrayed, McDaniel in her Oscar acceptance speech (said to have been written by her studio) announced that she hoped always to be a credit to her race and to her industry. Despite Holly-

The "Mammy" Stereotype

Hattie McDaniel and a number of other distinguished black actresses fashioned careers playing numerous incarnations and variations of the jolly, dependable house servant, a stereotype generally referred to as "Mammy." The Mammy stereotype emerged during the nineteenth century in diaries, novels, plays, lithographs, and advertising and extended well into the twentieth century in print, film, radio, and television. Throughout this period, the black woman was invariably portrayed as large girthed, wearing an apron and a bandanna, her faced wreathed in a smile, and her wisdom delivered in comical dialect. At various times, she was depicted as being tough and domineering, soft and judicious, slow-witted and comical, but she was always nonthreatening, hardworking, and nurturing—the one person on whom all others could depend. Margaret Mitchell's "Mammy" in her 1936 novel, *Gone With the Wind,* was the archetypal portrait. Mitchell's Mammy, portrayed by Hattie McDaniel in the 1939 film version, was firm, compassionate, morally exemplary, and privy to the inner workings of the white family. Her language was ungrammatical and provincial, and her name lacked family designation. This portrait of the black woman as being loyal without bound, caring solely for her white charges, cheerfully administering all duties regardless of personal circumstances, and fulfilling her own wants by being a slave and domestic worker was a creation arising out of needs of the white community. The Mammy stereotype was intended to legitimize enslavement and serve as a role model for all black women. After the 1950s, the civil rights and black nationalist movements provoked the gradual elimination of the Mammy stereotype from American culture. The rise to prominence of black legislators, writers, intellectuals, filmmakers, and performers also helped consign Mammy and her male counterpart, Sambo, to the historical dustbin.

wood's evident self-satisfaction with this award, it is important to note that McDaniel (along with the other black cast members) had been excluded from the Atlanta premiere of the film and that her portrait was removed from the promotional programs that the studio distributed in the South.

McDaniel continued to play similar roles throughout the 1940s despite increased criticism from the NAACP, which felt that McDaniel and the other black actors who played servile stereotypes were helping to perpetuate them. In 1947, after the controversy with the NAACP had passed, McDaniel signed her first contract for the radio show *Beulah*, in which she once again played a southern maid. In the contract McDaniel insisted that she would not use dialect, and she demanded the right to alter any script that did not meet her approval. Both of her demands were met.

McDaniel died in Los Angeles in 1952, after completing the first six episodes of the television version of *Beulah*. ◆

McMillan, Terry

OCTOBER 18, 1951 – ● WRITER

The eldest of five children, Terry McMillan was born in Point Huron, Michigan, where she spent much of her adolescence in a household headed by her mother. At seventeen, she left Point Huron for Los Angeles, and in 1978 received a bachelor's degree in journalism from the University of California at Berkeley. While she was at Berkeley, author and teacher Ishmael Reed convinced her to pursue a career in writing. She left California to pursue a master's degree in film at Columbia University, but she left there in 1979 still several credits short of the degree to join the Harlem Writers Guild.

The first story McMillan read aloud to the guild became the opening chapter of her first novel, *Mama* (1987), which thrust her into prominence. A semiautobiographical work, *Mama* earned critical praise for its depiction of one woman's struggle to provide for her family during the 1960s and 1970s. The success of the novel is largely due to its realistic, gritty portrayal of Mildred's attempts to cope with the care of five children single-handedly at the age of twenty-seven. McMillan established her reputation further in the genre of the popular novel through her second novel, *Disappearing Acts* (1989). In *Disappearing Acts*, McMillan continues to present strong African-American characters in a New York City setting. The work is a love story that manages to address numerous issues facing many urban African-American communities. The love story of Zora and Franklin becomes a vehicle for an exploration of the complex issues of class and culture that affect relationships between black professionals and working-class partners.

McMillan's third novel, *Waiting to Exhale* (1992), became a best-seller within the first week of its release. Though this novel deals with many African-American themes, McMillan's treatment of male-female relationships in a gripping narrative ensures a wide readership. The novel centers on the friendships among four African-American women in Phoenix, Arizona, and how each of them looks for and hides from love. McMillan's tough, sexy style clearly has a wide appeal; the paperback rights for *Waiting to Exhale* were auctioned in the

> *"The message to men is that tenderness, honesty and respect are what women want. To women, I'm saying, 'Relax. Stop blaming men and worrying about how long a relationship is going to last. Nothing's forever.'"*
>
> Terry McMillan, quoted in *People*, 1995

Terry McMillan (left) with Whoopi Goldberg (center) and Goldberg's daughter, Alex, at the premiere of the 1998 film *How Stella Got Her Groove Back*.

1951	McMillan is born in Michigan.
1978	McMillan graduates from University of California, Berkeley.
1979	McMillan joins Harlem Writers Guild.
1987	McMillan publishes first novel, *Mama*.
1989	McMillan publishes *Disappearing Acts*.
1991	McMillan edits an anthology of African-American fiction.
1992	McMillan publishes *Waiting to Exhale*.
1996	McMillan publishes *How Stella Got Her Groove Back*.

sixth week of its hardcover publication for $2.64 million. McMillan's fourth novel, *How Stella Got Her Groove Back* (1996), concerns a forty-two-year-old black professional woman who falls in love with a young Jamaican cook. Both *Waiting to Exhale* and *How Stella Got Her Groove Back* were made into successful films.

The commercial success of *Waiting to Exhale* has confirmed for some critics the belief that McMillan is more a writer of potboilers than she is a serious novelist. But McMillan, who lives in the San Francisco Bay area, hopes her success will open doors for other African-American writers. To this end, in 1991 McMillan edited *Breaking Ice: An Anthology of Contemporary African-American Fiction*, which includes short stories and book excerpts by fifty-seven African-American writers, ranging from well-known to new voices. ◆

McQueen, Thelma "Butterfly"

JANUARY 7, 1911 – DECEMBER 22, 1995 ● ACTOR

1911 McQueen is born in Tampa, Florida.

1937 McQueen debuts on Broadway in *Brown Sugar.*

1939 McQueen makes film debut in *Gone with the*

1947 McQueen walks out on the *Jack Benny Show.*

1968 McQueen appears off-Broadway in *Curly McDimple.*

1976 McQueen earns a college degree at age sixty-four.

1978 McQueen tours one-woman nightclub act.

1986 McQueen appears in *Mosquito Coast.*

1995 McQueen dies in a fire in her home.

Born in Tampa, Florida, Thelma McQueen grew up in New York City and Augusta, Georgia. She began her acting career in New York as part of Venezuela Jones's Theater Group for Negro Youth, appearing as part of the Butterfly Ballet in *A Midsummer Night's Dream*. From this ballet she earned the nickname Butterfly. In 1937 she made her Broadway debut in *Brown Sugar*, then went on to appear in other shows, including *What a Life* and *You Can't Take It with You*.

McQueen is best known for her Hollywood debut as the silly maid Prissy in *Gone with the Wind* (1939). McQueen was aware of the stereotypical nature of the role and worked successfully to lessen the offensive nature of the role, refusing, for example, to eat watermelon on camera. She was similarly reluctant to deliver her notorious line, "Lawdy, Miz Scarlett . . . I don't know nuthin' 'bout birthin' babies," feeling it was demeaning. McQueen played a variety of similar roles during the following years, in such films as *Duel in the Sun* (1945) and *Mildred Pierce* (1946), as well as in the independently produced, all-black film *Killer Diller* (1948). She also acted in radio and television roles. However, McQueen was so frustrated by being typecast in stereotypical black servant roles that in 1947, after walking out of the *Jack Benny Show*, she quit acting for a year, and in the 1950s gave up acting entirely. For some years she worked in factories and as a waitress; eventually she opened her own restaurant in Augusta, Georgia, where she also ran a radio talk show.

In 1968 McQueen made a well-publicized and well-received return to acting when she appeared in the off-Broadway play *Curly McDimple*. In 1972 she returned to school, and in 1976, at the age of sixty-four, McQueen received her bachelor's degree from the City College of New York. Beginning in 1978, she toured in a one-woman nightclub act. She also wrote, produced, and starred in a bilingual play tribute to Mary McLeod Bethune. Although she occasionally appeared in films such as *Mosquito Coast* (1986), during the 1980s and early 1990s McQueen was deeply involved in teaching drama to African-American and Latino children in pro-

Butterfly McQueen (right) as Prissy and Vivien Leigh as Scarlett O'Hara in a scene from the 1939 movie *Gone with the Wind.*

jects at the Marcus Garvey Mount Morris Welfare Center and P.S. 153 in the Bronx. McQueen died in 1995 from burns received when a kerosene heater caught fire in her home. ◆

McRae, Carmen

APRIL 8, 1922 – NOVEMBER 10, 1994 ● JAZZ SINGER

B orn in New York City, Carmen McRae studied piano as a child and won an Apollo Theater amateur night contest as a pianist-singer. She began her singing career with Benny Carter's orchestra in 1944. In 1948 she began performing regularly in Chicago, where she lived for nearly four years before returning to New York. By 1952 she was the intermission pianist at Minton's in Harlem, a birthplace of **bebop.** Married briefly to bop drummer Kenny Clarke, she made her first records under the name Carmen Clarke. Influenced by both Billie Holiday and Sarah Vaughan, she was named "best new female singer" by *Down Beat* in 1954, after which she signed a recording contract with Decca Records, for whom she recorded until 1959. Following a move to Los Angeles in the

bebop: jazz characterized by complex harmonies, often played very fast.

1960s, McRae made recordings for a number of different labels including Columbia, Mainstream, Atlantic, Concord, and Novus.

McRae remained an active presence on the international jazz scene, appearing regularly at clubs and festivals until May 1991, when she withdrew from public performance because of failing health. She is one of the important singers who integrated bebop into her vocal style, combining **bop** phrasing and **inflection** with sensitivity for the lyrics and dynamics of her material. Among her notable recordings are collections of songs associated with other jazz greats including Billie Holiday (released in 1962), Nat "King" Cole (1984), Thelonious Monk (1991), and Sarah Vaughan (1991). She died at her home in Beverly Hills, California, after suffering a stroke. ◆

bop: bebop.

inflection: change in pitch or tone in music and in speaking or singing.

Morrison, Toni

FEBRUARY 18, 1931 – ● WRITER

By the 1980s Toni Morrison was considered by the literary world to be one of the major American novelists. In 1992—five years after she received the Pulitzer Prize for *Beloved* and the year of publication both for her sixth novel, *Jazz*, and for a series of lectures on American literature, *Playing in the Dark*—Morrison was being referred to internationally as one of the greatest American writers of all time. In 1993 she became the first black woman in history to be awarded the Nobel Prize for literature.

The road to prominence began with Morrison's birth into a family she describes as a group of storytellers. Born Chloe Anthony Wofford in Lorain, Ohio, she was the second of four children of George Wofford (a steel-mill welder, car washer, and construction and shipyard worker) and Ramah Willis Wofford (who worked at home and sang in church).

Her grandparents came to the North from Alabama to escape poverty and racism. Her father's and mother's experiences with and responses to racial violence and economic inequality, as well as what Morrison learned about living in an economically cooperative neighborhood, have influenced the political edge of her art. Her early understanding of the "recognized and verifiable principles of Black art," principles she heard demonstrated in her family's stories and saw demonstrated in the art and play of black people around her, has also had its effect. Morrison's ability to manipulate the linguistic qualities of both black art and conventional literary form manifests itself in a prose that some critics have described as lyrical and vernacular at the same time.

After earning a B.A. from Howard University in 1953, Morrison moved to Cornell University for graduate work in English and received an M.A. in 1955. She taught at Texas Southern University from 1955 to 1957 and then at Howard University (until 1964), where she met and married Harold Morrison, a

"To get to a place where you could love anything you chose, not to need permission for desire, that was freedom."
Toni Morrison,
Beloved, 1987

Toni Morrison's Nobel Prize

When the Swedish Academy awarded the Nobel Prize for literature to Toni Morrison in 1993, she was the first African-American writer so honored. The Academy's award citation praised Morrison for "novels characterized by visionary force and poetic import," that give "life to an essential aspect of American reality." In her Nobel lecture, delivered as she accepted the award in Stockholm, Morrison told a parable about an elderly blind woman who is confronted by a group of young people. The youngsters ask the woman to tell them whether a bird that one of them holds is alive or dead. They laugh when the woman's blindness prevents her from answering, so the old woman reprimands them for asserting their power by taking control of the bird's frail life. The young people respond that their hands are empty, they have no bird at all, and had tricked her to get her to speak to them. Morrison explained that the bird may signify many things, but she chooses to interpret the bird as language and the old women as a practiced writer. The old woman sees language as "a living thing over which one has control" and she is worried about how the young people have used it to deceive and mock her. The children, however, remind her of her responsibility to speak to them and help them understand their lives. With this parable, Morrison expressed her sense of the responsibilities of those who use and control language, as well as the trust that must exist between writer and reader, and she acknowledged the Nobel Prize as a symbol of that responsibility and trust.

1931 Morrison is born in Lorain, Ohio.

1953 Morrison graduates from Howard University.

1955 Morrison earns an M.A. at Cornell University.

1964 Morrison moves to New York and begins working as an editor.

1970 Morrison publishes first novel, *The Bluest Eye*.

1977 Morrison publishes *Song of Solomon*.

1987 Morrison publishes *Beloved*, which wins the Pulitzer Prize.

1988 Morrison becomes professor at Princeton University.

1992 Morrison publishes *Jazz*.

1993 Morrison is awarded Nobel Prize for literature.

1998 Morrison publishes *Paradise*.

Jamaican architect, and gave birth to two sons. Those were years that Morrison has described as a period of almost complete powerlessness, when she wrote quietly and participated in a writers' workshop, creating the story that would become *The Bluest Eye*.

In 1964 Morrison divorced her husband and moved to Syracuse, New York, where she began work for Random House. She later moved to a senior editor's position at the Random House headquarters in New York City—continuing to teach, along the way, at various universities. Since 1988 she has been Robert F. Goheen Professor of the Humanities at Princeton University.

Morrison's first novel, *The Bluest Eye* (1970), is a text that combines formal "play" between literary aesthetics and pastoral imagery with criticism of the effects of racialized personal aesthetics. *Sula* (1973) takes the pattern of the heroic quest and the artist-outsider theme and disrupts both in a novel that juxtaposes those figurations with societal gender restrictions amid the historical constraint of racism. *Song of Solomon* (1977), *Tar Baby* (1981), and *Beloved* (1987) are engagements with the relation to history of culturally specific political dynamics, aesthetics, and ritualized cultural practices.

Song of Solomon sets group history within the parameters of a family romance; *Tar Baby* interweaves the effects of colonialism and multiple family interrelationships that are stand-ins for history with surreal descriptions of landscape; and *Beloved* negotiates narrative battles over story and history produced as a result of the imagination's inability to make sense of slavery. In *Jazz*, Morrison continues her engagement with the problems and productiveness of individual storytelling's relation to larger, public history.

Morrison's seventh novel, *Paradise* (1998), concerns an all-black township in Oklahoma and the interaction of its residents with four troubled women who live in an abandoned school nearby.

The lectures published as *Playing in the Dark* continue Morrison's interest in history and narrative. The collection abstracts her ongoing dialogue with literary criticism and history around manifestations of race and racism as narrative forms themselves produced by (and producers of) the social effects of racism in the larger public imagination.

Morrison's work sets its own unique imprimatur on that public imagination as much as it does on the literary world. A consensus has emerged that articulates the importance of Morrison to the world of letters and demonstrates the permeability of the boundary between specific cultural production—the cultural production that comes out of living as part of the African-American group—and the realm of cultural production that critics perceive as having crossed boundaries between groups and nation-states.

Morrison's ability to cross the boundaries as cultural commentator is reflected in *Race-ing Justice and Engendering Power: Essays on Anita Hill, Clarence Thomas, and the Construction of Social Reality*, a collection of essays about the nomination of Supreme Court Justice Clarence Thomas and the accusations of sexual harassment brought against him by law professor Anita Hill. The essays in the collection were written by scholars from various fields, then edited and introduced by Morrison. ◆

> *"At some point in life the world's beauty becomes enough. You don't need to photograph, paint or even remember it. It is enough."*
> Toni Morrison,
> *Tar Baby*, 1981

Moseley-Braun, Carol

AUGUST 16, 1947 – ● POLITICIAN

Carol Moseley was born and raised in Chicago, the daughter of a Chicago police officer. She was educated at public schools in Chicago and the University of Illinois at Chicago, and received a law degree from the University of Chicago in 1972. Although now divorced, she has used her married name throughout her public career but hyphenated it after joining the Senate.

Moseley-Braun worked for three years as a prosecutor in the U.S. Attorney's office in Chicago. For her work there she won the U.S. Attorney General's Special Achievement Award. She began her career in politics in 1978, when she successfully campaigned for a seat in the Illinois House of Representatives. While in the Illinois House she was an advocate for public education funding, particularly for schools in Chicago. She also sponsored a number of bills banning discrimination in housing and private clubs. After two terms Moseley-Braun became the

> *"It is not only our generational responsibility, but our patriotic duty to ensure that our children inherit no less from us than we did from our parents."*
> Carol Moseley-
> Braun

first woman and first African American elected assistant majority leader in the Illinois legislature.

In 1987 Moseley-Braun again set a precedent by becoming the first woman and first African American to hold executive office in Cook County government when she was elected to the office of Cook County Recorder of Deeds. She held the office through 1992, when she waged a campaign for the U.S. Senate. When she defeated two-term incumbent Alan Dixon and wealthy Chicago attorney Al Hofeld in the Democratic primary, Moseley-Braun became the first black woman nominated for the Senate by a major party in American history. Moseley-Braun then went on to defeat Republican nominee Rich Williamson in a close general election, becoming the first black woman to hold a seat in the U.S. Senate.

During her first year in the Senate Moseley-Braun sponsored several pieces of civil rights legislation, including the Gender Equity in Education Act and the 1993 Violence Against Women Act, and reintroduced the Equal Rights Amendment.

In 1993 Moseley-Braun made an impassioned speech in the Senate encouraging colleagues to vote against renewing a **patent** on the insignia of the United Daughters of the Confederacy, which featured the Confederate flag. Moseley-Braun implored the mainly white, male Senate to recognize the flag as a painful reminder of slavery to her people. The senate voted down the patent, and media sources applauded Moseley-Braun's success.

In 1994 Moseley-Braun authored and passed the Education **Infrastructure** Act to rebuild aging schools, and she cosponsored the Family and Medical Leave Act of 1994. She supported the North American Free Trade Agreement and worked to increase grants and loans for Illinois farmers.

In January 1995 Moseley-Braun became the first woman appointed to a full term on the powerful Senate Finance Com-

patent: an official document conferring an exclusive right or privilege.

infrastructure: the underlying framework of a system or organization.

mittee. She kept her seat on the Senate Banking Committee and gave up a spot on the Senate Judiciary Committee.

In spite of these accomplishments, controversies that began during her campaign grew around Moseley-Braun. Shortly after her election, the Federal Elections Commission audited her campaign, finding disorderly records but filing no charges. Allegations had surfaced that Moseley-Braun and Kgosie Matthews, her campaign manager and former fiancé, may have used hundreds of thousands of dollars of campaign money for expensive personal trips, clothing, and jewelry. The Internal Revenue Service sought to investigate her in 1995, but the U.S. Justice Department denied the request. However, the Congressional Accountability Project, a private watchdog group, filed a complaint against Moseley-Braun relating to the charges.

Moseley-Braun's most notorious misstep came in 1996, when she made trips to Nigeria and met with dictator Sani Abacha, who had been condemned by the Clinton administration for executing political opponents. Although Moseley-Braun defended her trip as a personal vacation, Matthews was registered with the U.S. Justice Department as a lobbyist for Nigeria.

By the 1998 senatorial race, when she was up for reelection, Moseley-Braun had lost many of the supporters who had voted her into the Senate—blacks and middle-class women. Her Republican opponent was Illinois state senator Peter Fitzgerald, a conservative banking heir who campaigned on a platform of lower taxes and family values. Fitzgerald spent lavishly on ads criticizing Moseley-Braun's controversial actions. Moseley-Braun called Fitzgerald a wealthy extremist trying to buy a U.S. Senate seat. Major Illinois newspapers endorsed Fitzgerald, though, and Moseley-Braun made a last-ditch effort to reach voters by acknowledging she had "made some mistakes" in office.

Many of Chicago's black voters turned out on November 3, 1998, and the election was close. Late into the night, the two candidates wavered around 5 to 10 percentage points apart in the vote tally. Finally, at 1:30 Wednesday morning, Moseley-Braun conceded defeat. She had earned 45 percent of the votes, but Fitzgerald won with 52 percent. It was a dramatic fall for Moseley-Braun, who had been swept into the Senate in what came to be called the "Year of the Woman."

1947 Moseley-Braun is born in Chicago.

1978 Moseley-Braun is elected to Illinois House of Representatives.

1987 Moseley-Braun is elected Cook County Recorder of Deeds.

1992 Moseley-Braun is elected to U.S. Senate.

1993 Moseley-Braun defeats patent featuring Confederate flag.

1994 Moseley-Braun passes the Education Infrastructure Act.

1995 Moseley-Braun becomes first full-term woman on Senate Finance Committee.

1996 Moseley-Braun visits Nigerian dictator.

1998 Moseley-Braun is defeated in reelection race.

On November 5, 1998, Moseley-Braun declared that she would never run for public office again. "Read my lips," she told a Chicago Tribune reporter. "Not. Never. Nein. Nyet." However, she reflected on her contribution as the first black female senator. "It seemed to me the whole idea was moving the American dream one step further, moving it closer to the level of inclusion that we'd all like to think that it really represents." ◆

Motley, Constance Baker

SEPTEMBER 14, 1921 – ● LAWYER AND JUDGE

1921 Motley is born in Connecticut.

1943 Motley graduates from New York University.

1945 Motley becomes law clerk for Thurgood Marshall.

1946 Motley graduates from Columbia Law School.

1954 Motley helps write briefs for *Brown* v. *Board of Education*.

1964 Motley is elected to the New York Senate.

1966 Motley is appointed a federal judge.

1982 Motley becomes chief judge of her court.

Constance Baker Motley was the first African-American woman to be elected to the New York State Senate, the first woman to be elected Manhattan borough president, and the first black woman to be appointed a federal judge. She was born in New Haven, Connecticut, to immigrants from the Caribbean island of Nevis. She graduated from high school with honors in 1939, but could not afford college. Impressed by her participation in a public discussion and by her high school record, Clarence Blakeslee, a local white businessman, offered to pay her college expenses.

Motley enrolled at Fisk University in February 1941, transferred to New York University, and received a bachelor's degree in economics in October 1943. She enrolled at Columbia Law School in February 1944 and graduated in 1946. In 1945, during her final year at Columbia, she began to work part-time as a law clerk for Thurgood Marshall at the NAACP Legal Defense and Educational Fund, and continued full-time after graduation, eventually becoming one of its associate counsels. Because Marshall's staff was small and there was little work being done in civil rights, Motley had the unusual opportunity to try major cases before circuit courts of appeal and the United States Supreme Court. From 1949 to 1964 she tried cases, primarily involving desegregation, in eleven southern states and the District of Columbia, including cases that desegregated the University of Mississippi (*Meredith* v. *Fair*, 1962) and the University of Georgia (*Homes* v. *Danner*, 1961). She helped write the briefs for the landmark desegregation case *Brown* v. *Board of Education*

(1954), and won nine of the ten cases she argued before the Supreme Court.

She left the NAACP in 1964 to run for the New York State Senate, to which she was elected in February 1964, becoming only the second woman elected to that body. She left the Senate in February 1965, when she was elected Manhattan **borough** president, becoming only the third black to hold this office. On January 25, 1966, President Lyndon B. Johnson appointed her to the bench of the United States District Court for the Southern District of New York. She was confirmed in August 1966, becoming both the first black and the first woman to be a federal judge in that district. On June 1, 1982, she became the chief judge of her court, serving in this position until October 1, 1986, when she became a senior judge. ◆

borough: one of five political divisions of New York City.

Nash, Diane Bevel

MAY 15, 1938 – ● CIVIL RIGHTS ACTIVIST

Diane Nash gained celebrity when she confronted the mayor of Nashville and forced him to admit that local lunch counters should be desegregated.

Diane Nash was born in Chicago. She was raised in a middle-class Roman Catholic household and attended Howard University in Washington, D.C. In 1959 she transferred to Fisk University in Nashville, Tennessee, majoring in English. In Nashville she was confronted by rigid racial segregation for the first time in her life, and later that year, she joined with other students from local colleges to organize protests against racism and segregation. She also began to attend nonviolence workshops led by James Lawson, a student of Mahatma Gandhi's theories of nonviolent resistance. Skeptical at first, Nash found the concept of moral resistance highly compatible with her strong religious beliefs and came to embrace nonviolence as a way of life.

Nash was elected chairperson of the Student Central Committee and was one of the key participants in sit-ins in local department stores in Nashville that began in February 1960. Nash's picture was printed in the local newspaper and she was often quoted as the spokesperson for the emerging student movement. She gained more celebrity when she confronted Nashville's mayor Ben West during a protest demonstration and forced him to admit that he felt local lunch counters should be desegregated.

In April 1960 Nash was one of the founding members of the Student Nonviolent Coordinating Committee (SNCC) in Raleigh, North Carolina. In February 1961 she and a group of ten other students were arrested in Rock Hill, South Carolina, for civil rights activities and refused the opportunity for bail.

Their actions dramatized racial injustice, popularized the plight of African Americans in the South, and set a precedent of "jail, no bail" that was followed by many other activists during the civil rights movement.

In May 1961 SNCC activists recommenced Freedom Rides, after the violent southern white response to the initial Freedom Rides led the Congress of Racial Equality (CORE) to discontinue them. Leaving Fisk to devote herself full time to the movement, Nash played a pivotal role as coordinator of the SNCC Freedom Rides, serving as liaison with governmental officials and the press. Later that year she was appointed head of direct action in SNCC, married James Bevel, a fellow civil rights activist, and moved to Jackson, Mississippi, where she continued her commitment to social activism. (She adopted her husband's last name as her middle name.) In August 1962 Nash and Bevel moved to Georgia and both became involved in the Southern Christian Leadership Conference (SCLC).

The couple proved to be a highly effective organizing team and played an integral role in organizing many SCLC campaigns including the 1964–65 Selma voting rights campaign. In 1965 they were awarded the Rosa Parks Award from SCLC for their commitment to achieving social justice through nonviolent direct action.

Diane Nash's prominent role in the student sit-in movement made her one of the few well-known female activists of the civil rights movement. She has maintained an unwavering commitment to black empowerment and over the years has broadened the scope of her activism to include antiwar protest and issues of economic injustice. Now divorced, Nash has remained politically active in the 1980s and '90s, living and teaching in Chicago, doing tenant organizing, and advocating housing reform. ◆

1938	Nash is born in Chicago.
1959	Nash attends James Lawson's nonviolence workshops.
1960	Nash helps establish SNCC.
1961	Nash refuses bail after being arrested in South Carolina sit-in.
1962	Nash becomes involved in the Southern Christian Leadership Conference.
1964	Nash begins work on the Selma voting rights campaign.
1965	Nash and husband James Bevel receive Rosa Parks Award.

Naylor, Gloria

JANUARY 25, 1950 – ● WRITER

Gloria Naylor was born in New York City to Roosevelt and Alberta Naylor. After traveling through New York, Florida, and North Carolina as a missionary for the

Jehovah's Witnesses (1968–75) she returned to New York, where she worked as a telephone operator at various hotels while she attended Brooklyn College (B.A., 1981). She received an M.A. in Afro-American Studies from Yale University in 1983.

Naylor's first published work, *The Women of Brewster Place* (1982), won the American Book Award for best first novel in 1983. Dealing with the lives of seven black women who live on one ghetto street, the novel conveys the oppression and spiritual strength that African-American women share. At the same time, by exploring the characters' differences, it emphasizes the variety of their experience. Naylor wrote a television screenplay adaptation of the novel, which starred Oprah Winfrey and appeared on *American Playhouse* in 1984. Her next novel, *Linden Hills* (1985), is concerned with the spiritual decay of a group of black Americans who live in an affluent community, having forsaken their heritage in favor of material gain. *Mama Day*, published in 1988, tells of an elderly lady with magical powers. The best-selling *Bailey's Cafe* (1992) takes place in a 1940s American diner where neighborhood prostitutes congregate. Naylor wrote a play based on the novel that was produced and performed by the Hartford Stage Company in 1994. She also wrote the screenplay for the PBS presentation *In Our Own Words* (1985). Naylor's 1998 novel, *The Men of Brewster Place*, is a collection of portraits featuring the male inhabitants of the urban neighborhood setting of her first novel.

Naylor has said that she writes because her perspective, that of the black American woman, has been "underrepresented in American literature." Her goal is to present the diversity of the black experience. Although she reworks traditional Western sources in her novels, borrowing the structure of Dante's *Inferno* for *Linden Hills*, and elements of Shakespeare's *The Tempest* for *Mama Day*, Naylor utilizes black vernacular and other aspects of her own heritage in her writing.

Naylor has taught at George Washington University, New York University, Princeton, Cornell, and Boston University. She has received a National Endowment for the Arts Fellowship (1985), the Distinguished Writer Award from the Mid-Atlantic Writers Association (1983), the Candace Award from the National Coalition of 100 Black Women (1986), and a Guggenheim Fellowship (1988). ◆

> *"Like an ebony phoenix, each in her own time and with her own season had a story."*
> Gloria Naylor, *The Women of Brewster Place*, 1982

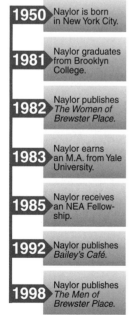

1950 Naylor is born in New York City.

1981 Naylor graduates from Brooklyn College.

1982 Naylor publishes *The Women of Brewster Place*.

1983 Naylor earns an M.A. from Yale University.

1985 Naylor receives an NEA Fellowship.

1992 Naylor publishes *Bailey's Café*.

1998 Naylor publishes *The Men of Brewster Place*.

Norman, Jessye

SEPTEMBER 15, 1945 – ● OPERA SINGER

Born in Augusta, Georgia, Jessye Norman was a soprano of promise from an early age. At sixteen she entered the Marian Anderson competitions, and although she did not win, she auditioned at Howard University with Carolyn Grant. Her acceptance was delayed until she completed high school. She followed her undergraduate training at Howard (B. Music, 1967) with summer study at the Peabody Conservatory under Alice Duschak before enrolling at the University of Michigan for study with Elizabeth Mannion and Pierre Bernac.

A travel grant allowed Norman to enter the International Music Competition in Munich in 1968, where she won first place with performances of Dido's Lament (Henry Purcell) and "Voi lo sapete" from Pietro Mascagni's *Cavalleria rusticana*. She was immediately engaged for her operatic debut as Elisabeth in Richard Wagner's *Tannhäuser* by the Deutsche Oper (1969), with which she later appeared in Giuseppe Verdi's *Aida* and *Don Carlo*, Meyerbeer's *L'Africaine*, and as the Countess in Mozart's *Le nozze di Figaro*. In 1972 she sang Aida at La Scala and Cassandre in Covent Garden's production of Berlioz's *Les Troyens*, making her recital debuts in London and New York the next year.

Norman's American stage debut came on November 22, 1982, when she appeared as both Jocasta in *Oedipus Rex* (Stravinsky) and Dido in Purcell's *Dido and Aeneas* with the Opera Company of Philadelphia. The following year, she made her debut with the Metropolitan Opera as Cassandre in Berlioz's *Les Troyens*, subsequently offering a performance as Didon in the same opera, as well as the Prima Donna and Ariadne in *Ariadne auf Naxos* (Richard Strauss).

> *"The very best that could happen to a voice if it shows any promise at all is to leave it alone when it is very young, to let it develop naturally and let the person go on for as long as possible with the sheer joy of singing."*
>
> Jessye Norman, quoted in *American Visions*, April 1988

1945 Norman is born in Georgia.

1967 Norman graduates from Howard University.

1968 Norman wins first place at Munich's International Music Competition.

1969 Norman debuts in Wagner's *Tannhäuser* at the Deutsche Oper.

1972 Norman stars in *Aida* at La Scala.

1982 Norman makes her American stage debut in Philadelphia.

1983 Norman debuts with the Metropolitan Opera in *Les Troyens*.

As recitalist, guest orchestral soloist, presenter of master classes, and recording artist, Norman was acknowledged as a musician of the highest rank. She was heard in nearly every major American city by 1990 and appeared frequently in telecasts starting in 1979 when she gave a concert version of the first act of Wagner's *Die Walküre* with the Boston Symphony Orchestra conducted by Seiji Ozawa.

Norman has excelled in French and German repertories, stylistically and linguistically, while remaining faithful to her roots in the spiritual. With a voice ranging from a dark mezzo-soprano to a dramatic soprano, she has not hesitated to reintroduce works outside of the mainstream repertory (e.g., Gluck and Haydn operas), or to perform songs of the musical theater. She has appeared on numerous recordings, including Beethoven's *Fidelio*; Berlioz's *Mort de Cléopatre*; Bizet's *Carmen*; Gluck's *Alceste*; Mahler's *Das Lied von der Erde*; Offenbach's *Tales of Hoffmann*; Purcell's *Dido and Aeneas*; Schoenberg's *Gurre-Lieder*; Strauss's *Four Last Songs* and *Ariadne auf Naxos*; Verdi's *Aida*, Wagner's *Lohengrin* and *Die Walküre*; and Weber's *Euryanthe*. Other notable recordings include *Spirituals*, *Spirituals in Concert* (with Kathleen Battle), and *Jessye Norman at Notre-Dame*. ◆

Norton, Eleanor Holmes

JUNE 13, 1937 – ● CIVIL RIGHTS LEADER

"This country would go bankrupt in a day if the Supreme Court suddenly ordained the powers that be to pay back wages to children of slaves and to women who have worked all their lives for half pay or no pay."
Eleanor Holmes Norton, 1970

Born in Washington, D.C., Eleanor Holmes graduated from Antioch College in 1960, and received an M.A. in American history from Yale University in 1963 and a law degree from Yale in 1965. Norton was a leader of the Student Non-Violent Coordinating Committee (SNCC), and was a participant in the Mississippi Freedom Democratic Party. In 1965 Holmes joined the American Civil Liberties Union (ACLU), where she served as a civil rights lawyer for five years. In 1967 she married Edward Norton, also a lawyer. The couple, who were separated in 1992, had two children. In 1968 Eleanor Holmes Norton gained attention for her active defense of freedom of speech when she represented segregationist presidential candidate George Wallace in his struggle to obtain permission

Eleanor Holmes Norton (front row, right) with President Carter and fellow cabinet members Patricia Derian and Virginia McCarty in 1977.

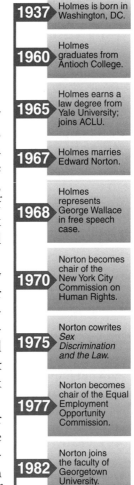

1937 Holmes is born in Washington, DC.

1960 Holmes graduates from Antioch College.

1965 Holmes earns a law degree from Yale University; joins ACLU.

1967 Holmes marries Edward Norton.

1968 Holmes represents George Wallace in free speech case.

1970 Norton becomes chair of the New York City Commission on Human Rights.

1975 Norton cowrites *Sex Discrimination and the Law.*

1977 Norton becomes chair of the Equal Employment Opportunity Commission.

1982 Norton joins the faculty of Georgetown University.

1990 Norton is elected to U.S. House of Representatives.

from the City of New York for a rally at Shea Stadium. Keenly interested in fighting both race and gender discrimination, Norton published an article on black women in the well-known anthology *Sisterhood Is Powerful* (1970). "If women were suddenly to achieve equality with men tomorrow," she wrote, "black women would continue to carry the entire array of utterly oppressive handicaps associated with race. . . . Yet black women cannot—must not—avoid the truth about their special subservience. They are women with all that that implies."

In 1970 Norton was appointed chair of the New York City Commission on Human Rights by Mayor John Lindsay. Her achievement in detailing and correcting discriminatory practices led to a position as cohost of a weekly local television program on civil rights. In 1973 Norton helped organize a National Conference of Black Feminists, and in 1975 she co-wrote *Sex Discrimination and the Law: Cases and Remedies*, a law textbook dealing with legal remedies to gender inequality.

In 1977 President Jimmy Carter appointed Norton as chair of the Equal Employment Opportunity Commission, a post she held until 1981. Charged with investigating complaints of discrimination, Norton was a visible and respected force within the Administration. In 1982 she accepted a post as professor of labor law at Georgetown University. Throughout the 1980s she was also a regular media commentator on civil rights and affirmative action issues.

In 1990 Norton announced her candidacy for the position of District of Columbia delegate to the U.S. House of Representatives. Despite the revelation during the campaign that she owed back taxes, she was elected to Congress. She soon won praise even from her opponents for her involvement in community affairs as well as for her work in assuring Washington's fiscal viability and cutting the District's budget. She also lobbied in Congress for District statehood. In 1992, the same year Norton won reelection, she won attention for her offer to escort women seeking abortion information at clinics past antiabortion picketers, and later for her denunciation of the verdict in the Rodney King trial, which she contended was as shameful as the actual beating of King. After the House vote in 1993 to give delegates limited voting privileges on the floor, Norton has become the first District representative to vote in Congress. In recognition of her prestige, President Bill Clinton agreed that as chair of the District of Columbia Subcommittee on Judiciary and Education, Norton would be responsible for the nomination of candidates for local U.S. Attorney and federal judgeships, the first elected District of Columbia official to be privileged.

Norton was reelected to a third term in 1994. When the Republican party took control of Congress in 1995, the Washington, D.C., delegate's floor voting privileges were rescinded. Norton won reelection in 1996 and 1998. She continued to fight for the return of the delegate vote on the house floor and for full congressional representation for Washington, D.C., residents. ◆

O'Leary, Hazel Rollins

MAY 17, 1937 – ● CORPORATE EXECUTIVE

Hazel Rollins was born and raised in the seaport city of Newport News, Virginia. She graduated from Fisk University in Nashville, Tennessee, in 1959 and earned a law degree from Rutgers in 1966. In New Jersey she began a career in law enforcement, serving as an assistant state attorney general and later as an Essex County prosecutor. In the early 1970s O'Leary moved to Washington and became a partner at the accounting firm of Coopers and Lybrand. She later joined the Federal Energy Administration during the Ford presidency. She served in Jimmy Carter's Energy Department as head of the Economic Regulatory Administration. While there, Rollins befriended John F. O'Leary, the deputy energy secretary. The couple married in 1980 and formed an energy consulting firm, O'Leary Associates. John O'Leary died in 1987, and Hazel O'Leary closed the consulting firm.

In 1989 O'Leary was named executive vice president for corporate affairs at the Minneapolis-based Northern States Power Company, one of the largest gas and electric

> *"We have proved we can deliver more for less, and this makes it possible for DOE to contribute $10.6 billion toward President Clinton's plan to provide tax relief to middle-income working taxpayers and to reduce the budget."*
>
> Hazel O'Leary, describing the Energy Department's 1996 budget.

utilities in the Midwest. She was in charge of environmental affairs, public relations, and lobbying. As an energy policy-maker O'Leary advocated decreased dependence on oil and coal, promoted fuel conservation, and helped develop a program at Northern States Power to generate electricity with windmills. She has also been a proponent of nuclear power, and her goals include the creation of safe storage methods for nuclear waste.

The policy of Northern States Power regarding the storage of nuclear waste earned her some criticism from environmental groups. In 1990 Northern States sought to build nuclear storage facilities at Prairie Island, Minnesota, next to the Mdewakan-ton Sioux Indian Reservation. After the Sioux protested, a judge prohibited an expansion of the nuclear waste site. O'Leary then drafted a compromise with regulators that permitted Northern States to open the storage facility on a reduced scale. Her background in energy regulation and her commitment to conservation attracted the attention of President Bill Clinton, who in 1993 offered O'Leary the post of secretary of energy. When confirmed, O'Leary became the first woman ever to hold that post.

During her tenure as secretary of energy, O'Leary promoted the development of alternative fuel and energy technologies. She resigned from the Department of Energy in January 1997 amid allegations that she had violated federal laws by soliciting a $25,000 contribution to Africare, a charitable organization, in return for a meeting with a group of Chinese **petrochemical** officials. In late 1997 Attorney General Janet Reno decided that the charges against O'Leary did not warrant an investigation by an independent counsel. ◆

petrochemical: a chemical derived from petroleum or natural gas.

Osborne, Estelle

1901 – DECEMBER 12, 1981 ● NURSE

Born Geneva Estelle Massey in 1901 in Palestine, Texas, the eighth of eleven children of Hall and Bettye Massey, Estelle Osborne completed Prairie View Teachers College at age sixteen. She taught for two years in rural schools before starting nursing education in October 1920 at St. Louis Hospital no. 2, which later became Homer G. Phillips Hospital. She began a discussion group, which, at her graduation in 1923, became the alumni association. She served as its first president. After achieving the highest score on the Missouri state nurses' examination, she pursued an active career that both enriched her profession and contributed to the health of many people in the South.

As an African-American nurse Osborne accomplished several notable firsts. She earned both bachelor's (1930) and master's (1931) degrees at Teachers College, Columbia University; she was appointed to a committee of the National Organization for Public Health Nursing (1934); she conducted Rosenwald-funded research on poverty and health in the South; she served as superintendent and director of nursing at the Homer G. Phillips School of Nursing in St. Louis (1940); she was a consultant with the National Nursing Council for War Service (1943); she taught at the schools of nursing at Harlem Hospital and New York University (1945); and she represented the American Nurses Association (ANA) at the International Council of Nurses in Stockholm (1949). Her marriage to Akron physician Bedford N. Riddle ended in divorce, and she later married Herman Osborne in New York. There were no children from either marriage.

Osborne filled leadership positions as president of the National Association of Colored Graduate Nurses (1934–39) and as Educational Director of the Freedman's Hospital School of Nursing in Washington, D.C. She was a member of the ANA board of directors (1948–52) and the board of directors of the American Journal of Nursing Company (1951); she was also assistant director for general administration of the National League for Nursing (1954).

In recognition of her achievements, Osborne was honored with the Mary Mahoney Award (1946), membership in the ANA Hall of Fame (1954), and honorary membership in Chi Eta Phi and the American Academy of Nursing (1975). After retirement in 1966, Osborne moved to Oakland, California, where she died on December 12, 1981. The Nurses Educational Fund, Inc., annually offers the Estelle Massey Osborne Memorial Scholarship for an outstanding African-American nurse seeking a master's degree. ◆

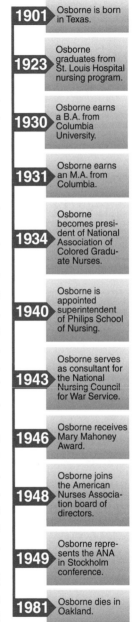

1901 Osborne is born in Texas.

1923 Osborne graduates from St. Louis Hospital nursing program.

1930 Osborne earns a B.A. from Columbia University.

1931 Osborne earns an M.A. from Columbia.

1934 Osborne becomes president of National Association of Colored Graduate Nurses.

1940 Osborne is appointed superintendent of Philips School of Nursing.

1943 Osborne serves as consultant for the National Nursing Council for War Service.

1946 Osborne receives Mary Mahoney Award.

1948 Osborne joins the American Nurses Association board of directors.

1949 Osborne represents the ANA in Stockholm conference.

1981 Osborne dies in Oakland.

Parks, Rosa Louise McCauley

FEBRUARY 4, 1913 – ● CIVIL RIGHTS LEADER

R osa McCauley was born in Tuskegee, Alabama. She lived with relatives in Montgomery, where she finished high school in 1933 and attended Alabama State College. She met her husband, Raymond Parks, a barber, and they married in 1932. Rosa Parks worked as a clerk, an insurance salesperson, and a tailor's assistant at a department store. She was also employed at the time as a part-time seamstress by Virginia and Clifford Durr, two white residents of Montgomery who were staunch supporters of the black freedom struggle.

> *"We didn't have any of what they called Civil Rights back then. It was just a matter of survival—existing from day to day."*
> Rosa Parks, *Blacks in Detroit*, 1980

Parks had been active in civil rights work since the 1930s. She and her husband supported the Scottsboro defendants, a notorious case in which nine young black men were convicted in 1931 on questionable evidence for raping two white women. In 1943 Parks became one of the first women to join the Montgomery NAACP. She worked as a youth adviser, served as secretary for the local group from 1943 to 1956, and helped operate the joint office of the NAACP and the Brotherhood of Sleeping Car Porters. In addition, she worked with the Montgomery Voters League to increase black voter registration. During the summer of 1955, with the encouragement of the Durrs, Parks accepted a scholarship for a workshop for community leaders on school integration at the Highlander Folk School in Tennessee. It was an important experience for Parks, not only for the practical skills of organizing and mobilizing she learned, but because the racial harmony she experienced there nurtured and sustained her activism.

224

Rose Parks in Montgomery, Alabama, in 1956.

1913	McCauley is born in Alabama.
1932	McCauley marries Raymond Parks.
1943	Parks joins Montgomery NAACP.
1955	Parks refuses to give up her seat on a bus.
1957	Parks moves to Detroit and begins working as a seamstress.
1965	Parks participates in the march from Selma to Montgomery.
1979	Parks is awarded the NAACP Spingarn Medal.
1987	Parks founds Rosa and Raymond Parks Institute for Self-Development.

Popularly known as the Mother of the Civil Rights Movement, Parks is best known for her refusal to give up her seat for a white man on a segregated bus in Montgomery on December 1, 1955, an incident that sparked the Montgomery Bus Boycott. Contrary to popular belief, Parks was not simply a tired woman who wanted to rest her feet, unaware of the chain of events she was about to trigger. As she wrote in *Rosa Parks: My Story*, "The only tired I was, was tired of giving in." Parks was a veteran of civil rights activity and was aware of efforts by the Women's Political Council and the local NAACP to find an incident with which they could address segregation in Montgomery.

Parks was actively involved in sustaining the boycott and for a time served on the executive committee of the Montgomery Improvement Association, an organization created to direct the boycott. The **intransigence** of the city council was met by conviction and fortitude on the part of African Americans. For over a year, black people in Montgomery car-pooled,

intransigence: refusal to compromise.

took taxis, and walked to work. The result was a ruling by the United States Supreme Court that segregation on city buses was unconstitutional.

As a result of her involvement in the bus boycott, Parks lost her job at the department store in Montgomery. In 1957 she and her husband moved to Detroit, where she worked as a seamstress for eight years before becoming administrative assistant for Congressman John Conyers, a position she held until 1988. After she moved to Detroit, Parks continued to be active in the Civil Rights Movement and joined the Southern Christian Leadership Conference (SCLC). She participated in numerous marches and rallies, including the 1965 march from Selma to Montgomery.

In the mid-1980s she was a supporter of the free South Africa movement and walked the picket lines in Washington, D.C., with other antiapartheid activists. She has made countless public appearances, speaking out on political issues as well as giving oral history lessons about the civil rights movement. In 1987, ten years after the death of her husband, she founded the Rosa and Raymond Parks Institute for Self-Development in Detroit, a center committed to career training for black youth. The institute, a dream of hers, was created to address the dropout rate of black youth.

Parks, an international symbol of African-American strength, has been given numerous awards and distinctions, including ten honorary degrees. In 1979 she was awarded the NAACP's prestigious Spingarn Medal. In 1980 she was chosen by *Ebony* readers as the living black woman who had done the most to advance the cause of black America. In the same year she was awarded the Martin Luther King Jr. Nonviolent Peace Prize by the Martin Luther King Jr. Center for Nonviolent Social Change. In addition, the SCLC has honored her by sponsoring the annual Rosa Parks Freedom award. ◆

> *"When one's mind is made up, this diminishes fear; knowing what must be done does away with fear."*
> Rosa Parks, *Quiet Strength*, 1994

Plato, Ann

C. 1820 – ? ● POET

All that is known about Ann Plato is that she was the author of *Essays; Including Biographies and Miscellaneous Pieces in Prose and Poetry* (1841) and that she was a member of the Colored Congregational Church, Hartford, Connecticut, of which James W. C. Pennington was pastor. Her birthdate is speculative, her date of death unknown. All other biographical data about Plato rests upon the content of her poems, and inferences based on such work are risky.

Using the evidence of the poems, scholars speculate that she may have had an American Indian father and a brother named Henry, that she joined the church when she was thirteen, that she was a teacher of very young children, and that she was in her early teens when she began to teach.

Essays, the second book published by a black American woman in the United States, is a slight but significant work containing sixteen essays, four biographical **eulogies,** and twenty poems. It is unique as the work of an African American during the mid-nineteenth century, neither slave narrative nor autobiography, decidedly apolitical in concerns and "ladylike" in tone. The content is historically informative, revealing through the brief biographies aspects of the lives of ordinary northern black women at the time and giving expression through the essays of the values espoused by many New England blacks at the time. The poems, of limited metrical variety and clearly the work of a young person, concern themselves largely with morality and mortality and show a lyric gift. ◆

eulogy: a written work highly praising a person.

Price, Mary Violet Leontyne

FEBRUARY 10, 1927 – ● OPERA SINGER

Born in Laurel, Mississippi, the soprano Leontyne Price came to be regarded as a *prima donna assoluta* during her exceptionally long operatic career (1952–85).

Her parents had been involved in the musical life of Laurel, and provided her with piano lessons from the age of four. Soon thereafter, she joined her mother in the church choir and, after attending a recital by Marian Anderson in Jackson, Mississippi, in 1936, she resolved on a career in music. At that time, African-American women could aspire in music only for roles in education, and it was with that major in mind that Price enrolled at Central State College in Ohio. Before she graduated in 1949, however, her vocal talent was manifest and she was encouraged to enter the Juilliard School of Music, where she

"Be black, shine, aim high."
Leontyne Price, 1990

studied with Florence Kimball. As Mistress Ford in a school production of Verdi's *Falstaff*, she attracted the attention of American composer Virgil Thomson, who enlisted her for the role of Cecilia in a 1952 revival of his *Four Saints in Three Acts* (1934), a work calling for an all-black cast, thus initiating her professional career and terminating her formal study.

Following this production in New York and performances at the Paris International Arts Festival, she was engaged for the role of Bess in George Gershwin's *Porgy and Bess,* with which she toured in Berlin, Paris, and Vienna into 1954. In November of that year, she made her New York debut at Town Hall. The following February she appeared in the title role of Puccini's *Tosca* on television, later adding Mozart's *Die Zauberflöte* and *Don Giovanni,* and Poulenc's *Dialogues des Carmélites* to her NBC telecasts. In 1956 she sang the role of Cleopatra in Handel's *Giulio Cesare.*

It was in the Poulenc opera as Madame Lidoine that she made her debut with the San Francisco Opera in 1957, following this with the leading soprano roles with that company in Verdi's *Il Trovatore* and Puccini's *Madama Butterfly* and debuts that year at the Arena di Verona, Covent Garden, and the Vienna Staatsoper (*Aida*). Her debut with the Lyric Opera of Chicago was as Liù in Puccini's *Turandot* (1959).

The Metropolitan Opera had only begun adding black singers to its roster in 1955 with Marian Anderson and Robert McFerrin, followed by the debuts of African-American artists Mattiwilda Dobbs (1956), Gloria Davy (1958), and Martina Arroyo (1959). Actually, Price had already appeared in the Metropolitan Opera Jamboree, a fund-raising broadcast from the Manhattan Ritz Theater, April 6, 1953, when she performed "Summertime" from *Porgy and Bess,* but her formal debut was as Leonora in Verdi's *Il Trovatore* on January 27, 1961, when she won an unprecedented forty-two-minute ovation, fully justifying her selection as the leading lady to open the next Met season (as Minnie in Puccini's *La Fanciulla del West*) and that of the next year (repeating her 1957 Vienna role of Aida, in which she was heard each season for the following five years). During the last six years of the "old Met," she particularly excelled in the Italian repertory (as Liù in Puccini's *Turandot*, Cio-Cio-San in Puccini's *Madama Butterfly*, and Elvira in Verdi's *Ernani*, which she had sung for Herbert von Karajan at the 1962 Salzburg Festival).

The new home of the Metropolitan Opera at Lincoln Center was inaugurated in 1966 with a new opera by Samuel Barber, *Antony and Cleopatra*, written specifically for her. When she concluded her career in opera performances on January 3, 1985, with *Aida* at the Metropolitan Opera, she had proved her interpretive leadership in the Italian repertories of Verdi and Puccini, but she has expanded the previously practiced limits to move far past any stereotypes, excelling in German, Spanish, French, and Slavic works, as well as in spirituals and other American literature. Her principal opera roles, in addition to those mentioned, were the Prima Donna and Ariadne (*Ariadne auf Naxos*), Amelia (*Un Ballo in Maschera*), Fiordiligi (*Così fan Tutte*), Donna Anna (*Don Giovanni*), Tatiana (*Eugene Onegin*), Minnie (*La Fanciulla del West*), Leonora (*La Forza del Destino*), Manon (*Manon Lescaut*), and the title role in *Tosca*.

Her recorded legacy is extensive. In addition to many of the operatic roles in which she appeared on stage—Bizet's *Carmen*, Mozart's *Don Giovanni* and *Così fan Tutte*, Puccini's *Madama Butterfly* and *Tosca*, Verdi's *Aida*, *Un Ballo in Maschera*, *Ernani*, *La Forza del Destino*, and *Il Trovatore*—she has recorded Samuel Barber's *Hermit Songs* and music of Fauré, Poulenc, Wolf, and R. Strauss, as well as Verdi's *Requiem* and Beethoven's *Ninth Symphony*. She has also recorded excerpts from *Porgy and Bess* (with her then-husband William Warfield), an album of popular songs with André Previn (*Right as Rain*), and *Swing Low, Sweet Chariot*, a collection of fourteen spirituals. In 1992 RCA reissued on compact disc forty-seven arias by Price under the title *Leontyne Price: The Prima Donna Collection*, arias that had been recorded between 1965 and 1979. ◆

1927 Price is born in Mississippi.

1936 Price hears Marian Anderson in recital and vows to become a singer.

1949 Price graduates from Central State College in Ohio.

1952 Price appears in *Four Saints in Three Acts* in New York.

1954 Price tours Europe in *Porgy and Bess*.

1957 Price debuts with San Francisco Opera in *Dialogues des Carmélites*.

1961 Price debuts with the Metropolitan Opera in *Il Trovatore*.

1966 Price opens new Metropolitan Opera House with *Antony and Cleopatra*.

1985 Price gives farewell performance in *Aida* at the Metropolitan Opera.

Rainey, Gertrude Pridgett "Ma"

APRIL 26, 1886 – DECEMBER 22, 1939 ● SINGER

Ma Rainey coined the term "blues" after she began singing the mournful songs she had heard a young woman sing along the tent show's route.

One of the most beloved blues and vaudeville singers of the first three decades in the twentieth century, Ma Rainey—"Mother of the Blues"—was born Gertrude Pridgett in Columbus, Georgia. Rainey was the second of five children born to Thomas and Ella Pridgett. She performed in a local show, "A Bunch of Blackberries," at fourteen and married a tent showman, Will Rainey, when she was eighteen. They performed together for several years as a comedy song and dance act, billed as the "Assassinators of the Blues," with the Rabbit Foot Minstrels.

Supposedly Rainey coined the term "blues" after she began singing the mournful songs that she had heard sung by a young woman along the tent show's route. Rainey left her husband after twelve years but continued to follow the TOBA (Theater Owner's Booking Association) circuit as a solo act because she was so popular with country folk, white and black. She sang with **jug bands** as well as small jazz bands, which included at times Tommy Ladnier, Joe Smith, and Coleman Hawkins. She was a seasoned performer who sang about the worries and tribulations of country folk in the traditional style of the rural South. Her subject matter was earthy, her renditions were often comedic, yet she did not resort to trivia.

Rainey's first recording, "Moonshine Blues," was produced by Paramount Records in 1923. She recorded a total of ninety-three songs, which included traditional country/folk blues,

jug band: a band that uses objects such as jugs and washboards and primitive instruments such as kazoos to play folk music.

vaudeville songs, and popular songs. Rainey wrote many of her songs, addressing topics as diverse as the impact of the boll weevil on cotton crops to homosexuality, prostitution, and jail. Although she was overshadowed by her younger counterpart, Bessie Smith, Rainey had a loyal following until her last days on the tent show circuit in the 1930s. She handled her business affairs well and retired to her native city of Columbus, Georgia, where she opened her own theater. She died there on December 22, 1939. ◆

vaudeville: theatrical shows featuring a variety of acts, including dancers, singers, and comedians.

Ray, Charlotte E.

JANUARY 13, 1850 – JANUARY 11, 1911 ● LAWYER

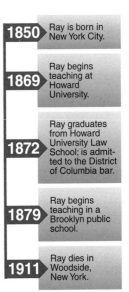

1850 — Ray is born in New York City.

1869 — Ray begins teaching at Howard University.

1872 — Ray graduates from Howard University Law School; is admitted to the District of Columbia bar.

1879 — Ray begins teaching in a Brooklyn public school.

1911 — Ray dies in Woodside, New York.

Born in New York City, Charlotte Ray was one of seven children of the Rev. Charles Bennett Ray and his second wife, Charlotte Augusta Burroughs. Her father was pastor of the Bethesda Congregational Church and publisher and editor of *Colored American*, an early African-American newspaper. Little is known about Ray's early life, but by 1869 she had secured a position teaching in the Normal and Preparatory Department at Howard University.

In February 1872, Ray graduated from Howard University's Law School, becoming the first African-American woman to receive a law degree from any law school in the nation. On March 2, 1872, she was admitted to the bar of the District of Columbia—just three years after the admission of George Boyer Vashon, the District of Columbia's first African-American lawyer. On April 23 she gained admittance to practice before the Supreme Court of the District of Columbia as well. She was the fifth woman in the United States admitted to the bar of any state.

Ray began a private practice in Washington, D.C., specializing in corporate and real estate law. Despite her abilities, the practice failed to attract sufficient clients. Details of her life after this point are vague. By 1879 she apparently had returned to the New York City area to live and had started teaching in a Brooklyn public school. Sometime before the mid-1880s, she was married to a man with the surname Fraim. By 1897 Ray was living in Woodside, New York, where she died in 1911 at the age of sixty. ◆

Remond, Sarah Parker

JUNE 6, 1826 – DECEMBER 13, 1894 ● ABOLITIONIST

1826 Remond is born in Salem.

1832 Remond's mother helps form the Salem Anti-Slavery Society.

1835 Because of her race, Remond is denied admission to the local high school.

1842 Remond begins antislavery lecture tours.

1853 Remond is arrested for refusing to vacate a whites-only seat in a Boston theater.

1859 Remond travels to England to fight for abolition.

1866 Remond returns to America and lobbies for voting rights.

1867 Remond settles in Italy.

1868 Remond receives diploma to practice medicine.

1894 Remond dies in Rome.

orn in Salem, Massachusetts, one of eight children, Sarah Remond was the daughter of John Remond, a black immigrant from Curaçao, and Nancy Lenox Remond, daughter of African-American Revolutionary War veteran Cornelius Lenox. The family was noted for its abolitionist activities. In 1832 Remond's mother helped found the Salem Anti-Slavery Society, and her sister Caroline became an active member. In 1835 her father became a life member of the Massachusetts Anti-Slavery Society, and three years later, her brother, Charles Lenox Remond, began lecturing for the Society. In 1835 Sarah Remond completed grade school, but she was denied admission to the local high school on racial grounds, whereupon the family moved to Newport, Rhode Island, returning to Salem after her graduation in 1841. In July 1842 Remond joined her brother as an antislavery lecturer, and began protesting segregation in churches, theaters, and other public places. In a well-publicized incident in 1853 at Boston's Howard Athenaeum, she refused to vacate a seat in the "whites-only" gallery during an opera. Arrested and thrown down the stairs, she subsequently won $500 in damages in a civil suit. In 1856 she was appointed a lecturing agent of the American Anti-Slavery Society and she and her brother covered the Northeast and Midwest. Antislavery leaders hailed her dignified bearing and eloquent speech.

In 1859 Sarah Remond and her brother left for England in order to further the cause of abolition. Denied a visa to France by the American legation in London, which claimed that because of her color she was not an American citizen, Remond toured Great Britain and Ireland. Bitter about the lack of educational opportunity in America, she welcomed the chance to study in Europe. She may have attended the Bedford College for Ladies in the years 1859 to 1861.

Remond stayed in England through the Civil War, urging the British to support the blockade of the Confederacy and raising money for freed slaves. In 1866 she returned to the United States. She attended the New York Constitutional Convention, where she lobbied unsuccessfully for universal suffrage. In 1867 Remond went back to Europe and settled in Italy, where she spent the rest of her life. She is believed to have studied medicine at the Santa Maria Nuova Hospital in Florence. Remond received her diploma for "Professional Medical Practice" in 1868, married Lorenzo Pintor in 1877, and died in Rome seven years later. ◆

Ringgold, Faith

OCTOBER 8, 1930 –   ● PAINTER AND SCULPTOR

Born in Harlem, Faith Ringgold was one of three children of Andrew Louis Jones Sr. and Willi Posey Jones, a fashion designer. She was married to Robert Earl Wallace, a pianist, from 1950 to 1956 and had two daughters in 1952: Michele, an author, and Barbara, a linguist. Ringgold graduated from City College, New York, in 1955, and taught art in New York public schools until 1973. In 1959 she received a master's degree, also from City College. She began spending summers in Provincetown, Massachusetts, in 1957, took her first trip to Europe in 1961, and married Burdette Ringgold in 1962.

Ringgold's work and life exemplify her interests in civil rights and feminism. Some of her early paintings, such as *The Flag Is Bleeding* (1967) are large with stylized figures; others are abstract, like *Flag for the Moon, Die Nigger* (1969). Her radical use of potent national symbols, such as the flag and, later, postage stamps and maps, fiercely counterpointed American values with their ingrained racism. To achieve greater recognition for blacks and women in the mainstream art world, Ringgold participated in demonstrations at the Whitney Museum (1968, 1970) and at the Museum of Modern Art (1968). She was a cofounder in 1971 of Where We At, a group of black women artists. The following year she created a mural at the Women's House of Detention in New York that used only images of women.

The women's movement and Ringgold's close relationship with her mother influenced her to begin using fabrics, traditionally a women's medium, to express her art. She began to make masks and dolls—soft sculptures. Her mother made the dolls' clothes. They portray, among others, the Rev. Dr. Martin

> *"I think about the characters and the story I want to tell and then I begin to write the chapters in segments. And then, just like the materials of a quilt, I piece the words together until they make a story."*
>
> Faith Ringgold

1930 Ringgold is born in New York City.

1955 Ringgold graduates from City College, New York.

1959 Ringgold earns an M.A. from City College.

1961 Ringgold travels to Europe.

1967 Ringgold paints *The Flag Is Bleeding.*

1971 Ringgold cofounds Where We At, a group for black women artists.

1972 Ringgold paints mural at New York's Women's House of Detention.

1979 Ringgold and her mother produce Sew Real doll kits.

1983 Ringgold produces first story quilt, *Who's Afraid of Aunt Jemima?*

1992 Ringgold publishes children's book, *Tar Beach.*

Luther King Jr., the murdered children of Atlanta (the Atlanta child murder cases of 1979–82), and various people in the community. Some of Ringgold's paintings were bordered in tankas, cloth frames made by her mother. Ringgold and her mother also collaborated on the production of Sew Real doll kits in 1979.

Ringgold then began working in the medium that brought her acclaim, story quilts. The first, *Who's Afraid of Aunt Jemima?* (1983), is a visual narrative of a woman restaurateur in painting, text, and patchwork. The quilts' stories vividly raise the issues of racism and feminism. As the stories became more complex, Ringgold began to create multiple quilts to encompass them. Each consists of a large painted panel bordered by printed patches pieced together, with text at the bottom. The quilt series are *The Bitter Nest* (1988), *Woman on the Bridge* (1988), and *The French Connection* (1991). Ringgold used one of her quilts as the basis for a children's book, *Tar Beach,* which was a Caldecott Honor Book and received the Coretta Scott King award in 1992. The original quilt was acquired by the Guggenheim Museum.

Ringgold's awards include a grant from the National Endowment for the Arts (1989), Warner Communications' Wonder Woman (1983), and the National Coalition of 100 Black Women's Candace (1986). She holds honorary degrees from Moore College of Art and the College of Wooster, Ohio. A twenty-five-year retrospective of her work traveled between 1990 and 1993. Ringgold has taught at the University of California at San Diego since 1984, spending half the year there. Her designs from *Street Story Quilt* were selected by Judith Lieber for a limited edition of jeweled evening bags. Some of Ringgold's works are in the High, Metropolitan, Newark, and Modern Art museums, as well as in private collections. ◆

Rolle, Esther

C. NOVEMBER 8, 1920 – NOVEMBER 17, 1998 ● ACTOR

Esther Rolle was born in Pompano Beach, California, probably in 1920, the tenth of eighteen children of parents of Bahamian descent. After her family relocated in Florida, she finished Booker T. Washington High School in

Miami, and attended Spelman College in Atlanta for one year before moving to New York City. There, Rolle supported herself by working at a pocketbook factory while trying to break into theater. She was taking drama classes at George Washington Carver School in Harlem when she obtained a scholarship to study acting at New York's innovative New School for Social Research.

During this time, Rolle was introduced to African dance master Asadata Dafora and became a member of his dance troupe, Shogola Oloba. After many years with the troupe, she became its director in 1960. During her dancing career Rolle continued to pursue her interest in theater, and in 1962 she made her professional acting debut as Felicity in Jean Genet's *The Blacks*. Rolle worked in theater throughout the early 1960s, appearing in such productions as *Blues for Mr. Charlie* (1964), *Amen Corner* (1965), and in Douglas Turner Ward's *Day of Absence* (1965). She made her film debut as Sister Sarah in 1964's *Nothing But a Man*, and in 1967 she became an original member of the Negro Ensemble Company.

Rolle continued to work steadily in the theater through the early 1970s. She was performing in Melvin Van Peebles's *Don't Play Us Cheap* (1972) when a casting director asked her to audition for the role of the maid on *Maude*, a Norman Lear television show being spun off from *All in the Family*. Rolle won the role and, that same year, with the understanding that her character, Florida Evans, would not be a typical maid, she proceeded to turn the limited role into a popular character. In 1974 the characters of Florida Evans and her husband were spun off into a new television series, *Good Times*.

Good Times depicted a lower-middle-class family living in a tenement on the South Side of Chicago as they struggled to survive economically in the face of layoffs and unemployment. Originally the show was praised for addressing the economic difficulties faced by many inner-city blacks. However, Rolle and costar John Amos constantly struggled with producers over the role of the oldest son, played by Jimmie Walker, who was portrayed as a fast-talking, womanizing buffoon, and who increasingly became the central figure of the show. Rolle left the show in 1977 over these and other disputes, but returned in 1978. *Good Times* was canceled in 1979.

Rolle continued to act in other roles on television and in the theater through the late 1970s and 1980s. She won an

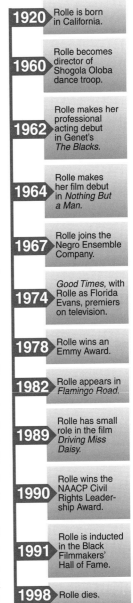

1920 Rolle is born in California.

1960 Rolle becomes director of Shogola Oloba dance troop.

1962 Rolle makes her professional acting debut in Genet's *The Blacks*.

1964 Rolle makes her film debut in *Nothing But a Man*.

1967 Rolle joins the Negro Ensemble Company.

1974 *Good Times*, with Rolle as Florida Evans, premiers on television.

1978 Rolle wins an Emmy Award.

1982 Rolle appears in *Flamingo Road*.

1989 Rolle has small role in the film *Driving Miss Daisy*.

1990 Rolle wins the NAACP Civil Rights Leadership Award.

1991 Rolle is inducted in the Black Filmmakers' Hall of Fame.

1998 Rolle dies.

Emmy Award for her performance as a housekeeper in the 1978 television movie *Summer of My German Soldier*. During the 1980s she appeared on such television shows as *Flamingo Road* (1982) and *The Love Boat* (1983, 1985). In 1989 she played a housekeeper in *The Member of the Wedding* at the Roundabout Theater, a role she had originated in Philadelphia four years earlier. Rolle played the matriarch in an American Playhouse remake of *A Raisin in the Sun* (1989) with Danny Glover as the errant son. That same year, she also played the maid, Idella, in the Academy Award-winning film *Driving Miss Daisy*.

In 1990 Rolle became the first woman to win the NAACP chairman's Civil Rights Leadership Award. For her achievements in film and television, Rolle was inducted into the Black Filmmakers Hall of Fame in 1991. She died in 1998. ◆

Ross, Diana

MARCH 26, 1944 –   ● SINGER AND ACTOR

Born Diane Ross in a low-income housing project in Detroit, Ross's interest in music began at an early age, when she sang with her parents in a church choir. In high school she studied dress design, illustration, and cosmetol-

---

The Supremes

The female soul vocal trio called the Supremes was one of the most successful recording groups of all time. They earned twelve Number-One hits and sold over twenty million records; their rise to national fame signaled the elimination of the color barrier in the pop market. The Supremes had several personnel changes during their eighteen-year history. At the height of their popularity from 1962 to 1967, the group included Diana Ross, Florence Ballard, and Mary Wilson. Their hits included "Where Did Our Love Go," "Baby Love," "Come See About Me," "Stop! In the Name of Love," and "Back in My Arms Again." The Supremes' earliest recordings featured Ballard's strong lead vocals, but the hits from 1964 to 1965 featured Ross's bright, cooing vocals. In 1967 Cindy Birdsong replaced Ballard, and the group was billed as Diana Ross and the Supremes. Their hits included "Love Child" and "I'm Gonna Make You Love Me." In 1970 Ross departed for a solo career and Jean Terrell led the trio, but their popularity declined by 1973. The 1981 Broadway show *Dreamgirls* depicts Ballard's perspective on the group, and in 1984 Wilson published her own memoir, *Dreamgirl: My Life as a Supreme*.

Left to right: Florence Ballard, **Diana Ross**, and Mary Wilson performing as the Supremes in 1965.

1944 Ross is born in Detroit.

1964 Ross records "Where Did Our Love Go" with the Supremes.

1970 Ross leaves Supremes to pursue solo career.

1972 Ross is nominated for Oscar for *Lady Sings the Blues.*

1975 Ross stars in *Mahagony.*

1978 Ross stars in the film version of *The Wiz.*

1983 Ross gives free concert in New York's Central Park.

1993 Ross publishes her memoirs, *Secrets of a Sparrow.*

ogy, spending her free time singing on Detroit street corners with her friends Mary Wilson and Florence Ballard. Betty McGlowan was soon added to the group, and the quartet became known as the Primettes. They came to the attention of Motown Records founder Berry Gordy, who used them as background singers for Mary Wells, Marvin Gaye, and the Shirelles. The group was renamed the Supremes, and from the mid-1960s until 1970 they were one of the most popular groups in pop music, with a string of influential hits. In 1970, however, Ross, who had always sought to dominate what was nominally a balanced trio, left to pursue a solo career.

After leaving the Supremes, Ross's popularity continued ("Ain't No Mountain High Enough," 1970), and she also began a career as a film actress. Ross was nominated for an Academy Award for her performance as Billie Holiday in *Lady Sings the Blues* (1972), and starred in *Mahagony* (1975), which yielded the hit ballad "Do You Know Where You're Going To?" the next year. By the mid-1970s Ross was also considered a top

> *"I am so excited to be on stage and in the lights, communicating with an audience. The magic lifts me. I feel as if I am levitating, floating out into the room, close to the people."*
>
> Diana Ross, *Secrets of a Sparrow*, 1993

disco diva, recording "Love Hangover" (1976) and "Upside Down" (1980). During this time she also had a starring role in the musical film *The Wiz* (1978). Ross reached the top of the pop charts again in 1981 with "Endless Love," a duet with Lionel Ritchie. Since then she has recorded less frequently (*Muscles*, 1982; *Eaten Alive*, 1985; and *Workin' Overtime*, 1989). Ross, who was married from 1971 to 1975 to Robert Silberstine, was remarried in 1985 to the Norwegian shipping tycoon and mountaineer Arne Naess. They have two sons and live in Norway and Connecticut. Ross has had nineteen Number-One recordings on the pop charts—the most to date for a solo performer—and continues to perform sporadically in concert and on television. ◆

Rudolph, Wilma Glodean

JUNE 23, 1940 – NOVEMBER 12, 1994 ● ATHLETE

> *"I had a series of childhood illnesses. The first was scarlet fever. Then I had pneumonia. Polio followed. I walked with braces until I was at least nine years old. My life wasn't like the average person who grew up and decided to enter the world of sports."*
>
> Wilma Rudolph, quoted in *USA Today*, 1987

Wilma Rudolph, the twentieth of twenty-two children, was born in Bethlehem, Tennessee, and raised in Clarksville. As a child, she suffered from scarlet fever and pneumonia and was stricken with polio, which left her without the use of her left leg. She wore a leg brace until the age of nine, when she was able to regain the strength in her legs. By age twelve, Rudolph was the fastest runner in her school. She entered Cobb Elementary School in 1947 and then attended Burt High School in Clarksville, Tennessee, where she played basketball and ran track.

Rudolph met Edward Temple, track coach at Tennessee State University, while at Burt. After her sophomore year, Temple invited Rudolph to a summer training camp and began to cultivate her running abilities. In 1956, at age sixteen, she participated in the Olympics in Melbourne, Australia, where her team won the bronze medal in the 4 × 100-meter relay race. Two years later Rudolph entered Tennessee State to run track and study elementary education and psychology. She was determined to return to the Rome Olympics in 1960. She trained and ran with the Tigerbelles, the Tennessee State University team, which was one of the premier teams in the country. In 1960 Rudolph became the first woman to receive three gold

medals, which she won for the 100-meter race, the 200-meter race, and the 4 × 100-meter relay. She instantly became a celebrity, drawing large crowds wherever she went. The French press called her "La Gazelle." Rudolph retired from amateur running at the height of her career, in 1962.

Rudolph graduated from Tennessee State in 1963 and accepted a job as teacher and track coach at Cobb Elementary School. Although she has lived in many places and has held a number of different jobs, she has invariably dedicated herself to youth programs and education. She worked as the director of a community center in Evansville, Indiana, with the Job Corps program in Boston and St. Louis, with the Watts Community Action Committee in California, and as a teacher at a high school in Detroit. In 1981 she started the Wilma Rudolph Foundation, a nonprofit organization that nurtures young athletes.

Wilma Rudolph received many awards and distinctions. She was chosen in 1960 as the United Press Athlete of the Year, and the next year she was designated Woman Athlete of the Year by the Associated Press. She was inducted in 1973 into the Black Sports Hall of Fame, seven years later into the Women's Sports Hall of Fame, and in 1983 into the U.S. Olympic Hall of Fame. In 1993 she became the only woman to be awarded the National Sports Award. In addition, her autobiography, *Wilma:*

1940 Rudolph is born in Tennessee.

1956 Rudolph wins Olympic bronze medal.

1960 Rudolph wins three Olympic gold medals.

1963 Rudolph graduates from Tennessee State University.

1973 Rudolph is inducted into Black Sports Hall of Fame.

1977 Rudolph publishes her biography, *Wilma: The Story of Wilma Rudolph.*

1981 Rudolph founds Wilma Rudolph Foundation.

1993 Rudolph is awarded National Sports Award.

1994 Rudolph dies from brain cancer.

The Story of Wilma Rudolph, published in 1977, was made into a television movie. Rudolph's achievements as a runner gave a boost to women's track in the United States and heightened awareness about racial and sexual barriers within sports. In addition, Rudolph served as a role model and inspiration to thousands of African-American and female athletes, as well as people trying to overcome physical disabilities. Rudolph died in Nashville in 1994 from brain cancer. ◆

Saar, Betye Irene

JULY 30, 1926 – ● ARTIST

Betye Brown was born in Los Angeles and moved to Pasadena, California, at age six following the death of her father. While her mother worked as a seamstress and receptionist to support her family, Brown attended public school in Pasadena and enrolled at Pasadena City College. She earned a B.A. degree in design from the University of California at Los Angeles in 1949 and married artist Richard Saar (pronounced "Say-er") shortly thereafter.

During her early career, Saar worked as a costume designer in theater and film in Los Angeles. In the late 1950s and early '60s, she resumed formal art training at California State University in Long Beach, at the University of Southern California, and at California State University in Northridge. In graduate school, Saar mastered the techniques of graphics, printmaking, and design, but after seeing a Joseph Cornell exhibition at the Pasadena Art Museum in 1967, she turned to what would become her signature work: three-dimensional **assemblage** boxes. Saar's encounter with Cornell's **surrealist** boxes led her away from her early, two-dimensional work in prints to her first landmark piece, *Black Girl's Window* (mixed media, 1969). Here Saar used Cornell-inspired elements like a segmented window and a surrealist combination of objects to explore issues of personal identity. The piece presents a black girl, possibly Saar, pressing her face and hands against a glass pane, surrounded by images of the occult.

During the late 1960s and '70s, Saar's boxes reflected her political engagement with the Civil Rights Movement by

assemblange: an artistic composition made from scraps, junk, and odds and ends.

surrealist: relating to an artistic style characterized by a dreamlike distortion of reality.

241

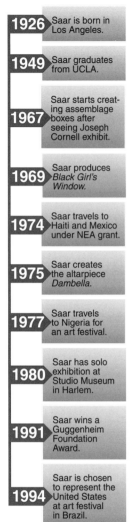

1926 Saar is born in Los Angeles.

1949 Saar graduates from UCLA.

1967 Saar starts creating assemblage boxes after seeing Joseph Cornell exhibit.

1969 Saar produces *Black Girl's Window.*

1974 Saar travels to Haiti and Mexico under NEA grant.

1975 Saar creates the altarpiece *Dambella.*

1977 Saar travels to Nigeria for an art festival.

1980 Saar has solo exhibition at Studio Museum in Harlem.

1991 Saar wins a Guggenheim Foundation Award.

1994 Saar is chosen to represent the United States at art festival in Brazil.

satirizing persistent derogatory images of African Americans. In *The Liberation of Aunt Jemima* (1972), Saar appropriated the racist stereotype of Aunt Jemima by transforming her from a passive black female into a militant revolutionary. Her later work took on a more personal, autobiographical dimension, exploring her own mixed heritage of Native American, Irish, and African descent, and her spiritual beliefs. The death of Saar's Aunt Hattie in particular pushed her work inward and inspired such nostalgic collages as *Keep for Old Memoirs* (1976), made from old family photographs and personal remnants such as gloves and handkerchiefs.

In 1974 Saar traveled to Haiti and Mexico under a National Endowment for the Arts grant, then to Nigeria for the second World Black and African Festival of Arts and Culture (1977). These trips, together with Saar's visits to the Egyptian, Oceanic, and African collections at the Field Museum of Natural History in Chicago, resulted in a series of altarpieces (1975–77) that combined personal emblems with totems from African, Caribbean, and Asian cultures. *Dambella* (1975) contains obvious references to Haitian voodoo with its ritualistic animal parts and snakeskin, while *Spiritcatcher* (1976–77), with its spiral structure and found objects, recalls Simon Rodia's Watts Towers in Los Angeles, which Saar had visited as a child.

In the 1980s and 1990s Saar continued to create assemblage boxes and collages while also experimenting with room-sized installations. As always, she works in materials culled and recycled from foreign markets, thrift shops, or her own personal history; she intends these "found treasures" to stir emotion and personal or collective memories in the viewer. Her *Mojotech* installation at the Massachusetts Institute of Technology (1988) explored the relationship between technology and magic, creating hybrid altars out of high-tech elements like computer-system circuit boards as well as traditional religious objects.

Saar's work has been shown at numerous solo exhibitions, including the Studio Museum in Harlem in New York (1980); the Museum of Contemporary Art, Los Angeles (1984); and the Pennsylvania Academy of the Arts, Philadelphia (1987). Since 1983, she has been awarded several commissions to create installations for public sites in Los Angeles, New Jersey, and Miami. Saar won a John Simon Guggenheim Memorial Foundation Award in 1991, and she was one of the two artists chosen to represent the United States in the 1994 São Paulo Biennial in Brazil. ◆

Sanchez, Sonia

SEPTEMBER 19, 1934 – ● POET

S onia Sanchez was born Wilsonia Benita Driver, the daughter of Wilson L. and Lena Jones Driver, in Birmingham, Alabama. During her childhood in the South as well as in Harlem, she was outraged by the way American society systematically mistreated black people. This sense of racial injustice transformed her from a shy, stuttering girl into one of the most vocal writer-activists in contemporary literature. In the early 1960s she began publishing poems under her married name, Sonia Sanchez, which she continued to use professionally after a divorce. Although best known for verse urging black unity and action, verse reflecting the cadences of African-American speech and music, she also became an accomplished dramatist, essayist, and editor, as well as an enduring proponent of black studies.

Sanchez studied at Hunter College in New York (B.A., 1955) and at New York University and has taught at many institutions, including Rutgers, the University of Pittsburgh, and Amherst College. She worked during the Civil Rights Movement as a supporter of the Congress of Racial Equality but in 1972 joined the Nation of Islam because she thought that it was doing more to instill cultural pride and morality in young people. In a 1983 interview, Sanchez said that her political and cultural affiliations, harassment by the FBI, and her insistence that black writers be included in curricula explained why she didn't gain a permanent academic position until 1978, when she became a professor at Temple University.

Homecoming (1969), her first collection of poetry, addressed racial oppression in angry voices derived from street talk. Sanchez soon became sought after for her passionate, confrontational readings. Although her use of profanity was shocking to some, she has never regretted her artistic approach: "There is vulgar stuff out there. One has got to talk about it in order for it not to be."

1934 Sanchez is born in Birmingham, Alabama.

1955 Sanchez graduates from Hunter College.

1969 Sanchez publishes her first poetry collection, *Homecoming*

1972 Sanchez joins the Nation of Islam; produces *Sister Sonji* off-Broadway.

1975 Sanchez leaves the Nation of Islam in protest over the role of women.

1978 Sanchez becomes a professor at Temple University.

While the plight of African Americans in a white society is her major subject, Sanchez has also critiqued struggles within the black community. *Sister Son / ji,* a play produced off-Broadway in 1972, is about a militant young woman fighting the sexism of the black revolutionary movement. Sanchez herself left the Nation of Islam in 1975 because the organization would not change the subservient role it assigned to women.

Books by Sanchez include poetry collections: *We a BadDDD People* (1970), *A Blues Book for Blue Black Magical Women* (1973), *homegirls & handgrenades* (1984), *Does Your House Have Lions* (1997); juvenile fiction: *A Sound Investment and Other Stories* (1979); plays: *Uh, Huh: But How Do It Free Us?* (1975), *Malcolm Man/Don't Live Here No More* (1979); as well as numerous contributions to journals, recordings, and anthologies as a poet, essayist, and editor.

Sanchez has received major awards from PEN (1969), the National Institute of Arts and Letters (1970), and the National Endowment for the Arts (1978–79). Other honors include the Lucretia Mott Award (1984), the Smith College Tribute to Black Women Award (1982), a doctorate from Wilberforce University (1972), and the American Book Award from the Before Columbus Foundation (1985). ◆

> *"There is vulgar stuff out there. One has got to talk about it in order for it not to be."*
>
> Sonia Sanchez

Savage, Augusta Christine Fells

FEBRUARY 29, 1892 – MARCH 26, 1962 ●
SCULPTOR AND EDUCATOR

The seventh of fourteen children, Augusta Savage was born in Green Cove Springs, Florida, to Cornelia and Edward Fells. Fells, a Methodist minister, initially punished his young daughter for making figurines in the local red clay, then came to accept her talent. Savage attended public schools and the state normal school in Tallahassee (now Florida A&M) briefly. At sixteen, she married John T. Moore, who died within a few years of the birth of their only child. In the mid-1910s she married James Savage, a laborer and carpenter; the two divorced in the early 1920s. In 1915 Savage moved to West Palm Beach, where one of her clay pieces won twenty-five dollars at a county fair. Public support encouraged Savage to move north in the Great Migration to New York, where she arrived in 1921 with just $4.60 and a letter of recommendation from the superintendent of the county fair to sculptor Solon Borglum, director of the School of American Sculpture.

Through Borglum's influence, Savage was admitted to the tuition-free college Cooper Union ahead of 142 women on the waiting list. She completed the four-year program in three years, specializing in portraiture. In the early 1920s she sculpted realistic busts of W. E. B. Du Bois, Frederick Douglass, W. C. Handy, and Marcus Garvey. In 1923 Savage married Robert L. Poston, a Garveyite journalist who died five months later. The same year, Savage was one of a hundred American women who received a $500 scholarship from the French government for summer study at the palace of Fontainebleau. However, when the American committee of seven white men discovered her racial identity, they withdrew the offer. One committee member, Hermon A. MacNeil, gave her private instruction instead. Two years later, Countess Irene Di Robilant of the Italian-American Society gave Savage a scholarship for study at the Royal Academy of Fine Arts in Rome, but Savage was unable to raise money for expenses abroad as she struggled to support her parents while working at a laundry.

In 1926 Savage exhibited her work in three locations—at the New York Public Library, at the Frederick Douglass High School in Baltimore, and at the **sesquicentennial** exhibition in Philadelphia. The following year, she studied privately with sculptor Onorio Ruotolo, former dean of the Leonardo da Vinci Art School. She also worked with sculptor Antonio Salemme and taught soap sculpture classes to children at Procter & Gamble.

sesquicentennial: a 150th anniversary.

In 1928 recognition from the Harmon Foundation, which exhibited her *Evening* and *Head of a Negro*, brought Savage sales. Eugene Kinckle Jones, executive secretary of the National

1892 Savage is born Augusta Fells in Florida.

1915 One of Savage's clay sculptures wins $25 at a fair.

1921 Savage moves to New York to attend Cooper Union.

1923 Savage receives a scholarship to study in Paris, but it is withdrawn when her race is revealed.

1926 Savage exhibits her work at the New York Public Library.

1929 Savage travels to Paris to study.

1932 Savage opens the Savage School for Arts and Crafts.

1934 Savage is elected to National Association of Women Painters and Sculptors.

1937 Savage becomes director of the Harlem Community Art Center.

1939 Savage opens the Salon of Contemporary Art.

1962 Savage dies in New York City.

Urban League, was so impressed with his purchase of a baby's bust that Savage had sculpted that he asked the Carnegie Corporation to sponsor her training. Through the Carnegie, Savage began study with sculptor Victor Salvatore, who urged her to continue her studies in France.

In fall 1929 Savage went to Paris with funds from both Carnegie and the Julius Rosenwald Fund. There, she studied privately with Felix Benneteau and created realistic portrait busts in plaster and clay. The most notable works Savage created abroad are of black female nudes, such as *Amazon* (a female warrior holding a spear) and *Mourning Victory* (a standing nude who gazes at a decapitated head on the ground) and works that celebrate her African heritage, such as *The Call* (in response to Alain Locke's call for racially representative art) and *Divinité nègre* (a female figurine with four faces, arms, and legs). In 1930 *La dépêche africaine*, a French journal, ran a cover story on Savage, and three of her figurative works were exhibited at the Salon d'Automne. Savage also sent works to the United States for display; the Harmon Foundation exhibited *Gamin* in 1930 and *Bust* and *The Chase* (in palm wood) in 1931. In 1931 Savage won a gold medal for a piece at the Colonial Exposition and exhibited two female nudes (*Nu* in bronze, and *Martiniquaise* in plaster) at the Société des Artistes Français.

After her return to New York, Savage exhibited three works (*Gamin, Envy,* and *Woman of Martinique*) at the American Art-Anderson Galleries in 1932. That same year, she opened the Savage School of Arts and Crafts. Some of her students, who included Jacob Lawrence, Norman Lewis, William Artis, and Ernest Crichlow, participated in Vanguard, a group Savage founded in 1933 to discuss art and progressive causes. She disbanded the group the following year when membership became communist controlled.

In 1934 Argent Galleries and the Architectural League exhibited Savage's work, and she became the first African American elected to the National Association of Women Painters and Sculptors. Two years later Savage supervised artists in the WPA's Federal Arts Project and organized classes and exhibitions at the Uptown Art Laboratory. In 1937 she became the first director of the Harlem Community Art Center. After receiving a commission from the New York World's Fair Board of Design, she left that position in 1938 to sculpt a sixteen-foot plaster harp, the strings of which were the folds of choir robes on singing black youths. Named after James Weldon Johnson's poem/song (also called the Negro National Anthem), *Lift Every Voice and Sing* was exhibited at the New York World's Fair of 1939 but was bulldozed afterward. (Savage could not afford to have it cast in bronze.)

In June 1939 Savage opened the Salon of Contemporary Art, the first gallery devoted to the exhibition and sale of works by African-American artists. It folded within a few months for lack of funds. The same year, Savage exhibited fifteen works in a solo show at Argent Galleries; among them were *Green Apples*, *Sisters in the Rain*, *Creation*, *Envy*, *Martyr*, *The Cat*, and a bust of James Weldon Johnson. She also exhibited at the American Negro Exposition and at Perrin Hall in Chicago in 1940.

About 1945, Savage retired to Saugerties, New York, where she taught children in nearby summer camps, occasionally sold her work, and wrote children's stories and murder mysteries. She died of cancer in New York City. ◆

> In 1938 Savage sculpted a sixteen-foot plaster harp, the strings of which were the folds of choir robes on singing black youths.

Shange, Ntozake

OCTOBER 18, 1948 – ● PLAYWRIGHT AND PERFORMER

N tozake Shange was born Paulette Williams in Trenton, New Jersey. She took the Zulu name Ntozake ("she who comes with her own things") Shange ("she who walks like a lion") in 1971. Shange grew up in an upper-middle-class family, very involved in political and cultural activities. She earned degrees in American studies from Barnard (1970) and the University of Southern California (1973). She lives in Philadelphia with her daughter.

Shange's writing is marked by unique spelling and punctuation, partly to establish a recognizable style, like that of a musician, but also as a reaction against Western culture. Much of her work is in the form of a "choreopoem," blending music, drama, and dance. Her work is brutally honest, reflective, and intense. She writes for those whose voices have often been ignored, especially young African-American women.

Her best-known work is the play *for colored girls who have considered suicide/when the rainbow is enuf* (1976). Despite many

> *"i found god in myself/and i loved her fiercely."*
> Ntozake Shange,
> *for colored girls, who have considered suicide/when the rainbow is enuf,*
> 1975

Ntozake Shange (right) in 1976 in a scene from *for girls who have considered suicide/when the rainbow is enuf.*

1948	Shange is born in New Jersey.
1971	Shange takes the Zulu name Ntozake Shange.
1973	Shange earns a degree from the University of California.
1976	Shange produces *for colored girls* on Broadway.
1981	Three of Shange's plays are published in *three pieces.*
1984	Shange publishes collected prose *See No Evil.*

harrowing scenes the work is essentially optimistic, showing the "infinite beauty" of black women. The play's conception took place over many years; it opened on Broadway in September 1976, and played there for almost two years before going on national and international tour.

Shange is a highly prolific author whose other published plays include *a photograph: lovers in motion, boogie woogie landscapes,* and *spell #7,* which were collected in *three pieces* (1981). Many other plays have not been published as yet, including a powerful adaptation of Bertolt Brecht's *Mother Courage* (1980).

Her volumes of poetry include *Nappy Edges* (1978), *A Daughter's Geography* (1983), *from okra to greens* (1984), *Ridin' the Moon in Texas: Word Paintings* (1987), and *The Love Space Demands: A Continuing Saga* (1991). She has written two novels, *Sassafrass, Cypress & Indigo* (1982) and *Betsey Brown* (1985). Many of these works have also been adapted into theatrical form. Her prose is collected in *See No Evil: Prefaces, Essays, and Accounts, 1976–83* (1984).

In 1998 Shange published a collection of recipes and essays about food and culture entitled *If I Can Cook/You Know God Can.* ◆

Simone, Nina (Waymon, Eunice Kathleen)

FEBRUARY 21, 1933 – ● SINGER

Born in Tryon, North Carolina, Simone was encouraged to study piano and organ starting at age three by her mother, an ordained Methodist minister. Simone was soon able to play hymns on the organ by ear, and at age six she became the regular pianist at her family's church. She studied privately, as well as at Asheville (North Carolina) High School, to become a classical pianist. She also studied at the Curtis Institute of Music in Philadelphia (1950–53) and the Juilliard School in New York (1954–56). Simone's career as a vocalist, which spans more than three decades and more than forty albums, came almost by accident, when, during a 1954 night-club engagement in Atlantic City, New Jersey, she was informed that in addition to playing piano she would have to sing. She adopted the stage name Nina Simone for this occasion, which marked the beginning of her career as a jazz singer.

1933	Simone is born in North Carolina.
1950	Simone begins studying at Philadelphia's Curtis Institute of Music.
1954	Simone enters Juilliard in New York.
1958	Simone releases *Jazz as Played*.
1963	Simone composes the civil rights anthem "Mississippi Goddam."
1987	Simone records *Let It Be Me*.
1991	Simone publishes her autobiography.

From the very start, Simone chafed under the restrictions of the label "jazz singer," and indeed, her mature style integrates classical piano techniques with a repertory drawn from sources as varied as the blues and folk music (*Jazz as Played*, 1958). Early in her career, Simone also began addressing racial problems in the United States. In 1963, angered by the death of Medgar Evers, and the bombing of an African-American church in Birmingham, Alabama, she composed her first civil rights anthem, "Mississippi Goddam," and during the next decade much of her work was explicitly dedicated to the civil rights movement, sung in her forceful and clear alto voice. In 1963 she composed "Four Women" with Langston Hughes. Her other popular songs from this time include "Young, Gifted, and Black," "Old Jim Crow," and "Don't Let Me Be Misunderstood." In the 1970s Simone continued to perform internationally and to record (*Baltimore*, 1978). Starting in the late 1970s she divided her time between Los Angeles and Switzerland. In more recent years she has lived in Paris, but she continues to appear regularly in New York. In 1987 she released *Let It Be Me*. Her autobiography, *I Put a Spell on You*, was published in 1991. ◆

Simpson, Coreen

FEBRUARY 18, 1942 – ● PHOTOGRAPHER

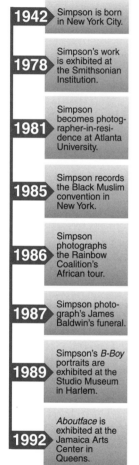

1942 Simpson is born in New York City.

1978 Simpson's work is exhibited at the Smithsonian Institution.

1981 Simpson becomes photographer-in-residence at Atlanta University.

1985 Simpson records the Black Muslim convention in New York.

1986 Simpson photographs the Rainbow Coalition's African tour.

1987 Simpson photograph's James Baldwin's funeral.

1989 Simpson's *B-Boy* portraits are exhibited at the Studio Museum in Harlem.

1992 *Aboutface* is exhibited at the Jamaica Arts Center in Queens.

Coreen Simpson was born in New York City and was raised with her brother in a foster home after her mother, who was Jewish, and her father, who was black, were divorced. Simpson became interested in photography as an adult when she was writing magazine articles and was dissatisfied with her editors' selection of images. From Walter Johnson, a local neighborhood photographer, and Frank Stewart, who taught at the Studio Museum in Harlem, Simpson learned how to use a camera, print her work, and recognize the styles of well-known photographers.

Simpson started her career as a photographer by covering fashion and cultural events for the *Village Voice* and the *Amsterdam News* in the early 1980s. She has provided extensive coverage of fashion shows in New York and Paris, and has photographed a diverse selection of cultural events in black communities including the Black Muslim convention at the Felt Forum in New York in 1985, the Rev. Jesse Jackson's Rainbow Coalition eight-nation African tour in 1986, and the funeral of writer James Baldwin in 1987.

In the early 1980s Simpson became interested in documenting Harlem at night, particularly the patrons and performers in the neighborhood's nightclubs. Her portrait series *B-Boys* (or *Break-Boys*) features large-scale prints (three by five feet) documenting the hairstyles and fashions worn by fans of hip-hop and rap music at night spots such as New York's Roxy Club during the 1980s (*Portrait of Vic*, 1986). Simpson has been compared to photographers Diane Arbus and Weegee for her ability to present uncommon individuals with depth of character and dignity in her portraits of punk rockers, transvestites, and cooks in Harlem's restaurants (*Portrait of Velma Jones*, 1978). Simpson also became an active jewelry maker in the early 1980s, selling her pieces outdoors on Fifty-seventh Street and in New York City department stores.

In the late 1980s Simpson began recombining the *B-Boy* portraits, creating collages, several of which were exhibited at the Studio Museum in Harlem in 1989. Simpson continued to draw upon the *B-Boys* series, as well as upon African traditions in the construction of headdresses and masks, in her project *Aboutface*, which was exhibited at the Jamaica Arts Center in New York in 1992. *Aboutface* looks at the relationship between identity and stylized self-presentation through the artist's symbolic use of masking. Simpson superimposes an individual's facial parts, as well as objects or patterns, onto the visage of someone else to show how the body is a site for adornment and performance.

Simpson's work has been shown in solo and group exhibitions at the Smithsonian Institution (1978–80), the Studio Museum in Harlem (1979, 1989), the Brooklyn Museum (1982), the Schomburg Center for Research in Black Culture (1982), the Tompkins Square Gallery in New York City (1988), and the Jamaica Arts Center in Queens, New York (1992). She was photographer-in-residence at the Studio Museum in Harlem (1978), Atlanta University (1981), and the Jamaica Arts Center (1991). Her photographs have been featured in such publications as *Vogue, Black Enterprise, American Art, Art News, Glamour, Ms.,* and *Essence.* ◆

> Coreen Simpson superimposes an individual's facial parts onto the visage of someone else to show how the body is a site for adornment and performance.

Simpson, Lorna

1960 – ● PHOTOGRAPHER

Born in Brooklyn, New York, Lorna Simpson enrolled as an undergraduate at the School of Visual Arts in New York City to study painting. She soon turned to documentary photography and received a B.F.A. in photography from the school in 1982. In 1985 Simpson earned an M.F.A. degree in visual arts from the University of California–San Diego (UCSD), where she also studied and taught film and became involved in performance art. Her first large-scale series of photographs, *Gestures and Reenactments* (1985), launched her ongoing project of rethinking the relationships among photographic images, textual description, and the representation of African Americans, particularly women.

Simpson's work reflects an awareness of the ways in which photography has been traditionally used by the social sciences and the media to classify, study, objectify, and ultimately control

> Lorna Simpson reexamines the relationships among photographic images, textual description, and the representation of African Americans, especially women.

black men and women. In large multipaneled or sequential works such as *You're Fine* (1988), *Stereo Styles* (1988), and *Guarded Conditions* (1989), Simpson typically presents a black Everywoman with her back turned to the viewer or her face deliberately obscured by **cropping**; the viewer is thus effectively denied access to the woman's identity and inner psychological state. Instead, Simpson provides clues as to subjective meaning in the accompanying captions, which usually refer to issues of gender and racial oppression. In contrast to the neutral, carefully controlled tone of her photographs, Simpson's captions can be emotionally charged, thereby creating an interpretive tension between word and image. In *You're Fine* Simpson presents an anonymous black woman lying on her side in a simple white shift, her back turned away from the viewer in a pose that recalls the reclining pose of the nineteenth-century female nude. The ominous text comments on the invasive and objectifying qualities of public surveillance.

Social commentary also informs Simpson's *Stereo Styles*, which consists of ten Polaroid prints in two tiers; each print shows the back of the same black woman's head done in a different hairstyle. Simpson here comments on the popular idea expressed in cosmetics advertisements that hairstyles can communicate personality traits. Since 1988 Simpson has abstracted the female body even further and combined its parts with such symbolic objects as African masks, black hair, and articles of women's clothing (*Flipside* 1991; *1978–88*, 1990; *Bio*, 1992).

In 1991 Simpson created *Five Rooms* with composer Alva Rogers, a site-specific, multimedia installation for the 1991 Spoleto Festival U.S. exhibition in Charleston, South Carolina, which presented a narrative of black slavery in America. She created another installation, *Standing in the Water*, for the Whitney Museum of American Art in New York City in 1994. Simpson's work has been shown in more than ninety major exhibitions throughout the United States and Europe; sites of solo exhibits include the Museum of Modern Art (1990) and the Museum of Contemporary Art, Chicago (1992–93), both of which have also acquired her work. Simpson was the first African-American woman ever chosen to exhibit in the Venice Biennale (1990). ◆

cropping: cutting out part of a photograph.

1960 — Simpson is born in Brooklyn.

1982 — Simpson graduates from New York's School of Visual Arts.

1985 — Simpson earns an M.F.A. degree from UCSD; produces *Gestures and Reenactments*.

1988 — Simpson begins to further abstract the female body in her art.

1990 — Simpson has solo exhibition at the Museum of Modern Art.

1991 — Simpson produces *Five Rooms* for Spoleto Festival.

1994 — Simpson creates an installation for New York's Whitney Museum.

Smith, Bessie

APRIL 15, 1894 – SEPTEMBER 26, 1937 ● BLUES SINGER

essie Smith, "Empress of the Blues," was the greatest woman singer of urban blues and, to many, the greatest of all blues singers. She was born in Chattanooga, Tennessee, the youngest of seven children of Laura and William Smith. Her father, a part-time Baptist preacher, died while she was a baby, and her early childhood, during which her mother and two brothers died, was spent in extreme poverty. Bessie and her brother Andrew earned coins on street corners with Bessie singing and dancing to the guitar playing of her brother.

The involvement of her favorite brother, Clarence, in the Moses Stokes Show was the impetus for Smith's departure from home in 1912. Having won local amateur shows, she was prepared for the move to vaudeville and tent shows, where her initial role was as a dancer. She came in contact with Gertrude "Ma" Rainey, who was also with the Stokes troupe, but there is no evidence to support the legend that Rainey taught her how to sing the blues. They did develop a friendship, however, that lasted through Smith's lifetime.

Smith's stint with Stokes ended in 1913, when she moved to Atlanta and established herself as a regular performer at the infamous Charles Bailey's 81 Theatre. By then the Theater Owners Booking Association (TOBA) **consortium** was developing into a major force in the lives and careers of African-American entertainers, and managers/owners often made the lives of performers miserable through low pay, poor working and living conditions, and curfews. Bailey's reputation in this regard was notorious. Smith became one of his most popular singers, although she was paid only ten dollars a week.

Smith's singing was rough and unrefined, but she possessed a magnificent vocal style and commanding stage presence, which resulted in additional money in tips. With the 81 Theatre as a home base, Smith traveled on the TOBA circuit throughout the South and up and down the eastern seaboard. By 1918 she was part of a duo-specialty act with Hazel Green but soon moved to her own show as a headliner.

"Nobody in town can bake a sweet jelly role like mine."
Bessie Smith

consortium: an organization formed to undertake an enterprise beyond the resources of any one member.

1894 — Smith is born in Chattanooga.

1912 — Smith leaves home to tour with the Moses Stokes Show.

1913 — Smith begins performing in Atlanta at Charles Bailey's 81 Theatre.

1923 — Smith records "Down Hearted Blues."

1924 — Smith becomes the highest-paid African American in America.

1929 — Smith appears in film short *St. Louis Blues.*

1933 — Okeh Records issues four Smith selections.

1937 — Smith dies in auto accident while on tour.

Smith attracted a growing number of black followers in the rural South as well as recent immigrants to northern urban ghettos who missed the down-home style and sound. She was too raw and vulgar, however, for the Tin Pan Alley black songwriters attempting to move into the lucrative world of phonograph recordings. White record company executives found Smith's (and Ma Rainey's) brand of blues too alien and unrefined to consider her for employment. As a result, Smith was not recorded until 1923, when the black buying public had already demonstrated that there was a market for blues songs and the companies became eager to exploit it.

Fortunately, Smith was recorded by the Columbia Gramophone Company, which had equipment and technology superior to any other manufacturer at the time. Columbia touted itself in black newspapers as having more "race" artists than other companies. Into this milieu came Bessie Smith singing "Down Hearted Blues" and "Gulf Coast Blues," the former written and previously performed by Alberta Hunter and the latter by Clarence Williams, studio musician for Columbia. Sales were astronomical. Advertisements in the black newspapers reported her latest releases, and Smith was able to expand her touring range to include black theaters in all of the major northern cities. By 1924 she was the highest-paid African American in the country.

Smith sang with passion and authenticity about everyday problems, natural disasters, the horrors of the workhouse, abuse and violence, unfaithful lovers, and the longing for someone, anyone, to love. She performed these songs with a conviction and dramatic style that reflected the memory of her own suffering, captured the mood of black people who had experienced pain and anguish, and drew listeners to her with empathy and intimacy. Langston Hughes said Smith's blues were the essence of "sadness . . . not softened with tears, but hardened with laughter, the absurd, incongruous laughter of a sadness without even a god to appeal to."

Smith connected with her listeners in the same manner as the southern preacher: they were her flock who came seeking relief from the burdens of oppression, poverty, endless labor, injustice, alienation, loneliness, and love gone awry. She was their spiritual leader who sang away the pain by pulling it forth in a direct, honest manner, weaving the notes into a tapestry of moans, wails, and slides. She addressed the vagaries of city life and its mistreatment of women, the depletion of the little respect women tried to maintain. She sanctioned the power of women to be their own independent selves, to love freely, to drink and party and enjoy life to its fullest, to wail, scream, and lambaste anyone who overstepped boundaries in relationships—all of which characterized Smith's own spirit and life.

Columbia was grateful for an artist who filled its coffers and helped move it to supremacy in the recording industry. Smith recorded regularly for Columbia until 1929, producing 150 selections, of which at least two dozen were her own compositions. By the end of the 1920s, women blues singers were fading in popularity, largely because urban audiences were becoming more sophisticated. Smith appeared in an ill-fated Broadway show, *Pansy*, and received good reviews, but the show itself was weak and she left almost immediately. Her single film, *St. Louis Blues* (1929), immortalized her, although time and rough living had taken a toll on her voice and appearance.

Because of the Great Depression, the recording industry was in disarray by 1931. Columbia dismantled its race catalog and dropped Smith along with others. She had already begun to shift to popular ballads and swing tunes in an attempt to keep up with changing public taste. Okeh Records issued four of her selections in 1933. She altered her act and costumes in an attempt to appeal to club patrons, but she did not live to fulfill her hope of a new success with the emerging swing ensembles. On a tour of southern towns, Smith died in an automobile accident. ◆

Bessie Smith sang with passion about everyday problems, natural disasters, the horrors of the workhouse, abuse and violence, unfaithful lovers, and the longing for someone, anyone, to love.

Smith, Mamie

MAY 26, 1883 – SEPTEMBER 16, 1946 ● BLUES SINGER

Many details surrounding the birth of Mamie Smith, the first African-American recording star, are uncertain. It is generally conceded that she was born in Cincinnati, Ohio, but it is not clear what her birth name was. Before reaching adulthood she sang, danced, and acted with white and black traveling vaudeville shows, including the Four Dancing Mitchells and the Salem Tutt-Whitney show. She married the singer William "Smitty" Smith in 1912 and came to New York the next year with the Smart Set revue.

1883 ▸ Smith is born in Cincinnati.

1912 ▸ Smith marries Smitty Smith.

1913 ▸ Smith travels to New York with the Smart Set revue.

1918 ▸ Perry Bradford hires Smith for his show *Made in Harlem*.

1920 ▸ Smith records "Crazy Blues."

1922 ▸ Smith records "Got to Cool My Doggies Now" with Coleman Hawkins.

1923 ▸ Smith records "Lady Luck Blues" with Sidney Bechet.

1944 ▸ Smith appears with Billy Holiday in New York.

1946 ▸ Smith dies in New York City.

In New York Smith met Perry Bradford, a minstrel performer and popular song composer, who eventually hired her for his show *Made in Harlem* (1918); he also launched her recording career in 1920 when he persuaded technicians at Okeh Records to let her record "That Thing Called Love" and "You Can't Keep a Good Man Down." This disc, one of the earliest known recordings by an African-American popular singer, sold well enough to allow Smith to return to Okeh's studios later that year to record "Crazy Blues," a Bradford composition backed by a jazz band whose members included Willie "The Lion" Smith. "Crazy Blues" is sometimes considered the first blues recording, but the performance shares less with other classic blues records from the 1920s than with popular musical and vaudeville theater songs from the time. Nonetheless, "Crazy Blues" was a huge success that sold more than one million copies and initiated the blues craze of the 1920s. "Crazy Blues" also inaugurated the "race music" industry, which marketed blues and jazz specifically for African-American audiences.

In the 1920s Smith worked extensively with some of the finest improvisers in blues and jazz, including Bubber Miley on "I'm Gonna Get You" (1922), Coleman Hawkins on "Got to Cool My Doggies Now" (1922), and Sidney Bechet on "Lady Luck Blues" (1923). She also continued to perform in vaudeville and stage acts, including *Follow Me* (1922), *Struttin' Along* (1923), *Dixie Revue* (1924), *Syncopated Revue* (1925), and *Frolicking Around* (1926). Smith became wealthy, lived lavishly, and toured and recorded frequently.

In the 1930s Smith sang at clubs and concerts with Fats Pichon, Andy Kirk, and the Beale Street Boys. She also performed in the shows *Sun Tan Follies* (1929), *Fireworks of 1930* (1930), *Rhumbaland Avenue* (1931), and *Yelping Hounds Revue* (1932–34). Smith's film career began in 1929 with *Jailhouse Blues* and continued with *Paradise in Harlem* (1939), *Mystery in Swing* (1940), *Murder on Lenox Avenue* (1941), and *Because I Love You* (1943). By the early 1940s Smith had lost much of her wealth. In 1944 she made her last appearance in New York with Billie Holiday. That year Smith fell ill, and she spent the last two years of her life in Harlem Hospital. Though the generally accepted date of Smith's death is September 16, 1946, it is possible that she died on October 30. ◆

Spencer, Anne
(Scales, Annie Bethel)

FEBRUARY 6, 1882 – JULY 27, 1975 ● POET

Born on a plantation in Henry County, Virginia, Annie Bethel Scales moved with her mother to Bramwell, West Virginia, a mining town, at the age of five when her parents separated. Her mother, Sarah Louise Scales, the proud daughter of a former slave and of a wealthy white Virginian, would not let Annie attend the local school with the miners' children. As a result, Annie barely knew how to read when she was enrolled, at age eleven, in the Virginia Seminary at Lynchburg, Virginia. She quickly made up for lost time and discovered a love for literature, writing her first poem, "The Skeptic," in 1896. As the valedictorian at her graduation in 1899, she gave a speech, "Through Sacrifice to Victory," about the plight of blacks in the United States.

This early concern for African Americans prompted Spencer to take an activist's role many times in her life, yet her poetry has been criticized for not reflecting activist issues. A strong individualist who was influenced by Ralph Waldo Emerson's theory of self-reliance, she felt no need to justify her choice of topics, saying simply, "I write about some of the things I love. But have no civilized articulation for the things I hate." In fact, although her poetry deals mostly with love and friendship, it does contain elements of racial pride and indignation, especially in "White Things," written in 1918, after Spencer read reports of the brutal lynching of a pregnant black woman.

After graduation, Scales taught in Maybeury, Elkhorn, and Naola, West Virginia, before marrying her high school sweetheart, Edward Spencer, in 1901, and settling with him at 1313 Pierce Street in Lynchburg. There she raised their three children and tended her famous garden, which figured prominently in much of her poetry. Her first poem was published in 1920, after James Weldon Johnson discovered her work. As field secretary for the NAACP, he met Annie Spencer when he helped her form a local chapter of the NAACP. He convinced her to use the pen name Anne Spencer, and forwarded her work to

1882 Spencer is born on a Virginia plantation.

1896 Spencer writes her first poem, "The Skeptic."

1899 Spencer graduates from high school as valedictorian.

1901 Spencer marries her high school sweetheart.

1918 Spencer writes "White Things."

1920 Spencer publishes her poetry for the first time.

1923 Spencer starts working at the town library.

1977 Spencer's house and garden are declared a historical landmark.

publishers. *The Crisis* published "Before the Feast at Shushan" in 1920, and subsequently Anne Spencer's work appeared in magazines and anthologies, including Johnson's *The Book of American Negro Poetry* (1922), Louis Untermeyer's *American Poetry Since 1900* (1923), Countee Cullen's *Caroling Dusk* (1927), and Richard Ellmann and Robert O'Clair's *The Norton Anthology of Modern Poetry* (1973). Fame brought friendships with such prominent figures as Paul Robeson, Langston Hughes, and W. E. B. Du Bois, who all found the Spencers' home a congenial place to stay in the South, where decent travel accommodations for blacks were scarce.

In 1923 Anne Spencer walked (she refused to ride in segregated buses) to Lynchburg's segregated Jones Memorial Library and applied for a job. She was hired, and, in 1924, at her urging, a new branch of the library was opened at Dunbar High School. Spencer served as librarian of this first public library facility available to blacks in Lynchburg until her retirement in 1945. In 1975, two months before her death, she was awarded an honorary Doctor of Letters degree from her alma mater. In 1977 her house and garden were declared a historical landmark. ◆

> *"I write about some of the things I love. But have no civilized articulation for the things I hate."*
>
> Anne Spencer

Stewart, Pearl

NOVEMBER 16, 1950 – ● JOURNALIST

Pearl Stewart is known primarily as the first African-American woman to edit a major national daily newspaper, but she also has had a long career as a journalist. A graduate of Howard University, Stewart's first important assignment came in 1978 when she moved to the San Francisco Bay area and was named features editor of the *Oakland Tribune,* owned by African-American editor Robert C. Maynard. Two years later, however, she moved to the *San Francisco Chronicle,* for which she worked as a reporter, amassing an impressive professional reputation. In 1991 Stewart left the *Chronicle* and took a position as regular columnist for a weekly Oakland community paper, and *East Bay Express.* In 1992, following the death of Robert Maynard, the *Tribune* was bought by the Alameda Newspaper Group, Inc., a newspaper chain. In accordance with

Maynard's previously expressed wishes, the group designated Stewart as his successor. On December 1, 1992, she assumed the editorship.

Stewart faced many challenges, notably that of reversing the *Tribune*'s decline in circulation from several hundred thousand in the 1970s to 114,000 in 1991, and encountered many obstacles. Her plan to transform the *Tribune* into a neighborhood paper led critics to accuse her of an overly suburban news focus. Similarly, her introduction of color photographs and improved graphics prompted complaints that the *Tribune* had become too slick. Stewart had a difficult working relationship with the Alameda Newspaper Group's members, especially after David Burgin took over as senior vice president and editor in chief in 1993. Worst of all, a contract dispute between the *Tribune*'s management and staff led employees to call for a boycott of the newspaper. The protest was officially endorsed by the Oakland City Council, which opposed Stewart's policies. Circulation continued to drop, reaching 91,000 by the end of 1993. On December 6, 1993, citing "differences of style" with Burgin, Stewart resigned as editor.

In 1994 Stewart was named journalist-in-residence at Howard University under a Freedom Forum grant. ◆

1950	Stewart is born.
1978	Stewart becomes features editor of the *Oakland Tribune*.
1980	Stewart becomes *San Francisco Chronicle* reporter.
1991	Stewart becomes a columnist for the *East Bay Express*.
1992	Stewart becomes editor of the *Oakland Tribune*.
1993	Stewart resigns as *Tribune* editor.
1994	Stewart becomes journalist-in-residence at Howard University.

Swoopes, Sheryl

MARCH 25, 1971 – ● BASKETBALL PLAYER

Even though basketball had become the world's most popular indoor sport in the mid 1990s, only men could compete as professionals in the United States. However, that changed dramatically in 1997, when the Board of Governors of the National Basketball Association (NBA) approved the Women's National Basketball Association (WNBA). Already a basketball legend, Sheryl Swoopes became one of the first two women the WNBA signed on.

Sheryl Denise Swoopes was born March 25, 1971, in Brownfield, Texas. She grew up with her mother, Louise, and three brothers. Swoopes played basketball with her brothers, and scoring against her 6′ 4″ brother taught Swoopes that she could take on any female. Swoopes grew to six feet and played

"I worked out the first six months of my pregnancy playing pickup games. Even after that, I still shot the ball."

Sheryl Swoopes,
1997

high school basketball. She became an All-State and All-American high school player, a remarkable beginning, as more American high schools compete in basketball than in any other sport.

College basketball teams recruited Swoopes, including the University of Texas in Austin, which was 400 miles from Brownfield. Impressed with that institution's reputation, she did not consider any other colleges. However, Swoopes became overwhelmed by homesickness and returned home after four days, dropping her full scholarship. She enrolled at nearby South Plains Junior College. Again Swoopes earned a national honor, becoming the National Junior College Player of the Year after her second season.

In 1991 Swoopes started at Texas Tech University in Lubbock, close to home. With her help, Texas Tech's Lady Raiders won two consecutive Southwest Conference titles. Swoopes delighted her coach and fans with her charisma and team spirit. She averaged 27 points per game as the team led by a 31 to 3 record. In a final game against the University of Texas at Austin, Swoopes scored an amazing 53 points.

In the NCAA tournament of 1993, Texas Tech won the championship in a final game against Ohio State University. Not only was the game a cliff-hanger with a final score of 84 to 82, Swoopes wowed the basketball world with an outstanding personal performance. She scored 47 points, breaking the record for most points scored in an NCAA final game. The record was previously held by Bill Walton, who had gone on to become a top-ranked NBA player.

Swoopes's big win brought her national attention and a number of awards. She was named Sportswoman of the Year by the Women's Sports Foundation and companies sought her endorsement for sports products. Eager to move up in the basketball world, she faced the hard reality of women's basketball:

"I have been playing since I was seven or eight years old and I've always loved it. There has never really been a point in time that I thought I was going to do something else. I always wanted to play basketball."

Sheryl Swoopes, quoted in *Lift*, March 1996

there were no professional women's teams in the United States. A man with her outstanding record would have entered the NBA draft, the process by which the NBA obtains new players from among former college players.

Swoopes's only option for professional play was an overseas team. In 1993 she played for an Italian professional women's league, but she only lasted ten games before returning home. She finished her college degree and volunteered as a coach.

Swoopes then played for the undefeated USA Basketball Women's National Team, playing around the world in preparation for the 1996 Summer Olympic Games. Swoopes earned a $50,000 salary as well as income from the first Nike shoe named for a woman, the Air Swoopes. She helped the USA Women's Olympic Team win the gold medal at the 1996 Summer Games in Atlanta.

In 1996 and 1997 Swoopes helped make basketball history. On April 24, 1996, the NBA Board of Governors approved the Women's National Basketball Association (WNBA), and on October 23, 1996, the first players, Sheryl Swoopes and Rebecca Lobo, were signed on. Eight cities were soon selected to be homes to the WNBA's charter teams.

The inaugural WNBA season began on June 21, 1997. In that same month, Swoopes and her husband, Eric Jackson, had their first child, a son they named Jordan, after her hero, basketball star Michael Jordan. Within six weeks of the birth, Swoopes was on the court with the Houston Comets. Commentators and players alike were amazed at her quick postpartum comeback. Swoopes told the press, "It's very important to me to show [young girls] that it is very possible to be able to manage being a mom and an athlete at the same time."

The Comets won the 1997 WNBA championship. In September 1998 the Comets repeated their victory, beating the Phoenix Mercury in an 80 to 71 final game. Swoopes told reporters, "I'm just really excited that I had the opportunity to come back and be a part of this wonderful organization. I want to say thank you, Houston, and I look forward to doing it again." ◆

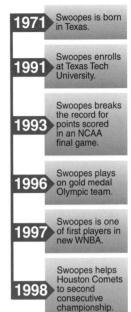

1971 Swoopes is born in Texas.

1991 Swoopes enrolls at Texas Tech University.

1993 Swoopes breaks the record for points scored in an NCAA final game.

1996 Swoopes plays on gold medal Olympic team.

1997 Swoopes is one of first players in new WNBA.

1998 Swoopes helps Houston Comets to second consecutive championship.

Taylor, Susie Baker King

AUGUST 6, 1848 – 1912 ● TEACHER, NURSE, AND WRITER

Susie Baker taught children during the day, adults at night, and black soldiers when they had a free moment. She also served as a laundress, cook, weapons cleaner, and nurse.

S usie Baker was born into slavery on Grest Farm, in Liberty County, Georgia, and secretly learned to read and write through the efforts of a neighboring free woman of color, a white female playmate, and the son of her family's white landlord. She put these skills to use by writing passes for African Americans, both slave and free.

At the opening of the Civil War, when the Union Army captured Fort Pulaski off the Georgia coast, Baker went with her uncle and his family to St. Simon's Island, on one of the Union-controlled Sea Islands. The men in her family became part of Company E of the First South Carolina Infantry, later the 33rd U.S. Colored Infantry commanded by Thomas Wentworth Higginson. Baker accompanied this regiment throughout the Civil War, going with the men to Camp Saxton in Beaufort, South Carolina, in late 1862 and joining them in their military expeditions up and down the coast.

Baker's literacy earned her the role of teacher; she taught children during the day, adults at night, and black soldiers when they had a free moment. She also served as laundress, cook, weapons cleaner, and nurse. As a nurse she worked with Clara Barton during the latter's stay at the Sea Islands in 1863. Baker was almost killed in a boating accident in 1864, but soon returned to service, where she tended to soldiers of the famous 54th Massachusetts Volunteers. All her labor was performed without pay.

Baker married Edward King, a black sergeant, in 1862, and after the war the couple lived in Savannah. As a means of support, and because there was no free school for black children, she ran a private school out of her home, teaching young students for a dollar a month, as well as adults in the evenings. She continued this work until a free school opened. Her husband, who worked as a carpenter and longshoreman, died in 1866, just before the birth of their only child.

In 1867 King opened a school in rural Liberty County, Georgia, in which she taught for a year, before deciding to return to city life. Upon her return to Savannah, she opened a private night school for adults, again until a free school was established. King then worked as a domestic servant, traveling to New England in the summer with a white family, and later seeking employment there on her own, in order to support herself and her son.

In 1879 she married Russell L. Taylor and moved to Boston where in 1886 she helped organize Corps 67, Women's Relief Corps, an auxiliary women's relief organization for Union Army veterans. She served as guard, secretary, treasurer, and in 1893, president. When Taylor traveled to Louisiana in 1898 to tend to her son, who had fallen ill, she was greatly affected by being forced to travel in segregated railway cars, and by witnessing a lynching.

Taylor is best remembered for her memoir, *Reminiscences of My Life in Camp with the 33rd United States Colored Troops*. Published in 1902, the work describes not only her labor for the Union Army and her memory of the reading of the Emancipation Proclamation, but also her observations and experiences of discrimination and violence in America after the Civil War. It is the only published account of the military experience of the Civil War from the perspective of a black female participant. ◆

1848	Baker is born a slave in Georgia.
1862	Baker joins Union soldiers at Camp Saxton.
1862	Baker marries Edward King.
1863	Baker works with Clara Barton in the Sea Islands.
1864	King Baker is almost killed in a boating accident.
1867	King Baker opens a school in rural Georgia.
1879	King Baker marries Russell Taylor; moves to Boston.
1886	Taylor organizes Corps 67, Women's Relief Corps.
1902	Taylor publishes *Remembrances of My Life in Camp.*
1912	Taylor dies.

Terrell, Mary Eliza Church

SEPTEMBER 26, 1863 – JULY 24, 1954 ● CIVIL RIGHTS ACTIVIST AND WOMEN'S RIGHTS ADVOCATE

Terrell was born in Memphis, into a prosperous family of former slaves; she graduated from Oberlin College (1884) at the head of her class, then taught at Wilberforce University (1885–87) and briefly in a high school in

National Association of Colored Women's Clubs

The National Association of Colored Women (NACW) was the first national black organization in the United States. The organization was rooted in decades of local political activity and reform efforts by African-American women's clubs after the Civil War. In 1895 the women's clubs, along with various black women's magazines in existence at the time, called a national convention of black women to respond to a racist letter sent by a southern journalist to a British reformer. The 1895 convention led to the formation of the NACW in 1896. Mary Church Terrell became the organization's first president, serving until 1901. Committed to welfare and social reform, the NACW was the primary organization through which black women channeled their reform efforts from the 1890s to the 1920s. NACW members built schools, ran orphanages and day care centers, opened health service facilities, founded homes for the aged, set up kindergarten programs, and formed agencies in New York and Philadelphia to help female migrants from the South find jobs and housing. Although never a militant organization, the NACW also took strong stands against racial injustice by opposing segregation, supporting women's suffrage, and crusading for passage of antilynching legislation. The stature of the NACW declined during the 1930s when many of its welfare and social services became available through local, state, and private agencies. In 1957 NACW changed its name to the National Association of Colored Women's Clubs (NACWC). Today, the NACWC is primarily involved in educational, social service, and fund-raising activities.

Washington, D.C. After receiving an M.A. from Oberlin (1888), she traveled in Europe for two years, studying French, German, and Italian. In 1891 she married Robert Terrell, who was appointed judge of District of Columbia Municipal Court in 1901.

"While most girls run away from home to marry, I ran away to teach."

Mary Church Terrell, *A Colored Woman in a White World*, 1940

The overlapping concerns that characterized Terrell's life—public-education reform, women's rights, and civil rights—found expression in community work and organizational activities. She served as the first woman president of Bethel Literary and Historical Association (1892–93). She was the first black woman appointed to the District of Columbia Board of Education (1895–1901, 1906–11).

In spite of elements of racism and nativism, Terrell was an active member of the National American Woman Suffrage Association and addressed their convention in 1898 and 1900. She joined the Woman's Party picket line at the White House, and, after the achievement of suffrage, was active in the Republican party.

Women's international affairs involved her as well. She addressed the International Council of Women (Berlin, 1904) in English, German, and French, the only American to do so; she was a delegate to the Women's International League for Peace and Freedom (Zurich, 1919) and a vice president of the International Council of Women of the Darker Races; and addressed the International Assembly of the World Fellowship of Faiths (London, 1937).

Terrell participated in the founding of the National Association for the Advancement of Colored People (NAACP) and was vice president of the Washington, D.C., branch for many years. Her various causes coalesced around her concern with the quality of black women's lives. In 1892 she helped organize and headed the National League for the Protection of Colored Women in Washington, D.C.; she was the first president of the National Association of Colored Women, serving three terms (1896–1901) before being named honorary president for life and a vice president of the National Council of Negro Women.

Terrell worked for the unionization of black women and for their inclusion in established women's affairs. In 1919 she campaigned, unsuccessfully, for a Colored Women's Division within the Women's Bureau of the Department of Labor, and to have the First International Congress of Working Women directly address the concerns of black working women.

Age did not diminish Terrell's activism. Denied admission to the Washington chapter of the American Association of University Women (AAUW) in 1946 on racial grounds, she entered a three-year legal battle that led the national group to clarify its bylaws to read that a college degree was the only requirement for membership. In 1949 Terrell joined the sit-ins, which challenged segregation in public accommodations, a landmark civil rights case, as well as serving as chairwoman of the Coordinating Committee for the Enforcement of the District of Columbia Anti-Discrimination Laws.

In addition to her picketing and sit-ins, Terrell wrote many magazine articles treating disfranchisement, discrimination, and racism, as well as her autobiography, *A Colored Woman in a White World* (1940). ◆

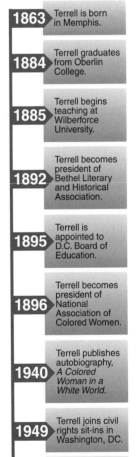

"Keep on moving, keep on insisting, keep on fighting injustice."
Mary Church Terrell, in *Journal of Negro History*, 1938

1863 Terrell is born in Memphis.

1884 Terrell graduates from Oberlin College.

1885 Terrell begins teaching at Wilberforce University.

1892 Terrell becomes president of Bethel Literary and Historical Association.

1895 Terrell is appointed to D.C. Board of Education.

1896 Terrell becomes president of National Association of Colored Women.

1940 Terrell publishes autobiography, *A Colored Woman in a White World.*

1949 Terrell joins civil rights sit-ins in Washington, DC.

1954 Terrell dies.

Tharpe, Sister Rosetta

MARCH 20, 1915 – OCTOBER 9, 1973 ● GOSPEL SINGER AND GUITARIST

1915 Tharpe is born in Arkansas.

1938 Tharpe makes a mark as a singer in New York City.

1943 Tharpe becomes the first major gospel singer to perform at the Apollo Theater.

1944 Tharpe records "Strange Things Happen Every Day."

1949 Tharpe records Daniel in the Lion's Den" with her mother.

1960 Tharpe records "I Have Good News to Bring" with the Sally Jenkins Singers.

1973 Tharpe dies in Philadelphia.

Sister Rosetta Tharpe was born Rosetta Nubin in Cotton Plant, Arkansas. She began her musical apprenticeship playing guitar and singing in the Church of God in Christ, a Pentecostal church, and gained professional experience traveling with her mother, Katie Bell Nubin, a missionary. In her teens she followed her mother to Chicago. It is not clear whether she took a new last name as the result of a marriage, but it was as Sister Rosetta Tharpe that she came to prominence in 1938 in New York. At first she was known for performing in secular venues, a controversial practice for a gospel singer. In that year she performed at Harlem's Cotton Club with bandleader Cab Calloway and at the famous "Spirituals to Swing" concert at Carnegie Hall. Those performances helped her land a contract with Decca, making her the first gospel singer to record for a major label. In 1943 she performed at the Apollo Theater, the first time that a major gospel singer had appeared there. Her 1944 rendition of "Strange Things Happen Every Day" was widely popular.

Starting in the 1940s, Tharpe performed in churches, concert halls, nightclubs, on the radio, and later even on television. She gained fame not only because of her practice of playing secular venues, a practice she defended by calling all of her music evangelical, but also because of her jazz and blues-influenced guitar playing. Tharpe, who recorded "Daniel in the Lion's Den" in 1949 with her mother, eventually toured with such jazz and blues groups as those led by Benny Goodman, Count Basie, Muddy Waters, Sammy Price, and Lucky Millinder, as well as with gospel groups such as the Caravans, the James Cleveland Singers, the Dixie Hummingbirds, the Richmond Harmonizing Four, and the Sally Jenkins Singers, with whom she recorded "I Have Good News to Bring" in 1960. Tharpe, who was the first major gospel singer to tour Europe, was also widely known for her live performances and recordings of "That's All," "I Looked Down the Line," "Up Above My Head," and "This Train." She died in Philadelphia. ◆

Thomas, Alma

SEPTEMBER 22, 1891 – FEBRUARY 24, 1978 ● ARTIST

Alma Thomas was born in Columbus, Georgia; her family moved to Washington, D.C., in 1907 after the Atlanta race riots (1906) to seek better educational opportunities. In Washington, D.C., Thomas attended Armstrong Technical High School, from which she graduated in 1911. That year she began studying at Miner Teachers Normal School in Washington, D.C., and received a certificate to teach kindergarten in 1913. From 1915 to 1921 she taught art at Thomas Garrett Settlement House in Wilmington, Delaware.

Thomas attended Howard University from 1921 to 1924. There she pursued a B.S. in fine arts as one of the first students in the newly organized department of fine arts. In 1924 she began teaching art at Shaw Junior High School in northwest Washington and she remained there until her retirement in 1960. From 1930 to 1934 she pursued a master's degree at Columbia University's Teachers College, where she studied puppet making. In 1943 Thomas became one of the founders of the Barnett-Aden Gallery in Washington, D.C. The gallery exhibited works by men and women of all races, and Thomas remained active as its codirector for twenty years.

Thomas's early work was largely representational, reflecting her academic training. Although she was influenced by abstract expressionism in the 1950s, she maintained an interest in depicting forms as they appeared in the world as in her work *Joe Summerford's Still Life Study* (1952). After 1960, when she retired from teaching and began to paint full time, her work became more abstract and was comprised of patterns and textures of color (*Watusi*, 1963). Working with a palette knife rather than a brush, Thomas painted abstract impressions of her grandfather's plantation in Alabama, the view of a tree from her kitchen window, the flower garden in her backyard, and the blossoms around Washington, D.C., in a work entitled *Earth Paintings* from the late 1960s. Thomas used the white of the canvas as a backdrop for splotches of color and long horizontal

1891 Thomas is born in Georgia.

1907 Thomas's family moves to Washington, DC, to seek better schools.

1913 Thomas earns a certificate to teach kindergarten.

1921 Thomas enters Howard University.

1924 Thomas joins faculty of Shaw Junior High School in Washington.

1930 Thomas enters Columbia University Teachers College.

1943 Thomas helps found the Barnett-Aden Gallery in Washington.

1952 Thomas paints *Joe Summerford's Still Life Study.*

1963 Thomas paints *Watusi.*

1972 Thomas's work is exhibited at New York's Whitney Museum.

1978 Thomas dies.

strips made from short brush strokes in paintings such as *A Joyful Scene of Spring* (1968). In 1970 she created a series of *Space Paintings*, which were inspired by the U.S. Space Program (*The Eclipse*, 1970). Other works from the 1970s include *Wind and Crepe Myrtle Concerto* (1973), and *Red Azaleas Singing and Dancing Rock and Roll* (1976).

Thomas's exhibitions included shows at Howard University organized by James Porter in 1966, the Whitney Museum of American Art (1972), Corcoran Gallery in Washington, D.C. (1972), Martha Jackson Gallery in New York City (1973), and the Franz Bader Gallery in Washington, D.C. (1974). ◆

Thomas, Debra J. "Debi"

MARCH 25, 1967 – ● ICE SKATER

1967 — Thomas is born in New York.

1986 — Thomas wins U.S. and Women's World Figure Skating Championships.

1987 — Thomas develops tendinitis.

1988 — Thomas wins Olympic bronze medal; turns professional.

1991 — Thomas wins World Challenge of Champions; graduates from Stanford University.

tendinitis: inflammation of the tissue that connects muscles to the bones.

A native of Poughkeepsie, New York, Debi Thomas moved to northern California with her family when she was a small child. Fascinated by an ice show she watched at the age of three, Thomas had become a competitive skater by the time she was in junior high school.

Thomas began to achieve national honors as a skater while a student at San Mateo High School and moved quickly to the senior women's division before graduating. She excelled academically as well as on the ice and became the first prominent female skater to attend college since Tenley Albright in the 1950s; Thomas graduated from Stanford in 1991.

At 5' 6", Thomas was taller than most of her competitors, with extra height on her double and triple jumps. She thrilled audiences and pleased judges with her graceful choreography blended with a powerful athleticism. She also excelled in the mandatory school figures required during her years of competition. In 1985 she was named Figure Skater of the Year, and in 1986 she became the first black woman to win the United States and Women's World Figure Skating Championships. That same year she was named Amateur Female Athlete of the Year and Wide World of Sports Athlete of the Year. She developed **tendinitis** in 1987 but managed to place second in the U.S. and World Championships. In 1988 she placed third in both the World Championships and at the Winter Olympics in Calgary, Alberta.

Thomas turned professional in 1988, winning the World Professional Championships in 1988, 1989, and 1991. In 1991 she also won the World Challenge of Champions and entered Northwestern University Medical School that same year to study orthopedic and sports medicine. ◆

Thornton, Willie Mae "Big Mama"

DECEMBER 11, 1926 – JULY 25, 1984   ● BLUES SINGER

Born in Montgomery, Alabama, the daughter of a minister, Willie Mae Thornton left home after her mother died. She joined Sammy Green's Hot Harlem Revue at the age of fourteen. In 1948 she moved to Houston, where Peacock Records owner Don Robey arranged for her to sing with the Johnny Otis Rhythm and Blues Caravan. Her 250-pound size earned her the nickname "Big Mama," and she became popular for her boisterous, shouting style. "Hound Dog" (1953), a blues song later made famous by Elvis Presley, was her only hit, but it enabled her to tour nationally with Johnny Ace as the "reigning king and queen of the blues" until Ace's Russian roulette death in 1954. Thornton's career never recovered from that event.

Thornton struggled in the San Francisco Bay area until the blues revival of the mid-1960s created a demand for older blues singers after which time she performed at jazz, folk, and blues festivals in the United States and abroad. The rock singer Janis Joplin remade Thornton's "Ball and Chain" into her signature song in 1968, but Thornton had signed away the copyright to the tune years before, and she earned no money for Joplin's version. Thornton's recordings include *In Europe* (1965), *Ball and Chain* (1968), *Stronger Than Dirt* (1969), *Saved* (1973), *Jail* (1975), and *Mama's Pride* (1978).

Throughout her career, Thornton drank heavily and dressed in men's clothing, sometimes wearing a dress over trousers and brogans. Her audiences, however, forgave the eccentricity. She was frail from **cirrhosis** and weighed only ninety-five pounds when she died of a heart attack at the age of

cirrhosis: chronic liver disease.

fifty-seven in a Los Angeles boarding house. At a funeral conducted by the Rev. Johnny Otis, money was raised to pay for her burial expenses. ◆

Truth, Sojourner

C. 1797 – NOVEMBER 26, 1883 ● ABOLITIONIST, SUFFRAGIST, AND SPIRITUALIST

Sojourner Truth was born Isabella Bomefree in Ulster County, New York, the second youngest of thirteen children born in slavery to Elizabeth (usually called Mau-Mau Bett) and James Bomefree. The other siblings were either sold or given away before her birth. The family was owned by Johannes Hardenbergh, a patroon and Revolutionary War patriot, the head of one of the most prominent Dutch families in late eighteenth-century New York.

Mau-Mau Bett was mystical and unlettered but imparted to her daughter strong faith, filial devotion, and a strong sense of individual integrity. Isabella Bomefree, whose first language was Dutch, was taken from her parents in 1808 and sold to an English-speaking owner, who maltreated her because of her inability to understand English. Through her own defiance—what she later called her "talks with God"—and her father's intercession, a Dutch tavern keeper soon purchased her. Kindly treated but surrounded by the rough tavern culture and probably sexually abused, the girl prayed for a new master. In 1810 John I. Dumont of New Paltz, New York, purchased Isabella Bomefree for three hundred dollars.

Isabella remained Dumont's slave for eighteen years. Dumont boasted that Belle, as he called her, was "better to me than a man." She planted, plowed, cultivated, and harvested crops. She milked the farm animals, sewed, weaved, cooked, and cleaned house. But Mrs. Dumont despised and tormented her, possibly because Dumont fathered one of her children.

Isabella had two relationships with slave men. Bob, her first love, a man from a neighboring estate, was beaten senseless for "taking up" with her and was forced to take another woman. She later became associated with Thomas, with whom she remained until her freedom. Four of her five children survived to adulthood.

Although New York slavery ended for adults in 1827, Dumont promised Isabella her freedom a year earlier. When he refused to keep his promise, she fled with an infant child, guided by "the word of God" as she later related. She took refuge with Isaac Van Wagenen, who purchased her for the remainder of her time as a slave. She later adopted his family name.

Isabella Van Wagenen was profoundly shaped by a religious experience she underwent in 1827 at Pinkster time, the popular early summer African-Dutch slave holiday. As she recounted it, she forgot God's deliverance of his people from bondage and prepared to return to Dumont's farm for Pinkster: "I looked back in Egypt," she said, "and everything seemed so pleasant there." But she felt the mighty, luminous, and wrathful presence of an angry God blocking her path. Stalemated and momentarily blinded and suffocated under "God's breath," she claimed in her *Narrative*, Jesus mercifully intervened and proclaimed her salvation. This conversion enabled Isabella Van Wagenen to claim direct and special communication with Jesus and the Trinity for the remainder of her life, and she subsequently became involved with a number of highly spiritual religious groups.

A major test of faith followed Isabella Van Wagenen's conversion when she discovered that Dumont had illegally sold her son Peter. Armed with spiritual assurance and a mother's rage, she scoured the countryside, gaining moral and financial support from prominent Dutch residents, antislavery Quakers, and local Methodists. She brought suit, and Peter was eventually returned from Alabama and freed.

In 1829 Isabella, now a Methodist, moved to New York City. She joined the African Methodist Episcopal Zion Church, where she discovered a brother and two sisters. She also began

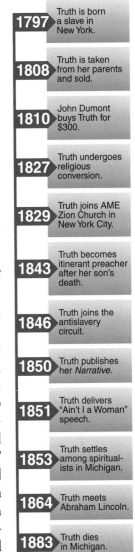

1797 Truth is born a slave in New York.

1808 Truth is taken from her parents and sold.

1810 John Dumont buys Truth for $300.

1827 Truth undergoes religious conversion.

1829 Truth joins AME Zion Church in New York City.

1843 Truth becomes itinerant preacher after her son's death.

1846 Truth joins the antislavery circuit.

1850 Truth publishes her *Narrative*.

1851 Truth delivers "Ain't I a Woman" speech.

1853 Truth settles among spiritualists in Michigan.

1864 Truth meets Abraham Lincoln.

1883 Truth dies in Michigan.

> *"Look at me! Look at my arms! I have plowed and planted, and gathered into barns, and no man could head me—and ain't I a woman? I could work as much and eat as much as a man (when I could get it) and bear de lash as well—and ain't I a woman?"*
> Sojourner Truth, 1851

millenarian: someone who believes in a coming ideal society.

to attract attention for her extraordinary preaching, praying, and singing, though these talents were mainly employed among the Perfectionists (a sect of white radical mystics emerging from the Second Great Awakening who championed millennial doctrines and equated spiritual piety with morality and social justice with true Christianity). As housekeeper for Perfectionist Elijah Pierson, Isabella was involved in "the Kingdom," a sect organized by the spiritual zealot Robert Matthias. Among other practices he engaged in "spirit-matching," or wife swapping, with Ann Folger, wife of Pierson's business partner. Elijah Pierson's unexplained death brought public outcries of foul play. To conceal Ann Pierson's promiscuity, the Folgers suggested that there had been an erotic attachment between Matthias and Isabella Van Wagenen and that they murdered Pierson with poisoned blackberries. Challenging her accusers, Isabella Van Wagenen vowed to "crush them with the truth." Lack of evidence and prejudice about blacks testifying against whites led to dismissal of the case. Isabella Van Wagenen triumphed by successfully suing the Folgers for slander. Though chastened by this experience with religious extremism, the association with New York Perfectionists enhanced her biblical knowledge, oratorical skills, and commitment to reform.

Isabella Van Wagenen encouraged her beloved son Peter to take up seafaring to avoid the pitfalls of urban crime. In 1843 his vessel returned without him. Devastated by this loss, facing (at forty-six) a bleak future in domestic service, and influenced by the **millenarian** (known as the Millerite movement) ferment sweeping the Northeast at the time, she decided to radically change her life. She became an itinerant preacher and adopted the name Sojourner Truth because voices directed her to sojourn the countryside and speak God's truth. In the fall of 1843 she became ill and was taken to the Northampton utopian community in Florence, Massachusetts, where black abolitionist David Ruggles nursed her at his water-cure establishment. Sojourner Truth impressed residents, who included a number of abolitionists, with her slavery accounts, scriptural interpretations, wit, and simple oral eloquence.

By 1846 Sojourner Truth had joined the antislavery circuit, traveling with Abby Kelly Foster, Frederick Douglass, William Lloyd Garrison, and British M.P. George Thompson. An electrifying public orator, she soon became one of the most popular speakers for the abolitionist cause. Her fame was heightened by the publication of her *Narrative* in 1850, related and transcribed by Olive Gilbert. With proceeds from its sale she purchased a Northampton home. In 1851, speaking before a National Women's Convention in Akron, Ohio, Sojourner Truth defended the physical and spiritual strength of women in her famous "Ain't I a Woman?" speech. In 1853 Sojourner's anti-slavery, spiritualist, and temperance advocacy took her to the Midwest, where she settled among spiritualists in Harmonia, Michigan.

"I cannot read a book," said Sojourner Truth, "but I can read the people." She dissected political and social issues through parables of everyday life. The Constitution, silent on black rights, had a "little weevil in it." She was known for her captivating one-line retorts. An Indiana audience threatened to torch the building if she spoke. Sojourner Truth replied, "Then I will speak to the ashes." In the late 1840s, grounded in faith that God and moral **suasion** would eradicate bondage, she challenged her despairing friend Douglass with "Frederick, is God dead?" In 1858, when a group of men questioned her gender, claiming she wasn't properly feminine in her demeanor, Sojourner Truth, a bold early feminist, exposed her bosom to the entire assembly, proclaiming that shame was not hers but theirs.

During the Civil War Sojourner Truth recruited and supported Michigan's black regiment, counseled freedwomen, set up employment operations for freedpeople willing to relocate, and initiated desegregation of streetcars in Washington, D.C. In 1864 she had an audience with Abraham Lincoln. Following the war, Sojourner Truth moved to Michigan, settling in Battle Creek, but remained active in numerous reform causes. She supported the Fifteenth Amendment and women's suffrage.

Disillusioned by the failure of Reconstruction, Sojourner Truth devoted her last years to the support of a black western homeland. In her later years, despite decades of interracial cooperation, she became skeptical of collaboration with whites and became an advocate of racial separation. She died in 1883 in Battle Creek, attended by the famous physician and breakfast cereal founder John Harvey Kellogg. ◆

"I have borne thirteen children and seen them most all sold off into slavery, and when I cried out with a mother's grief, none but Jesus heard—and ain't I a women?"
Sojourner Truth, 1851

suasion: urging.

Tubman, Harriet Ross

C. 1820 – MARCH 10, 1913 ● ABOLITIONIST, NURSE, AND FEMINIST

H arriet Ross, one of eleven children born to slaves Benjamin Ross and Harriet Green, was born about 1820 in Dorchester County in Maryland. Although she was known on the plantation as Harriet Ross, her family called her Araminta, or "Minty," a name given to her by her mother.

Like most slaves, Ross had no formal education and began work on the plantation as a child. When she was five years old, her master rented her out to a neighboring family, the Cooks, as a domestic servant. At age thirteen, Ross suffered permanent neurological damage after either her overseer or owner struck her in the head with a two-pound lead weight when she placed herself between her master and a fleeing slave. For the rest of her life, she experienced sudden blackouts.

In 1844 she married John Tubman, a free black who lived on a nearby plantation. Her husband's free status, however, did not transfer to Harriet upon their marriage. Between 1847 and 1849, after the death of her master, Tubman worked in the household of Anthony Thompson, a physician and preacher. Thompson was the legal guardian of Tubman's new master, who was still too young to operate the plantation. When the young master died, Tubman faced an uncertain future, and rumors circulated that Thompson would sell slaves out of the state.

In response, Tubman escaped from slavery in 1849, leaving behind her husband, who refused to accompany her. She settled in Philadelphia, where she found work as a scrubwoman. She returned to Maryland for her husband two years later, but John Tubman had remarried.

Tubman's successful escape to the free state of Pennsylvania, however, did not guarantee her safety, particularly after the passage of the Fugitive Slave Law of 1850, which facilitated southern slave-holding efforts to recover runaway slaves. Shortly after her escape from slavery, Tubman became involved in the abolitionist movement, forming friendships with one of the black leaders of the Underground Railroad, William Still, and white abolitionist Thomas Garrett. While many of her abolitionist colleagues organized antislavery societies, wrote and spoke against slavery, and raised money for the cause, Tubman's abolitionist activities were more directly

> *"I started with this idea in my head: There was two things I had a right to, liberty or death. If I could not have one, I would have the other, for no man should take me alive."*
>
> Harriet Tubman,
> c. 1868

Harriet Tubman
(at left, holding a pan)
with a group of slaves
she helped rescue.

1820	Tubman is born a slave in Maryland.
1844	Tubman marries John Tubman.
1849	Tubman escapes to Philadelphia.
1850	Tubman makes first rescue mission to the South.
1851	Tubman travels to the South to rescue her brother and his wife.
1857	Tubman rescues her parents.
1859	Tubman helps John Brown plan Harper's Ferry raid.
1862	Tubman nurses Union soldiers during the Civil War.
1869	Tubman publishes *Scenes in the Life of Harriet Tubman.*
1890	Congress awards Tubman a monthly pension as a war widow.
1896	Tubman is delegate to National Federation of Afro-American Women convention.
1913	Tubman dies in New York.

related to the actual freeing of slaves on the Underground Railroad. She worked as an agent on the railroad, assuming different disguises to assist runaways in obtaining food, shelter, clothing, cash, and transportation. Tubman might appear as a feeble, old woman or as a demented, impoverished man, and she was known for the rifle she carried on rescue missions, both for her own protection and to intimidate fugitives who might become fainthearted along the journey.

Tubman traveled to the South nineteen times to rescue approximately three hundred African-American men, women, and children from bondage. Her first rescue mission was to Baltimore, Maryland, in 1850 to help her sister and two children escape from slavery. Her notoriety as a leader of the Underground Railroad led some Maryland planters to offer a $40,000 bounty for her capture. Having relocated many runaways to Canada, Tubman herself settled in the village of St. Catharines, Canada West (now Ontario), in the early 1850s. She traveled to the South in 1851 to rescue her brother and his wife, and returned in 1857 to rescue her parents, with whom she resettled in Auburn, New York, shortly thereafter.

Tubman's involvement in the abolitionist movement placed her in contact with many progressive social leaders in the North, including John Brown, whom she met in 1858. She helped Brown plan his raid on Harpers Ferry, Virginia, in 1859, but illness prevented her from participating. Tubman's last trip

"When I found I had crossed that line, I looked at my hands to see if I was the same person. There was such a glory over everything; the sun came like gold through the trees, and over the fields, and I felt like I was in Heaven."

Harriet Tubman, c. 1868, describing her first escape from slavery

to the South took place in 1860, after which she returned to Canada. In 1861 she moved back to the United States as the last of eleven southern states seceded from the Union.

When the Civil War broke out, Tubman served in the Union Army as a scout, spy, and nurse. In 1862 she went to Beaufort, South Carolina, where she nursed both white soldiers and black refugees from neighboring southern plantations. Tubman traveled from camp to camp in the coastal regions of South Carolina, Georgia, and Florida, administering her nursing skills wherever they were needed. Tubman also worked as a scout for the Union Army, traveling behind enemy lines to gather information and recruit slaves. She supported herself by selling chickens, eggs, root beer, and pies. After returning briefly to Beaufort, Tubman worked during the spring and summer of 1865 at a freedman's hospital in Fortress Monroe, Virginia.

After the war's end, Tubman eventually returned to Auburn to care for her elderly parents. Penniless, she helped support her family by farming. In 1869 Tubman married Nelson Davis, a Civil War veteran. That same year, she published *Scenes in the Life of Harriet Tubman*, written for her by Sarah H. Bradford and printed and circulated by Gerrit Smith and Wendall Phillips. Tubman received some royalties from the book, but she was less successful in her effort to obtain financial compensation for her war work. She agitated for nearly thirty years for $1,800 compensation for her service as a Civil War nurse and cook. In 1890 Congress finally awarded Tubman a monthly pension of $20 as a widow of a war veteran.

Tubman's activism continued on many fronts after the Civil War ended. She was an ardent supporter of women's suffrage and regularly attended women's rights meetings. To Tubman, racial liberation and women's rights were inextricably linked. Tubman formed close relationships with Susan B. Anthony and other feminists. She was a delegate to the first convention of the National Federation of Afro-American Women in 1896 (later called the National Association of Colored Women). The following year, the New England Women's Suffrage Association held a reception in Tubman's honor.

While living in Auburn, Tubman continued her work in the black community by taking in orphans and the elderly, often receiving assistance from wealthier neighbors. She helped establish schools for former slaves and wanted to establish a permanent home for poor and sick blacks. Tubman secured twenty-five acres in Auburn through a bank loan, but lacked the necessary funds to build on the land. In 1903 she deeded the land to the African Methodist Episcopal Zion Church, and five years later the congregation built the Harriet Tubman Home for Indigent and Aged Negroes, which continued to operate for several years after Tubman's death and was declared a National Historic Landmark in 1974.

Tubman died on March 10, 1913, at the age of ninety-three. Local Civil War veterans led the funeral march. The National Association of Colored Women later paid for the funeral and for the marble tombstone over Tubman's grave. A year after her death, black educator Booker T. Washington delivered a memorial address in celebration of Tubman's life and labors and on behalf of freedom. In 1978 the United States Postal Service issued the first stamp in its Black Heritage USA Series to honor Tubman.

Tubman, dubbed "the Moses of her people," had obtained legendary status in the African-American community within ten years of her escape to freedom. Perhaps more than any other figure of her time, Tubman personified resistance to slavery, and she became a symbol of courage and strength to African Americans—slave and free. The secrecy surrounding Tubman's activities on the Underground Railroad and her own reticence to talk about her role contributed to her mythic status. Heroic images of the rifle-carrying Tubman have persisted well into the twentieth century as Tubman has become the leading symbol of the Underground Railroad. ◆

To Harriet Tubman, racial liberation and women's rights were inextricably linked.

Turner, Tina

NOVEMBER 26, 1939 – ● SINGER

Tina Turner was born Annie Mae Bullock in Brownsville, Tennessee, where she lived until the age of eleven when her parents separated. As a child she sang and danced with Bootsie Whitelaw, a local trombonist. She lived with her grandmother until the age of sixteen, and then moved to St. Louis to live again with her mother. With her older sister Alline, she frequented nightclubs across the river in East St. Louis to see the popular Kings of Rhythm band, led by the rhythm and blues singer, guitarist, producer, and disc jockey Ike

Turner. One night Annie Mae took the stage and sang with Turner, and, soon after, she joined the group and went on tour with Ike and the Kings of Rhythm.

In 1960 Ike Turner declared that Annie Mae Bullock would be publicly known as "Tina" and announced that her first lead-vocal debut, "A Fool in Love" (1960), would be credited to Ike and Tina Turner. In 1962 Ike and Tina were married. The couple toured and recorded until 1974 as the "Ike and Tina Turner Revue," which featured Tina with her flamboyant backup singers and dancers, the Ikettes, accompanied by the Kings of Rhythm. They became one of the foremost rhythm and blues groups of the 1960s, distinguished by Ike's hard-driving accompaniment and Tina's hard-edged singing and seductive dancing. Their most important and popular recordings from the 1960s include "It's Gonna Work Out Fine" (1961) and "River Deep, Mountain High" (1966). A tour of the United States with the Rolling Stones in 1969 launched Ike and Tina Turner into the rock mainstream, and in 1970 they recorded Sly Stone's "I Want to Take You Higher." The next year they won a Grammy Award for "Proud Mary." Their other hits from this period include "Nutbush City Limits" (1973) and "Sweet Rhode Island Red" (1974). In 1974 Tina Turner embarked upon an acting career, starring in the movie version of the Who's rock opera, *Tommy*.

Ike and Tina Turner separated in 1975, with Tina claiming she was the victim of frequent domestic abuse. Their divorce came in 1978, and Tina built her solo career. Her appearances with Rod Stewart and the Rolling Stones led to her signing with Capitol Records in 1983. Her 1984 album, *Private Dancer*, including a revival of Al Green's "Let's Stay Together," marked her arrival as a solo performer. Turner won three Grammys for *Private Dancer* (1984), which included "What's Love Got to Do with It?"

By the mid-1980s Turner had become a major pop singer in her own right, and was famed for her towering mane of hair, revealing costumes, and sexually charged strutting dances. In 1985 she resumed her acting career with the film *Mad Max 3: Beyond Thunderdome*, whose sound track included her performances of "We Don't Need Another Hero" and the Grammy-winning "One of the Living." After publishing her autobiography, *I, Tina*, in 1986, Turner released *Break Every Rule*, a best-selling album that won another Grammy. Turner then went on a 145-city tour, parts of which were released as *Tina Live in Europe!* (1988). In 1988 Turner announced that she was retiring from touring to focus on her acting career, but the following year she toured to promote her *Foreign Affair* album (1989). She continues to tour and record and has also remained involved in film, serving as consultant for the feature film *What's Love Got to Do with It?* (1993), which was based on her autobiography. Turner released the album *Wildest Dream* in 1996. ◆

1939 Turner is born in Tennessee.
1862 Tina marries Ike Turner.
1869 Turners tour with the Rolling Stones.
1971 Turners win Grammy Award for "Proud Mary."
1975 Turners separate.
1984 Turner records *Private Dancer*.
1986 Turner publishes her autobiography: *I, Tina*.

Tyson, Cicely

DECEMBER 19, 1939 – ● ACTOR

Born to immigrant parents from Nevis, one of the Leeward Islands in the Caribbean, Cicely Tyson grew up in East Harlem in New York City. Her father worked as a carpenter, at times selling fruit and vegetables from a pushcart, while her mother worked as a domestic. After the divorce of her parents she lived with her mother, who forbade **secular** theatrical entertainment such as movies. It was in Saint John's Episcopal Church in Harlem, where she sang and played the organ, that Tyson's theatrical talents surfaced.

secular: not connected to religion.

After graduating from high school and taking a job as a secretary with the American Red Cross, Tyson was asked to model hairstyles by her hairdresser. He encouraged her to enroll in the Barbara Watson Modeling School where she met *Ebony* fashion editor Freda DeKnight. Soon Tyson was appearing on the cov-

1939 Tyson is born.

1957 Tyson is cast in *Twelve Angry Men* with Henry Fonda.

1959 Tyson makes her stage debut in *Dark of the Moon*.

1962 Tyson appears in Genet's *The Blacks*, and wins a Vernon Rice Award.

1963 Tyson stars in the TV series *East Side/West Side*.

1968 Tyson appears in *The Heart Is a Lonely Hunter*.

1972 Tyson earns an Academy Award nomination for *Sounder*.

1974 Tyson wins an Emmy Award for *The Autobiography of Miss Jane Pittman*.

1977 Tyson plays Kunte Kinte's mother in *Roots*.

1981 Tyson marries Miles Davis.

1989 Tyson appears in *The Women of Brewster Place*.

ers of the major fashion magazines in the United States, such as *Vogue* and *Harper's Bazaar*.

In 1957 Tyson had a small part in the film *Twelve Angry Men* with Henry Fonda. Two years later she made her stage debut, starring in *Dark of the Moon* directed by Vinnette Carroll and produced by the Harlem YMCA's Drama Guild. In 1962 she appeared in both *Moon on the Rainbow Shawl* and Jean Genet's *The Blacks*, for which she received a Vernon Rice Award.

Tyson was recruited in 1963 for a lead role in the CBS television series *East Side/West Side*, becoming the first African-American actress to be a regular on a dramatic television series. The same year she appeared on stage with Alvin Ailey in the Broadway production of *Tiger, Tiger, Burning Bright* and in the off-Broadway production of *The Blue Boy in Black*, playing opposite Billy Dee Williams. In 1968 she appeared in the film *The Heart Is a Lonely Hunter*, for which she received critical and public acclaim for her performance.

Tyson waited four years before doing film work again because of her decision not to accept roles that added to the negative stereotypes of African Americans. Then, in 1972, she accepted the role of Rebecca in the film *Sounder*. Her performance earned her an Academy Award nomination for best actress.

In 1974 Tyson received two Emmy awards—one for best lead actress in a drama and the other for actress of the year—for her portrayal of aged ex-slave Jane Pittman in *The Autobiography of Miss Jane Pittman*. She went on to play other socially conscious roles for television, including the part of Harriet Tubman in *A Woman Called Moses* (1976), Kunte Kinte's mother in *Roots* (1977), and Coretta Scott King in *King* (1978).

On Thanksgiving Day 1981, Tyson married jazz trumpeter Miles Davis. Davis's third attempt at marriage and Tyson's first, the arrangement lasted seven years. Tyson continues to be active in film and television, appearing with Oprah Winfrey in the television miniseries *The Women of Brewster Place* in 1989 and in the film *Fried Green Tomatoes* in 1991. ◆

Vaughan, Sarah

MARCH 29, 1924 – APRIL 3, 1990 ● JAZZ SINGER

Nicknamed "Sassy" and "the Divine One," Sarah Vaughan is considered one of America's greatest vocalists and part of the **triumvirate** of women jazz singers that includes Ella Fitzgerald and Billie Holiday. A unique stylist, she possessed vocal capabilities—lush tones, perfect pitch, and a range exceeding three octaves—that were matched by her adventurous, sometimes radical sense of improvisation. Born in Newark, New Jersey, she began singing and playing organ in the Mount Zion Baptist Church when she was twelve.

triumvirate: a group of three rulers.

In October 1942 she sang "Body and Soul" to win an amateur-night contest at Harlem's Apollo Theater. Billy Eckstine, the singer for Earl "Fatha" Hines's big band, happened to hear her and was so impressed that he persuaded Hines to hire Vaughan as a second pianist and singer in early 1943. Later that year, when Eckstine left Hines to organize his own big band, she went with him. In his group, one of the incubators of bebop jazz, Vaughan was influenced by Eckstine's vibrato-laced baritone, and by the innovations of such fellow musicians as Dizzy Gillespie and Charlie Parker. Besides inspiring her to forge a personal style, they instilled in her a lifelong desire to improvise. ("It was just like going to school," she said.)

Vaughan made her first records for the Continental label on New Year's Eve 1944, and began working as a solo act the following year at New York's Cafe Society. At the club she met trumpeter George Treadwell, who became her manager and the first of her four husbands. Treadwell promoted Vaughan and helped create her glamorous image. Following hits on Musicraft (including "It's Magic" and "If They Could See Me Now") and Columbia ("Black Coffee"), her success was assured. From 1947 through 1952 she was voted top female vocalist in polls in *Down Beat* and *Metronome* jazz magazines.

Throughout the 1950s Vaughan recorded pop material for Mercury records, including such hits as "Make Yourself Comfortable" and "Broken-Hearted Melody" and songbooks (like those made by Ella Fitzgerald) of classic American songs by George Gershwin and Irving Berlin; she also recorded jazz sessions on the EmArcy label (Mercury's jazz label) with trumpeter Clifford Brown, the Count Basie Orchestra, and other jazz musicians. By the mid-1960s, frustrated by the tactics of record companies trying to sustain her commercially, Vaughan took a five-year hiatus from recording. By the 1970s her voice had become darker and richer.

contralto: the lowest female singing voice.

Vaughan was noted for a style in which she treated her voice like a jazz instrument rather than as a conduit for the lyrics. A **contralto,** she sang wide leaps easily, improvised sometimes subtle, sometimes dramatic melodic and rhythmic lines, and made full use of **timbral** expressiveness—from clear tones to bluesy growls with **vibrato.** By the end of her career, she had performed in more than sixty countries, in small clubs and in football stadiums, with jazz trios as well as symphony orchestras. Her signature songs, featured at almost all of her shows, included "Misty," "Tenderly," and "Send in the Clowns." She died of cancer in 1990, survived by one daughter. ◆

timbral: the distinctive tone quality of a particular singing voice.

vibrato: slight, rapid variations in pitch.

Verrett, Shirley

MAY 31, 1931 – ● OPERA SINGER

Born in New Orleans, Shirley Verrett grew up in Los Angeles. She studied music in her youth and received a degree from Venture College in Los Angeles in 1951. After her performance of "Mon coeur s'ouvre à ta voix" from

Saint-Saëns's *Samson et Dalila* earned her first prize in Arthur Godfrey's 1955 Talent Scout competition, she was invited to study at the Juilliard School of Music in New York City. Before receiving a degree in 1961, she debuted in Benjamin Britten's *The Rape of Lucretia* at Yellow Springs, Ohio, in 1957; appeared at New York's Town Hall in 1958; and performed in the New York City Opera's 1958 production of Kurt Weill's *Lost in the Stars*.

Verrett first came to international acclaim as a mezzo-soprano after singing the title role in Bizet's *Carmen* at the 1962 Spoleto Festival in Italy. She made her Covent Garden debut to critical acclaim in 1966 as Ulrica in Verdi's *Un Ballo in Maschera*, and returned to England the next year as Queen Elizabeth in Donizetti's *Maria Stuarda*. Verrett made her Metropolitan Opera debut in 1968 as Carmen. In 1972 she performed the role of Queen Selika in Meyerbeer's *L'Africaine* in San Francisco. At the Metropolitan's 1973 premiere of Berlioz's *Les Troyens* she created a sensation by singing the roles of both Cassandra and Dido. Thereafter Verrett concentrated on soprano roles. In 1976 she sang in Verdi's *Macbeth* in Washington, D.C., and in 1978 and 1979 Verrett performed in Donizetti's *La Favorita* and the title role in Bellini's *Norma* at the Metropolitan Opera.

By the 1980s Verrett's magnetic stage presence and her ability to sing both soprano and mezzo-soprano roles made her one of the leading divas of the international opera stage. She sang in Puccini's *Tosca* at Tanglewood in 1980, and returned the next year to perform in Verdi's *Requiem*. In 1982 Verrett performed Chausson's song cycle *Poème de l'amour et de la mer* with the New York Philharmonic. That same year she participated in a Carnegie Hall tribute to Marian Anderson. In 1986 she sang the Verdian role of Lady Macbeth in San Francisco. In the 1990s Verrett branched out of the operatic repertory. In 1991 she performed songs by George Gershwin in Moscow, and in 1994 she sang the role of Nettie in the Lincoln Center production of Rodgers and Hammerstein's *Carousel*. ◆

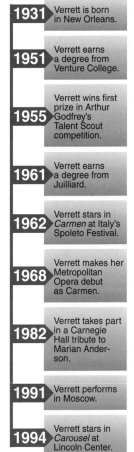

1931 Verrett is born in New Orleans.

1951 Verrett earns a degree from Venture College.

1955 Verrett wins first prize in Arthur Godfrey's Talent Scout competition.

1961 Verrett earns a degree from Juilliard.

1962 Verrett stars in *Carmen* at Italy's Spoleto Festival.

1968 Verrett makes her Metropolitan Opera debut as Carmen.

1982 Verrett takes part in a Carnegie Hall tribute to Marian Anderson.

1991 Verrett performs in Moscow.

1994 Verrett stars in *Carousel* at Lincoln Center.

Walker, A'Lelia

JUNE 6, 1885 – AUGUST 17, 1931 ● ENTREPRENEUR

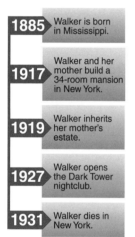

1885	Walker is born in Mississippi.
1917	Walker and her mother build a 34-room mansion in New York.
1919	Walker inherits her mother's estate.
1927	Walker opens the Dark Tower nightclub.
1931	Walker dies in New York.

Through the lavish parties she hosted, A'Lelia Walker made herself the center of elite social life during the Harlem Renaissance. She was born Lelia Walker to Sarah and Moses McWilliams in Vicksburg, Mississippi. (She changed her name to "A'Lelia" as an adult.) After her father died when she was two, her mother took her to St. Louis. She attended public schools there and graduated from Knoxville College, a private black school in Knoxville, Tennessee.

She and her mother then moved to Denver, where her mother married C. J. Walker, from whom they took their surnames. A'Lelia also married, but while she took the surname Robinson from her husband, she only occasionally used it, and the marriage was as short-lived as two subsequent unions. While in Denver, the Walkers began their hair care business. Madame C. J. Walker developed products that straightened and softened African-American women's hair, and assisted by her daughter, she quickly created a vast empire. She moved parts of her operations and her residence to Pittsburgh and Indianapolis before finally settling in New York. In 1917 the Walkers built a thirty-four-room mansion in Irvington-on-Hudson, New York, which A'Lelia's friend, the opera singer Enrico Caruso, dubbed "Villa Lewaro" (short for Lelia Walker Robinson).

With her mother's death on May 25, 1919, A'Lelia inherited the bulk of her mother's estate, including Villa Lewaro and two twin brownstones at 108–110 West 136th St. in Harlem. Soon after her mother's death, Walker also bought an apartment at 80 Edgecombe Avenue, in Harlem. While she was the

titular director of the Walker business interests, A'Lelia Walker devoted most of her money and attention to social life. She threw parties at Villa Lewaro and in Harlem. She established "at-homes" at which she introduced African-American writers, artists, and performers to each other and to such white celebrities as Carl Van Vechten. Her "salon" was regarded as a place where artistic people, particularly male and female homosexuals, could go to eat and drink and hear music. In 1927 and 1928 she turned part of the brownstones into a nightclub, which she named "The Dark Tower."

titular: bearing the title but not the responsibilities.

When the Depression came, Walker experienced grave financial difficulties. She was forced to close her nightclub, and she mortgaged Villa Lewaro. When she died suddenly on August 17, 1931, Langston Hughes wrote that this "was really the end of the gay times of the New Negro era in Harlem." The NAACP, to whom Walker had willed Villa Lewaro, was unable to keep up the payments on the estate and ended up putting it on the auction block. ◆

Walker, Alice

FEBRUARY 9, 1944 –   ● NOVELIST

Alice Walker was born in Eatonton, Georgia, the eighth child of sharecroppers Willie Lee and Minnie Lou Grant Walker. The vision in Walker's right eye was destroyed when she was eight years old by a brother's BB-gun shot, an event that caused her to become an introverted child. Six years later, Walker's self-confidence and commitment to school increased dramatically after a minor surgical procedure removed disfiguring scar tissue from around her injured eye. Encouraged by her family and community, Walker won a scholarship for the handicapped and matriculated at Spelman College in 1961.

"Wherever I have knocked, a door has opened. Wherever I have wandered, a path has appeared. I have been helped, supported, encouraged, and nurtured by people of all races, creeds, colors, and dreams."

Alice Walker, *In Search of Our Mothers' Gardens,* 1983

After two years Walker transferred to Sarah Lawrence College because she felt that Spelman stifled the intellectual growth and maturation of its students, an issue she explores in the novel *Meridian*. At Sarah Lawrence, Walker studied works by European and white American writers, but the school failed to provide her with an opportunity to explore the intellectual and cultural traditions of black people. Walker sought to broaden her education by traveling to Africa during the summer before her senior year. During her stay there, Walker became pregnant, and the urgency of her desire to terminate the pregnancy (she was prepared to commit suicide had she not been able to get an abortion), along with her experiences in Africa and as a participant in the Civil Rights Movement, became the subject of her first book, a collection of poems entitled *Once* (1968).

Walker moved to Mississippi in 1965, where she taught, worked with Head Start programs, and helped to register voters. There she met and married Melvyn Leventhal, a civil rights lawyer whom she subsequently divorced (a daughter, Rebecca, was born in 1969), and wrote her first novel, *The Third Life of Grange Copeland* (1970), a chilling exploration of the causes and consequences of black intrafamilial violence. While doing research on black folk medicine for a story that became "The Revenge of Hannah Kemhuff," collected in *In Love and Trouble* (1973), Walker first learned of Zora Neale Hurston.

In Hurston, Walker discovered a figure who had been virtually erased from American literary history in large part because she held views—on the beauty and complexity of black southern rural culture; on the necessity of what Walker termed a "womanist" critique of sexism; and on racism and sexism as intersecting forms of oppression—for which she had herself been condemned. In Hurston, Walker found legitimacy for her own literary project. Walker obtained a tombstone for Hurston's grave, which proclaimed her "A Genius of the South," and focused public attention on her neglected work, including the novel *Their Eyes Were Watching God*.

In her influential essay "In Search of Our Mothers' Gardens" Walker asked, with Hurston and other marginalized women in mind, "How was the creativity of the black woman kept alive, year after year and century after century?" Some of the most celebrated of Walker's works—from the short stories "Everyday Use" and "1955" to the novel *The Color Purple*

1944 Walker is born in Georgia.

1961 Walker enters Spelman College on scholarship.

1963 Walker transfers to Sarah Lawrence College.

1968 Walker publishes her first poetry book, *Once*.

1970 Walker publishes *The Third Life of Grange Copeland.*

1982 Walker is awarded Pulitzer Prize for *The Color Purple.*

(1982)—explore this question. By acknowledging her artistic debt to writers like Phillis Wheatley, Virginia Woolf, and Hurston, as well as to her own verbally and horticulturally adept mother, Walker encouraged a generation of readers and scholars to question traditional evaluative norms.

After *In Love and Trouble*, Walker published several novels (including *Meridian, The Temple of My Familiar, Possessing the Secret of Joy,* and *By the Light of My Father's Smile*), volumes of poetry (including *Horses Make a Landscape Look More Beautiful*), collections of essays, and another short story collection, *You Can't Keep a Good Woman Down* (1981). In all these works, she examined the racial and gendered inequities that affect black Americans generally and black women in particular. The most celebrated and controversial of these works is her Pulitzer Prize- and National Book Award-winning **epistolary** novel, *The Color Purple*, which explores, among other matters, incest, marital violence, lesbianism, alternative religious practices, and black attitudes about gender. Since the early 1980s Walker has lived in northern California and continues to produce work that challenges and inspires its readers. ◆

> *"No song or story will bear my mother's name. Yet, so many of the stories I write, that we all write, are my mother's stories."*
> Alice Walker, *In Search of Our Mothers' Gardens*, 1983

epistolary: told through letters.

Walker, Madame C. J.

DECEMBER 23, 1867 – MAY 25, 1919 ● ENTREPRENEUR AND PHILANTHROPIST

Born Sarah Breedlove to ex-slaves Owen and Minerva Breedlove on a Delta, Louisiana, cotton plantation, she was orphaned by age seven. She lived with her sister, Louvenia, in Vicksburg, Mississippi, until 1882, when she married Moses McWilliams, in part to escape Louvenia's cruel husband. In 1887, when her daughter, Lelia (later known as A'Lelia Walker), was two years old, Moses McWilliams died. For the next eighteen years she worked as a laundress in St. Louis. But in 1905, with $1.50 in savings, the thirty-seven-year-old McWilliams moved to Denver to start her own business after developing a formula to treat her problem with baldness—an ailment common among African-American women at the time, brought on by poor diet, stress, illness, damaging hair-care treatments, and scalp disease. In January 1906 she married Charles

Madame C. J. Walker developed a formula to treat her problem with baldness—an ailment common among African-American women at the time.

1867 Walker is born Sarah Breedlove in Louisiana.

1905 Walker founds hair-care business in Denver.

1906 Walker marries Charles Joseph Walker.

1908 Walker establishes the Lelia College of Hair Culture in Pittsburgh.

1910 Walker moves the business to Indianapolis.

1917 Walker joins the Negro Silent Protest Parade.

1919 Walker rewrites her will, making numerous donations to charity.

1992 Walker is elected to National Business Hall of Fame.

Joseph Walker, a newspaper sales agent, who helped design her advertisements and mail-order operation.

While Madame Walker is often said to have invented the "hot comb," it is more likely that she adapted metal implements popularized by the French to suit black women's hair. Acutely aware of the debate about whether black women should alter the appearance of their natural hair texture, she insisted years later that her Walker System was not intended as a hair "straightener," but rather as a grooming method to heal and condition the scalp to promote hair growth and prevent baldness.

From 1906 to 1916 Madame Walker traveled throughout the United States, Central America, and the West Indies promoting her business. She settled briefly in Pittsburgh, establishing the first Lelia College of Hair Culture there in 1908, then moved the company to Indianapolis in 1910, building a factory and vastly increasing her annual sales. Her reputation as a philanthropist was solidified in 1911, when she contributed one thousand dollars to the building fund of the Indianapolis YMCA. In 1912 she and C. J. Walker divorced, but she retained his name. Madame Walker joined her daughter, A'Lelia, and A'Lelia's adopted daughter, Mae (later Mae Walker Perry), in Harlem in 1916. She left the daily management of her manufacturing operation in Indianapolis to her longtime attorney and general manager, Freeman B. Ransom, factory forewoman Alice Kelly, and assistant general manager Robert L. Brokenburr.

Madame Walker's business philosophy stressed economic independence for the 20,000 former maids, farm laborers, housewives, and schoolteachers she employed as agents and factory and office workers. To further strengthen her company, she created the Madame C. J. Walker Hair Culturists Union of America and held annual conventions.

During World War I she was among those who supported the government's black recruitment efforts and War Bond drives. But after the bloody 1917 East St. Louis riot, she joined the planning committee of the Negro Silent Protest Parade, traveling to Washington to present a petition urging President Wilson to support legislation that would make lynching a federal crime. As her wealth and visibility grew, Walker became increasingly outspoken, joining those blacks who advocated an alternative peace conference at Versailles after the war to monitor proceedings affecting the world's people of color. She intended her estate in Irvington-on-Hudson, New York—Villa Lewaro, which was designed by black architect Vertner W. Tandy—not only as a showplace but as an inspiration to other blacks.

During the spring of 1919, aware that her long battle with hypertension was taking its final toll, Madame Walker revamped her will, directing her attorney to donate five thousand dollars to the National Association for the Advancement of Colored People's antilynching campaign and to contribute thousands of dollars to black educational, civic, and social institutions and organizations.

When she died at age fifty-one, at Villa Lewaro, she was widely considered the wealthiest black woman in America and was reputed to be the first African-American woman millionaire. Her daughter, A'Lelia Walker—a central figure of the Harlem Renaissance—succeeded her as president of the Mme. C. J. Walker Manufacturing Company.

Walker's significance is rooted not only in her innovative (and sometimes controversial) hair-care system, but also in her advocacy of black women's economic independence and her creation of business opportunities at a time when most black women worked as servants and sharecroppers. Her entrepreneurial strategies and organizational skills revolutionized what would become a multibillion-dollar ethnic hair-care and cosmetics industry by the last decade of the twentieth century. Having led an early life of hardship, she became a trailblazer of black philanthropy, using her wealth and influence to leverage social, political, and economic rights for women and blacks. In 1992 Madame Walker was elected to the National Business Hall of Fame. ◆

> *"I am a woman who came from the cotton fields of the South. I was promoted from there to the washtub. Then I was promoted to the cook kitchen, and from there I promoted myself into the business of manufacturing hair good and preparations."*
> Madame Walker, 1912

Walker, Maggie Lena

JULY 15, 1867 – DECEMBER 15, 1934 ● BUSINESS AND NEWSPAPER EXECUTIVE

Maggie Lena Walker was born in Richmond, Virginia. Her mother, Elizabeth Draper, was a former slave who worked as a cook in the home of Elizabeth Van Lew, a

1867 ▶ Walker is born in Virginia.

1880 ▶ Walker joins the Grand United Order.

1883 ▶ Walker graduates from teachers college.

1899 ▶ Walker becomes secretary and treasurer of the Independent order of St. Luke.

1902 ▶ Walker founds the *St. Luke Herald.*

1907 ▶ Walker becomes confined to a wheelchair.

1912 ▶ Walker joins the National Association of Colored Women.

1929 ▶ Walker becomes chair of the Consolidated Bank and Trust Company.

1934 ▶ Walker dies.

wealthy abolitionist from Virginia. Her Irish-born father, Eccles Cuthbert, was a Union sympathizer and reporter for the *New York Herald*. Walker's stepfather, William Mitchell, worked as a butler in the Van Lew household.

Walker attended Richmond's Armstrong Normal School. Upon graduation in 1883, she taught at the Lancaster School for three years. In 1886 she married Armstead Walker, who worked with his father's prosperous bricklaying and construction business. Together the couple had three sons and adopted a daughter.

In 1880 Walker joined the Grand United Order of St. Luke in Richmond, a mutual aid society established by Mary Prout in 1867 to ensure health benefits and proper burial for African-American veterans of the Civil War. At a time of little government relief and assistance for the poor and elderly, these societies were important in the lives of African Americans. In the late 1880s and 1890s, the Richmond order grew and slowly came to resemble a diversified business that included a bank, a real estate division, a newspaper, a hotel, and a grocery store.

In 1899 Walker became executive secretary and treasurer of the consolidated and renamed Independent Order of St. Luke in Richmond. Under her leadership the organization grew rapidly. Walker's goal was to create businesses that would provide employment for African Americans, especially African-American women, through cooperative effort and mutual support. In 1902 she founded the *St. Luke Herald*, a paper addressing business as well as political issues, such as lynching and economic independence of the African-American community. The following year, she founded the St. Luke Penny Savings Bank, and was probably the first woman bank president in the United States. When, in 1929, the St. Luke Bank merged with other African-American banks in Richmond to become the Consolidated Bank and Trust Company, Walker became chairperson of the board.

In addition to these activities, in 1912 Walker joined the National Association of Colored Women and was a member of the executive committee for the remainder of her life. In the same year, she founded and became president of the Richmond's Council of Colored Women and helped raise $5,000 for the Virginia Industrial School for Colored Girls. Although she was confined to a wheelchair after an accident in 1907, she continued until her death in 1934 to work unrelentingly to improve job opportunities for African Americans, to speak out against black political disfranchisement, and to advocate the cooperative enterprising and economic independence of African Americans. ◆

Walker, Margaret

JULY 7, 1915 – DECEMBER 4, 1988 ● WRITER

Margaret Abigail Walker was born in Birmingham, Alabama. She received her early education in New Orleans, and completed undergraduate work at Northwestern University at the age of nineteen. Although Walker had published some of her poems before she moved to Chicago, it was there her talent matured. She wrote as a college student and as a member of the federal government's works project administration, and she shared cultural and professional interests with black and white intellectuals in Chicago, the best known of whom was Richard Wright. Wright and Walker were close friends until Walker left Chicago for graduate work at the University of Iowa in 1939, by which time she was on her way to becoming a major poet.

In 1942 Walker completed the manuscript of a collection of poems entitled *For My People*, the title poem of which she had written and published in Chicago in 1937. The book served as her master's thesis at the Iowa Writers Workshop, and won a measure of national literary prominence. In 1942 *For My People* won the Yale Younger Poets Award. About the same time, Walker began work on a historical novel based on the life of her grandmother, Elvira Dozier Ware, a work she did not finish until she returned to Iowa in the 1960s to complete her Ph.D. In the interim, she joined the faculty at Jackson State University in Jackson, Mississippi, where she and her husband, Firnist James Alexander, raised their four children.

Walker played an active role in the civil rights movement in Mississippi, and continued to write. The novel she created from her grandmother's stories was published in 1966 as *Jubilee*, and received the Houghton Mifflin Literary Award. It was translated into seven languages and enjoyed popularity as one of the first modern novels of slavery and the Reconstruction South told from an African-American perspective. Other books

> *"The mind is the only place I can exist and feel free. In my mind I am absolutely free."*
> Margaret Walker, 1983

> *"There were bizarre beginnings in old lands for the making of me."*
>
> Margaret Walker, "Dark Blood," *For My People*, 1942

followed: *Prophets for a New Day* (1970), *How I Wrote Jubilee* (1972), *October Journey* (1973), and *A Poetic Equation: Conversations Between Nikki Giovanni and Margaret Walker* (1974). Throughout her long career, Walker received numerous awards and honors for her contribution to American letters. She held several honorary degrees and in 1991 received a Senior Fellowship from the National Endowment for the Arts.

Walker retired from full-time teaching in 1979, remained in Jackson, and worked on several projects, especially a controversial biography of Richard Wright, published in 1988 as *Richard Wright: Daemonic Genius*. In 1989 Walker brought together new and earlier poems in *This Is My Century: New and Collected Poems*. A year later she published her first volume of essays, *How I Wrote Jubilee and Other Essays on Life and Literature*.

Throughout her work, Walker incorporated a strong sense of her own humanistic vision together with an autobiographical recall of her own past and cogent themes from black history. Her artistic vision recognized the distinctiveness of black cultural life and the values associated with it. She was outspoken on matters of political justice and social equality, for women as well as for men.

Jubilee tells the story of Vyry, a slave on an antebellum Georgia plantation, the unacknowledged daughter of the master, who aspires to freedom. She marries a fellow slave, and assumes responsibility for the plantation during the Civil War. After the war she moves away and discovers that her courage and determination make it possible for her to triumph over numerous adversities. In a 1992 interview Walker stated, "The body of my work springs from my interest in the historical point of view that is central to the development of black people as we approach the twenty-first century." ◆

1915 Walker is born in Birmingham, Alabama.

1939 Walker enters the University of Iowa.

1942 Walker completes *For My People*.

1966 Walker publishes the novel *Jubilee*.

1991 Walker receives a Senior Fellowship from the NEA.

1998 Walker dies in Chicago.

Warwick, Dionne

DECEMBER 12, 1941 – ● SINGER

Marie Dionne Warwick, one of the most important African-American pop soul artists outside Motown in the 1960s, was born in East Orange, New Jersey. Warwick studied voice at the Hartt College of Music in Connecticut, but decided to pursue her interests in gospel music with the Drinkard Singers and the Gospelaires, a trio she formed with her sister Dee Dee and cousin Cissy Houston. In 1960 she met the songwriters Burt Bacharach and Hal David while supporting herself in New York as a studio session vocalist. They helped Warwick obtain a contract with Scepter Records, for whom she recorded from 1962 to 1971. Bacharach and David wrote sophisticated songs for her that were well suited to her dark, warm alto voice and impeccable diction. She was particularly adept at conveying the immediacy and emotionalism of David's lyrics to a wide audience.

Bacharach and David wrote and produced most of her hit songs, including "Anyone Who Had a Heart" (Number One, 1964), "A House Is Not a Home" (1964), and "Do You Know the Way to San Jose?" (Number Ten, 1968). During the 1970s Warwick had the hit "Then Came You" with the Spinners (Number One, 1974); her next major hit was on Arista Records with "I'll Never Love This Way Again" (Number Five, 1979; produced by Barry Manilow), which sold one million copies. Other hits include "Déjà Vu" (1979) and "That's What Friends Are For" (1986). The proceeds from the latter were donated for AIDS research. She also participated in the famine effort U.S.A. for Africa, which resulted in the worldwide hit "We Are the World." ◆

1941	Warwick is born in New Jersey.
1960	Warwick meets Burt Bacharach and Hal David.
1968	Warwick records "Do You Know the Way to San Jose."
1979	Warwick records "I'll Never Love This Way Again."
1986	Warwick records "That's What Friends Are For."

Washington, Dinah (Jones, Ruth Lee)

AUGUST 19, 1924 – DECEMBER 14, 1963 ● SINGER

Dinah Washington's versatile, commanding, expressive delivery allowed her to cross over from rhythm and blues to pop, earning her the **sobriquet** of "Queen of the Blues" or simply "the Queen." "I can sing anything," she once claimed, for anything she sang sounded deeply felt. Clarion-clear, yet edged with emotion, her voice recalled both the gospel "shout" and the rawness of the blues.

Born Ruth Jones in Tuscaloosa, Alabama, Washington was raised in Chicago and sang both in Saint Luke's Baptist Church

sobriquet: a nickname.

1924 ▶ Washington is born in Alabama.

1943 ▶ Washington starts singing with Lionel Hampton's band; cuts her first records.

1946 ▶ Washington signs with Mercury.

1959 ▶ Washington records "What a Difference a Day Makes."

1963 ▶ Washington dies from a drug and alcohol overdose.

and Sallie Martin's Gospel Group. At fifteen, she won an amateur-night contest at the Regal Theater and began appearing in local nightclubs. During an engagement at the Garrick Lounge, Washington was recommended by agent Joe Glaser to bandleader Lionel Hampton, who hired her as a vocalist from 1943 until 1946, when she left to sing solo.

On December 29, 1943, Washington cut her first records, "Evil Gal Blues" and "Salty Papa Blues," for the Keynote label. In 1946 she contracted with Mercury, for which she made over four hundred recordings before signing with Roulette. Between 1949 and 1954, ten of her singles were in the Top Five of the R&B charts. Following her 1959 breakthrough, "What a Difference a Day Makes," Washington regularly reached the pop Top Twenty. Alternating between jazz and orchestral accompaniments, she often completed recordings in one take. Her demeanor was feisty and uninhibited, and she was married (at best count) seven times. Her death in 1963 came from an accidental overdose of pills and liquor. ◆

Washington, Margaret Murray

C. 1861 – JUNE 4, 1925 ● EDUCATOR AND CLUBWOMAN

The child of a black mother, Lucy Murray, and a white father, Margaret Murray was born in Macon, Mississippi. March 9, 1865, is inscribed on her gravestone as her birthday, but she was listed as being nine years old in the census of 1870. She may have lowered her age in 1881, when she began Fisk Preparatory School in Nashville, Tennessee. Taken in by a Quaker brother and sister after her father's death when she was seven, Washington was educated by them, and it was they who suggested she become a teacher.

Margaret Murray became Booker T. Washington's third wife. After completing her Fisk University education in 1889, she joined the Tuskegee faculty and the next academic year became dean of the women's department. Washington, who was recently widowed and had three small children, proposed to her in 1891 and they married on October 12, 1892. Margaret Murray Washington advised her husband in his speaking and fund-raising work, and she shared his advocacy of accommodation with whites while uplifting the black race. As an educated woman, Margaret Washington believed she had a responsibility to help those of her race who had fewer opportunities. She pursued her own work at Tuskegee and was a leader in the black women's club movement.

Washington was the director of the Girls' Institute at Tuskegee, which provided courses in laundering, cooking, dressmaking, sewing, **millinery,** and mattress making, skills students were to use in maintaining healthy, efficient, and gracious homes. She founded the women's club at Tuskegee for female faculty and faculty wives, which was especially active in the temperance movement. She also worked with people in the surrounding rural area on self-improvement. By 1904 nearly 300 women attended her mothers' meetings each Sunday. Especially concerned about high rates of black mortality and illegitimate births, Washington instructed the women on diet and personal hygiene for better health and urged them to set good moral examples at home for both boys and girls.

millinery: hat making.

These sentiments found expression in the motto of the influential National Association of Colored Women (NACW)— "Lifting as we climb." Washington was one of the women invited by Josephine St. Pierre Ruffin to meet in Boston in July 1895 to form the National Federation of Afro-American Women. She became vice president and then, in 1896, president of the federation, which was now sixty-seven clubs strong; it joined with the Colored Women's League to form the NACW that year. In 1914 Washington was elected president of the NACW after holding numerous other offices and served two terms. She also edited the NACW's *National Notes* until her death.

President of the Alabama Association of Women's Clubs from 1919 until her death in 1925, Margaret Murray Washington led the movement to establish a boys' reform school as an alternative to prison, and later the Rescue Home for Girls, both in Mt. Meigs, Alabama. Through the AAWC, she worked with the Commission on Interracial Cooperation to provide educational opportunities for blacks in Alabama. A lifelong friend of W. E. B. Du Bois, in 1920 Margaret Washington helped found the International Council of Women of the Darker Races to promote race pride through knowledge of black culture around the world. ◆

Waters, Ethel

OCTOBER 31, 1896? – SEPTEMBER 1, 1977 ● SINGER AND ACTOR

Ethel Waters was born in Chester, Pennsylvania. She came from a musical family; her father played piano, and her mother and maternal relatives sang. Her first public performance was as a five-year-old billed as Baby Star in a church program. Waters began her singing career in Baltimore with a small vaudeville company where she sang W. C. Handy's "St. Louis Blues," becoming, apparently, the first woman to sing the song professionally. She was billed as Sweet Mama Stringbean.

"When I was a honky-tonk entertainer, I used to work from nine to unconscious."
Ethel Waters

About 1919 Waters moved to New York and became a leading entertainer in Harlem, where her first engagement was at a small black club, Edmond's Cellar. As an entertainer, she reached stardom during the Harlem Renaissance of the 1920s. In 1924 Earl Dancer, later the producer of the Broadway musical *Africana,* got her a booking in the Plantation Club as a

replacement for Florence Mills, who was on tour. When Mills returned, Waters toured in Dancer's *Miss Calico.* By then, Waters had begun to establish herself as an interpreter of the blues with such songs as Perry Bradford's "Messin' Around." In 1921 she recorded "Down Home Blues" and "Oh Daddy" for Black Swan Records. The success of her first recording led her to embark on one of the first personal promotion tours in the United States.

In 1932 and 1933 Waters recorded with Duke Ellington and Benny Goodman, respectively. Her renditions of "Stormy Weather," "Taking a Chance on Love," and "Lady Be Good" were closer stylistically to jazz than to popular music. She sang with the swing orchestra of Fletcher Henderson, who was her conductor on the Black Swan tours. Though her performances were un-

Black Swan Records

In 1921 music publisher and entrepreneur Harry Pace founded Pace Phonographic Records, the first black-owned record label. He named his recording label Black Swan, after the nineteenth-century opera singer Elizabeth Taylor Greenfield. Black Swan's first office was on West 138th street in New York's Harlem, but it soon moved to the Times Square area. Pace hired composer William Grant Still as arranger and music director. Bandleader Fletcher Henderson was hired as recording director, and began his recording career as pianist and conductor for the label. The label's first record was released in September 1921. The company was renamed the Black Swan Phonograph Company in 1923. Black Swan recorded black performers in many different musical styles, including opera singers, classical soloists, choruses, vaudeville duos, jazz bands, and dance orchestras. The label became best known for recording blues singers such as Alberta Hunter, Trixie Smith, and Ethel Waters. Waters's recording of "Down Home Blues" was a sensation, prompting the founding of a vaudeville group, the Black Swan Troubadours, led by Waters and Henderson. Black Swan played an important role in developing the market for popular music recorded by African Americans. Nevertheless, the label failed within two years. In 1923 Black Swan went bankrupt; its catalogue was leased by Paramount in 1924. There were no other black-owned record companies until the mid-1940s.

questionably potent, many critics did not consider her a real jazz performer but rather a singer who possessed a style that was more dramatic and **histrionic** than jazz-oriented. However, Waters, along with Billie Holiday and Louis Armstrong, significantly influenced the sound of American popular music. Though generally regarded as blues or jazz singers, all of them sang the popular songs of their day like no other singers of the period.

histrionic: theatrical.

"Dinah" (first performed in 1925), "Stormy Weather," and "Miss Otis Regrets" were among Waters's most popular songs. Later she recorded with Russell Wooding and Eddie Mallory, among others. Beginning in 1927 she appeared in Broadway musicals, including *Africana* (1927), Lew Leslie's *Blackbirds of 1930*, *Rhapsody in Black* (1931), *As Thousands Cheer* (1933), *At Home Abroad* (1936), and *Cabin in the Sky* (1940). All these roles primarily involved singing.

It was not until the Federal Theatre Project (FTP) that she had the chance to do more serious and dramatic roles. Waters received excellent reviews for her performance in Shaw's *Androcles and the Lion*, which led to her being cast as Hagar in Dubose and Dorothy Heyward's *Mamba's Daughters* (1939), for which she again received good notices. Ten years later, she was

1921 Waters records "Down Home Blues."

1940 Waters appears on Broadway in *Cabin in the Sky*.

1949 Waters is nominated for Oscar for *Pinky*.

1951 Waters publishes *His Eye Is on the Sparrow*.

1977 Waters dies from cancer.

acclaimed for her performance as Berenice in Carson McCullers's *The Member of the Wedding* (which won the Drama Critics Circle Award for Best American Play of the Year in 1950).

Waters appeared in nine films between 1929 and 1959, the most popular being *Pinky*, which garnered her an Academy Award nomination as Best Supporting Actress (1949). From 1957 to 1976 she toured with evangelist Billy Graham's religious crusades in the United States and abroad and became celebrated for singing "His Eye Is on the Sparrow." This song became the title of her first autobiography, which was published in 1951. A second autobiography, *To Me It's Wonderful*, was published in 1972. Waters died in 1977, following a long bout with cancer. ◆

Waters, Maxine Moore

AUGUST 15, 1938 –   ● POLITICIAN

"As public policymakers we must insist that current laws dealing with discrimination be enforced. As a country, we cannot afford to backslide in our commitment to end all forms of discrimination whether at the federal, state, or local level."

Maxine Waters, 1997

The daughter of Remus Carr and Velma Moore, Maxine Moore was born in St. Louis, Missouri. She attended the public schools in St. Louis and married Edward Waters immediately upon graduation from high school. In 1961

she moved with her husband and two children to the Watts section of Los Angeles. After working at a garment factory and as an operator for Pacific Telephone, Waters was hired in 1966 as an assistant teacher in a local Head Start program and later was promoted to supervisor.

In 1971 Waters received her bachelor's degree in sociology from California State University at Los Angeles. She became active in local and state politics, serving as a chief advisor for David S. Cunningham's successful race for a city council seat in 1973. After Cunningham's election, Waters became his chief deputy.

In 1976 Waters was elected to the California State Assembly, where she served for fourteen years. She represented the Watts area and was a noted spokesperson for women's issues. In 1978 she cofounded the Black Women's Forum, a national organization designed to provide a platform for the discussion of issues of concern to black women—programs for the poor and minorities, and divestiture of investments in South Africa. Among her many achievements, Waters helped establish the Child Abuse Prevention Training Program and sponsored legislation to protect tenants and small businesses, to impose stringent standards on vocational schools, and to limit police

1938 — Waters is born in St. Louis.

1961 — Waters moves to Los Angeles.

1971 — Waters earns a B.A. from California State University.

1976 — Waters is elected to California State Assembly.

1990 — Waters is elected to U.S. House of Representatives.

1996 — Waters chairs Congressional Black Caucus.

Congressional Black Caucus

The Congressional Black Caucus (CBC) is an organization made up of black members of Congress that promotes legislation of interest to African Americans. The CBC was a product of the growth in black political power in the 1960s and 1970s. The creation of an institutional base for black Americans within Congress had been encouraged by the passage of the Civil Rights Act of 1965. In 1969 Representative Charles Diggs, a Democrat from Michigan, formed the Democratic Select Committee, the precursor of the CBC, as a means by which the nine black members of the House of Representatives could address their common political concerns. In 1971 the group was formally organized as the Congressional Black Caucus, and Diggs became its first chairperson. Since its formation, the CBC has been involved in numerous legislative initiatives including welfare reform, minority business development, the passage of sanctions against South Africa, the establishment of the Martin Luther King holiday, and the expansion of educational opportunities for minorities. Over the years, the growth of black political power has expanded the size of the CBC. By the 1990s the CBC had become one of the most influential voting blocks in Congress. In 1996 Representative Maxine Waters was chosen to chair the CBC for the 105th congressional term. The CBC had thirty-eight members, including twelve women, following the 1998 midterm elections.

strip-and-search authority. Waters served as the assembly's first black female member of the Rules Committee and the first non-lawyer on the Judiciary Committee.

In 1990 Waters was elected to represent a wide area of South Central Los Angeles in the United States House of Representatives. In the ensuing years, she voiced her criticism of the United States involvement in the Persian Gulf War and advocated a number of reintegration services for black troops upon their return home.

Following the outbreak of riots in her Los Angeles district after the acquittal of the police officers charged in the Rodney King case in April 1992, Waters received national attention for her statements about the root social causes of the riots. In 1993 Waters proposed legislation for the Youth Fair Chance Program, an inner-city job training program, and supported passage of AIDS and abortion-rights legislation. Over the course of her first two terms, Waters rapidly emerged as a major spokesperson for the black community and one of the most prominent women in Congress. In 1996 Waters was chosen by her House colleagues to chair the Congressional Black caucus for the 105th congressional term. ◆

Wattleton, Faye

July 8, 1943 – ● Activist

Faye Wattleton has dedicated her career to securing reproductive rights and equal access to health care for poor women and men. Wattleton was born and raised in St. Louis, Missouri, in a working-class home. She received a degree in nursing in 1964 from Ohio State University and an M.S. degree in maternal and infant health care from Columbia University. While studying at Columbia, Wattleton interned at Harlem Hospital and began to focus her attention on the devastating effects of illegal abortions. She went on to work for the public health department in Dayton, Ohio, and there became involved with the local Planned Parenthood. Soon she was head of this local organization.

In 1978 Wattleton became president of the Planned Parenthood Federation of America, the oldest organization in the country to provide information on birth control, and one that serves millions of people around the world each year. As the head of this organization, Wattleton has confronted the federal and state governments and the courts on the issue of abortion, protesting restrictions on women's health choices. She has also made Planned Parenthood an important resource for information on AIDS prevention.

Wattleton is the author of *How to Talk to Your Children About Sex*, and has received many honors for her years of service. In 1992 she resigned her position at Planned Parenthood to pursue other career interests that would give her experience in a broader range of issues. She published her autobiography, *Life on the Line*, in 1996. ◆

Weems, Carrie Mae

APRIL 20, 1953 – ● PHOTOGRAPHER

Born in Portland, Oregon, Carrie Mae Weems began taking pictures in 1976 after a friend gave her a camera as a gift. Weems worked as a professional modern dancer and also held odd jobs on farms and in restaurants and offices until 1979, when she began taking classes in art, folklore, and literature at the California Institute of the Arts (B.F.A., 1981). She traveled to Mexico and Fiji, and then studied photography at the University of California, San Diego, where she worked with Fred Lonidier (M.F.A., 1984).

In 1978 Weems began taking her first series of images, *Environmental Profits*, which focused on life in Portland. Weems continued to develop her interest in autobiographical images in *Family Pictures and Stories* (1978–84), which took the format of

"The focus of my work is to describe simply and directly those aspects of American culture in need of deeper illumination."
Carrie Mae Weems

a family photo album and featured images of relatives at their jobs and at home, often with accompanying narrative text and audio recordings. *Family Pictures* was Weems's response to the Moynihan Report of ten years earlier, which claimed that a **matriarchal** system of authority was responsible for a systemic crisis in the black family (*Mom at Work*). Images in the series were arranged to look like snapshots of ordinary moments to show that the process of passing on family history is an aspect of everyday life.

Weems's work on *Family Pictures* intensified her interest in folklore, and she took graduate classes in the folklore program at University of California, Berkeley, during 1984–87. Her work *Ain't Jokin* (1987–88), which grew out of her studies at the university, was a series of captioned photographs that prompts viewers to question racial stereotypes (*Black Woman with Chicken*).

In 1990 Weems explored the conflict between a woman's political ideals and her emotional desires in *Untitled (Kitchen Table Series)*. Shot with a large-format camera, the images record episodes in the relationship between a woman and man; they are taken from a single vantage point in front of the receding kitchen table.

In the same year, Weems completed *Then What? Photographs and Folklore*, a collection of images that illustrates or comments upon folk sayings, signs, and omens. Weems's image of a coffeepot highlights a superstition by quoting parents who tell their child not to drink coffee because "coffee'll make you black." *Then What?* also includes *Colored People* (1989–90), a series of front- and sideview mug shots of girls and boys that explores the process of color stereotyping.

In 1991 Weems began creating large-scale color still lifes and portraits that were included in *And 22 Million Very Tired and Angry People* (1992). Selecting a title that echoes Richard Wright's 1941 work *12 Million Black Voices*, Weems combines photos of ordinary objects such as an alarm clock (*A Precise Moment in Time*), a fan (*A Hot Day*), and a typewriter (*An Informational System*) with text from thinkers such as Ntozake Shange, Malcolm X, and Fannie Lou Hamer, to educate viewers about historical causes of political change. In 1992 Weems exhibited a series of images on the Gullah culture of the Sea Islands, located off the coast of South Carolina and Georgia, at the P.P.O.W. Gallery in New York City.

matriarchal: a family, group, or state governed by women.

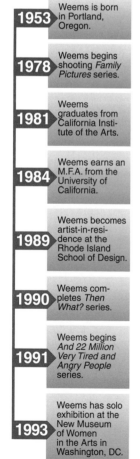

1953 Weems is born in Portland, Oregon.

1978 Weems begins shooting *Family Pictures* series.

1981 Weems graduates from California Institute of the Arts.

1984 Weems earns an M.F.A. from the University of California.

1989 Weems becomes artist-in-residence at the Rhode Island School of Design.

1990 Weems completes *Then What?* series.

1991 Weems begins *And 22 Million Very Tired and Angry People* series.

1993 Weems has solo exhibition at the New Museum of Women in the Arts in Washington, DC.

Weems has taught photography at institutions such as San Diego City College in California (1984); Hampshire College in Amherst, Massachusetts (1987–92), Hunter College in New York City (1988–89), and California College of Arts and Crafts in Oakland, California (1991). She has been artist-in-residence at the Visual Studies Workshop in Rochester, New York (1986); Rhode Island School of Design in Providence, Rhode Island (1989–90); and the Art Institute of Chicago (1990).

Weems's work has been shown in solo exhibitions at the Alternative Space Gallery, San Diego (1984); Hampshire College Art Gallery (1987), CEPA Gallery, Buffalo (1990); P.P.O. W. Gallery (1990, 1992); New Museum of Contemporary Art, New York City (1991); and the National Museum of Women in the Arts, Washington, D.C. (1993). ◆

Wells-Barnett, Ida Bell

JULY 6, 1862 – MARCH 25, 1931 ● JOURNALIST AND
CIVIL RIGHTS ACTIVIST

I da Bell Wells was born to Jim and Elizabeth Wells in Holly Springs, Mississippi, the first of eight children. Her father, the son of his master and a slave woman, worked on a plantation as a carpenter. There he met his future wife, who served as a cook. After Emancipation, Jim Wells was active in local Reconstruction politics.

Young Ida Wells received her early education in the grammar school of Shaw University (now Rust College) in Holly Springs, where her father served on the original board of trustees. Her schooling was halted, however, when a yellow fever epidemic claimed the lives of both her parents in 1878 and she assumed responsibility for her siblings. The next year, the family moved to Memphis, Tennessee, with an aunt. There Wells found work as a teacher. She later studied at Fisk University and Lemoyne Institute.

A turning point in Wells's life occurred on May 4, 1884. While riding a train to a teaching assignment, she was asked to leave her seat and move to a segregated car. Wells refused, and she was physically ejected from the railway car. She sued the

> "We must do something and we must do it now. We must educate the white people out of their two hundred fifty years of slave history."
>
> Ida B. Wells,
> *Crusade for Justice*,
> 1928

1862 Wells is born in Mississippi.

1878 Wells's parents die from yellow fever.

1884 Wells sues for ejection from railway car.

1892 Wells becomes co-owner of Memphis *Free Speech;* joins antilynching crusade.

1893 Wells tours Europe fighting for civil rights.

1895 Wells publishes *A Red Record;* marries Ferdinand L. Barnett.

1896 Wells-Barnett helps organize National Association of Colored Women.

1901 Well-Barnett meets with President McKinley.

1913 Wells-Barnett organizes Alpha Suffrage Club in Chicago.

1916 Wells-Barnett becomes involved with Marcus Garvey's organization.

1930 Wells-Barnett runs for the Senate.

1931 Wells-Barnett dies in Chicago.

railroad, and though she was awarded $500 by a lower court, the Tennessee Supreme Court reversed the decision in 1887. In the same year, she launched her career in journalism, writing of her experiences in an African-American weekly called *The Living Way.* In 1892 she became the co-owner of a small black newspaper in Memphis, the *Free Speech.* Her articles on the injustices faced by southern blacks, written under the pen name "Iola," were reprinted in a number of black newspapers, including the *New York Age,* the *Detroit Plain-Dealer,* and the *Indianapolis Freeman.*

In March 1892 the lynching of three young black businessmen, Thomas Moss, Calvin McDowell, and Henry Steward, in a suburb of Memphis focused Wells's attention on the pressing need to address the increasing prevalence of this terrible crime in the post–Reconstruction South. Her approach was characteristically forthright. She argued that though most lynchings were fueled by accusations of rape, they actually were prompted by economic competition between whites and blacks. Wells infuriated most whites by asserting that many sexual liaisons between black men and white women were not rape but mutually consensual.

She urged African Americans in Memphis to move to the West (where, presumably, conditions were more favorable) and to boycott segregated streetcars and discriminatory merchants. Her challenges to the prevailing racial orthodoxy of the South were met by mob violence, and in May 1892, while she was out of town, the offices of the *Free Speech* were destroyed by an angry throng of whites.

After her press was destroyed, Wells began to work for the *New York Age*. There, Wells continued to write extensively on lynching and other African-American issues. She penned exposés of southern injustice and decried the situation before European audiences in 1893 and 1894. During these European tours, she criticized some white American supporters of black causes for their halfhearted opposition to lynching. Wells's most extended treatment of the subject, *A Red Record: Tabulated Statistics and Alleged Causes of Lynchings in the United States*, appeared in 1895. This was the first serious statistical study of lynchings in the post–Emancipation South. She continued this work for the rest of her life. Some of her more widely read articles in this area include "Lynching and the Excuse for It" (1901) and "Our Country's Lynching Record" (1913). Perhaps her greatest effort in this arena was her tireless campaign for national antilynching legislation. In 1901 she met with President McKinley to convince him of the importance of such legislation. Her appeal was to no avail.

Another issue that provoked Wells's ire was the decision not to permit an African-American pavilion at the 1893 World's Fair. Wells, with the financial support of Frederick Douglass, among others, published a widely circulated booklet entitled *The Reason Why the Colored American Is Not in the World's Exposition* (1893).

In 1895 Wells married Chicago lawyer-editor Ferdinand L. Barnett, who was appointed assistant state attorney for Cook County in 1896. The couple had four children. Chicago would remain their home for the rest of their lives, and though she was a devoted mother and homemaker, Wells-Barnett's political and reform activities were unceasing. She served as secretary of the National Afro-American Council from 1898 to 1902 and headed its Antilynching Speakers Bureau. She organized and played an important role in, the founding of the National Association of Colored Women in 1896. In 1910 she founded the Negro Fellowship League in Chicago, which provided housing and employment for black male migrants. As early as 1901 the

> *"I had to become a mother before I realized what a wonderful place in the scheme of things the Creator has given woman."*
> Ida B. Wells,
> *Crusade for Justice*,
> 1928

Barnetts challenged restrictive housing covenants when they moved to the all-white East Side of Chicago. Her concern for the welfare of Chicago's black community led Wells-Barnett to become, in 1913, the first black woman probation officer in the nation. She lost her appointment in 1916, when a new city administration came to power.

Wells-Barnett was also active in the fight for women's suffrage. In 1913 she organized the Alpha Suffrage Club, the first black women's **suffrage** club in Illinois. That year, and again in 1918, she marched with suffragists in Washington, D.C. On the former occasion she insisted on marching with the Illinois contingent, integrating it over the objection of many white women marchers.

suffrage: the right to vote.

Wells-Barnett's militant opposition to the southern status quo placed her at odds with Booker T. Washington and his strategy of **accommodationism.** She was much more sympathetic to the ideology of W. E. B. Du Bois and in 1906 she attended the founding meeting of the Niagara Movement. She was a member of the original Executive Committee of the National Association for the Advancement of Colored People (NAACP) in 1910. She was, however, uneasy about the integrated hierarchy at the organization and felt their public stance was too **tempered,** and she ceased active participation in 1912.

accommodationism: the attitude that blacks should gradually adapt to white society.

tempered: mild, restrained.

In 1916 Wells-Barnett began an affiliation with Marcus Garvey's Universal Negro Improvement Association (UNIA). In December 1918, at a UNIA meeting in New York, Wells-Barnett was chosen along with A. Philip Randolph to represent the organization as a delegate to the upcoming Versailles Conference. Both representatives were repeatedly denied U.S. State Department clearance, however, so they never attended the meeting. Wells-Barnett, however, did speak on behalf of the UNIA at Bethel AME Church in Baltimore at the end of December 1918. Her continued affiliation with the organization after this was less public.

In the last decades of her life, Wells-Barnett continued to write about racial issues and American injustice. The East St. Louis race riot of July 1917 and the Chicago riot of July and August 1919 provided the impetus for impassioned denunciations of the treatment of African Americans in the United States. She wrote *The Arkansas Race Riot* in 1922 in response to the accusation of murder aimed at several black farmers, an accusation that was said to have instigated the disturbance. Most of her later work targeted social and political issues in

Chicago. In 1930 Wells-Barnett ran unsuccessfully as an independent candidate for the Senate from Illinois.

She died the next year, on March 25, 1931. In 1941 the Chicago Housing Authority named one of its first low-rent housing developments the Ida B. Wells Homes. In 1990 the U.S. Postal Service issued an Ida B. Wells stamp. ◆

West, Dorothy

1907 – AUGUST 16, 1998 ● WRITER

D orothy West was born to Rachel Pease West and Isaac Christopher West in Boston, where she attended Girls' Latin School and Boston University. Hers was a long and varied writing career that spanned over seventy years, beginning with a short story she wrote at age seven. When she was barely fifteen, she was selling short stories to the *Boston Post*. And before she was eighteen, already living in New York, West had won second place in the national competition sponsored by *Opportunity* magazine, an honor she shared with Zora Neale Hurston. The winning story, "The Typewriter," was later included in Edward O'Brien's *The Best Short Stories of 1926*.

As friend of such luminaries as Countee Cullen, Langston Hughes, Claude McKay, and Wallace Thurman, Dorothy West judged them and herself harshly for "degenerat[ing] through [their] vices" and for failing, in general, to live up to their promise. Thus, in what many consider the waning days of the Harlem Renaissance and in the lean years of the Depression, West used personal funds to start *Challenge*, a literary quarterly, hoping to recapture some of this failed promise. She served as its editor from 1934 until the last issue appeared in the spring of 1937. It was succeeded in the fall of that year by *New Challenge*. The renamed journal listed West and Marian Minus as coeditors and Richard Wright as associate editor, but West's involvement with the new project was short-lived.

The shift from *Challenge* to *New Challenge* is variously explained but can perhaps be summed up in Wallace Thurman's observation to West that *Challenge* had been too "high schoolish" and "pink tea." Whether *Challenge* was to *New Challenge* what "pink tea" was to "red" is debatable, but West has admitted

> *"I went to the Harlem Renaissance and never said a word. I was young and a girl so they never asked me to say anything. I didn't know I had anything to say."*
> Dorothy West

1907 West is born in Boston.

1926 West's story *The Typewriter* is included in *The Best Short Stories of 1926.*

1934 West begins editing *Challenge.*

1948 West publishes *The Living Is Easy.*

1995 West publishes *The Wedding.*

1998 West dies.

insularity: narrow-mindedness.
bourgeoisie: the middle class.

that *New Challenge* turned resolutely toward a strict Communist party line that she found increasingly difficult to toe. Despite her resistance to this turn in the journal's emphasis, *Challenge*, under West's editorship, succeeded in encouraging and publishing submissions that explored the desperate conditions of the black working class.

Because of her involvement with *Challenge* and her early associations with the figures and events that gave the period its singular status and acclaim, West was designated the "last surviving member of the Harlem Renaissance" before her death in 1998. The bulk of her writing, however, actually began to be published long after what most literary historians consider the height of the movement.

In the more than sixty short stories written throughout her career, West showed that form to be her forte. Many of these stories were published in the *New York Daily News*. The first to appear there was "Jack in the Pot" (retitled "Jackpot" by the editors), which won the Blue Ribbon Fiction contest and was anthologized in John Henrik Clarke's 1970 collection *Harlem: Voices from the Soul of Black America*. Another story, "For Richer, for Poorer," has been widely anthologized in textbooks and various collections.

Although the short story was the mainstay of her career, West is best known for her novel, *The Living Is Easy*. Published in 1948, the novel has been praised for its engaging portrayal of Cleo Judson, the unscrupulous and manipulative woman who brings ruin on herself as well as on family members who fall under her domination and control. But the novel has also earned West high marks for its treatment of the class snobbery, **insularity,** and all-around shallowness of the New England black **bourgeoisie,** whom West termed the "genteel poor." While Mary Helen Washington commends *The Living Is Easy* for its array of feminist themes—"the silencing of women, the need for female community, anger over the limitations and restrictions of women's lives"—in the final analysis she faults it for silencing the mother's voice.

For more than forty years, Dorothy West lived on Martha's Vineyard, contributing after 1968 a generous sampling of occasional pieces and columns to its newspaper, the *Vineyard Gazette*. In 1995 West published *The Wedding*, a novel about middle-class African Americans living on Martha's Vineyard during the 1950s. It was her first novel in forty-seven years. ◆

Wheatley, Phillis

C. 1753 – DECEMBER 5, 1784 ● POET

Phillis Wheatley was born, according to her own testimony, in Gambia, West Africa, along the fertile lowlands of the Gambia River. She was abducted as a small child of seven or eight, and sold in Boston to John and Susanna Wheatley on July 11, 1761. The horrors of the middle passage very likely contributed to the persistent asthma that plagued her throughout her short life. The Wheatleys apparently named the girl, who had nothing but a piece of dirty carpet to conceal her nakedness, after the slaver, the *Phillis*, that transported her. Nonetheless, unlike most slave owners of the time, the Wheatleys permitted Phillis to learn to read, and her poetic talent soon began to emerge.

Her earliest known piece of writing was an undated letter from 1765 (no known copy now exists) to Samson Occom, the Native American Mohegan minister and one of Dartmouth College's first graduates. The budding poet first appeared in print on December 21, 1767, in the *Newport Mercury* newspaper, when the author was about fourteen. The poem, "On Messrs. Hussey and Coffin," relates how the two gentlemen of the title narrowly escaped being drowned off Cape Cod in Massachusetts. Much of her subsequent poetry deals, as well, with

> *"Imagination! who can sing thy force?*
> *Or who describe the swiftness of thy course?"*
> Phillis Wheatley, "On Imagination," 1773

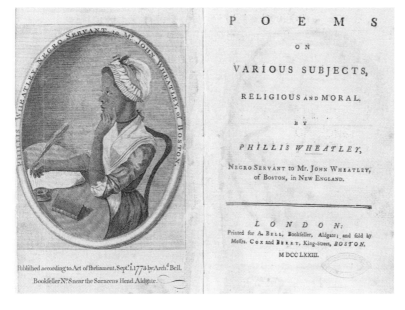

The title page from **Phillis Wheatley**'s *Poems on Various Subjects*, printed in London in 1773.

elegy: a poem expressing sorrow, usually for a dead person.

privy: private.

events occurring close to her Boston circle. Of her fifty-five extant poems, for example, nineteen are **elegies;** all but the last of these are devoted to commemorating someone known by the poet. Her last elegy is written about herself and her career.

In early October 1770 Wheatley published an elegy that was pivotal to her career. The subject of the elegy was George Whitefield, an evangelical Methodist minister and **privy** chaplain to Selina Hastings, countess of Huntingdon. Whitefield made seven journeys to the American colonies, where he was known as "the Voice of the Great Awakening" and "the Great Awakener." Only a week before his death in Newburyport, Massachusetts, on September 30, 1770, Whitefield preached in Boston, where Wheatley very likely heard him. As Susanna Wheatley regularly corresponded with the countess, she and the Wheatley household may well have entertained the Great Awakener. Wheatley's vivid, ostensibly firsthand account in the elegy, replete with quotations, may have been based on an actual acquaintance with Whitefield. In any case, Wheatley's deft elegy became an overnight sensation and was often reprinted.

It is almost certain that the ship that carried news of Whitefield's death to the countess also carried a copy of Wheatley's elegy, which brought Wheatley to the sympathetic attention of the countess. Such an acquaintance ensured that Wheatley's elegy was also reprinted many times in London, giving the young poet the distinction of an international reputation. When Wheatley's *Poems* was denied publication in Boston for racist reasons, the countess of Huntingdon generously financed its publication in London by Archibald Bell.

Wheatley's support by Selina Hastings and her rejection by male-dominated Boston signal her nourishment as a literary artist by a community of women. All these women—the countess, who encouraged and financed the publication of her *Poems* in 1773; Mary and Susanna Wheatley, who taught her the rudiments of reading and writing; and Obour Tanner, who could empathize probably better than anyone with her condition as a slave—were much older than Wheatley and obviously nurtured her creative development.

During the summer of 1772 Wheatley actually journeyed to England, where she assisted in the preparation of her volume for the press. While in London she enjoyed considerable recognition by such dignitaries as Lord Dartmouth, Lord Lincoln, Granville Sharp (who escorted Wheatley on several tours about

1753 Wheatley is born in the Gambia, West Africa.

1761 Wheatley is sold as a slave in Boston.

1767 Wheatley publishes "On Messrs. Hussey and Coffin."

1770 Wheatley publishes elegy to George Whitefield.

1773 Wheatley publishes *Poems* in London.

1775 Wheatley publishes "To His Excellency General Washington."

1784 Wheatley dies in poverty in Boston.

London), Benjamin Franklin, and Brook Watson, a wealthy merchant who presented Wheatley with a folio edition of John Milton's *Paradise Lost* and who would later become lord mayor of London. Wheatley was to have been presented at court when Susanna Wheatley became ill. Wheatley was summoned to return to Boston in early August 1773. Sometime before October 18, 1773, she was granted her freedom, according to her own testimony, "at the desire of my friends in England." It seems likely, then, that if Selina Hastings had not agreed to finance Wheatley's *Poems* and if the poet had not journeyed to London, she would never have been manumitted.

As the American Revolution erupted, Wheatley's patriotic feelings began to separate her even more from the Wheatleys, who were loyalists. Her patriotism is clearly underscored in her two most famous Revolutionary War poems. "To His Excellency General Washington" (1775) closes with this justly famous encomium: "A crown, a mansion, and a throne that shine, / With gold unfading WASHINGTON! be thine." "Liberty and Peace" (1784), written to celebrate the Treaty of Paris (September 1783), declares: "And new-born Rome [i.e., America] shall give *Britannia* Law."

Phillis Wheatley's attitude toward slavery has also been misunderstood. Because some of her antislavery statements have been recovered only in the 1970s and '80s, she has often been criticized for ignoring the issue. But her position was clear: in February 1774, for example, Wheatley wrote to Samson Occom that "in every human breast, God has implanted a Principle, which we call Love of Freedom; it is impatient of Oppression, and pants for Deliverance." This letter was reprinted a dozen times in American newspapers over the course of the next twelve months. Certainly Americans of Wheatley's time never questioned her attitude toward slavery after the publication of this letter.

In 1778 Wheatley married John Peters, a free African American who was a jack-of-all-trades, serving in various capacities from storekeeper to advocate for African Americans before the courts. But given the turbulent conditions of a nation caught up in the Revolution, Wheatley's fortunes began to decline steadily. In 1779 she published a set of *Proposals* for a new volume of poems. While the *Proposals* failed to attract subscribers, these *Proposals* attest that the poet had been diligent with her pen since the 1773 *Poems* and that she had indeed

"O Virtue, smiling in immortal green,
Do thou exert thy pow'r, and change the scene;
Be thine employ to guide my future days,
And mine to pay the tribute of my praise."
Phillis Wheatley, "On Recollection," 1773

produced some 300 pages of new poetry. This volume never appeared, however, and most of its poems are now lost.

Phillis Wheatley Peters and her newborn child died in a shack on the edge of Boston on December 5, 1784. Preceded in death by two other young children, Wheatley's tragic end resembles her beginning in America. Yet Wheatley has left to her largely unappreciative country a legacy of firsts: she was the first African American to publish a book, the first woman writer whose publication was urged and nurtured by a community of women, and the first American woman author who tried to earn a living by means of her writing. ◆

Williams, Mary Lou
(Scruggs, Mary Elfrieda)

MAY 8, 1910 – MAY 28, 1981 ● JAZZ PIANIST

swing: a style of jazz popular in the 1930s and 1940s.

Although she never led her own big band, and recorded only occasionally as a leader, Mary Lou Williams is generally acknowledged as the most significant female instrumentalist in the history of jazz, composing and arranging works that exemplify the rhythmic drive and harmonic sophistication of the **swing** era. Born Mary Elfrieda Scruggs in Atlanta, Georgia, she moved to Pittsburgh, Pennsylvania, with her mother in 1914, and performed professionally on piano at age six. Using the surname of her two stepfathers, she performed as Mary Lou Burley and Mary Lou Winn at private parties in Pittsburgh and in East Liberty, Pennsylvania, before the age of ten. At fifteen, while a student at Pittsburgh's Lincoln High School, she played piano on the Theater Owners Booking Association (TOBA) black vaudeville circuit. Two years later she married John Williams, a baritone saxophonist, and moved with him to Memphis. They next lived in Oklahoma City and then Kansas City, where Mary Lou Williams quickly became a prominent member of the developing swing scene. In 1929 her husband arranged for her to have an audition with bandleader Andy Kirk. Williams became a full-time member of Kirk's Clouds of Joy in 1930, and its star soloist, composer, and arranger, one of the few well-known instrumentalists of the swing era.

Although Williams's early style as a soloist was influenced by Earl Hines, Jelly Roll Morton, and Fats Waller, by the late 1920s she was a well-known exponent of Kansas City swing, a somewhat lighter style of swing derived from stride influences. As one of her Kirk recordings pointed out in its title, Williams was "The Lady Who Swings the Band" (1936). She was significant as both a composer and arranger, lending harmonic sophistication and a bold sense of swing to Kirk's repertory, including "Mess-a-Stomp" (1929 and 1938), "Walkin' and Swingin'" (1936), "Froggy Bottom" (1936), "Moten Swing" (1936), "In the Groove" (1937), and "Mary's Idea" (1938). In the mid-1930s the Clouds of Joy moved to New York, where Williams also worked as an

arranger for Louis Armstrong, Earl Hines, Tommy Dorsey, and Benny Goodman, for whom she arranged the famous 1937 versions of "Roll 'Em," "Camel Hop," and "Whistle Blues." In 1940 she arranged and recorded "Baby Dear" and "Harmony Blues" as Mary Lou Williams and Her Kansas City Seven, an ensemble drawn from the Kirk band. Williams, who had divorced her husband in the late 1930s, left Kirk's band in 1942. That year she married and began performing with trumpeter Shorty Baker. That marriage also ended in divorce. Throughout the 1940s Williams continued to work as an arranger, again with Goodman, as well as on "Trumpets No End," her 1945 arrangement of "Blue Skies" for Duke Ellington. She also continued to perform, as a solo act in the mid-to-late 1940s at both the uptown and downtown Cafe Society in New York, and with an all-female group (1945–46). At Carnegie Hall in 1946 the New York Philharmonic performed three movements of her *Zodiac* suite, a version of which she had recorded the year before.

While many giants of the swing era failed to make the transition to **bebop,** Williams readily assimilated into her playing

bebop: style of jazz characterized by complex melody and constant shifting of accent, played very fast.

1910 Williams is born in Atlanta.

1930 Williams joins Andy Kirk's Clouds of Joy.

1946 Williams's *Zodiac* suite is performed by the New York Philharmonic.

1957 Williams performs at the Newport Jazz Festival.

1969 Williams composes *Mary Lou's Mass.*

1977 Williams performs with Cecil Taylor at Carnegie Hall.

1981 Williams dies in Durham, NC.

the developments of Thelonious Monk and Bud Powell, both of whom were regular guests at the informal piano salon she held at her Harlem home throughout the 1940s and 1950s. In 1952 Williams began a two-year tour of England and France. In 1954 she underwent a religious experience while performing at a Paris nightclub, and walked off the bandstand in mid-set. Back home in Harlem, Williams, who had been raised a Baptist, joined a Roman Catholic church because she was allowed to pray there at any time of the day or night. She refused to play in public until 1957, when, urged on by Dizzy Gillespie, she performed at the Newport Jazz Festival. From the late 1950s on, she regularly toured and performed, including a concert with fellow pianists Willie "The Lion" Smith, Duke Ellington, Earl Hines, and Billy Taylor in Pittsburgh in 1965.

In the 1960s Williams, who had become a devout Roman Catholic, composed several large-scale liturgical works (*Black Christ of the Andes*, 1963; *St. Martin de Porres*, 1965), culminating in *Mary Lou's Mass* (1969), which was commissioned by the Vatican and choreographed by Alvin Ailey. In the 1970s she continued to perform and record (*Solo Recital*, 1977), particularly with the intention of educating listeners about the history of jazz. She also performed with avant-garde pianist Cecil Taylor at Carnegie Hall (*Embraced*, 1977), and in that year became an artist in residence at Duke University in Durham, North Carolina, where she died. ◆

Williams, Venus

JUNE 17, 1980 – ●   TENNIS PLAYER

> *"I'm tall. I'm black. Everything's different about me. Just face the facts."*
> Venus Williams, 1997

W omen have held a key place in the sport of tennis ever since the first amateur world championships for women took place in Wimbledon, England, in 1884. Following in these footsteps, but bringing a bold new energy to the "country-club sport," seventeen-year-old Venus Williams made her Wimbledon debut in 1997. With long, nimble limbs and beaded braids flashing, Williams created a sensation on the courts.

Venus Ebone Starr Williams was born June 17, 1980, in Los Angeles, the fourth of five daughters of Richard and Oracene

(Price) Williams. Michigan-born Oracene practiced nursing, and Richard, son of a Louisiana share-cropper, headed a security business. By the time Venus was five, Richard had her on the courts in their Compton neighborhood hitting tennis balls. All the daughters played tennis, but Richard concentrated on Venus and Serena, her younger sister.

Venus began competing in 1989. By the age of ten she had won numerous titles on the Southern California junior tennis circuit and soon became the No. 1 player in her age group in California. Serena also competed, and the girls soon tasted minor celebrity.

In 1991, accepting scholarships for Venus and Serena at the tennis academy of coach Rick Macci, the family relocated to Florida, eventually purchasing a home in Palm Beach Gardens. Richard then made an unusual move by withdrawing the girls from junior competitions.

Instead they practiced six hours a day, six days a week. The Williamses also home schooled the sisters.

In October 1994 Venus emerged on the professional circuit, playing a tournament in Oakland, California. Although the fourteen-year-old had not competed in three years, she beat the fifty-ninth ranked woman in the world and also gave a close game to Arantxa Sanchez-Vicario, the No. 2 player. Puzzled by Richard Williams's change of mind, observers guessed that new rules from the World Tennis Association lay behind it. After 1994, fourteen-year-olds would no longer be allowed to enter the pros. Also, women under eighteen entering the pros after 1995 would be limited to a certain number of tournaments. After Oakland, though, Venus did not compete again until August 1995.

In the spring of 1997 Venus made her debut at the French Open, and a month later she debuted at Wimbledon. She did

1980 — Williams is born in Los Angeles.

1989 — Williams begins competing in tennis.

1991 — Williams family moves to Florida.

1994 — Williams enters the ranks of professional tennis players.

1997 — Williams makes her first appearance at Wimbledon.

1998 — Williams reaches the semifinals of the U.S. Open.

not do well, but the world had seen her talent. That summer, Venus performed better at the U.S. Open, advancing from 66th to 25th in the rankings in one day. Williams became the first African-American female to appear in the finals of the U.S. Open since Althea Gibson won the title in 1958. Martina Hingis beat Williams; however, Williams created more of a stir than any other player. She defeated 8th-seeded Anke Huber in the third round and toppled No. 11, the Romanian Irina Spirlea, in a tight semifinal round. In that match, an incident occurred in which Williams and Spirlea appeared deliberately to bump into each other. Afterwards, Richard Williams proclaimed Spirlea a racist, though he later retracted his accusation. At 1998's U.S. Open, Venus, eighteen, made it to the semifinals and by autumn she was ranked No. 5 in the world.

At 6′ 2″ and 168 pounds, Venus powers a serve that has reached 125 mph, equal to the standing women's record. Richard Williams often boasted that someday Venus and Serena would go head-to-head for first place. The sisters played each other for the first time at the Australian Open in January 1998. Venus won. Off court, the girls are best friends and close to their family. As practicing Jehovah's Witnesses, Serena and Venus visit door-to-door to discuss the Bible. While they abstain from alcohol, tobacco, and premarital sex, the sisters are famous for skintight tennis dresses and beaded braids. They have been called cocky, and Venus has displayed emotional outbursts on court. However, both Venus and Serena are considered well spoken and intelligent by the press as well as many enthusiastic fans. The *New York Times* once quoted Venus as saying, "I never thought anyone was better than me. Once you do that, you lose." ◆

Wilson, Harriet E. Adams

C. 1830 – 1870 ● WRITER

Harriet E. Wilson is believed to be the pseudonymous "Our Nig," who wrote what may have been the first novel by an African American published in the United States: *Our Nig; or, Sketches from the Life of a Free Black, in a Two-Story White House, North. Showing That Slavery's Shad-*

ows Fall Even There (1859). Some scholars also include her with Maria F. dos Reis, who in 1859 published a novel in Brazil, as the first two women of African descent to publish a novel in any language. "Our Nig's" work describes the life of Alfredo, a mulatto indentured servant, and condemns Northern whites for a magnitude of racial prejudice and cruelty more commonly associated with slavery and the South. Three letters presumably written by friends of the novelist are appended to the novel, and it is because of the correspondences between the seemingly supplementary biographical information included there that the novel has been considered semiautobiographical.

Despite these letters, however, little definite is known about Harriet Wilson's life. For instance, according to the 1850 federal census for the state of New Hampshire, a twenty-two-year-old "Black" (not "mulatto") woman originally from New Hampshire named Harriet Adams lived in the town of Milford with the family of Samuel Boyles, which in part corresponds to information included in the novel. This suggests that Wilson was born about 1827–28. However, the 1860 federal census for the city of Boston, where Wilson moved in approximately 1855, and where she had her novel printed, lists a "Black" woman named Harriet E. Wilson born in Fredericksburg, Virginia, in about 1807–08.

The appended letters, as well as the end of *Our Nig*, provide details of the author's life between 1850 and 1860, when she lived in Massachusetts and worked as a weaver of straw hats. About 1851 Harriet Adams met Thomas Wilson, a fugitive slave from Virginia, and together they moved to Milford, New Hampshire, and married, perhaps on October 6, 1851. By the time Harriet Wilson gave birth in May or June of 1852 to their son, George Mason Wilson, Thomas Wilson had abandoned his wife and she had gone to a charity establishment in Goffstown, New Hampshire, the Hillsborough County Farm. Thomas Wilson returned and supported his wife and child for a short time, but then suddenly left them again and never returned.

Harriet Wilson, whose health had been bad since she was eighteen, was rescued by a couple who took in and cared for her and her son. When her health failed, Wilson began writing her novel in an effort to make money: "Deserted by kindred, disabled by failing health," she wrote in her preface to *Our Nig*, "I am forced to some experiment, which shall aid me in maintaining myself and child without extinguishing this feeble life."

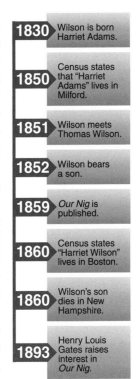

1830 Wilson is born Harriet Adams.

1850 Census states that "Harriet Adams" lives in Milford.

1851 Wilson meets Thomas Wilson.

1852 Wilson bears a son.

1859 *Our Nig* is published.

1860 Census states "Harriet Wilson" lives in Boston.

1860 Wilson's son dies in New Hampshire.

1893 Henry Louis Gates raises interest in *Our Nig*.

Little is known of Wilson's life after the publication of *Our Nig*, on September 5, 1859. Her son died in New Hampshire in February 1860, and Harriet Wilson died sometime between the death of her son and January 1870.

For more than 100 years, *Our Nig* was barely noticed. In 1983, however, the critic Henry Louis Gates Jr. raised scholarly interest in Wilson and the novel by arranging to have the book republished, the text being an exact reprint of the 1859 edition. ◆

Winfrey, Oprah Gail

JANUARY 29, 1954 –   ● TALK-SHOW HOST AND ACTOR

Born on a farm in Kosciusko, Mississippi, to Vernita Lee and Vernon Winfrey, Oprah Winfrey was reared by her grandmother for the early part of her life. At age six, she was sent to live with her mother, who worked as a domestic, and two half brothers in Milwaukee, Wisconsin. It was in Milwaukee that Winfrey began to display her oratorical gifts, reciting poetry at socials and teas. During her adolescence, Winfrey began to misbehave to such a degree that she was sent to live with her father in Nashville, Tennessee. Under the strict disciplinary regime imposed by her father, Winfrey started to flourish, distinguishing herself in debate and oratory. At sixteen, she won an Elks Club oratorical contest that awarded her a scholarship to Tennessee State University.

While a freshman in college, Winfrey won the Miss Black Nashville and Miss Black Tennessee pageants. As a result of this exposure, she received a job offer from a local television station and in her sophomore year became a news anchor at WTVF-TV in Nashville. After graduating in 1976, Winfrey took a job with WJZ-TV in Baltimore as a reporter and coanchor of the evening news. In 1977 she was switched to updates on local news, which appeared during the ABC national morning show *Good Morning America*. That same year she found her niche as a talk-show host, cohosting WJZ-TV's morning show *Baltimore Is Talking*.

In 1984 Winfrey moved to Chicago to take over *A.M. Chicago*, a talk show losing in the ratings to Phil Donahue's popular morning program. Within a month Winfrey's ratings were equal to Donahue's. In three months she surpassed him. A year and a half later the show extended to an hour and was renamed *The Oprah Winfrey Show*. The show, which covers a wide range of topics from the lighthearted to the sensational or the tragic, was picked up for national syndication by King World Productions in 1986. By 1993 *The Oprah Winfrey Show* was seen in 99 percent of U.S. television markets and sixty-four countries. Since the show first became eligible in 1986, it has won Emmy Awards for best talk show, or best talk-show hostess each year except one.

In 1985 Winfrey was cast as the strong-willed Sofia in the film version of Alice Walker's *The Color Purple*, for which she received an Oscar nomination. The following year she formed her own production company, HARPO Productions, to develop projects. In 1989 Winfrey produced and acted in a television miniseries based on Gloria Naylor's novel *The Women of Brewster Place*, and in 1993 she starred in and produced the television drama *There Are No Children Here*. That same year *Forbes* magazine listed Winfrey as America's richest entertainer based on her 1992 and 1993 earnings of approximately $98 million.

In September 1996 Winfrey launched Oprah's Book Club to encourage her audiences to read books. In its first year, each of the on-air book club's first eight selections shot to the top of best-seller lists, and publishing experts estimated that Oprah's Book Club generated the sale of twelve million books.

In 1997 *Forbes* magazine ranked Winfrey as the wealthiest woman in the entertainment industry. She continued her relationship with Stedman Graham, forty-six, head of a marketing consulting firm and an advertising agency, whom she had met at a friend's party in 1986. The couple own a Chicago condominium and, though engaged for a while, have dropped their marriage plans. They share a commitment to charitable giving.

The Oprah Winfrey Show kicked off its thirteenth season in syndication in early September 1998. Carried by 206 television

1954 Winfrey is born in Mississippi.

1976 Winfrey graduates from Tennessee State University.

1977 Winfrey begins cohosting *Baltimore Is Talking*.

1984 Winfrey begins hosting *A.M. Chicago*.

1985 Winfrey is nominated for Oscar for *The Color Pur-*

1986 Winfrey's *The Oprah Winfrey Show* is syndicated nationally.

1989 Winfrey produces and performs in *The Women of Brewster Place*.

1993 *Forbes* magazine lists Winfrey as American's wealthiest entertainer.

1996 Winfrey launches "Oprah's Book Club."

1998 Winfrey produces and stars in *Beloved*.

stations nationwide and in 135 international territories, it was promoted as the most popular talk show in the world and the highest-rated talk show in television history. In late September 1998 HARPO and King World agreed that Winfrey would continue to host and produce the show through the 2001 to 2002 broadcast season.

Winfrey began her 1998 season proclaiming a "renewed mission to enlighten, educate and entertain viewers." She unveiled a new set and premiered a new theme song performed by herself. She called her new concept "Change Your Life TV" and introduced a daily spiritual segment called "Remembering Your Spirit." Some media critics reacted to Winfrey's latest persona negatively. One nicknamed her "Saint Oprah" and several commented on her tendency to preach. Winfrey also posed on the covers of fashionable women's magazines with her newly slimmed and professionally trained figure. Some viewers did not identify with the super-wealthy Oprah as they had with the cheery, overweight, sisterly Oprah of earlier years who had shared with audiences painful personal stories of childhood abuse.

In October of 1998 Touchstone Pictures released *Beloved*, a movie based on the novel by Nobel prize-winning author Toni Morrison. Winfrey had been deeply moved by the novel when it came out in 1988 and bought the rights to film the story. She starred as the runaway slave in post–Civil War Ohio who struggles with a past of unspeakable brutality. Reviewers were respectful of the work, but the film met a lukewarm response from critics and audiences. The film's three-hour length and grim subject matter contributed to a lack of box-office fervor. Producers predicted the movie would see longevity in video sales and rentals.

Winfrey timed the sale of her book *Journey to Beloved* with the movie's release. The book consisted of journal entries she made on the set of the movie. Winfrey said that few events in her life had affected her as powerfully as playing the part of Sethe, the former slave. "The whole purpose for life on Earth is to attach yourself to that force which is divine and let yourself be released to that," Winfrey said. "I felt that way about making the movie *Beloved*. It was divine—I know no other word to use." ◆

Wright, Jane Cooke

NOVEMBER 17, 1919 – ● CANCER RESEARCHER AND
MEDICAL SCHOOL ADMINISTRATOR

Born in New York City, Jane Cooke Wright's choice of a medical career was inspired by the accomplishments of her father, physician Louis T. Wright. After graduating from Smith College (B.A., 1938) and New York Medical College (M.D., 1945), she completed residencies in internal medicine at Bellevue Hospital and at Harlem Hospital in New York.

As a medical researcher, Wright worked on many types of cancer, from skin cancer and breast cancer to leukemia. In the 1950s she did pioneering research in the use of chemicals (chemotherapy) to treat the disease in humans. Her method of using human tissue cultures from cancer patients, rather than laboratory mice, to test the effects of drugs on cancer cells was a significant contribution to the field. She is credited with being the first to use the drug methotrexate to gain remissions in patients with mycosis fungoides (a skin cancer) and solid-tumor breast cancer. The Damon Runyon fund awarded her $25,000 in 1955 to continue her cancer research at Bellevue. In 1961 she was part of a medical group sponsored by the African Research Foundation that treated some 340 cancer patients in Kenya using a mobile medical unit.

Wright has been active in a number of national medical associations, including the American Association for Cancer Research and the New York Academy of Sciences. In 1964 she was one of the seven founding members of the American Society of Clinical Oncology, a preeminent organization in the field of cancer research. In 1967 Wright was appointed associate dean and professor of surgery at New York Medical College. That same year, President Lyndon Johnson appointed her to the National Cancer Advisory Council. In 1971 Wright became the first woman elected president of the New York Cancer Society. As she moved toward retirement in 1985, she led delegates to Ghana, China, Eastern Europe, and the Soviet Union to learn the latest knowledge and techniques in cancer chemotherapy research and treatment. ◆

1919 Wright is born in New York City.

1938 Wright graduates from Smith College.

1945 Wright receives M.D. from New York Medical College.

1955 Damon Runyon fund awards Wright $25,000 for research.

1961 Wright travels to Kenya to treat cancer patients.

1964 Wright helps found the American Society of Clinical Oncology.

1967 Wright is appointed to National Cancer Advisory Council.

1971 Wright is elected president of New York Cancer Society.

Young, Roger Arliner

1899 – NOVEMBER 9, 1964 ● ZOOLOGIST

Roger Arliner Young was the first African-American woman to earn a doctoral degree in zoology, which she received from the University of Pennsylvania in 1940. In an era when few black scientists had the opportunity to conduct scientific research, Young published a number of papers on marine eggs based on experiments she had conducted at the Marine Biological Laboratory in Woods Hole, Massachusetts, the premier biological research institute in the country. She was the first black woman to do experimental biology at this institution.

Young was born in Clifton Forge, Virginia. She entered Howard University in 1916 and studied zoology under the eminent black scientist Ernest Everett Just, one of the leading zoologists in the United States. When she completed her undergraduate work at Howard, she was hired as an assistant professor of zoology in 1924. During that same year she published the results of her observations on the **morphology** of the contractile **vacuole** and feeding canals in the microorganism in *Paramecium caudatum*.

Young received a master's degree in zoology in 1926 from the University of Chicago, where she was elected to Sigma Xi, the national science honors society. From 1927 until 1939 she taught at Howard, serving as acting head of the zoology department in Just's absence in 1929. She spent her summers doing research at Woods Hole.

Young's research, both alone and under Just, the leading biologist of his time in the study of normal marine eggs, was

morphology: the form and structure.

vacuole: a small hole.

noteworthy. Her work on the paramecium challenged the prevailing theory on the role of the contractile vacuole and received favorable comments from scientists in both the United States and Europe. Burdened by a heavy teaching load and few financial resources, Young saw her career begin to flounder in the 1930s. After losing her position at Howard in 1936, she rallied to continue her research, publishing three papers between 1936 and 1938 and completing her doctoral work at the University of Pennsylvania under L. V. Heilbrunn in 1940.

Much of Young's research during this time continued the work she had begun with Just consisting of studies of the effects of ultraviolet radiation on sea-urchin eggs. From 1940 until her death she taught at a number of black colleges in the South, including the North Carolina College for Negroes, Shaw University (where she served as chair of the biology department), and Southern University in Louisiana.

1899 Young is born in Virginia.

1924 Young joins faculty of Howard University.

1926 Young earns a master's degree from the University of Chicago.

1940 Young is awarded Ph.D. in zoology from University of Pennsylvania.

1964 Young dies.

Time Line: The Accomplishments of Black Women in the Context of African-American History

1619	Twenty Africans arrive at Jamestown, Virginia, aboard a Dutch ship, the first Africans to enter an English colony.
1634	The first African child is born in the Jamestown Colony and is named William by officials of the Anglican Church.
1651	Anthony Johnson, an African from Jamestown, is given a land grant of 250 acres in Northampton County, Virginia.
1676	African Americans take a leading role in Bacon's Rebellion in Virginia.
1688	Quakers in Philadelphia make the first formal protest against enslavement of African Americans.
1712	African Americans revolt against enslavement in New York City, killing nine whites.
1739	Violent African-American revolt in South Carolina; thirty white slave owners and overseers are killed.
1741	African Americans in New York City set numerous fires, leading to panic, confusion, and increased tension between enslaved Africans and whites. Nearly 30 African Americans are executed for participation in the general insurrection.
1760	Jupiter Hammons from New York publishes the poem "An Evening Thought: Salvation by Christ, with Penitential Cries," the first poem published by a black person in North America.
1770	During a demonstration on March 5, African-American dockworker Crispus Attucks is gunned down by British soldiers in Boston, becoming the first person to give his life for the American Revolution.
1773	Phillis Wheatley publishes *Poems on Various Subjects Religious and Moral* in London.
1775	African soldiers fight on the side of the Americans at the Battle of Bunker Hill. African Americans also fight on the side of the British, who represent the colonial government.
1776	The Americans declare independence from England.
1777	Vermont becomes the first territory to abolish the enslavement of black people.
1783	Massachusetts abolishes slavery.
1787	The Northwest Ordinance prohibits slavery in the Northwest Territories.

1790	Sally Hemings gives birth to the first of her seven children, whom some believe to be the offspring of Thomas Jefferson.
1793	Richard Allen founds Mother Bethel African Methodist Episcopal Church in Philadelphia.
1800	Gabriel Prosser organizes a massive slave uprising involving nearly 1,000 African Americans in Richmond, Virginia. The revolt is betrayed and 16 African Americans, including Prosser, are hanged.
1804	Ohio enacts "Black Laws" preventing the movement of free African Americans in the state.
1807	The European slave trade on the high seas comes to an end; however, the importation of Africans continues.
1808	A U.S. law prohibiting the importation of African slaves goes into effect, but is widely circumvented.
1812	African Americans comprise nearly 20 percent of the United States Navy during the War of 1812 against the British. Some accept the British offer for freedom and escape to Nova Scotia, Jamaica, and eventually Sierra Leone.
1816	Wealthy whites from the American Colonization Society repatriate free and intransigent African Americans to Africa.
1817	African Americans in Philadelphia under the leadership of John Russwurm and Samuel Cornish form a powerful and united opposition to the American Colonization Society.
1821	Thomas L. Jennings becomes the first African American in North America to receive a patent for an invention, a dry-cleaning system.
1827	Sojourner Truth undergoes religious conversion.
	John Russwurm and Samuel Cornish publish *Freedom's Journal*, the first African-American-owned newspaper in the United States.
1828	William Lloyd Garrison begins publishing an abolitionist newspaper in Bennington, Vermont.
1830	First national convention of African Americans is held in Philadelphia; the purpose of the meeting is to assess conditions of African Americans until 1864.
1831	Nat Turner leads the most successful slave insurrection in the United States; nearly 60 white people are killed in Southhampton County, Virginia.
1841	Ann Plato publishes *Essays*.
1842	Sarah Parker Remond begins antislavery lecture tours.
	Henry Highland Garnet calls for enslaved Africans to revolt at a meeting in Buffalo, New York.

1843   Henry Blair receives a patent for a corn planter.

Sojourner Truth starts her travels and lectures against slavery.

1847   Rebecca Cox Jackson joins Shakers at Watervliet, New York.

Frederick Douglass publishes his paper, *North Star.*

1848   Harriet Tubman escapes from enslavement in Maryland.

1850   Fugitive Slave Act is passed making it a crime to help a runaway slave.

Ellen Craft flees to England.

Harriet Tubman makes her first rescue mission to the South.

1851   Sojourner Truth delivers the famous "Ain't I a Woman" speech in Akron, Ohio.

1852   Institute for Colored Youth, forerunner of Cheyney University, is founded in Philadelphia.

1853   William Wells publishes the first novel, *Clotel,* by an African American.

1854   Frances Ellen Watkins Harper publishes *Poems on Miscellaneous Subjects.*

Ashmun Institute, the country's first African-American college, is formed; renamed Lincoln University in 1866.

1855   Celia stands trial for murder of her slavemaster.

1857   Dred Scott decision denies African Americans rights by law, declaring that African Americans are not and cannot be citizens of the United States and that slavery cannot be prohibited in the western states.

1859   John Brown leads a band of 12 whites and 5 African Americans in a raid on the United States arsenal at Harpers Ferry, Virginia.

The last ship to bring slaves to the United States, the *Clothilde,* anchors in Mobile Bay, Alabama.

1860   South Carolina secedes from the Union, followed in 1861 by the other states that were to comprise the Confederacy.

1861   Harriet Ann Jacobs publishes *Incidents in the Life of a Slave Girl.*

Elizabeth Keckley is retained as Mary Todd Lincoln's dressmaker.

Confederate forces attack Fort Sumter in South Carolina; the Civil War begins.

1863   President Lincoln signs the Emancipation Proclamation freeing slaves in states that had rebelled against the federal government.

White officer Robert Gould Shaw leads the 54th Regiment of Massachusetts, an African-American unit, on a suicide mission against Fort Wagner in Charleston, South Carolina.

1864   Rebecca Lee receives an M.D. from the New England Female Medical College.

New Orleans Tribune becomes the first black daily newspaper in the South.

1865 General Robert E. Lee surrenders on April 8, ending the Civil War.

Nathan B. Forrest organizes the Ku Klux Klan.

Congress establishes the Freedmen's Bureau to provide health care, education, and other assistance to newly freed slaves.

The Thirteenth Amendment to the Constitution, outlawing slavery in the United States, is ratified.

1866 Biddy Mason purchases property in downtown Los Angeles.

Fisk University opens in Nashville, Tennessee.

1867 Rebecca J. Cole receives an M.D. from Women's Medical College of Pennsylvania.

Congress requires the former Confederate states to approve the right of African Americans to vote.

1868 Howard, Morehouse, and Talladega colleges are founded.

The Fourteenth Amendment to the Constitution, granting citizenship to African Americans, is ratified.

1869 Ebenezer Don Carlos Bassett becomes first African-American diplomat when he is appointed minister to Haiti.

1870 Hiram Rhodes Revel is elected to fill Jefferson Davis's Senate seat, thereby becoming the first African American to sit in the U.S. Senate.

The Fifteenth Amendment to the Constitution, ensuring black men the right to vote, is ratified.

1872 Charlotte Ray graduates from Howard University Law School, becoming the first African-American woman lawyer.

1876 Edmonia Lewis sculpts *Death of Cleopatra* for Philadelphia Centennial Exposition.

Edward Boucher earns doctorate from Yale University, becoming the first African American to receive an advanced degree from an American University.

Frederick Douglass becomes marshal of the District of Columbia.

Henry Flipper becomes the first African American to graduate from the United States Military Academy at West Point.

1878 Mary Ann Shadd Cary addresses National Woman Suffrage Association convention.

Lewis Latimer works with Hiram Maxim in invention of the incandescent electric light.

1879 Mary Eliza Mahoney completes nursing program at New England Hospital for Women and Children.

1880	Burrett Lewis becomes the first black jockey to win the Kentucky Derby.
1881	Booker T. Washington opens Tuskegee Institute in Alabama.
1883	Spelman College opens in Atlanta, Georgia.
1892	Ida B. Wells begins her campaign against lynching.
1893	Daniel B. Wells performs the first open-heart surgery in Chicago.
1895	W. E. B. Du Bois becomes the first African American to receive a Ph.D. from Harvard University.
1896	*Plessy* v. *Ferguson* case establishes the "separate but equal" doctrine on which segregation is based.
	Mary Eliza Church Terrell becomes president of National Association of Colored Women.
1897	Victoria Earle Matthews founds the White Rose Mission.
1902	Annie Turnbo Malone establishes hair-care product company in St. Louis.
1903	W. E. B. Du Bois publishes *Souls of Black Folks*.
1905	Madame C. J. Walker founds hair-care business in Denver.
	Niagara Movement organized to fight for social and civil justice, forerunner to the National Association for the Advancement of Colored People.
1907	Alain Locke, a Harvard graduate, becomes first African-American Rhodes scholar.
1909	Du Bois and others found the National Association for the Advancement of Colored People.
	Matthew Henson reaches the North Pole with the Robert Peary expedition.
1911	The National Urban League is established to help African Americans deal with the social and economic problems they encountered in American cities.
1913	Ida B. Wells-Barnett organizes Alpha Suffrage Club in Chicago.
1915	Carter G. Woodson institutes the Association for the Study of Negro Life.
1917	United States enters World War I; 300,000 African Americans serve.
1919	Eighty-three African Americans are lynched during the "Red Summer of Hate" as the Ku Klux Klan holds 200 meetings throughout the nation.
1920	Mamie Smith records "Crazy Blues."
	Marcus Garvey convenes an international gathering of Africans in Harlem under the banner of the Universal Negro Improvement Association and African Communities League.
1921	Ethel Waters records "Down Home Blues."
	The Harlem Renaissance begins.
	Sadie Tanner Mossell Alexander earns a Ph.D. from the University of Pennsylvania.

1922	Bessie Coleman obtains an international pilot's license.
	Dyer antilynching bill is passed in the U.S. House of Representatives but is defeated in the Senate.
1923	Ma Rainey records "Moonshine Blues."
	Bessie Smith records "Down Hearted Blues."
1924	A. Phillip Randolph organizes the Brotherhood of Sleeping Car Porters union.
1925	Lil Armstrong joins Louis Armstrong in Hot Fives and Hot Sevens jazz ensembles.
	Josephine Baker opens in Paris in *La Revue Nègre*.
1926	Dorothy West publishes prize-winning short story, *The Typewriter*.
1932	Jane Mathilda Bolin joins New York bar.
1933	Billie Holiday is discovered by John Hammond of Columbia Records.
	Myra Adele Logan is awarded an M.D. from New York Medical College.
1934	Ella Fitzgerald wins Harlem amateur contest.
	Augusta Savage is elected to National Association of Women Painters and Sculptors.
1935	Mary McLeod Bethune founds National Council of Negro Women.
1936	Jesse Owens captures four gold medals at the Berlin Olympics.
	Elijah Muhammad establishes the Nation of Islam headquarters in Chicago.
1937	Meta Vaux Warrick Fuller sculpts *The Talking Skull*.
	Zora Neale Hurston publishes *Their Eyes Were Watching God*.
	Joe Louis becomes the heavyweight boxing champion of the world.
	William H. Hastie is the first African American to be appointed a federal judge.
1938	Crystal Bird Fauset is elected to Pennsylvania House of Representatives.
1939	Marian Anderson gives Easter Sunday concert at Lincoln Memorial.
	Hattie McDaniel wins Academy Award for *Gone with the Wind*.
	Eleanor Roosevelt resigns from the Daughters of the American Revolution when they prevent Marian Anderson from singing in Constitution Hall.
1940	Estelle Osborne is appointed superintendent of Philips School of Nursing.
	Roger Arliner Young is awarded a Ph.D. in zoology from University of Pennsylvania.
	Richard Wright's *Native Son* is published.
	Benjamin O. Davis Sr. becomes the first black general in the U.S. Army.

1941   Scientist Charles Drew develops techniques to separate and preserve blood; organizes the first blood bank.

1942   Lena Horne stars in *Cabin in the Sky*.

Sarah Vaughan wins amateur-night contest at Harlem's Apollo Theater.

1943   Sadie Tanner Mossell Alexander is elected secretary of National Bar Association.

1944   Adam Clayton Powell Jr. is elected to the U.S. House of Representatives from Harlem.

The United Negro College Fund is founded.

1945   Katherine Dunham opens Dunham School of Dance and Theater.

Jane Cooke Wright receives an M.D. from New York Medical College.

More than one million African Americans are inducted into the U.S. armed forces by the end of World War II.

Ebony magazine, published by John H. Johnson, makes its debut.

1946   Dorothy Height helps organize YWCA conference on racial integration.

Clementine Clemence Rubin Hunter produces first painting.

Mary Lou Williams's *Zodiac* suite is performed by the New York Philharmonic.

1947   Butterfly McQueen walks out on the *Jack Benny Show*.

Jackie Robinson joins the Brooklyn Dodgers baseball team.

1949   Marjorie Lee Brown receives a Ph.D. in mathematics from University of Michigan.

Alice Childress produces first major play, *Florence*.

Evelyn Boyd Granville receives a Ph.D. in mathematics from Yale University.

1950   Helen Octavia Dickens is admitted to the American College of Surgeons.

Ralph J. Bunche wins the Nobel Peace Prize for his work as a mediator in Palestine.

1952   Gladys Knight forms "The Pips."

1954   Dorothy Dandridge receives Oscar nomination for *Carmen Jones*.

Etta James records "Roll With Me Henry."

U. S. Supreme Court decision in the *Brown v. Board of Education of Topeka, Kansas* says separate but equal doctrine is invalid.

1955   Rosa Parks is arrested for refusing to give up her seat on a bus to a white man in Montgomery, Alabama.

1957   Althea Gibson wins women's singles at Wimbledon.

Federal troops enforce court order to integrate Little Rock Central High School in Arkansas.

Leontyne Price debuts with San Francisco Opera in *Dialogues des Carmélites*.

Congress passes the Voting Rights Bill of 1957.

1959   Elizabeth Catlett heads sculpture department at National University of Mexico.

Lorraine Hansberry's first play, *A Raisin in the Sun*, opens on Broadway starring Ruby Dee.

Martin Luther King Jr. organizes the Southern Christian Leadership Conference.

1960   Wilma Rudolph wins three gold medals in Rome Olympics.

Tina Turner begins touring with Ike Turner.

1961   Mahalia Jackson sings at inauguration of John F. Kennedy.

1962   Fannie Lou Hamer attempts to register to vote in Indianola, Mississippi.

James Meredith fights to enter the University of Mississippi; federal troops are ordered to protect him.

Moms Mabley performs at New York's Carnegie Hall.

1963   Medgar Evers is assassinated.

More than 250,000 people march on Washington and hear Martin Luther King Jr.'s "I Have a Dream" speech.

1964   Martin Luther King Jr. wins Nobel Peace Prize.

Malcolm X is assassinated.

The federal Civil Rights Act of 1964 is passed.

Twenty-fourth Amendment to the Constitution outlaws poll taxes for national elections.

1965   Unita Blackwell initiates *Blackwell* v. *Board of Education* case.

Judith Jamison joins Alvin Ailey American Dance Theater.

Riots erupt in the Watts section of Los Angeles after police kill a black motorist; 35 people are killed.

The federal Voting Rights Act is passed.

1966   Aretha Franklin records "Respect."

Constance Baker Motley is appointed federal judge of U.S. District Court.

Bobby Seale and Huey Newton found the Black Panther Party of Oakland, California.

Stokely Carmichael (Kwame Toure) becomes head of the Student Nonviolent Coordinating Committee.

Edward Brooke, a Massachusetts Republican, becomes the first African American elected to the Senate since Reconstruction.

Robert Weaver becomes the first African American appointed to the presidential cabinet when he is made head of the Department of Housing and Urban Development.

1967 Thurgood Marshall becomes the first African American appointed to the Supreme Court.

1968 Martin Luther King Jr. is assassinated in Memphis, Tennessee.

Pearl Bailey receives special Tony Award for appearance in *Hello, Dolly!*

Nikki Giovanni publishes her first book of poetry, *Black Judgment.*

Shirley Chisholm becomes the first African-American woman elected to the U.S. House of Representatives.

Congress passes the federal Civil Rights Act of 1968.

1969 Coretta Scott King cofounds Martin Luther King Jr. Center for Nonviolent Social Change.

Jessye Norman debuts in Wagner's *Tannhäuser* at the Deutsche Oper.

Sonia Sanchez publishes poetry collection *Homecoming.*

Moneta Sleet of *Jet* magazine becomes the first African-American photographer to win a Pulitzer Prize for photojournalism.

1970 June Jordan publishes *Voice of the Children.*

Toni Morrison publishes her first novel, *The Bluest Eye.*

Essence and *Black Enterprise* magazines debut.

1971 The Congressional Black Caucus is formally organized.

1972 Shirley Chisholm seeks Democratic nomination for president.

Barbara Jordan is elected to the U.S. House of Representatives.

Alma Thomas's paintings are exhibited at Whitney Museum in New York.

National Black Panther Political Convention takes place in Gary, Indiana.

1973 Marian Wright Edelman founds Children's Defense Fund.

Coleman Young is elected mayor of Detroit.

Thomas Bradley is elected the first black mayor of Los Angeles.

Maynard H. Jackson is elected the first black mayor of Atlanta.

1975 General Daniel C. James of the U.S. Air Force becomes the first African-American four-star general.

1976 Septima Poinsette Clark is elected to Charleston, South Carolina, school board.

Patricia Harris is appointed Secretary of Housing and Urban Development.

Jamaica Kincaid becomes staff writer at the *New Yorker.*

Ntozake Shange's play *for colored girls who have considered suicide/when the rainbow is enuf* opens on Broadway.

1977   Toni Morrison publishes *Song of Solomon.*

Eleanor Holmes Norton is appointed to chair Equal Employment Opportunity Commission.

Andrew Young becomes first African-American U.S. ambassador to the United Nations.

1978   Kathleen Battle debuts at the Metropolitan Opera in Wagner's *Tannhäuser.*

Faye Wattleton becomes president of Planned Parenthood.

Carrie Mae Weems begins shooting *Family Pictures* photograph series.

1979   Amalya Lyle Kearse is appointed U.S. Appeals Court judge.

Franklin Thomas is named Ford Foundation president, the first black to head a major foundation.

Arthur Lewis is awarded the Nobel prize for economics.

1980   Toni Cade Bambara's novel *Salt Eaters* receives American Book Award.

1981   Suzanne De Passe is named president of Motown Productions.

1982   Charles Fuller wins Pulitzer Prize for his play *A Soldier's Story.*

Michael Jackson's *Thriller* becomes the best selling record of all time.

1983   Gloria Naylor wins American Book Award for *The Women of Brewster Place*.

Faith Ringgold produces first story quilt, *Who's Afraid of Aunt Jemima?*

Lt. Colonel Guion Bluford becomes the first African American in space.

Alice Walker becomes the first African American woman to win the Pulitzer Prize for fiction with the book *The Color Purple.*

Harold Washington is elected the first black mayor of Chicago.

1984   Jesse Jackson campaigns for the Democratic nomination for president.

Evelyn Ashford wins two gold medals at Los Angeles Olympics.

1985   Gwendolyn Brooks is named consultant in poetry at Library of Congress.

1986   Whitney Houston receives her first Grammy for best pop vocal performance.

Charlayne Hunter-Gault receives Peabody Award.

Jackie Joyner-Kersee sets world record for heptathlon at Goodwill Games.

Debra Thomas wins U.S. and women's world figure skating championships.

The Oprah Winfrey Show begins national syndication.

1987   Terry McMillan publishes her first novel, *Mama.*

Playwright August Wilson wins his first Pulitzer Prize for *Fences.*

1988   Florence Griffith-Joyner wins three Olympic gold medals and one silver medal.

Temple University becomes the first university to offer the Ph.D. in African-American studies.

1989   David Dinkins is elected first African-American mayor of New York City.

Douglas Wilder of Virginia becomes first African-American governor.

Ronald H. Brown is elected chair of the Democratic National Committee.

General Colin Powell is named chairman of the Joint Chiefs of Staff, the highest military position after the president.

1990   Whoopi Goldberg wins Academy Award for *Ghost*.

Lorna Simpson has solo exhibition at the Museum of Modern Art in New York.

Maxine Waters is elected to U.S. House of Representatives.

1991   Sharon Pratt Kelly begins term as mayor of Washington, D.C.

Audre Lorde is named poet laureate of New York State.

Clarence Thomas is confirmed for the Supreme Court despite Anita Hill's charges of sexual harassment.

1992   Julie Dash's acclaimed film *Daughters of the Dust* opens.

Mae Carol Jemison becomes the first African-American woman to travel in space when she serves on the crew of the shuttle *Endeavour*.

Carol Moseley-Braun becomes the first African-American woman elected to the U.S. Senate.

Riots erupt in Los Angeles and other U.S. cities after a jury acquits the Los Angeles police officers who beat Rodney King.

Sheila Jackson Lee begins her first term as a representative from Texas in the U.S. House.

1993   Maya Angelou recites a new poem at the inauguration of President Bill Clinton.

Angela Bassett is nominated for an Academy Award for *What's Love Got to Do with It?*

Betty Currie becomes President Bill Clinton's executive assistant.

Rita Dove is appointed Poet Laureate of the United States.

President Clinton nominates Lani Guinier to the nation's top civil rights post.

Toni Morrison becomes the first African-American writer to be awarded the Nobel prize for literature.

President Bill Clinton appoints five African Americans to his cabinet and other high government positions: Michael Espy, agriculture; Ronald H.

Brown, commerce; Hazel O'Leary, energy; Jesse Brown, veterans affairs; and Joycelyn Elders, surgeon general.

1994   Sharon Sayles Belton begins first term as mayor of Minneapolis.

Venus Williams enters the professional ranks of tennis players.

Beverly J. Harvard becomes the first African-American woman to head a major urban police department when she accepts the post in Atlanta.

1995   Shirley Ann Jackson becomes chair of U.S. Nuclear Regulatory Commission.

The NAACP elects Myrlie Evers as chair and Kweisi Mfume as executive director and national president.

More than one million African Americans march on Washington, DC.

1996   Tyra Banks appears on cover of *Sports Illustrated* swimsuit issue.

Dominique Dawes wins bronze medal at Summer Olympics and helps team win gold.

1997   Farai Chideya becomes an ABC News correspondent.

Phile Choinesu and Barbara Smith organize the million woman march on the Benjamin Franklin Mall in Philadelphia.

Alexis Herman becomes the first African-American woman to serve as U.S. secretary of energy.

1998   Carol Moseley-Braun is defeated in Senate reelection race.

Sheryl Swoopes helps Houston Comets to second consecutive championship

Venus Williams wins IGA Tennis Classic.

Oprah Winfrey produces and stars in film adaptation of Toni Morrison's novel *Beloved*.

Angela Bassett and Whoopi Goldberg star in successful film adaptation of Terry McMillan's novel *How Stella Got Her Groove Back*.

Article Sources

Most of the biographies in **Macmillan Profiles**: *Black Women in America* were extracted from the *Encyclopedia of African American Culture and History*, published by Macmillan Library Reference in 1996. Extracted articles were written by

ARTICLE	AUTHOR
Alexander, Sadie Tanner Mossell	Siraj Ahmed and Pam Nadasen
Allen, Debbie	Zita Allen
Anderson, Marian	Dominique-Rene de Lerma
Angelou, Maya	Barbara T. Christian
Armstrong, Lillian Hardin "Lil"	Elizabeth Muther
Ashford, Evelyn	Peter Schilling
Bailey, Pearl	Krista Whetstone
Baker, Ella J.	Joanne Grant
Baker, Josephine	Barbara Chase-Riboud
Bambara, Toni Cade	Elizabeth Brown-Guillory
Battle, Kathleen	A. Louise Toppin
Bethune, Mary McLeod	Judith Weisenfeld
Blackwell, Unita	Nancy Yousef and Greg Robinson
Bolin, Jane Mathilda	Qadri Ismail
Brooks, Gwendolyn	D. H. Melhem
Brown, Charlotte Hawkins	Judith Weisenfeld
Browne, Marjorie Lee	William T. Fletcher
Burke, Yvonne Brathwaite	Siraj Ahmed
Burroughs, Nannie Helen	Pam Nadasen
Butler, Octavia Estelle	Sandra Y. Govan
Carroll, Dianne	Vasanti Saxena
Cary, Mary Ann Shadd	Quandra Prettyman
Catlett, Elizabeth	Jeanne Zeidler
Celia	Melton A. McLaurin
Chase-Riboud, Barbara Dewayne	Pamela Wilkinson
Childress, Alice	Elizabeth Brown-Guillory
Chisholm, Shirley	Judith Weisenfeld
Clark, Septima Poinsette	Chana Kai Lee
Cole, Rebecca J.	Gerard Ferguson
Coleman, Bessie	Siraj Ahmed
Cooper, Anna Julia Haywood	Pam Nadasen
Craft, Ellen	Sabrina Fuchs

ARTICLE	AUTHOR
Dandridge, Dorothy	Pamela Wilkinson
Dash, Julie	Farah Jasmine Griffin
Davis, Angela	Christine A. Lunardini
De Passe, Suzanne	Jonathan Gill
Dee, Ruby	Susan McIntosh
Dickens, Helen Octavia	Vanessa Northington Gamble
Dove, Rita	Gina Dent
Dunbar-Nelson, Alice	Michael Fabre
Dunham, Katherine	Sally Sommer
Edelman, Marian Wright	Sabrina Fuchs
Elders, M. Joycelyn Jones	Greg Robinson
Fauset, Crystal Dreda Bird	Greg Robinson
Fitzgerald, Ella	Bud Kliment
Flack, Roberta	Bud Kliment
Franklin, Aretha Louise	Bud Kliment
Fuller, Meta Vaux Warrick	Theresa Leininger-Miller
Garrison, Zina	Shipherd Reed
Gibson, Althea	Arthur R. Ashe, Jr.
Giovanni, Yolanda Cornelia "Nikki"	Michael Paller
Goldberg, Whoopi	Susan McIntosh
Granville, Evelyn Boyd	Sylvie Trimble Boseman
Griffith-Joyner, Florence	Cindy Himes Gissendanner
Grimké, Angelina Weld	Dickson D. Bruce, Jr.
Grimké, Charlotte L. Forten	Dickson D. Bruce, Jr.
Hamer, Fannie Lou	Chana Kai Lee
Hansberry, Lorraine	Lily Phillips
Harper, Frances Ellen Watkins	Judith Weisenfeld
Harris, Barbara Clementine	Debi Broome
Harris, Patricia Roberts	James Bradley
Height, Dorothy	Judith Weisenfeld
Holiday, Billie	Bud Kliment
Horne, Lena	James E. Mumford
Horn, Rosa Artemis	Harold Dean Trulear
Hunter, Clementine Clemence Rubin	Regina A. Perry
Hunter-Gault, Charlayne	Charlayne Hunter-Gault
Huston, Zora Neale	Nellie Y. McKay
Jackson, Mahalia	Horace Clarence Boyer
Jackson, Rebecca Cox	Jean McMahon Humez
Jackson, Shirley Ann	Robert C. Hayden
Jacobs, Harriet Ann	Jean Fagan Yellin
James, Etta	Robert W. Stephens
Jamison, Judith	Thomas F. DeFrantz

ARTICLE	AUTHOR
Jemison, Mae Carol	Michael Cassutt; Lydia McNeill
Jordan, Barbara Charline	Christine A. Lunardini
Jordan, June	Barbara T. Christian
Joyner-Kersee, Jackie	Benjamin K. Scott
Kearse, Amalya Lyle	Joseph W. Lowndes
Keckley, Elizabeth	Thaddeus Russell
Kincaid, Jamaica	Gina Dent
King, Coretta Scott	Louise P. Maxwell
Kitt, Eartha Mae	Susan McIntosh and Thaddeus Russell
Knight, Gladys	Thaddeus Russell
LaBelle, Patty	Pamela Wilkinson
Lampkin, Daisy Elizabeth Adams	Durahn Taylor
Lee, Rebecca	Lydia McNeill
Lewis, Edmonia	Marilyn Richardson
Lloyd, Ruth Smith	Kenneth R. Manning
Logan, Myra Adele	Lydia McNeill
Lorde, Audre Geraldine	Nicole R. King
Mabley, Jackie "Moms"	Pamela Wilkinson
Mahoney, Mary Eliza	Thaddeus Russell
Malone, Annie Turnbo	Walter Friedman
Marshall, Paule	Joseph T. Skerrett, Jr.
Mason, Biddy Bridget	Sabrina Fuchs
Matthews, Victoria Earle (Smith)	Sabrina Fuchs and Pam Nadasen
McDaniel, Hattie	Matthew Buckley
McMillan, Terry	Amritjit Singh
McQueen, Thelma "Butterfly"	Evan A. Shore
McRae, Carmen	Bud Kliment
Morrison, Toni	Wahneema Lubiano
Moseley-Braun, Carol	Thaddeus Russell (updated by Mary Carvlin)
Motley, Constance Baker	Siraj Ahmed
Nash, Diane Bevel	Lydia McNeil and Robyn Spencer
Naylor, Gloria	Lily Phillips and Lydia McNeill
Norman, Jessye	Dominique-Rene de Lerma
Norton, Eleanor Holmes	Evan A. Shore and Greg Robinson
O'Leary, Hazel Rollins	Greg Robinson
Osborne, Estelle	Patricia E. Sloan
Parks, Rosa Louise McCauley	Pam Nadasen
Plato, Ann	Clint C. Wilson II
Price, Mary Violet Leontyne	Dominique-Rene de Lerma
Rainey, Gertrude Pridgett "Ma"	Daphne Duval Harrison
Ray, Charlotte E.	Jo H. Kim

ARTICLE	AUTHOR
Remond, Sarah Parker	Kim Robbins
Ringgold, Faith	Betty Kaplan Gubert
Rolle, Esther	Kenya Dilday
Ross, Diana	Karen Bennett Harmon
Rudolph, Wilma Glodean	Pam Nasaden
Saar, Betye Irene	Tamara L. Felton
Sanchez, Sonia	Derek Scheips
Savage, Augusta Christine Fells	Theresa Leininger-Miller
Shange, Ntozake	Louis J. Parascandola
Simone, Nina	Rosita M. Sands
Simpson, Coreen	Melissa Rachleff
Simpson, Lorna	Deirdre A. Scott
Smith, Bessie	Daphne Duval Harrison
Smith, Mamie	Bud Kliment
Spencer, Anne	Lydia McNeill
Stewart, Pearl	Greg Robinson
Taylor, Susie Baker King	Martha E. Hodes
Terrell, Mary Eliza Church	Quandra Prettyman
Tharpe, "Sister" Rosetta	Irene V. Jackson
Thomas, Alma	Jane Lusaka
Thomas, Debra	Gayle Pemberton
Thornton, Willie Mae "Big Mama"	James M. Salem
Truth, Sojourner	Margaret Washington
Tubman, Harriet	Louise P. Maxwell
Turner, Tina	Kyra D. Gaunt
Tyson, Cicily	Sabrina Fuchs and Joseph W. Lowndes
Vaughan, Sarah	Bud Kliment
Verrett, Shirley	A. Louise Toppin
Walker, A'Lelia	Sarij Ahmed
Walker, Alice	Michael Awkward
Walker, Madame C. J.	A'Lelia Perry Bundles
Walker, Maggie Lena	Sabrina Fuchs and Pam Nadasen
Walker, Margaret	Maryemma Graham
Warwick, Dionne	Kyra D. Gaunt
Washington, Dinah	Bud Kliment
Washington, Margaret Murray	Alana J. Erickson
Waters, Ethel	James E. Mumford
Waters, Maxine Moore	Louise P. Maxwell
Wattleton, Faye	Judith Weisenfeld
Weems, Carrie Mae	Renee Newman
Wells-Barnett, Ida Bell	Margaret L. Dwight
West, Dorothy	Deborah McDowell

ARTICLE	AUTHOR
Wheatley, Phillis	John C. Shields
Williams, Mary Lou	S. Antoinette Handy
Wilson, Harriet E. Adams	Peter Schilling
Winfrey, Oprah	Kenya Dilday (updated by Mary Carvlin)
Wright, Jane Cooke	Robert C. Hayden
Young, Roger Arliner	Evelynn M. Hammonds.

The following articles were newly written for **Macmillan Profiles**: *Black Women in America.*

ARTICLE	AUTHOR
Banks, Tyra	Patty Ohlenroth
Bassett, Angela	Kaye Foran
Belton, Sharon Sayles	Mary Carvlin
Berry, Halle	Kaye Foran
Chideya, Farai	Patty Ohlenroth
Curry, Betty	Patty Ohlenroth
Dawes, Dominique	Mary Carvlin
Guinier, Lani	Mary Carvlin
Hill, Anita	Mary Carvlin
Houston, Whitney	Patty Ohlenroth
Jackson, Janet	Patty Ohlenroth
Kelly, Sharon Pratt	Mary Carvlin
Swoopes, Sheryl	Mary Carvlin
Williams, Venus	Mary Carvlin

The following sidebars in *Black Women in America* were adapted from articles in the *Encyclopedia of African American Culture and History*:

African-American Autobiography (page 8) was adapted from an article by William L. Andrews.

Bethune Cookman College (page 32) was adapted from an article by Margaret D. Jacobs.

Black Scholar (page 37) was adapted from an article by Mansur M. Muruddin and Robyn Spencer.

Howard University (page 51) was adapted from an article by Esme Bhan.

American Negro Theatre (page 58) was adapted from an article by Michael Paller.

Avery Normal Institute (page 61) was adapted from an article by Jocelyn Bryant Harden.

National Council of Negro Women (page 129) was adapted from an article by Judith Weisenfeld.

Black English Vernacular (page 145) was adapted from an article by Cassandra A. Stancil.

Spingarn Medal (page 162) was adapted from an article by Greg Robinson.

The "Mammy" Stereotype (page 201) was adapted from an article by Joseph Boskin.

The Supremes (page 236) was adapted from an article by Kyra D. Gaunt.

National Association of Colored Women's Clubs (page 264) was adapted from an article by Pam Nasadem

Black Swan Records (page 297) was adapted from an article by Greg Robinson.

Congressional Black Caucus (page 299) was adapted from an article by Durahn Taylor.

Marian Anderson (page 5): National Archives

Maya Angelou (page 7): CORBIS/Leif Skoogfors

Lil Armstrong (page 10): National Archives

Pearl Bailey (page 13): CORBIS/Bettmann

Josephine Baker (page 19): National Archives

Tyra Banks (page 22): CORBIS/Mitchell Gerber

Angela Bassett (page 24): CORBIS/Mitchell Gerber

Kathleen Battle (page 26): Ira Nowinski/CORBIS

Sharon Sayles Belton (page 28): Office of the Mayor, Minneapolis, Minnesota

Halle Berry (page 29): CORBIS/Mitchell Gerber

Mary McLeod Bethune (page 31): National Archives

Farai Chideya (page 56): Lorenzo Bevilaqua/ABC News

Shirley Chisholm (page 60): UPI/CORBIS-Bettmann

Bessie Coleman (page 64): CORBIS/Underwood & Underwood

Dorothy Dandridge (page 73): UPI/CORBIS-Bettmann

Dominque Dawes (page 77): CORBIS

Ruby Dee (page 81): CORBIS/Bettmann

Rita Dove (page 83): CORBIS/Tim Wright

Katherine Dunham (page 87): CORBIS/Bettmann

Marian Wright Edelman (page 92): UPI/CORBIS-Bettmann

Crystal Dreda Bird Fauset (page 95): National Archives

Ella Fitzgerald (page 97): CORBIS/Bettmann

Aretha Franklin (page 99): CORBIS/Bettmann

Meta Warrick Vaux Fuller's *Talking Skull* (page 101): National Archives

Zina Garrison (page 104): CORBIS/S. Carmona

Althea Gibson (page 105): UPI/CORBIS-Bettmann

Whoopi Goldberg (page 109): CORBIS/Mitchell Gerber

Florence Griffith-Joyner (page 112): CORBIS/Neal Preston

Fannie Lou Hamer (page 119): UPI/CORBIS-Bettmann

Lorraine Hansberry (page 121): UPI/CORBIS-Bettmann

Patricia Harris (page 127): Jimmy Carter Library

Anita Hill (page 131): National Archives

Billie Holiday (page 134): UPI/CORBIS-Bettmann

Lena Horne (page 137): CORBIS/Bettmann

Whitney Houston (page 139): CORBIS/Mitchell Gerber

Zora Neale Hurston (page 143): Library of Congress/CORBIS

Janet Jackson (page 147): CORBIS/Mitchell Gerber

Mahalia Jackson (page 149): UPI/CORBIS-Bettmann

Shirley Ann Jackson (page): United States Nuclear Regulatory Commission

Etta James (page 156): CORBIS/Craig Lovell

Mae Jemison (page160): CORBIS/NASA

Barbara Jordan (page 161): UPI/CORBIS-Bettmann

Jackie Joyner-Kersee (page 166): CORBIS/Gilbert Iundt; TempSport

Coretta Scott King (page 174): CORBIS/Bettmann

Gladys Knight (page 178): UPI/CORBIS-Bettmann

Patti LaBelle (page 180): CORBIS/ Matthew Mendelsohn

Hattie McDaniel (page 200): National Archives

Terry McMillan (page 203): CORBIS/Mitch Gerber

Butterfly McQueen (page 205): UPI/CORBIS-Bettmann

Toni Morrison (page 206): CORBIS/Bettmann

Carol Moseley-Braun (page 210): Office of Senator Carol Moseley-Braun

Jessye Norman (page 217): CORBIS/Hulton-Deutsch Collection

Eleanor Holmes Norton (page 219): Jimmy Carter Library

Hazel Rollins O'Leary (page 221): United States Department of Energy

Rosa Parks (page 225): UPS/Corbis-Bettmann

Leontyne Price (page 228): UPS/Corbis-Bettmann

Diana Ross (page 237): UPS/Corbis-Bettmann

Wilma Rudolph (page 239): UPS/Corbis-Bettmann

Augusta Savage (page 245): National Archives

Ntozake Shange (page 248): UPS/Corbis-Bettmann

Sheryl Swoopes (page 260): Andrew W. Bernstein/WNBA Photos

Sojourner Truth (page 270): National Archives

Harriet Tubman (page 275): CORBIS/Bettmann

Tina Turner (page 278): CORBIS/Neal Preston

Sarah Vaughan (page 281): UPS/Corbis-Bettmann

Alice Walker (page 285): UPS/Corbis-Bettmann

Ethel Waters (page 296): CORBIS/Bettmann

Maxine Waters (page 298): CORBIS/Joseph Sohm; ChromoSohm Inc.

Faye Wattleton (page 301): UPS/Corbis-Bettmann

Ida B. Wells-Barnett (page 304): UPS/Corbis-Bettmann

Phillis Wheatley (page 309): Library of Congress/CORBIS

Mary Lou Williams (page 313): CORBIS/Bettmann

Venus Williams (page 315): CORBIS/S. Carmona

Oprah Winfrey (page 318): CORBIS/Mitchell Gerber

Suggested Reading

MARIAN ANDERSON

Anderson, Marian. *My Lord, What a Morning: An Autobiography*. University of Wisconsin Press, reissue 1993.

Ferris, Jeri. *What I Had Was Singing: The Story of Marian Anderson*, First Avenue Editions, 1994.

Tedards, Anne. *Marian Anderson*. Chelsea House Publishing Paperbacks, 1989.

Vehanen, Kosti, and George J. Barnett. *Marian Anderson: A Portrait*. Greenwood Publishing Group, 1970.

MAYA ANGELOU

Angelou, Maya. *All God's Children Need Traveling Shoes*. Random House, 1997.

Angelou, Maya. *A Brave and Startling Truth*. Random House, 1995.

Angelou, Maya. *The Complete Collected Poems of Maya Angelou*. Random House, 1994.

Angelou, Maya. *Even the Stars Look Lonesome*. Random House, 1997.

Angelou, Maya. *I Know Why the Caged Bird Sings*. Random House, reissue 1996.

Pettit, Jayne. *Maya Angelou: Journey of the Heart*. Puffin, reissue 1998.

Spain, Valerie. *Meet Maya Angelou*. Bullseye Books, 1994.

Williams, Mary E. *Readings on Maya Angelou*. Greenhaven Press, 1997.

LILLIAN ARMSTRONG

Bergreen, Laurence. *Louis Armstrong: An Extravagant Life*. Broadway Books, 1997.

Unterbrink, Mary. *Jazz Women at the Keyboard*. 1983.

EVELYN ASHFORD

Connolly, Pat. *Coaching Evelyn: Fast, Faster, Fastest Woman in the World*. 1991.

Davis, Michael D. *Black American Women in Olympic Track and Field: A Complete Illustrated Reference*. McFarland & Company, 1992.

Wickham, Martha. *Superstars of Women's Track and Field*. Chelsea House, 1997.

PEARL BAILEY

Bailey, Pearl. *Between You and Me: A Heartfelt Memoir of Learning, Loving and Living*. 1989.

Bailey, Pearl. *Raw Pearl*. 1968.

Brandt, Keith. *Pearl Bailey: With a Song in Her Heart*. Troll Associates, 1992.

ELLA BAKER

Dallard, Shyrlee. *Ella Baker: A Leader Behind the Scenes*. Silver Burdett Press, 1990.

Grant, Joanne. *Ella Baker: Freedom Bound*. John Wiley & Sons, 1998.

TONI CADE BAMBARA

Bambara, Toni Cade. *Gorilla, My Love*. Vintage Books, 1992.

Bambara, Toni Cade. *The Salt Eaters*. Vintage Books, reissue 1992.

Bambara, Toni Cade. *The Sea Birds Are Still Alive*. Random House, 1982.

TYRA BANKS

Tyra Banks, *Tyra's Beauty Inside & Out*. HarperCollins, 1998.

MARY MCLEOD BETHUNE

Anderson, Lavere. *Mary McLeod Bethune*. Chelsea House Publishing, 1991.

Halasa, Malu. *Mary McLeod Bethune*. Chelsea House Publishing, 1993.

Kelson, Richard, and Debbie Heller. *Building a Dream: Mary Bethune's School*. Raintree/Steck-Vaughn, 1996.

Meltzer, Milton. *Mary McLeod Bethune: Voice of Black Hope*. Puffin, 1996.

GWENDOLYN BROOKS

Kent, George E. *A Life of Gwendolyn Brooks*. University Press of Kentucky, 1994.

Madhubuti, Haki R. *Say That the River Turns: The Impact of Gwendolyn Brooks*. Third World Press, 1991.

Wheeler, Jill C. *Gwendolyn Brooks*. Abdo & Daughters, 1997.

MARY ANN SHADD CARY

Rhodes, Jane. *Mary Ann Shadd Cary: The Black Press and Protest in the Nineteenth Century*. Indiana University Press, 1998.

CELIA

McLaurin, Melton Alonza. *Celia: A Slave*. University of Georgia Press, 1991.

FARAI CHIDEYA

Chideya, Farai. *The Color of Our Future: Our Multiracial Future*. William Morrow & Company, 1999.

Chideya, Farai. *Don't Believe the Hype: Fighting Cultural Misinformation About African Americans*. Plume, 1995.

ALICE CHILDRESS

Childress, Alice. *A Hero Ain't Nothin' but a Sandwich*. Avon, reissue 1995.

Childress, Alice. *Rainbow Jordan*. Avon, reissue 1997.

Childress, Alice. *Those Other People*. Putnam Publishing Company, 1989.

Jennings, La Vinia Delois. *Alice Childress*. Twayne, 1995.

SHIRLEY CHISHOLM

Chisholm, Shirley. *Unbought and Unbossed*. 1972.

Duffy, Susan. *Shirley Chisholm: A Bibliography of Writing By and About Her*. Scarecrow Press, 1988.

Hicks, Nancy. *The Honorable Shirley Chisholm, Congresswoman from Brooklyn*. Lion Books, 1971.

Jackson, Garnet N. *Shirley Chisholm, Congresswoman*. Modern Curriculum Press, 1994.

SEPTIMA POINSETTE CLARK

Clark, Septima Poinsette, and Cynthia Stokes Brown. *Ready from Within: A First Person Narrative*. Red Sea Press, Inc., 1990.

BESSIE COLEMAN

Fisher, Lillian M. *Brave Bessie: Flying Free*. Hendrick-Long Publishing Company, 1995.

Freydberg, Elizabeth Hadley. *Bessie Coleman: The Brownskin Lady Bird*. Garland Publishing,1994.

Johnson, Dolores. *She Dared to Fly: Bessie Coleman*. Benchmark Books, 1997.

Rich, Doris L. *Queen Bess: Daredevil Aviator*. Smithsonian Institution Press, 1995.

ELLEN CRAFT

Craft, Ellen, William Craft, and R. J. M. Blackett. *Running a Thousand Miles for Freedom: The Escape of William and Ellen Craft from Slavery*. Louisiana State University Press, reissue 1999.

DOROTHY DANDRIDGE

Bogle, Donald. *Dorothy Dandridge: A Biography*. Amistad Press, 1997.

JULIE DASH

Dash, Julie, bell hooks, and Toni Cade Bambara. *Daughters of the Dust: The Making of an African American Woman's Film*. New Press, 1992.

DOMINIQUE DAWES

Kleinbaum, Nancy H., Amy Chow, Amanda Borden, and Dominique Moceanu. *Magnificent Seven: The Authorized Story of American Gold*. Bantam Doubleday Dell Publishing,1996.

SUZANNE DE PASSE

Mussari, Mark. *Suzanne De Passe: Motown's Boss Lady*. Garrett Educational Corp., 1991.

RUBY DEE

Dee, Ruby, and Ossie Davis. *With Ossie and Ruby: In This Life Together.* William Morrow & Company, 1998.

RITA DOVE

Dove, Rita. *The Darker Face of the Earth.* Story Line Press, 1996.

Dove, Rita. *Grace Notes: Poems.* W. W. Norton & Company, 1991.

Dove, Rita. *Mother Love: Poems.* W. W. Norton & Company, 1995.

Dove, Rita. *Museum.* University of Pittsburgh Press, 1997.

Dove, Rita. *The Poet's World.* Library of Congress, 1995.

Dove, Rita. *Selected Poems.* Pantheon Books, 1993.

Dove, Rita. *Thomas and Beulah.* Carnegie-Mellon University Press, 1987.

Dove, Rita. *Through the Ivory Gate: A Novel.* Vintage Books, 1993.

Dove, Rita. *The Yellow House on the Corner.* Carnegie-Mellon University Press, 1989.

KATHERINE DUNHAM

Donloe, Darlene. *Katherine Dunham.* Holloway House Publishing Company, 1993.

Dunham, Katherine. *A Touch of Innocence: Memoirs of Childhood.* University of Chicago Press, 1994.

Harnan, Terry. *African Rhythm—American Dance: A Biography of Katherine Dunham.* 1974.

Rose, Albirda. *Dunham Technique: A Way of Life.* Kendall/Hunt Publishing Company, 1990.

MARIAN WRIGHT EDELMAN

Edelman, Marian Wright. *Guide My Feet: Prayers and Meditations on Loving and Working for Children.* Beacon Press, 1995.

Edelman, Marian Wright. *The Measure of Our Success: A Letter to My Children and Yours.* HarperCollins, 1993.

Edelman, Marian Wright, and James P. Comer. *School Power: Implications of an Intervention Project.* Free Press, 1995.

Edelman, Marian Wright, and Adrienne Yorinks, illus. *Stand for Children.* Hyperion Press, 1998.

Edelman, Marian Wright. *The State of America's Children: A Report from the Children's Defense Fund.* Beacon Press, 1999.

Old, Wendie C. *Marian Wright Edelman: Fighter for Children's Rights.* Enslow Publishers, Inc., 1995.

Siegel, Beatrice. *Marian Wright Edelman: The Making of a Crusader.* Simon & Schuster, 1995.

JOYCELYN ELDERS

Elders, Joycelyn. *Joycelyn Elders, M.D.: From Sharecropper's Daughter to Surgeon General of the United States of America.* Avon Books, 1997.

ELLA FITZGERALD

Fidelman, Geoffrey Mark. *First Lady of Song: Ella Fitzgerald for the Record.* Citadel Press, 1996.

Leslie Gourse, ed. *The Ella Fitzgerald Companion: Seven Decades of Commentary.* Schirmer Books, 1998.

Nicholson, Stuart. *Ella Fitzgerald: A Biography of the First Lady of Jazz.* Da Capo Press, 1995.

Wyman, Carolyn. *Ella Fitzgerald: Jazz Singer Supreme.* Franklin Watts, 1993.

ARETHA FRANKLIN

Bego, Mark. *Aretha Franklin: The Queen of Soul.* 1989.

Gourse, Leslie. *Aretha Franklin, Lady Soul.* Franklin Watts, Inc., 1995.

Sheafer, Silvia Anne. *Aretha Franklin: Motown Superstar.* Enslow Publishers, Inc., 1996.

ZINA GARRISON

Porter, A. P. *Zina Garrison: Ace.* First Avenue Editions, 1992.

ALTHEA GIBSON

Beracree, Tom. *Althea Gibson.* Holloway House Publishing Company, 1990.

Davidson, Sue. *Changing the Game: The Stories of Tennis Champions Alice Marble and Althea Gibson.* Seal Press Feminist Publishing,1997.

Gibson, Althea. *I Always Wanted to Be Somebody.* 1958.

NIKKI GIOVANNI

Fowler, Virginia C. *Nikki Giovanni.* Twayne, 1992.

Giovanni, Nikki. *Cotton Candy on a Rainy Day.* William Morrow & Company, 1980.

Giovanni, Nikki. *Ego-Tripping and Other Poems for Young People.* Lawrence Hill & Company, 1993.

Giovanni, Nikki. *Gemini: An Extended Autobiographical Statement on My First Twenty Five Years of Being a Black Poet.* Viking Press, 1976.

Giovanni, Nikki. *Grand Mothers: Poems Reminiscences, and Short Stories About the Keepers of Our Traditions.* Henry Holt & Company, Inc., 1994.

Giovanni, Nikki. *Love Poems.* William Morrow & Company, 1997.

Giovanni, Nikki. *Racism 101.* Quill, 1995.

Giovanni, Nikki. *The Selected Poems of Nikki Giovanni.* William Morrow & Company, 1996.

Giovanni, Nikki, and Margaret Walker. *A Poetic Equation: Conversations Between Nikki Giovanni and Margaret Walker.* Howard University Press, 1983.

WHOOPI GOLDBERG

Adams, Mary Agnes. *Whoopi Goldberg: From Street to Stardom.* Dillon Press, 1993.

Caper, William. *Whoopi Goldberg: Comedian and Movie Star.* Enslow Publishers, Inc, 1999.

Deboer, Judy. *Whoopi Goldberg.* Creative Education, 1998.

Goldberg, Whoopi. *Book.* Avon, 1997.

Katz, Sandor. *Whoopi Goldberg.* Chelsea House Publishing Paperbacks, 1996.

Parish, James Robert. *Whoopi Goldberg: Her Journey from Poverty to Megastardom.* Birch Lane Press, 1997.

FLORENCE GRIFFITH-JOYNER

Aaseng, Nathan. *Florence Griffith Joyner: Dazzling Olympian.* Demco Media, 1991.

Koral, April. *Florence Griffith Joyner: Track and Field Star.* Franklin Watts, 1992.

CHARLOTTE L. FORTEN GRIMKÉ

Grimké, Charlotte L. Forten, and Brenda Stevenson, ed. *Journals of Charlotte Forten Grimké.* Oxford University Press, 1988.

LANI GUINIER

Guinier, Lani. *Lift Every Voice: Turning a Civil Rights Setback into a New Vision of Social Justice.* Simon & Schuster, 1998.

Guinier, Lani. *The Tyranny of the Majority: Fundamental Fairness in Representative Democracy.* Free Press, 1995.

FANNIE LOU HAMER

Mills, Kay. *This Little Light of Mine: The Life of Fannie Lou Hamer.* Plume, 1994.

Rubel, David. *Fannie Lou Hamer: From Sharecropping to Politics.* Silver Burdett Press, 1990.

LORRAINE HANSBERRY

Cheney, Anne. *Lorraine Hansberry.* Twayne, 1984.

Domina, Lynn. *Understanding A Raisin in the Sun: A Student Casebook to Issues, Sources, and Historical Documents.* Greenwood Publishing Group, 1998.

Hansberry, Lorraine. *To Be Young, Gifted and Black: Lorraine Hansberry in Her Own Words.* Vintage Books, reissue 1995.

McKissack, Pat et al. *Young, Black, and Determined: A Biography of Lorraine Hansberry.* Holiday House, 1998.

Scheader, Catherine. *Lorraine Hansberry: Playwright and Voice of Justice.* Enslow Publishers, 1998.

Tripp, Janet. *The Importance of Lorraine Hansberry.* Lucent Books, 1997.

FRANCIS ELLEN WATKINS HARPER

Boyd, Melba Joyce. *Discarded Legacy: Politics and Poetics in the Life of Frances E.W. Harper, 1825–1911.* Wayne State University Press, 1994.

Harper, Francis Ellen Watkins. *Iola.* X-Press, reissue 1996.

Harper, Francis Ellen Watkins, and Frances Smith Foster, ed. *Minnie's Sacrifice, Sowing and Reaping, Trial and Triumph: Three Rediscovered Novels.* Beacon Press, 1994.

DOROTHY HEIGHT

Fitzgerald, Tracey A. *The National Council of Negro Women and the Feminist Movement, 1935–1975.* Georgetown University Press. 1985.

ANITA HILL

Hill, Anita. *Speaking Truth to Power.* Doubleday, 1997.

Hill, Anita, and Emma Coleman Jordan, eds. *Race, Gender, and Power in America: The Legacy of the Hill-Thomas Hearings.* Oxford University Press, 1995.

Italia, Bob. *Anita Hill.* Abdo & Daughters, 1993.

Morrison, Toni, ed., Nellie McKay, and Micheal Thelwell (contributors). *Racing Justice, En-Gendering Power: Essays on Anita Hill, Clarence Thomas, and the Construction of Social Reality.* Pantheon Books, 1992.

Smitherman, Geneva. *African American Women Speak Out on Anita Hill-Clarence Thomas.* Wayne State University Press, 1995.

BILLIE HOLIDAY

Chilton, John. *Billie's Blues: The Billie Holiday Story, 1933-1959.* Da Capo Press, 1989.

Gourse, Leslie. *Billie Holiday: The Tragedy and Triumph of Lady Day.* Franklin Watts, 1995.

Gourse, Leslie. *Billie Holiday Companion: Seven Decades of Commentary.* Schirmer Books, 1997.

Kliment, Bud. *Billie Holiday: Singer.* Chelsea House Publishing, 1990.

O'Meally, Robert. *Lady Day: The Many Faces of Billie Holiday.* Arcade Publishing, 1993.

LENA HORNE

Haskins, James. *Lena: A Biography of Lena Horne.* Scarborough House, 1991.

Howard, Brett. *Lena Horne.* Holloway House Publishing Company, 1991.

Palmer, Leslie. *Lena Horne: Entertainer.* Chelsea House Publishing, 1989.

WHITNEY HOUSTON

Cox, Ted. *Whitney Houston.* Chelsea House Publishing, 1998.

Savage, Jeff. *Whitney Houston.* Silver Burdett Press, 1998.

Wallner, Rosemary. *Whitney Houston.* Abdo & Daughters, 1994.

CLEMENTINE CLEMENCE RUBIN HUNTER

Cook, Sterling. *2 Black Folk Artists: Clementine Hunter and Nellie Mae Rowe.* Miami University Art Museum, 1986.

Henkes, Robert. *The Art of Black American Women: Works of Twenty-Four Artists of the Twentieth Century.* McFarland & Company, 1993.

Hunter, Clementine, and Mary E. Lyons. *Talking With Tebe: Clementine Hunter, Memory Artist.* Houghton Mifflin Company, 1998.

Wilson, James. *Clementine Hunter: American Folk Artist*. Pelican Publishing Company, 1988.

CHARLAYNE HUNTER-GAULT

Hunter-Gault, Charlayne. *In My Place*. Vintage Books, 1993.

Trillin, Calvin, and Charlayne Hunter-Gault. *An Education in Georgia: Charlayne Hunter, Hamilton Holmes, and the Integration of the University of Georgia*. University of Georgia Press, 1991.

ZORA NEALE HURSTON

Bloom, Harold, ed. *Zora Neale Hurston* (Modern Critical Views). Chelsea House Publishing, 1986.

Gates, Henry Louis, and K. A. Appiah, eds. *Zora Neale Hurston: Critical Perspectives Past and Present*. Amistad Press, 1993.

Hurston, Zora Neale. *Dust Tracks on a Road*. HarperCollins, reissue 1996.

Hurston, Zora Neale, and Cheryl A. Wall, ed. *Folklore, Memoirs, and Other Writings: Mules and Men, Tell My Horse, Dust Tracks on a Road, Selected Articles*. Library of America, 1995.

Hurston, Zora Neale, and Cheryl A. Wall, ed. *Novels and Stories: Jonah's Gourd Vine; Their Eyes Were Watching God; Moses, Man of the Mountain; Seraph on the Suwanee; Selected Stories*. Library of America, 1995.

Lyons, Mary E. *Sorrow's Kitchen: The Life and Folklore of Zora Neale Hurston*. Atheneum, 1990.

Porter, A. P. *Jump at De Sun: The Story of Zora Neale Hurston*. First Avenue Editions, 1992.

Witcover, Paul. *Zora Neale Hurston*. Holloway House Publishing Company, 1994.

JANET JACKSON

Robinson, Nancy. *Janet Jackson: In Control*, 1987.

MAHALIA JACKSON

Donloe, Darlene. *Mahalia Jackson*. Holloway House Publishing Company, 1992.

Gourse, Leslie. *Mahalia Jackson: Queen of Gospel Song*. Franklin Watts, 1996.

Jackson, Jesse. *Make a Joyful Noise Unto the Lord! The Life of Mahalia Jackson, Queen of Gospel Singers*. 1974.

Schwerin, Jules. *Got to Tell It: Mahalia Jackson, Queen of Gospel*. Oxford University Press, 1992.

Wolfe, Charles K. *Mahalia Jackson*. Chelsea House Publishing, 1990.

SHIRLEY ANN JACKSON

Jenkins, Edward Sidney, Patricia Stohr-Hunt, and Exyie C. Ryder. *To Fathom More: African American Scientists and Inventors*. University Press of America, 1996.

HARRIET ANN JACOBS

Brent, Linda (Harriet Ann Jacobs). *Incidents in the Life of a Slave Girl*. Harcourt Brace, reissue 1989.

Catherine Clinton. *The Plantation Mistress: Woman's World in the Old South*. Random House, 1984.

Fleischner, Jennifer. *I Was Born a Slave: The Story of Harriet Jacobs*. Millbrook Press, 1997.

Gates, Henry Louis. *The Classic Slave Narratives*. New American Library, 1987.

Jones, Jacqueline. *Labor of Love, Labor of Sorrow: Black Women, Work, and the Family from Slavery to the Present*. Vintage Books, 1986.

Lyons, Mary E. *Letters from a Slave Girl: The Story of Harriet Jacobs*. Atheneum, 1992.

White, Deborah Gray. *Ar'n't I a Woman? Female Slaves in the Plantation South*. W. W. Norton & Company, 1987.

Zafar, Rafia, and Deborah Garfield, eds. *Harriet Jacobs and Incidents in the Life of a Slave Girl: New Critical Essays*. Cambridge University Press, 1996.

ETTA JAMES

James, Etta. *Rage to Survive: The Etta James Story*. Da Capo Press, 1998.

JUDITH JAMISON

Ailey, Alvin, and A. Peter Bailey (contributor). *Revelations: The Autobiography of Alvin Ailey*. Citadel Press, 1997.

Dunning, Jennifer. *Alvin Ailey: A Life in Dance*. Perseus Press, 1996.

Jamison, Judith. *Dancing Spirit: An Autobiography*. Anchor, 1994.

Mitchell, Jack (photographer), and Richard Philip (designer). *Alvin Ailey American Dance Theater: Jack Mitchell Photographs*. Andrews & McMeel, 1993.

MAE JEMISON

Burns, Khephra, and William Miles. *Black Stars in Orbit: NASA's African American Astronauts*. Gulliver Books, 1995.

Ceaser, Ebraska D. *Mae C. Jemison: 1st Black Female Astronaut*. New Day Press, 1992.

Jones, Stanley, and Octavia Tripp. *African-American Astronauts*. Capstone Press, 1998.

Yannuzzi, Della A. *Mae Jemison: A Space Biography*. Enslow Publishers, Inc., 1998.

BARBARA JORDAN

Jeffrey, Laura S. *Barbara Jordan: Congresswoman, Lawyer, Educator*. Enslow Publishers, Inc., 1997.

Johnson, Linda Carlson. *Barbara Jordan: Congresswoman*. Blackbirch Marketing, 1997.

Jordan, Barbara. *Selected Speeches*. Howard University Press, 1999.

Patrick-Wexler, Diane. *Barbara Jordan*. Raintree/Steck-Vaughn, 1995.

Rhodes, Lisa Renee. *Barbara Jordan: Voice of Democracy*. Franklin Watts, 1998.

Rogers, Mary Beth. *Barbara Jordan: American Hero*. Bantam Doubleday Dell Publishing, 1998.

Teutsch, Austin. *Barbara Jordan: The Biography*. Golden Touch Press, 1997.

JUNE JORDAN

Jordan, June. *Affirmative Acts: Political Essays*. Doubleday, 1998.

Jordan, June. *Kissing God Goodbye: Poems, 1991–1997*. Doubleday, 1997.

JACKIE JOYNER-KERSEE

Goldstein, Margaret J., and Jennifer Larson. *Jackie Joyner-Kersee: Superwoman*. Lerner Publications Company, 1994.

Green, Carl R. *Jackie Joyner-Kersee*. Crestwood House, 1994.

Harrington, Geri. *Jackie Joyner Kersee*. Chelsea House Publishing, 1995.

Joyner-Kersee, Jackie. *A Kind of Grace: The Autobiography of the World's Greatest Female Athlete*. Warner Books, 1997.

AMALYA LYLE KEARSE

Kearse, Amalya. *Bridge Conventions Complete*. Devyn Press, 1990.

Kearse, Amalya. *Bridge at Your Fingertips*. Devyn Press, 1980.

ELIZABETH KECKLEY

Keckley, Elizabeth. *Behind the Scenes, Or, Thirty Years a Slave, and Four Years in the White House*. Oxford University Press, reissue 1989.

JAMAICA KINCAID

Bloom, Harold, ed. *Jamaica Kincaid* (Modern Critical Views). Chelsea House Publishing, 1998.

Kincaid, Jamaica. *Annie John*. Noonday Press, 1997.

Kincaid, Jamiaca. *At the Bottom of the River*. Plume, 1992.

Kincaid, Jamaica. *Lucy*. Farrar, Straus & Giroux, 1990.

Kincaid, Jamaica. *My Brother*. Farrar, Straus & Giroux, 1997.

Kincaid, Jamaica. *A Small Place*. Farrar, Straus & Giroux, 1988.

Mistron, Deborah. *Understanding Annie John: A Student Casebook to Issues, Sources and Historical Documents*. Greenwood Publishing Group, 1998.

Simmons, Diane. *Jamaica Kincaid*. Twayne, 1994.

CORETTA SCOTT KING

King, Coretta Scott. *My Life With Martin Luther King*. 1969.

Medearis, Angela Shelf. *Dare to Dream: Coretta Scott King and the Civil Rights Movement*. Lodestar Books, 1994.

Rhodes, Lisa Renee. *Coretta Scott King*. Chelsea House Publishing, 1998.

Schraff, Anne. *Coretta Scott King: Striving for Civil Rights*. Enslow Publishers, Inc., 1998.

Turk, Ruth. *Coretta Scott King: Fighter for Justice*. Branden Publishing Company, 1997.

EARTHA KITT

Kitt, Eartha. *Alone With Me: A New Autobiography*. 1976.

Kitt, Eartha. *Confessions of a Sex Kitten*. 1991.

GLADYS KNIGHT

Knight, Gladys. *Between Each Line of Pain and Glory: My Life Story*. Hyperion, 1997.

PATTI LABELLE

LaBelle, Patti, and Laura B. Randolph. *Don't Block the Blessings: Revelations of a Lifetime*. Boulevard, 1997.

EDMONIA LEWIS

Wolfe, Rinna Evelyn. *Edmonia Lewis: Wildfire in Marble*. Silver Burdett Press, 1998.

AUDRE LORDE

Lorde, Audre. *A Burst of Light*. Firebrand Books, 1988.

Lorde, Audre. *The Cancer Journals*. Aunt Lute Books, reissue 1997.

Lorde, Audre. *The Collected Poems of Audre Lorde*. W. W. Norton & Company, 1997.

Lorde, Audre. *The Marvelous Arithmetics of Distance: Poems 1987–1992*. W. W. Norton & Company, 1993.

Lorde, Audre. *Undersong: Chosen Poems Old and New*. W. W. Norton & Company, 1992.

Lorde, Audre. *Zami: A New Spelling of My Name*. Crossing Press, 1982.

JACKIE "MOMS" MABLEY

Wiliams, Elsie A. *The Humor of Jackie Moms Mabley: An African American Comedic Tradition*. Garland Publishing, 1995.

MARY ELIZA MAHONEY

Miller, Helen S. *Mary Eliza Mahoney 1845–1926: America's First Black Professional Nurse—A Historical Prospective*. Wright Publishing Company, 1997.

PAULE MARSHALL

Marshall, Paule. *Brown Girl, Brownstones*. Feminist Press, 1996.

Marshall, Paule. *The Chosen Place, the Timeless People*. Vintage Books, 1992.

Marshall, Paule. *Daughters*. Plume, 1992.

Marshall, Paule. *Praisesong for the Widow*. Plume, 1992.

Marshall, Paule. *Soul Clap Hands and Sing*. Howard University Press, 1988.

HATTIE MCDANIEL

Jackson, Carlton. *Hattie: The Life of Hattie McDaniel*. Madison Books, 1990.

TERRY MCMILLAN

McMillan, Terry. *Disappearing Acts*. Viking Press, 1987.

McMillan, Terry. *How Stella Got Her Groove Back*. Viking Press, 1996.

MacMillan, Terry. *Mama*. Pocket Books, reissue 1995.

McMillan, Terry. *Waiting to Exhale*. Viking Press, 1992.

MCRAE, CARMEN

Gourse, Leslie. *Carmen McRae: A Biography*. Holiday House Inc, 1999.

TONI MORRISON

Bloom, Harold, ed. *Toni Morrison* (Modern Critical Views). Chelsea House Publishing, 1991.

Century, Douglas. *Toni Morrison*. Chelsea House Publishing, 1994.

Kramer, Barbara. *Toni Morrison: Nobel Prize-Winning Author*. Enslow Publishers, Inc., 1996.

McKay, Nellie, ed. *Critical Essays on Toni Morrison*. G. K. Hall, 1988.

Morrison, Toni. *Beloved*. Knopf, reissue 1998.

Morrison, Toni. *The Bluest Eye*. Knopf, reissue 1993.

Morrison, Toni. *Jazz*. Knopf, 1992.

Morrison, Toni. *Paradise*. Knopf. 1998.

Morrison, Toni. *Song of Solomon*. Random House, 1977.

Morrison, Toni. *Sula*. Knopf, 1973.

Morrison, Toni. *Tar Baby*. Knopf, 1981.

Patrick-Wexler, David. *Toni Morrison*. Raintree/Steck Vaughn, 1997.

Peach, Lindon, ed. *Toni Morrison: Contemporary Critical Essays*. St. Martin's Press, 1998.

CONSTANCE BAKER MOTLEY

Motley, Constance Baker. *Equal Justice Under Law: An Autobiography*. Farrar, Straus & Giroux, 1998.

GLORIA NAYLOR

Fowler, *Gloria Naylor: In Search of Sanctuary*. Twayne, 1996.

Gates, Henry Louis, and K. A. Appiah, eds. *Gloria Naylor: Critical Perspectives Past and Present*. Amistad Press, 1993.

Naylor, Gloria. *Bailey's Café*. Vintage Books, 1993.

Naylor, Gloria. *Lindon Hills*. Viking Press, 1995.

Naylor, Gloria. *Mama Day*. Vintage Books, 1989.

Naylor, Gloria. *The Men of Brewster Place*. Hyperion, 1998.

Naylor, Gloria. *The Women of Brewster Place*. Penguin USA, 1982.

JESSYE NORMAN

Story, Rosalyn M. *And So I Sing: African-American Divas of Opera and Concert*. Amistad Press, 1993.

ESTELLE OSBORNE

Carnegie, Mary Elizabeth. *Path We Tread: Blacks in Nursing 1854–1990*. 1991.

Hine, Darlene Clark. *Black Women in White: Racial Conflict and Cooperation in the Nursing Profession, 1890–1950*. Indiana University Press, 1989.

ROSA PARKS

Celsi, Teresa. *Rosa Parks and the Montgomery Bus Boycott*. Demco Media, 1994.

Friese, Kai Jabir. *Rosa Parks: The Movement Organizes*. Silver Burdett Press, 1990.

Greenfield, Eloise. *Rosa Parks*. Harpercrest, 1996.

Hull, Mary. *Rosa Parks*. Chelsea House Publishing, 1994.

Parks, Rosa, and Jim Haskins. *Rosa Parks: Mother to a Movement*. Dial Books for Young Readers, 1992.

Parks, Rosa, and Gregory J. Reed. *Dear Mrs. Parks: A Dialogue With Today's Youth*. Lee & Low Books, 1996.

Siegel, Beatrice. *The Year They Walked: Rosa Parks and the Montgomery Bus Boycott*. Charro Book Company, 1991.

ANN PLATO

Plato, Ann, and Kenny J. Williams, illus. *Essays: Including Biographies and Miscellaneous Pieces, in Prose and Poetry*. Oxford University Press, 1988.

LEONTYNE PRICE

Steins, Richard. *Leontyne Price: Opera Superstar*. Blackbirch Marketing, 1994.

Story, Rosalyn M. *And So I Sing: African-American Divas of Opera and Concert*. Amistad Press, 1993.

GERTRUDE PRIDGETT "MA" RAINEY

Harris, Sheldon. *Blues Who's Who: A Biographical Dictionary of Blues Singers*. Da Capo Press, 1988.

Lieb, Sandra R. *Mother of the Blues: A Study of Ma Rainey*. University of Massachusetts Press, 1983.

Santelli, Robert. *The Big Book of Blues: A Biographical Encyclopedia.* Penguin USA, 1994.

CHARLOTTE E. RAY

Smith, J. Clay, ed. *Rebels in Law: Voices in History of Black Women Lawyers.* University of Michigan Press, 1998.

SARAH PARKER REMOND

Yee, Shirley J. *Black Women Abolitionists: A Study in Activism, 1828–1860.* University of Tennessee Press, 1992.

FAITH RINGGOLD

Flomenhaft, Eleanor, ed. *Faith Ringgold: A 25 Year Survey.* 1990.

Ringgold, Faith. *Aunt Harriet's Underground Railroad in the Sky.* Crown Publishing, 1995.

Ringgold, Faith. *May Dream of Martin Luther King.* Crown Publishing, 1995.

Ringgold, Faith. *Tar Beach.* Crown Publishing, 1991.

Ringgold, Faith. *We Flew over the Bridge: The Memoirs of Faith Ringgold.* Little Brown & Company, 1995.

Ringgold, Faith, and Dan Cameron, ed. *Dancing at the Louvre: Faith Ringgold's French Collection and Other Story Quilts.* University of California Press, 1998.

Ringgold Faith, and Linda Freeman. *Talking to Faith Ringgold.* Crown Publishing, 1995.

DIANA ROSS

Huggins, Nathan Irvin, ed. *Diana Ross: Entertainer.* Chelsea House Publishing, 1995.

Ross, Diana. *Secrets of a Sparrow.* Villard Books, 1993.

Whithall, Susan. *Women of Motown: An Oral History.* Avon Books, 1998.

WILMA RUDOLPH

Biracree, Tom. *Wilma Rudolph.* Chelsea House Publishing, 1992.

Coffey, Wayne. *Wilma Rudolph.* Blackbirch Marketing, 1997.

Rudolph, Wilma. *Wilma: The Story of Wilma Rudolph.* 1977.

Sherrow, Victoria. *Wilma Rudolph/Olympic Champion.* Chelsea House Publishing, 1995.

BETYE SAAR

Saar, Betye. *Betye Saar: Digital Griot* (CD-ROM). Voyager Company, 1998.

Sills, Leslie. *Visions: Stories About Women Artists.* Albert Whitman & Company, 1993.

SONIA SANCHEZ

Joyce, Ann Joyce. *Ijala: Sonia Sanchez and the African Poetic Tradition.* Third World Press, 1996.

Sanchez, Sonia. *Does Your House Have Lions?* Beacon Press, 1997.

Sanchez, Sonia. *Like the Singing Coming Off the Drums: Love Poems*. Beacon Press, 1998.

Sanchez, Sonia. *Shake Loose My Skin: New and Selected Poems*. Beacon Press, 1999.

Sanchez, Sonia. *Wounded in the House of a Friend*. Beacon Press, 1995.

AUGUSTA SAVAGE

Henkes, Robert. *The Art of Black American Women: Works of Twenty-Four Artists of the Twentieth Century*. McFarland & Company, 1993.

NTOZAKE SHANGE

Lester, Neal. *Ntozake Shange: A Critical Study of the Plays*. Garland Publishing, 1994.

Shange, Ntozake. *for colored girls who have considered suicide/when the rainbow is enuf*. Scribner, reissue 1997.

Shange, Ntozake. *I Live in Music: Poem*. Stewart Tabori & Chang, 1994.

Shange, Ntozake. *If I Can Cook, You Know God Can*. Beacon Press, 1998.

Shange, Ntozake. *Liliane: Resurrection of the Daughter*. Picador USA, 1995.

NINA SIMONE

Simone, Nina, and Stephen Cleary. *I Put a Spell on You: The Autobiography of Nina Simone*. Da Capo Press, 1993.

CORREEN SIMPSON

Moutoussamy-Ashe, Jeanne. *Viewfinders: Black Women Photographers*. Writers & Readers, 1993.

LORNA SIMPSON

Moutoussamy-Ashe, Jeanne. *Viewfinders: Black Women Photographers*. Writers & Readers, 1993.

Willis, Deborah, Andy Grundberg, and Michael Read, eds. *Lorna Simpson (Untitled; 54)*. Art Publishers, 1993.

BESSIE SMITH

Brooks, Edward. *Bessie Smith Companion*. Da Capo Press, 1983.

SHERYL SWOOPES

Butman, Bill. *Shooting Stars: The Women of Pro Basketball*. Random House, 1998.

Kelly, J. *Superstars of Women's Basketball*. Chelsea House Publishing, 1997.

Rutledge, Rachel. *The Best of the Best in Basketball* (Women of Sports). Millbrook Press, 1998.

Sehnert, Chris W. *Sheryl Swoopes*. Abdo & Daughters, 1998.

Swoopes, Sheryl, and Doug Keith, illus. *Bounce Back*. Taylor Publishing, 1996.

Vaderveer, Tara, and Joan Ryan. *Shooting from the Outside: How a Coach and Her Olympic Team Transformed Women's Basketball*. Avon Books, 1997.

SUSIE BAKER KING TAYLOR

Jordan, Denise, and Higgins Bond, illus. *Susie King Taylor: Destined to Be Free*. Just Us Books, 1994.

Taylor, Susie Baker King. *A Black Woman's Civil War Memoirs: Reminiscences of My Life in Camp With the 33rd U.S. Colored Troops, Late 1st South Carolina Volunteers*. Markus Wiener Publishing, reissue 1988.

MARY ELIZA CHURCH TERRELL

Terrell, Mary Church. *A Colored Woman in a White World*. G. K. Hall, reissue 1996.

Washington, Beverly Jones. *Quest for Equality: The Life and Writings of Mary Eliza Church Terrell, 1863–1954*. 1990.

DEBRA THOMAS

Smith, Pohla, and Joel H. Cohen. *Superstars of Women's Figure Skating*. Chelsea House Publishing, 1998.

SOJOURNER TRUTH

Fitch, Suzanne Pullon, and Roseann M. Mandziuk. *Sojourner Truth As Orator: Wit, Story, and Song*. Greenwood Publishing Group, 1997.

Krass, Peter. *Sojourner Truth*. Chelsea House Publishing, 1988.

McKissack, Patricia C., and Fredrick L. McKissack. *Sojourner Truth: Ain't I A Woman?* Scholastic Paperbacks, 1994.

Painter, Nell Irvin. *Sojourner Truth: A Life, a Symbol*. W. W. Norton & Company, 1996.

Taylor-Boyd, Susan. *Sojourner Truth: The Courageous Former Slave Whose Eloquence Helped Promote Human Equality*. Morehouse Publishing Company, 1997.

Truth, Sojourner, and Margaret Washington, ed. *The Narrative of Sojourner Truth*. Vintage Books, reissue 1993.

HARRIET TUBMAN

Bradford, Sarah H. *Harriet Tubman: The Moses of Her People*. Applewood Books, 1994.

Burns, Bree. *Harriet Tubman*. Chelsea House Publishing, 1994.

Elish, Dan. *Harriet Tubman and the Underground Railroad*. Demco Media, 1994.

Petry, Ann Lane. *Harriet Tubman: Conductor on the Underground Railroad*. Harper Trophy, 1996.

McClard, Megan. *Harriet Tubman: Slavery and the Underground Railroad*. Silver Burdett Press, 1991.

Sawyer, Kem Knapp. *The Underground Railroad in American History*. Enslow Publishers, Inc., 1997.

TINA TURNER

Turner, Tina, and Kurt Loder. *I, Tina: My Life Story*. Avon, reissue 1993.

SARAH VAUGHAN

Grouse, Leslie. *Sassy: The Life of Sarah Vaughan*. Da Capo Press, 1994.

Ruuth, Marianne. *Sarah Vaughan*. Holloway House Publishing Company, 1994.

SHIRLEY VERRETT

Story, Rosalyn M. *And So I Sing: African-American Divas of Opera and Concert*. Amistad Press, 1993.

ALICE WALKER

Gentry, Tony. *Alice Walker*. Chelsea House Publishing, 1993.

Howard, Lillie P. *Alice Walker and Zora Neale Hurston: The Common Bond*. Greenwood Publishing Group, 1993.

Kramer, Barbara. *Alice Walker: Author of the Color Purple*. Enslow Publishers, Inc., 1995.

Winchell, Donna Haisty. *Alice Walker*. Twayne, 1992.

Walker, Alice. *By the Light of My Father's Smile*. Random House, 1998.

Walker, Alice. *The Color Purple*. Harcourt Brace, reissue 1992.

Walker, Alice. *In Search of Our Mothers' Gardens*. Harcourt Brace, 1984.

Walker, Alice. *Meridian*. Pocket Books, reissue 1996.

Walker, Alice. *Possessing the Secret of Joy*. Harcourt Brace, 1992.

MADAME C. J. WALKER

Ballard, Donna. *Doing It for Ourselves: Success Stories of African-American Women in Business*. Berkley Publishing Group, 1997.

Bundles, A'lelia Perry. *Madame C. J. Walker*. Chelsea House Publishing, 1991.

Lommel, Cookie. *Madame C . J. Walker*. Holloway House Publishing Company, 1993.

MAGGIE LENA WALKER

Branch, Muriel Miller, and Dorothy Marie Rice. *Pennies to Dollars: The Story of Maggie Lena Walker*. Linnet Books, 1997.

MARGARET WALKER

Walker, Margaret. *How I Wrote Jubilee and Other Essays on Life and Literature*. Feminist Press, reissue 1990.

Walker, Margaret. *Jubilee*. Mariner Books, reissue 1999.

Walker, Margaret. *This Is My Century: New and Collected Poems*. University of Georgia Press, 1989.

Walker, Margaret, and Nikki Giovanni. *A Poetic Equation: Conversations Between Nikki Giovanni and Margaret Walker*. Howard University Press, 1983.

ETHEL WATERS

Waters, Ethel, and Charles T. Samuels. *His Eye Is on the Sparrow: An Autobiography*. De Capo Press, 1992.

MAXINE WATERS

Gill, Laverne McCain. *African American Women in Congress: Forming and Transforming History*. Rutgers University Press, 1997.

FAYE WATTLETON

Wattleton, Faye. *Life on the Line*. Ballantine Books, 1996.

IDA BELL WELLS-BARNETT

Haynes, Richard M. *Ida B. Wells: Antilynching Crusader*. Raintree/Steck Vaughn, 1993.

Lisandrelli, Elaine Slivinski. *Ida B. Wells-Barnett: Crusader Against Lynching*. Enslow Publishers, Inc., 1998.

McMurry, Linda O. *To Keep the Waters Troubled: The Life of Ida B. Wells, Agitator*. Oxford University Press, 1998.

Wells, Ida B., and Alfreda M. Duster, ed. *Crusade for Justice: The Autobiography of Ida B. Wells*. University of Chicago Press, 1991.

DOROTHY WEST

West, Dorothy. *The Living Is Easy: A Novel*. Feminist Press, reissue 1996.

West, Dorothy. *The Richer, the Poorer: Stories, Sketches, and Reminiscences*. Anchor, 1996.

West, Dorothy. *The Wedding: A Novel*. Anchor, 1995.

PHILLIS WHEATLEY

Richmond, M. A. *Phillis Wheatley*. Chelsea House Publishing, 1992.

Rinaldi, Anne. *Hang a Thousand Trees With Ribbons: The Story of Phillis Wheatley*. Harcourt Brace, 1996.

Wheatley, Phillis, and John C. Shields, ed. *The Collected Works of Phillis Wheatley*. Oxford University Press, 1989.

MARY LOU WILLIAM

Unterbrink, Mary. *Jazz Women at the Keyboard*, 1983.

VENUS WILLIAMS

Aronson, Virginia. *Venus Williams*. Chelsea House Publishing, 1999.

Rutledge, Rachel. *The Best of the Best in Tennis*. Millbrook Press, 1998.

Teitelbaum, Michael. *Grand Slam Stars: Martina Hingis, Venus Williams*. HarperCollins, 1998.

HARRIET E. ADAMS WILSON

Wilson, Harriet E. Adams, and Henry Louis Gates Jr., ed. *Our Nig; Or, Sketches from the Life of a Free Black, in a Two-Story White House, North. Showing That Slavery's Shadows Fall Even There: Or, Sketches.* Random House, reissue 1983.

OPRAH WINFREY

Nicholson, Lois P. *Influential Voice: Oprah Winfrey.* Chelsea House Publishing, 1997.

Presnall, Judith Janda. *Oprah Winfrey.* Lucent Books, 1999.

Ruuth, Marianne. *Oprah Winfrey: Entertainer.* Holloway House Publishing Company, 1996.

Saidman, Ann. *Oprah Winfrey: Media Success Story.* First Avenue Editions, 1993.

Winfrey, Oprah, and Ken Regan (photographer). *Journey to Beloved.* Hyperion, 1998.

JANE COOKE WRIGHT

Jenkins, Edward Sidney, Patricia Stohr-Hunt, and Exyie C. Ryder. *To Fathom More: African American Scientists and Inventors.* University Press of America, 1996.

abolitionist Most commonly used to refer to a person or policy that supported the abolition of slavery in the southern United States prior to the Civil War.

activist A person involved, or "active," in political affairs such as protests or demonstrations, designed to bring about change.

affirmative action The collective term for government policies in the United States intended to promote opportunities for minorities by setting specific goals or quotas. Affirmative Action favors minorities in hiring, promotion, college admissions, and government contracts to offset the effects of past discrimination against a group. The term was first used by President Lyndon B. Johnson in 1965, and the first federal policies designed to guarantee minority hiring were implemented by President Richard Nixon in 1969.

amateur In athletics, a person involved in a sport or activity as a pastime rather than as a profession; an athlete who is not paid for his or her participation in a sport.

ambassador A diplomat of the highest rank, usually assigned to a specific foreign country, accredited as an official representative of another country in matters of foreign relations.

antebellum A term most often used to refer to the group of southern states that formed the Confederate States of America; the period of prosperity in the South before the Civil War.

anthologized In literary terms, used to refer to a work, often a short story, that has been collected into a larger volume featuring a number of different writers, often with a central theme, known as an anthology.

aria In music, a solo vocal piece, usually a portion of a larger work, with an instrumental accompaniment. Arias are most often featured in operas and oratorios.

assemblage In general, any large group of people who have come or been brought together for a single purpose. The term is also used to refer to a political body, such as the Congress.

athenaeum From the Greek word *Athenaion*, meaning "temple of Athena," a formal, archaic name for an institution or academy for the promotion of learning, such as a college or university, or a library.

be-bop (also **bebop**) A style of jazz first made popular in the early 1940s by Charlie Parker. It is based on improvisation over chord progression, characterized by fast tempos, long phrases, and greater emotional ranges than were common in jazz before that time.

black separatism A politicle principle, or movement, advocated by the Black Muslim organization under the leadership of Elijah Muhammad, to establish a separate homeland for African Americans in the United States. After Elijah Muhammad's death in 1975, his son and successor, Wallace D. Muhammad, downplayed black separatism and nationalism, but in the late 1970s, a dissident faction led by current Nation of Islam leader Louis Farrakhan reasserted the principle of black separatism.

blacklist Meaning literally a list of disapproved persons or organizations, the term is often used to refer to those persecuted against and denied the right to practice their trade because of political or religious beliefs that are in conflict with those of the persons in power. The term is best known from the McCarthy-era "blacklisting" of entertainers who were not allowed to work because of their suspected ties to communism or communist sympathizers.

bootlegger Most often used to refer to a person who illegally transported or sold liquor during the Prohibition era. It may also refer to anyone who makes illegal copies of copyrighted works, such as music albums or videotaped music, for unauthorized distribution or sale.

boycott A form of protest in which a person or group refuses to buy products from or support companies, individuals, nations, or other groups with which they disagree. The intent of a boycott is to bring about or force change. It is used as a tool or weapon in labor disputes, by consumers, and in international affairs.

cadence In poetry or music, a term used to refer to the balance, rhythm, or flow of a spoken or performed work. The term refers both to the beat, as in marching, and to the inflection or modulation of sound, as in singing or speaking, and to both vocal and instrumental progressions.

caseworker Most often used to refer to a government employee involved in social work who is assigned to a specific case or person.

celestial Used to refer to objects of or relating to the sky or the heavens. It is commonly used as a superlative.

centrist   A person whose political views are for the most part at equal extremes from the right (conservatism) and the left (liberalism), as in "in the center."

Civil Rights Movement (also **civil rights**)   The overall name given to the political, legal, and social struggle by African Americans to challenge and bring an end to segregation and segregation laws, and to establish full citizenship rights and racial equality. In a number of different ways, and under many different leaders, the Civil Rights Movement sought an end to racial discrimination in the United States, and to eliminate laws and customs, prevalent in some southern states after the Reconstruction, that promoted segregation and differentiation between races. The beginning of the most active phase of the Civil Rights Movement is considered to be the Montgomery bus boycott, in 1955, and it achieved its greatest objectives with the passage of the Voting Rights Act of 1965.

coachman   Literally, a person who drives a coach (usually, a large, four-wheeled carriage with doors on the side and an elevated seat for the driver).

coalition   An alliance or union of two or more parties, usually temporary, established for the purpose of attaining goals favorable to those involved. The term is most often used to refer to political alliances.

coiffure   From the French word *coiffer*, meaning to arrange hair, a term used to refer to a hairstyle or to the overall presentation of the hair, most often in women.

colonialism   A political philosophy or policy by which a governing nation maintains control over its foreign possessions or colonies. The term is also used to refer to an attitude in which a citizen of the ruling country may view citizens of a subject nation with a certain disdain or sense of superiority.

coloratura   In music, a term used to refer to ornamental trills and runs in a vocal performance.

compulsories   In a sporting event, such as the Olympics, a predetermined routine of exercises or elements that must be performed by all participants.

concubine   A woman who lives with a man. The term is often used to refer to a woman who has a sexual or conjugal relationship with a man outside of marriage.

Congress of Racial Equality (CORE)   A civil rights organization founded in 1942 by James Leonard Farmer to protect the rights of black Americans and seek equal opportunity in jobs,

housing, and education for them. CORE advocates a policy of nonviolent, direct action, including sit-ins, voter registration drives, and large public demonstrations.

consortium   A group or association of businesses, investors, or banking institutions involved in a joint financial venture.

Constitutional amendment   The process by which changes are made, or new legislation is added, to the Constitution of the United States. Because the U.S. Congress does not have the authority to alter the Constitution itself, provision was made in Article V, which states that an amendment passes after a two-thirds vote of both houses of Congress or after the petition of two-thirds of the state legislatures. An amendment must then be ratified by the legislatures of three-fourths of the states or by "constitutional conventions" in three-fourths of the states. There are currently 27 amendments to the Constitution, of which the first ten, added immediately after the ratification of the Constitution itself, are referred to as the Bill of Rights.

contralto   The lowest female voice or vocal part.

credo   A creed or belief by which a person or organization may be said to be spiritually or philosophically governed.

creole   Most often used to refer to a person descended from the original French settlers of Louisiana, the term also describes the French dialect or culture of these people, or a person of mixed black and European descent.

Daughters of the American Revolution (DAR)   A patriotic organization, founded in Washington, D.C., in 1890, to preserve the memory of those who had fought for American independence. To qualify for membership, a woman must be a direct descendent of a man or woman who actively participated in the American Revolution. Approximately 200,000 women belong to the society.

delegation   A group of representatives from a specific group or organization that speaks for the whole in matters dealing with outside groups.

demonstration   An organized form of protest, often political in nature, in which a public display of opposition is made.

depiction   The representation, in words or in a picture, of someone or something. For example, *Uncle Tom's Cabin* may be said to be a depiction of the time and people that it portrays.

desegregation   The opposite of segregation, which separates one group from another, desegregation refers to the end of the separation. Most often used in reference to the civil rights struggles of the 1960s, which sought to end the forced segregation of blacks and whites in schools, public accommodations, and the like.

diaspora The dispersion or separation of culture. The term is often used to refer to the pattern of immigration that spreads an ethnic group beyond its native land.

diction Used to refer both to the choice and use of words in speech and writing, and to the clarity and distinctness in pronunciation.

diorama A three-dimensional scene or depiction, complete with background and modeled figures.

discrimination An action or situation in which an individual or group is treated differently from another based on factors other than individual or personal reasons, usually because of membership in a social or racial group or category. The term is most often used to refer to the preferential treatment given to white Americans as opposed to black Americans on the basis of race, or to men as opposed to women. In the United States, discrimination due to such factors is illegal.

disfranchise In general, meaning to deprive of any of the rights and privileges of citizenship, but used most often to refer specifically to taking away the right to vote.

divestiture In business, a term often used to refer to the sale or spin-off of a portion of a company, often a subdivision or subsidiary.

EEOA The Equal Educational Opportunity Act of 1974, under which provision no state may deny educational opportunities to any student because of language barriers. Along with Title VI of the Civil Rights Act of 1964, the EEOA established minimum standards for the education of "limited English proficient" (LEP) students, who by some estimates make up 7 to 10 percent of the U.S. student population.

elegy From the Greek word *elegos*, meaning song, a mournful poem or song, often lamenting a death.

emancipation Literally meaning to free from bondage, oppression, or restraint, most often used to refer to freedom from slavery, as in the Emancipation Proclamation.

Emancipation Proclamation Proclamation issued by U.S. president Abraham Lincoln on January 1, 1863, effectively ending slavery in the United States. Although excluding some slaves in areas of the Confederacy held by Union armies, the Emancipation Proclamation was a radical change in governmental policy, and was instrumental in leading to the enact-

ment of the 13th Amendment to the Constitution in 1865, by which slavery was wholly abolished.

entrepreneur A person who organizes and operates a business venture; commonly used to refer to people who seek business opportunities on their own rather than as part of an organization or corporation.

envoy A messenger or agent sent from a group or organization to another. In political terms, an envoy is often a diplomat or other government representative who represents his nation on a special mission or in negotiations.

equality In a political and social sense, the right of each individual to the same opportunities and legal protections as any other, without regard to race, religion, or other differences.

ethnicity A sociological classification referring to a person's ethnic character, background, or affiliation.

ethnocentric The belief or philosophy that one's ethnic or racial heritage is superior to another's.

ethnology A subdivision of anthropology concerned with the study of cultures in their traditional form, and their adaptation to modern influences.

eulogy A spoken or written tribute, most often given when a person has died.

excise A term that means the cutting out or removal of something. Also used to refer to a type of tax on the production, sale, or consumption of goods or commodities within a country.

exclusionary A type of act or practice that by design excludes or removes something or someone from its effects.

exile A person who has been forced out of his or her home or country and must reside elsewhere. The term often refers to political or social activists who might face criminal charges upon their return.

expressionism A movement in the fine arts, most commonly used in reference to painting, that emphasized the subjective expression through the work of the artist's inner experiences and emotional responses over a literal or objective depiction. It began in the late 19th and early 20th centuries in reaction to the prevailing academic standards in Europe. Among its earliest and most famous practitioners are the painter Vincent van Gogh and the sculptor Auguste Rodin.

expropriation The taking or acquiring of property belonging to another. The term often refers to the taking of private property, such as land, by the government for public use.

falsetto   A musical term used to classify a voice that produces tones in a range higher than the normal range.

Father Diviners   Followers of Father Divine (George Baker, c. 1880–1965), a charismatic storefront minister and preacher whose mission to channel his spirit to generate health, prosperity, and salvation reached its height in the years of the Great Depression. His social programs included sponsorship of a national network of relief shelters, encouraging the opening new businesses, and running an employment agency.

feminist (also **feminism**)   A person who believes in the social, political, and economic equality of both sexes, and the political or philosophical belief that people of both sexes should be treated equally socially and under the law.

folio   A publication on which the text is printed onto a large sheet folded into fourths that forms a small book or pamphlet.

folklore   The overall name for the traditions, beliefs, legends, and practices of a people or ethnic group, most often passed from generation to generation through the oral tradition.

forte   Something in which one excels, or an area of expertise.

Fulbright Scholarship   A type of scholarship provided for under the Fulbright Act of 1946, amended by the Fulbright-Hays Act in 1961, that provides funds for the exchange of students between the United States and other countries. It is named for politician and educator J. William Fulbright (1905–95), who sponsored the initial legislation while serving as a U.S. senator from Arkansas from 1944 to 1974, and as chairman of the Senate Committee on Foreign Relations from 1959 to 1974.

Garveyites   Followers of black political leader Marcus Garvey (1887–1940), who in 1914 founded the Universal Negro Improvement Association and the African Communities League. Born in Jamaica, Garvey moved to the United States in 1916. His political philosophies included the "Back to Africa" movement, which urged Americans of African descent to take pride in their heritage and return to their ancestral homelands. At its height, the UNIA claimed two million members, but Garvey suffered a series of economic setbacks and went to prison in 1925 for mail fraud. He was released two years later and deported to Jamaica, but he was unable to regain his former influence.

gender   A term categorizing an item by its sex or sexual identity as it relates to society or culture.

ghetto   An Italian term used originally to refer to a specific area of a city where Jews were required by law to reside, it has come to mean any section of a city, often depressed, occupied primarily by one or more minority groups, who live there because of social, economic, or legal pressure.

gospel   A style of music, usually religious in lyrical content, sung by a choir or group of people.

grassroots   A term used to describe people or a society living at a common, local level. In politics, a "grassroots campaign" is one that takes place at a basic level, dealing directly with individuals and communities, and gains power and influence through word of mouth.

gullah   A member of the community of people of African ancestry living in the coastal areas of South Carolina, Georgia, and northern Florida. The term also refers to their English-based creole dialect.

haute couture   Meaning "high fashion" in French, the process and creators of exclusive, often expensive fashions for women. The term refers both to the creators and to the fashions themselves.

heptathlon   An all-around track and field event in amateur sports, especially the Olympic Games, that requires skill in seven different individual events.

humanism   A philosophy or belief that emphasizes the dignity and worth of individual human beings.

idealism   The philosophy or practice of envisioning things in the best possible, or perfect, form. The term is often used to describe the subject of a piece of artwork or literature.

ideology   The collective term for the body of ideas and principles reflecting the social needs and aspirations of an individual, group, or culture.

idyll   A term used to refer both to a type of poetry, characterized by an idealized portrayal of rural life, and to a romantic interlude or event of a tranquil nature.

impetus   A compelling or stimulating force that incites a person or object to action.

impresario   A person who sponsors or produces entertainment. The term is frequently associated with the director of an opera company.

inaugurate   To induct a person, often a member of government, into office by a formal ceremony.

insignia   Most often used to refer to the distinguishing badges or decorations associated with military rank or nationalistic allegiance.

integration   The incorporation of diverse ethnic or social groups into a unified society. The term is most often used to refer to the process of racial integration, by which black Americans and other ethnic minorities are afforded the same rights, status, and opportunities as whites. True integration implies that an individual's ability to enjoy any benefits of society are not denied or restricted by reason of race, religion, or national origin.

interracial   Of or pertaining to relations and interaction between different ethic races and social groups.

intransigence   The refusal to modify or compromise an existing position or opinion, often an extreme political view.

Jim Crow laws   A slang term describing the group of laws that enforced the segregation of blacks in the South.

Ku Klux Klan   A social group characterized as being white supremacists, who adhere to the belief that the white, Aryan race is superior, and that blacks are inferior and unequal.

lambaste   Most commonly used to refer to a verbal berating or scolding; to criticize a person's political or social views.

legal brief   A short or condensed statement or paper in a legal case or argument, that presents the purported facts or details in a specific aspect of the proceedings.

leonine   Possessing the characteristics, usually in a symbolic sense, of a lion.

lexicon   A group of terms used in a specific profession, often in the form of a dictionary.

licentious   From the Latin word *licentia*, meaning license, a type of person or behavior lacking moral and/or sexual restraint.

linguistics   A term that refers to the science or study of the nature and structure of human languages.

lobby   A political term referring to a group of people whose goal is to influence legislators to favor a specific cause.

lobbyist   A person, often a hired professional, who lobbies for and represents the interests of an organization, group, or individual.

luminarie (also **luminary**)   Literally meaning an object, such as a star, that gives off light, the term is most often used to refer to a person recognized as outstanding or highly influential in a specific field, or a celebrity.

lynching   The execution, usually by hanging, of a person without a legal trial.

macabre   Something that suggests the horror or frightening aspects of death and decay.

manifest   An adjective that means clearly apparent, or obvious, to the sight or to understanding. For example, the idea of "Manifest Destiny" in the United States, which maintained that the country was "destined" to extend itself from the Atlantic to the Pacific Ocean.

manumitted (also **manumission**)   To free or be freed from slavery or bondage.

materialism   A philosophical theory or doctrine that states that physical matter is the ultimate reality, and that everything else, including human consciousness, can be explained in physical terms.

matriarchy   A familial or social system in which the mother or eldest female relative is the head of the family or group, and descent is traced through the maternal, or female, line.

maverick   In sociology or politics, a person who avoids association with or membership in a specific group or political party. The term is often used to describe people with a history of making independent decisions.

mentor   A trusted counselor or teacher. The term is most often used to describe the teacher who has had significant impact or provided great guidance in the shaping or a career or lifestyle.

Methodism (also **Methodist**)   A Protestant religious movement that began in Oxford, England, in 1729. The name refers to the methodical manner in which the first members carried out their religious duties and rituals. Among the founders of Methodism were John and Charles Wesley. Among its primary tenets are a belief in free will, Christian perfection, and personal salvation through faith.

mezzo-soprano   A musical term that describes a woman's singing voice having a range between soprano and contralto. The term is also used to refer to the singer herself.

militant   A person, political party, or course of action that is combative or aggressive, usually for a cause or to achieve a specific objective.

Millerite   An early name for Adventists, members of a number of related Protestant denominations, followers of the American Baptist preacher William Miller. Adventists stress the imminent second coming of Christ, and Miller originally proclaimed that it would occur between March 21, 1843, and March 21, 1844. When it did not, many left the movement, though there are branches of the original organization—most notably, the Seventh-day Adventists, with worldwide membership in the early 1990s in excess of 5.5 million—that continue to flourish.

missionary   A member of a particular religious organization whose tradition is to "witness" by word and deed to the beliefs of his or her religion, so that others may come to know and understand it.

mulatto   A term used to describe someone with one white parent and one black parent.

NAACP   An acronym for the National Association for the Advancement of Colored People, an organization founded in 1909 to protect the rights and improve the living and working conditions of black Americans. Over the years, the NAACP has been an effective force in promoting and protecting the civil rights of African Americans, leading the efforts that resulted in the enacting of the Civil Rights Acts of 1957 and 1964, along with other important regulations aimed at overcoming discrimination and abuse in business as well as social affairs.

nationalism   The devotion to the beliefs and interests of a specific nation.

nativist   A person opposed to the presence of foreigners and immigrants in the United States.

novel   In literature, a work of fiction of some length in which characters and situations are depicted within the framework of a plot.

oppression   To be kept down or denied rights through an unjust use of force or authority. The term is often used to refer to social and legal discrimination against certain ethic groups.

oral tradition   The term used to refer to the preservation of personal or cultural history by word of mouth, without written document, usually in the form of epic songs, stories, or poetry.

oratory   The art of speaking or speechmaking, especially speeches designed to influence the judgments or feelings of those listening.

orthodoxy   An accepted or established doctrine or creed, and the adherence to it. The term "orthodox" is also often used to refer to the most conservative or traditional element, especially of a religion.

Pan-Africanism   A movement that seeks to unite and promote the welfare and unity of all people of African descent or race. Among its early adherents was civil rights leader W. E. B. Du Bois (1868–1963), who maintained a cultural and political interest in Africa throughout his life, and was called the "father of Pan-Africanism."

pastoral   Most often used to refer to a lifestyle or setting that is simple, serene, or idyllic, usually possessing elements of rural life.

patroon   A Dutch term, based on the French word *patron*, that refers to a landholder in New Netherland (later New York) under Dutch colonial rule, who was granted rights to large tracts of land. Under the provisions established by the Dutch West India company, members were granted tracts of land if they would establish a colony of 50 persons on the land within a specified time period. The result was a patroon/tenant relationship with some similarities to the feudal system in medieval Europe. Patroonships were continued after the English took possession of New Netherland in 1664, and, with some modifications, continued through the early part of the 19th century.

pen name   A pseudonym used by a writer to disguise his or her real identity.

philanthropy   In business, a term used to describe the ongoing practice or philosophy, usually of an individual, of giving to or establishing charitable or humanistic causes or foundations. Many wealthy persons who express a desire to "give something back" to their communities or to the general public support or create such public-serving organizations as charities, scholarships, libraries, and museums, either during the course of their lifetimes, or in the form of behests made in wills and estates.

pilgrimage   The voyage taken by a traveler to a site of spiritual or political importance. Most often used to refer to a religious journey.

pitch   A slang term for the way in which a salesman attempts to interest potential buyers in a product or service. Also, a music term that refers to the lowness or highness of a specific sound, dependent primarily on frequency.

plantation   A term originating in colonial times, a plantation is a settlement or piece of land used to grow crops and that houses the workers who tend the crops. The land was independently owned and self-contained, often housing the owner of the land as well.

pliant   From the Old French word *plier*, meaning to fold or bend, a term used to refer to a person who adapts easily or is receptive to change or argument.

poet laureate   A formal title, used both in the United States and Great Britain, that designates an "official" or state poet. In Great Britain, the poet laureate is appointed, for life, by the king or queen, becomes a member of the royal household, and is responsible for composing suitable verse for royal and state occasions. The first to officially fill the post was John Dryden, in 1668; the most recent was Ted Hughes. In the United States, the position was created by Congress in 1985, and the poet laureate serves for one year as a poetry consultant to the Library of Congress.

polio   The common term for the infectious virus poliomyelitis, a disease of the central nervous system. Polio sometimes results in paralysis, and its greatest instance is in children between the ages of five and ten years, and is more prevalent in temperate zones. It was first described in 1840, and there is no known cure, although a vaccine was developed by epidemiologist Jonas Salk, and widespread inoculation began in 1954. Since 1960, an oral vaccine containing attenuated, live polio virus, developed by virologist Albert Sabin, has replaced the Salk vaccine as the immunizing standard in the United States.

poll tax A type of tax levied on citizens when they are preparing to vote. It has occasionally been used as a political tool to prevent lower income citizens from voting.

poverty An economic condition in which people lack the income to obtain the minimal levels of such essentials as food, clothing, medical services, and housing necessary to maintain an adequate standard of living. In a strict sense, the "poverty line" is defined as those households earning a certain percentage below the average family income. In the United States, the group that currently makes up the largest portion of the population living in poverty are single mothers, who account for roughly one-third of all poor people in the country.

Prohibition The legal ban on the production and sale of alcoholic beverages. The Prohibition Act, also referred to as the Volstead Act, was ratified on January 16, 1919. It was repealed in 1933.

prose A literary term referring to spoken language, without metrical structure or rhyme.

protagonist The main character in a literary work, usually possessing good qualities. The protagonist is often the hero of the work.

pseudonym Similar to a pen name, a fictious name assumed by an author.

quadrille A type of square dance performed by four couples. The term also refers to the music that accompanies the dance.

Quaker A member of the Society of Friends, a Christian denomination of the mid-17th century that rejected formal sacraments, creeds, priesthood, and violence.

racism The belief that a racial or ethnic group is inferior due to its race or nationality.

radicalism A term that refers collectively to the actions or philosophies of those espousing extremist positions or taking using extreme measures to effect their views.

ragtime An American musical genre, mostly written for piano, that combined 19th-century African-American musical styles with the chromatic harmonies of contemporary European music. It is characterized by synco-pated melodies, usually in 2/4 time, over a regularly accented base.

Rastafarianism A religion or movement, considered to have had a profound influence on reggae music. Among other beliefs, Rastafarianism praises the spiritual effects of marijuana and endorses black racial superiority. Among the most famous and influential members of the movement was Jamaican reggae artist Bob Marley (1945–81).

realism A philosophical discipline inclined toward truth and pragmatism. In art, the representation of objects as they actually appear.

Reconstruction The term used for the rebuilding plan established for the southern, formerly Confederate states following the American Civil War.

Red Cross An international humanitarian organization, dedicated in wartime to relieving the suffering of wounded soldiers, civilians, and prisoners of war, and in peace to the relief and aid of people affected by natural disasters such as earthquakes, floods, and famine. It was founded in the 19th century at the initiative of Swiss philanthropist Jean Henri Dunet, with a committee of five Swiss citizens who would later become the International Committee of the Red Cross. An international conference was held in Geneva in 1863, and was attended by delegates from 16 nations. The following year, the first Geneva Convention was signed, creating for the first time a set of rules for the treatment of the wounded and for the protection of medical personnel and hospitals. The familiar symbol of a red cross on a white background (which is modified in non-Christian countries) was created at this time. The organization is known as the Red Crescent in most Muslim countries. Among the foremost leaders of the Red Cross in the United States was Clara Barton (1821–1912), who founded the American Red Cross in 1881 and served as its first president until 1904.

reformer In political terms, a person who seeks to bring about change, often in laws and government policies, by means of the established political systems.

repertoire (also **repertory, repertory theater**) The stock of performance numbers, such as songs or plays, performed by a player or company. The terms repertory and repertory theater refer to the players and to the type of entertainment in general.

resonance In music, the intensification of sound in a musical instrument or vocal performance, by sympathetic vibration.

revivalist Someone who revives or restores a belief no longer in use. Also used to refer to a minister or preacher who operates in a carnival-like atmosphere.

rhythm-and-blues music (R&B, rhythm and blues)   The overall term for a variety of different but related types of popular music. Among the genres included are jump and club blues, doo wop, soul, funk, disco, Motown, and rap. Beginning in the 1940s, R&B was primarily produced and supported by black Americans, but the tremendous popularity of white performers such as Elvis Presley brought certain aspects into the mainstream, where it was commonly referred to as rock 'n' roll. R&B is recognized as one of the most profound influences on popular music in the 20th century.

sadism   A psychological disorder in which someone enjoys inflicting abuse and physical pain as a means of sexual gratification.

sanctioned   In a legal or political sense, activities or policies that are formally supported by the government or other powerful agency.

scarlet fever   An infectious disease, caused by the same bacteria as strep throat, transmitted from person to person through direct contact. Symptoms include headache, sore throat, chills, and fever. From two to three days after the initial appearance of symptoms, red spots or eruptions may appear on the head, tongue, and all parts of the body except for the face. The disease most often affects children between the ages of two and ten years, and may be treated with the use of penicillin or other antibiotics.

segregation   To be separated, usually through force, from the mainstream for reasons of race or creed. The term is most often used to refer to the forced separation of blacks and whites, most notable in the southern United States.

septet   A term that most commonly refers to a musical group comprised of seven members. It may consist of all vocalists or all instruments, or a combination of both.

sharecropper   A person who is placed in a position of servitude by which he or she provides labor for the landowner in return for a share of the profits of the merchandise, usually an agricultural crop. The landowner not only provides the land to be tended, but also the equipment, animals and seed, and housing to the sharecropper.

siren   Based on a character from Greek mythology, one of a group of sea nymphs whose sweet singing lured ships and sailors to their destruction, the term commonly refers to a beautiful, alluring, or tempting woman.

sit-in   A nonviolent protest during which the protesters literally sit as a means of reaching their goal. By the protesters physically being in place, the normal process of events is interrupted, therefore creating the obstacle that in turn gets results.

slavery   A social institution that is considered to be the most involuntary form of human servitude. The people, or slaves, are obtained by force, are property of an owner, and are subject to perform whatever work the owner demands.

sociology   The science or study of human social relations or group life and interaction. It examines the ways in which social structures, institutions, and social problems influence society. It is considered one of the social sciences, along with such studies and sciences as psychology, economics, and anthropology.

sojourn   A colorful term used to refer to a brief stay. It is often used to describe a vacation or religious or spiritual pilgrimage.

soprano   A musical term used to classify a voice with the highest tonal range, usually achieved by a woman or a young boy.

speakeasy   A slang term for an illegal bar or club that served alcohol during the time of Prohibition.

spiritualism   The belief that the dead can and do manifest themselves to living people, usually with the assistance of a clairvoyant or medium. The term is also used to refer to the practices of those who believe in such manifestations. Modern spiritualism in the United States and Great Britain became popular in the 19th century, with a series of occurrences and research into popular claims, many of which were proved false, and there are several organizations espousing spiritualism, with a membership of more than 180,000, that exist today.

status quo   The state of affairs as they exist.

strike   An organized work stoppage carried out by a group of employees, usually as a tactic to enforce demands or to protest unfair labor conditions. Strikes are most frequently conducted by workers organized into trade unions, and are often used as a bargaining tool during contract negotiations. A strike made primarily for symbolic purposes may have a set duration, but most often strikes are continued until an agreement is reached between labor and management representatives. A strike carried out for the purpose of obtaining better relations for employees is considered an economic strike, and an employer may then seek to hire replacements for the striking workers, and is not obligated to rehire those who have been replaced. In a strike called because of alleged unfair labor practices, the employer loses the right of replacement and is obligated to rehire any workers who were discharged or replaced during the strike. One of the most feared and effective tools available to organized labor, strikes have been instrumental in changing the course of labor relations in the United States and Europe.

subjective   A term used to describe an opinion or interpretation of events that takes place or proceeds from a person's mind, unaffected by or with disregard to the external world.

subpoena   A legal document, issued by a court of law, requiring an appearance before the court to give testimony. The term also refers to the act of serving or summoning with a subpoena.

subversive   Policies or actions that are intended to undermine, or subvert, established systems. The term is most often used to refer to oppositional or confrontational political activity.

suffrage   The right or privilege of voting.

suffragette   A person who advocates the right of women to vote.

surrealism   A movement in literature and fine arts that emphasized the role of the unconscious in creative activity, and employed it in an orderly and serious manner. Surrealism was founded by French critic and poet Andre Breton (1896–1966), and grew out of the movement known as Dadaism. Artists associated with surrealism include Salvador Dali, William Blake, photographer Man Ray, and Pablo Picasso.

symposium   A meeting or conference, arranged specifically for the discussion of a specific topic.

tendinitis   The pain associated with a muscular injury that occurs from overuse, or misuse, a muscle. Tendinitus often afflicts athletes who constantly use the same muscles in training for their specific sport.

tenure   The status associated with holding one's position in a specific job or function, for a specific length of time or on a permanent basis.

timbre   A musical term referring to the quality of a sound or tone that distinguishes it from others of the same pitch and volume.

trailblazer   A slang term used for someone who is a leader in his or her particular area of expertise.

trajectory   A physics term referring to the path of a projectile, or other moving object, through space or air.

transracial   A term usually associated with adoption, in which parents of one culture and race adopt a child from a different culture or race. In society, the children are not often accepted in the cultural circles of their parents due to their racial differences.

triumvirate   From the Latin terms *trium*, meaning of three, and *vir*, meaning man, a group or political alliance composed of three men. The term was first used in ancient Rome, and is used casually to refer to any central administration of three holding power over a specific group or organization.

truant   From the Old French word for "beggar," the term refers to one who shirks work and responsibilities. Truant is more commonly used in the education system for a student who is absent without permission.

Underground Railroad   A network of anti-slavery northerners that illegally helped black southern slaves escape slavery and reach safety in free states and Canada. The refugees traveled from "station" to "station" (usually farms), aided by a "conductor" who helped them find safe places to hide during their journey.

United Negro College Fund   An organization established in 1944, made up of an alliance of 41 black colleges, that raises all the funds for operating expenses including teachers salaries, scholarships, and equipment. The organization was initially established to financially aid black institutions of higher learning during World War II, a time when wartime shortages had slowed contributions. Today, the United Negro College Fund remains the premier nongovernmental funding source for historically black colleges, providing an alternative education source to its students.

urban   A classification for an area that refers to its characteristics of a city.

vacuole   A biological term for a small cavity, usually filled with fluid, that is found in the liquid outside a cell. Microscopic organisms, such as amoebas, form a vacuole as a means of ingesting food, using the cavity to store the particles they have absorbed until a digestive enzyme can break down the food.

valedictorian   The term given to the student with the highest academic rank in the class. This person usually delivers the valedictory speech at graduation.

vaudeville   A type of theatrical entertainment, most often made up of a variety of separate elements, popular in the United States in the late 19th and early 20th centuries.

verisimilitude   Something that possesses the qualities of being true or real.

vibrato   A musical term used to refer to a tremulous or pulsating effect in voice or instrument caused by slight, rapid variations in pitch.

virtuoso   Most often used to refer to a person with exceptional or masterful musical skills in instrument or voice.

vodoun   A religious sect, African in origin, that is similar to voodoo in its practices and beliefs.

voodoo   The primary religion of Haiti, voodoo combines elements of Roman Catholicism with tribal religions of Africa. The religions beliefs include cult worship of a high god (Bon Dieu), the dead, twins, and spirits called Ioa. As in Roman Catholicism the use of candles, prayer, crosses, and the sign of the cross are common elements. African elements include dancing, drumming, and the worship of ancestors and twins. Voodoo rituals are conducted by a priest, called a houngan, or a priestess, called a mambo, during which spirits are invoked and "possess" each of the dancers. While in this trance, the dancer performs the called upon cure or gives advice on the subject in question.

xenophobia   A sociological term referring to a fear or contempt of strangers or foreigners.

YWCA (Young Women's Christian Association)   One of the oldest women's organizations in the United States, the YWCA was founded in 1858 by 35 women who were devoted to helping women and girls adjust to urban life. Today, the organization operates on an international, national, and local level providing women with source materials on women's issues. The organization also works with state and federal lawmakers in an effort to raise the consciousness of women's public-policy concerns.

Zulu   The sociological term for a member of a people from southeast Africa. A dominant tribe in the nineteenth century, the Zulu defeated numerous tribes in an effort to settle in an area rich in land and food.

Index

A

Abolitionists
  Crafts, Ellen, 67–69
  Grimké, Charlotte L.
    Forten, 114–115
  Harper, Frances Ellen
    Watkins, 123–124
  Jacobs, Harriet Ann, and,
    154
  Keckley, Elizabeth, and,
    170
  Remond, Sarah Parker,
    232–233
  Truth, Sojourner, 270–273
  Tubman, Harriet Ross,
    274–277
Academics. *See also* Educators
  Browne, Marjorie Lee,
    41–43
Activists. *See also* Civil rights
    activists; Women's
    rights activists
  Alexander, Sadie Tanner
    Mossell, 1–2
  Baker, Ella J., 14–17
  Bethune, Mary McLeod,
    31–34
  Brown, Charlotte
    Hawkins, 40
  Burroughs, Nannie Helen,
    44–46
  Cary, Mary Ann Shadd, 50
  Davis, Angela Yvonne,
    75–76
  Dunbar-Nelson, Alice, 86
  Dunham, Katherine,
    90–91
  Edelman, Marian Wright,
    92–93

Harper, Frances Ellen
    Watkins, 122–124
Height, Dorothy, 128–130
Sanchez, Sonia, 243–244
Walker, Maggie Lena,
    290–291
Wattleton, Faye, 300–301
Actors
  Angelou, Maya, and, 8
  Bailey, Pearl, 13–14
  Bassett, Angela, 23–25
  Berry, Halle, 29–31
  Carroll, Diahann, 48–49
  Dandridge, Dorothy,
    72–74
  Dee, Ruby, 80–81
  Goldberg, Whoopi,
    109–110
  Horne, Lena, 137–138
  Houston, Whitney,
    138–140
  Jackson, Janet, 147–149
  Kitt, Eartha Mae, 176–177
  Mabley, Jackie "Moms,"
    190–191
  McDaniel, Hattie,
    199–201
  McQueen, Thelma
    "Butterfly," 204–205
  Rolle, Esther, 234–236
  Ross, Diana, 236–238
  Tyson, Cicely, 279–280
  Waters, Ethel, 296–298
  Winfrey, Oprah Gail,
    318–320
African culture, Dunham,
    Katherine, and, 86–91
Alexander, Sadie Tanner
    Mossell, 1–2
Allen, Debbie, 2–4

Alvin Ailey American Dance
    Theater (AAADT),
    157, 158
Ambassadors
  Harris, Patricia Roberts,
    127
American Negro Theatre
    (ANT), 58
American Nurses Association
    (ANA), 191–192
American Tennis Association
    (ATA), 105–106
Anatomists
  Lloyd, Ruth Smith,
    186–187
Anderson, Marian, 4–6
Angelou, Maya, 6–9
ANT. *See* American Negro
    Theatre (ANT)
Antislavery movement. *See*
    Abolitionists
Armstrong, Lillian Hardin
    "Lil," 9–11
Armstrong, Louis, 9
Arrangers (musical)
  Williams, Mary Lou,
    312–314
Artists. *See specific types of*
    artists
Ashford, Evelyn, 11–12
Astronauts
  Jemison, Mae Carol,
    159–161
Athletes
  Ashford, Evelyn, 11–12
  Dawes, Dominique,
    76–78
  Garrison, Zena, 104–105
  Gibson, Althea,
    105–107

Griffith-Joyner, Florence Delorez, 111–113
Joyner-Kersee, Jacqueline, 165–167
Rudolph, Wilma Glodean, 238–240
Swoopes, Sheryl, 259–261
Thomas, Debra J. "Debi," 268–269
Williams, Venus, 314–316
Authors. *See* Writers
Autobiography
  Angelou, Maya, 6–8
  in black America, 8
Avery Normal Institute, 61
Aviators
  Coleman, Bessie, 64–65

B

Bailey, Pearl, 13–14
Baker, Ella J., 14–17
Baker, Josephine, 18–20
Bambara, Toni Cade, 20–21
Bank presidents
  Walker, Maggie Lena, 290
Banks, Tyra, 21–23
Basketball players
  Swoopes, Sheryl, 259–261
Bassett, Angela, 23–25
Battle, Kathleen, 25–27
Belton, Sharon Sayles, 27–28
Berry, Halle, 29–31
Bethune, Mary McLeod, 31–34, 129
Bethune-Cookman College, 32, 33
BEV. *See* Black English Vernacular (BEV)
Black Arts Movement (1960s), 38
Black Cabinet, of Roosevelt, Franklin D., 34

Black English Vernacular (BEV), 145
Black Scholar (journal), 37
Black Swan Records, 296, 297
Blackwell, Unita, 34–35
Blackwell v. Board of Education, 35
Black women's club movement. *See* Women's club movement
Blues singers. *See* Singers
Bolin, Jane Mathilda, 35–36
Bridge players
  Kearse, Amalya Lyle, 168–169
Brooks, Gwendolyn Elizabeth, 36–39
Brown, Charlotte Hawkins, 39–41
Browne, Marjorie Lee, 41–43
Burke, Yvonne Braithwaite, 43–44
Burroughs, Nannie Helen, 44–46
Businesswomen
  Malone, Annie Turnbo, 192–193
  Mason, Biddy Bridget, 196–197
  O'Leary, Hazel Rollins, 221–222
  Walker, A'Lelia, 284–285
  Walker, Madame C. J., 287–289
  Walker, Maggie Lena, 289–291
Butler, Octavia Estelle, 46–47

C

Cabinet
  Black Cabinet as, 34

Harris, Patricia Roberts, in, 126–128
O'Leary, Hazel Rollins, in, 222
Cade, Toni. *See* Bambara, Toni Cade
Cancer researchers
  Wright, Jane Cooke, 321
Carroll, Diahann, 48–49
Cary, Mary Ann Shadd, 49–50
Catlett, Elizabeth, 51–53
CBC. *See* Congressional Black Caucus (CBC)
CDF. *See* Children's Defense Fund (CDF)
Celia, 53–54
Chase-Riboud, Barbara Dewayne, 54–56
Chideya, Farai, 56–57
Children's Defense Fund (CDF), Edelman, Marian Wright, and, 92–93
Childress, Alice, 57–59
Chisholm, Shirley, 59–60
Choreographers
  Dunham, Katherine, 86–91
  Jamison, Judith, 158
Citizenship schools, 62
Civil rights activists
  Alexander, Sadie T. M., 1
  Angelou, Maya, 7
  Baker, Ella J., 14–17
  Baker, Josephine, and, 20
  Bethune, Mary McLeod, 31–34
  Blackwell, Unita, 34–35
  Clark, Septima Poinsette, 60–63
  Dee, Ruby, 80
  Guinier, Lani, 115–117
  Hamer, Fannie Lou, 118–121

Harris, Barbara
    Clementine, 124–125
King, Coretta Scott,
    173–176
Lampkin, Daisy Elizabeth
    Adams, 181–183
Nash, Diane Bevel,
    214–215
Norton, Eleanor Holmes,
    218–220
Parks, Rosa Louise
    McCauley, 224–226
Ringgold, Faith, and,
    233–234
Terrell, Mary Eliza Church,
    263–265
Wells-Barnett, Ida Bell,
    303–307
Clark, Septima Poinsette,
    60–63
Club movement. *See* Women's
    club movement
Cole, Rebecca J., 63–64
Coleman, Bessie, 64–65
College professors. *See also*
    Educators
    Guinier, Lani, 115–117
    Hill, Anita, 130–134
    Jordan, Barbara Charline,
        161–163
    Jordan, June, 164
    Lloyd, Ruth Smith,
        186–187
    Marshall, Paule, 194
Comediennes
    Goldberg, Whoopi,
        109–110
    Mabley, Jackie "Moms,"
        190–191
Communists
    Davis, Angela Yvonne,
        75–76
Congressional Black Caucus
    (CBC), 299

Congress of Racial Equality
    (CORE), Nash, Diane
    Bevel, and, 215
Congresswomen
    Burke, Yvonne
        Braithwaite, 43–44
    Chisholm, Shirley,
        59–60
    Jordan, Barbara Charline,
        161–163
    Waters, Maxine Moore,
        298–300
Cooper, Anna Julia Haywood,
    65–67
CORE. *See* Congress of Racial
    Equality (CORE)
Corporate executives
    O'Leary, Hazel Rollins,
        221–222
Craft, Ellen, 67–69
Currie, Betty, 69–71

D

Dancers
    Allen, Debbie, 2–3
    Dunham, Katherine,
        86–91
    Jamison, Judith, 157–159
Dandridge, Dorothy, 72–74
Dash, Julie, 74–75
Daughters of the American
    Revolution (DAR),
    Anderson, Marian, and,
    4–5
Davis, Angela Yvonne,
    75–76
Dawes, Dominique, 76–78
Daytona Institute, 33
Death of Cleopatra, The (sculp-
    ture by Lewis),
    184–185
Dee, Ruby, 80–81

De Passe, Suzanne, 78–79
Dickens, Helen Octavia,
    81–82
Dixon, Sharon Pratt. *See*
    Kelly, Sharon Pratt
Doctors. *See* Physicians
Dove, Rita, 82–84
Dressmakers
    Keckley, Elizabeth,
        169–170
Dunbar-Nelson, Alice, 84–86
Dunham, Katherine, 86–91

E

Ebonics, 145
Edelman, Marian Wright,
    92–93
Educators. *See also* College pro-
    fessors; Teaching;
    Universities and colleges
    Alexander, Sadie T. M.,
        and, 1–2
    Bethune, Mary McLeod
        and, 32–33
    Brooks, Gwendolyn
        Elizabeth, 36–39
    Brown, Charlotte
        Hawkins, 39–41
    Browne, Marjorie Lee,
        41–43
    Burroughs, Nannie Helen,
        44–46
    Cary, Mary Ann Shadd,
        49–50
    Clark, Septima Poinsette,
        60–63
    Cooper, Anna Julia
        Haywood, 65–67
    Dickens, Helen Octavia,
        81–82
    Granville, Evelyn Boyd,
        110–111

Grimké, Charlotte L.
Forten, 114–115
Harris, Patricia Roberts,
126–128
Hill, Anita, and, 132
Lorde, Audre Geraldine,
188–189
Savage, Augusta Christine
Fells, 244–247
Taylor, Susie Baker King,
262–263
Washington, Margaret
Murray, 294–295
Elders, M. Joycelyn Jones,
93–94
Entertainers. *See also*
Actors; Comediennes;
Dancers; Singers
Allen, Debbie, 2–4
Baker, Josephine, 18–20
Shange, Ntozake,
247–248
Winfrey, Oprah Gail,
318–320
Entertainment executives
De Passe, Suzanne, 78–79
Entrepreneurs
Malone, Annie Turnbo,
192–193
Walker, A'Lelia, 284–285
Walker, Madame C. J.,
287–289
Episcopal bishops
Harris, Barbara
Clementine, 124–125
Executive assistant to the
president
Currie, Betty, 69–71

F

Fauset, Crystal Dreda Bird,
95–96
Feminists. *See also* Women's
rights activists
Hurston, Zora Neale, and,
144

Ringgold, Faith, and,
233–234
Tubman, Harriet Ross,
274–277
Filmmakers
Dash, Julie, 74–75
Fitzgerald, Ella, 96–98
Flack, Roberta, 98–99
"Flo-Jo." *See* Griffith-Joyner,
Florence Delorez
Folklorists
Hurston, Zora Neale,
142–146
Franklin, Aretha Louise,
99–100
Fuller, Meta Vaux Warrick,
100–103

G

Garrison, Zina, 104–105
Gibson, Althea, 105–107
Giovanni, Yolanda Cornelia
"Nikki," 107–108
Goldberg, Whoopi, 109–110
Gospel singers. *See also*
Singers
Jackson, Mahalia,
149–151
Tharpe, Sister Rosetta,
266
Government workers
Currie, Betty, 69–71
Granville, Evelyn Boyd,
110–111
Graphic arts
Catlett, Elizabeth, 52
Griffith-Joyner, Florence
Delorez, 111–113
Grimké, Angelina Weld,
113–114
Grimké, Charlotte L. Forten,
114–115
Guinier, Lani, 115–117
Gymnasts
Dawes, Dominique,
76–78

H

Hair-care industry pioneer
Walker, Madame C. J.,
287–289
Hamer, Fannie Lou, 118–121
Hansberry, Lorraine, 121–122
Harlem Renaissance. *See spe-
cific individuals*
Harper, Frances Ellen
Watkins, 122–124
Harris, Barbara Clementine,
124–125
Harris, Patricia Roberts,
126–128
Health, Education, and
Welfare Department,
Harris, Patricia Roberts,
and, 127
Height, Dorothy, 128–130
Hill, Anita, 130–134
Holiday, Billie, 134–135
Holt, Patricia Louise. *See*
LaBelle, Patti
Horn, Rosa Artimus, 135–137
Horne, Lena, 137–138
Housing and Urban
Development,
Department of (HUD),
126, 127, 128
Houston, Whitney, 138–140
Howard University, Catlett,
Elizabeth, and, 51
Hunter, Clementine
Clemence Rubin,
140–142
Hunter-Gault, Charlayne, 142
Hurston, Zora Neale,
142–146

I

Ice skaters
Thomas, Debra J. "Debi,"
268–269
*I Know Why the Caged Bird
Sings* (Angelou), 6, 8

Inauguration (presidential), Angelou, Maya, and, 9

J

Jackson, Janet, 147–149
Jackson, Mahalia, 149–151
Jackson, Rebecca Cox, 151–152
Jackson, Shirley Ann, 152–153
Jacobs, Harriet Ann, 153–155
James, Etta, 156–157
Jamison, Judith, 157–159
Jazz singers. *See* Singers
 Armstrong, Lillian Hardin "Lil," and, 9–11
 Bailey, Pearl, 13–14
 Fitzgerald, Ella, 96–98
 Holiday, Billie, 134–135
 McRae, Carmen, 205–206
 Simone, Nina, 249
 Vaughan, Sarah, 281–282
 Williams, Mary Lou, 312–314
Jemison, Mae Carol, 159–161
Johnson, Marguerite Annie. *See* Angelou, Maya
Jones, Ruth Lee, Washington, Dinah (Jones, Ruth Lee), 293–294
Jordan, Barbara Charline, 161–163
Jordan, June, 163–165
Journalists
 Cary, Mary Ann Shadd, 49–50
 Chideay, Farai, 56–57
 Hunter-Gault, Charlayne, 142
 Matthews, Victoria Earle (Smith), 197–199
 Stewart, Pearl, 258–259
 Wells-Barnett, Ida Bell, 303–307
Joyner-Kersee, Jacqueline, 165–167

Judges
 Bolin, Jane Mathilda, 35–36
 Kearse, Amalya Lyle, 168–169
 Motley, Constance Baker, 212–213

K

Kearse, Amalya Lyle, 168–169
Keckley, Elizabeth, 169–170
Kelly, Sharon Pratt, 170–172
Kincaid, Jamaica, 172–173
King, Coretta Scott, 173–176
King, Martin Luther, Jr., 5
Kitt, Eartha Mae, 176–177
Knight, Gladys, 177–179

L

LaBelle, Patti, 180–181
Lampkin, Daisy Elizabeth Adams, 181–183
Law. *See also* Judges
 Alexander, Sadie T. M., 1–2
 Burke, Yvonne Braithwaite, 43–44
 Hill, Anita, 130–134
Law school deans
 Harris, Patricia Roberts, 127
Lawyers
 Guinier, Lani, 115–117
 Harris, Patricia Roberts, 126–128
 Jordan, Barbara Charline, 161–163
 Motley, Constance Baker, 212–213
 Ray, Charlotte E., 231
Lee, Rebecca, 183
Lewis, Edmonia, 183–186

Lincoln Memorial, Anderson, Marian, at, 5
Literature. *See* Poets; Writers
Lloyd, Ruth Smith, 186–187
Logan, Myra Adele, 187–188
Lorde, Audre Geraldine, 188–189

M

Mabley, Jackie "Moms," 190–191
Mahoney, Mary Eliza, 191–192
Malone, Annie Turnbo, 192–193
"Mammy" stereotype, 201
Marshall, Paule, 193–196
Mason, Biddy Bridget, 196–197
Mathematicians
 Browne, Marjorie Lee, 41–43
 Granville, Evelyn Boyd, 110–111
Matthews, Victoria Earle (Smith), 197–199
Mayors
 Belton, Sharon Sales, 27–28
 Blackwell, Anita, 35
 Kelly, Sharon Pratt, 170–172
McDaniel, Hattie, 199–201
McMillan, Terry, 202–203
McQueen, Thelma "Butterfly," 204–205
McRae, Carmen, 205–206
Medical school administrators
 Wright, Jane Cooke, 321
Medicine. *See* Anatomists; Nurses; Physicians; Scientists
MFDP. *See* Mississippi Freedom Democratic Party (MFDP)

Ministers
  Harris, Barbara
    Clementine, 124–125
  Horn, Rosa Artimus,
    135–137
Mississippi Freedom
    Democratic Party
    (MFDP), 35
  Baker, Ella J., and, 17
  Hamer, Fannie Lou, and,
    120
Models
  Banks, Tyra, 21–23
Modern dance, Dunham,
    Katherine, and, 86–91
Morrison, Toni, 206–209
Moseley-Braun, Carol,
    209–212
Mossell, Aaron Albert, 2
Motley, Constance Baker,
    212–213
Movies. *See* Actors;
    Entertainers; Filmmakers
Music. *See* Entertainers;
    Singers

N

NAACP. *See* National
    Association for the
    Advancement of
    Colored People
    (NAACP)
NACW. *See* National
    Association of Colored
    Women (NACW)
Nannie Helen Burroughs
    School, 46
Nash, Diane Bevel,
    214–215
National Association for the
    Advancement of
    Colored People
    (NAACP)
  Baker, Ella J., and, 15–16
  Jordan, Barbara Charline
    and, 162

Lampkin, Daisy Elizabeth
    Adams, and, 182–183
Motley, Constance Baker,
    and, 212–213
Terrell, Mary Eliza Church,
    and, 265
National Association of
    Colored Graduate
    Nurses (NACGN),
    192, 223
National Association of
    Colored Women
    (NACW), 264, 295
  Burroughs, Nannie Helen,
    and, 44–46
National Bar Association, 2
National Council of Negro
    Women (NCNW), 34,
    128, 129, 130
National Political Congress of
    Black Women, 60
National Youth
    Administration (NYA),
    34
Naylor, Gloria, 215–216
NCNW. *See* National Council
    of Negro Women
    (NCNW)
Newspapers
  Cary, Mary Ann Shadd,
    50
  Walker, Maggie Lena,
    289–291
Nobel Prize winners
  Morrison, Toni, 206, 207
  Norman, Jessye, 217– 218
Norton, Eleanor Holmes,
    218–220
Novelists
  Butler, Octavia Estelle,
    46–47
  Chase-Riboud, Barbara
    Dewayne, 54–56
  Childress, Alice, 59
  Lorde, Audre Geraldine,
    188–189
  Marshall, Paule, 193–196
  McMillan, Terry, 202–203

Morrison, Toni, 206–209
Walker, Alice, 285–287
Nurses
  Mahoney, Mary Eliza,
    191–192
  Osborne, Estelle, 222–223
  Taylor, Susie Baker King,
    262–263
  Tubman, Harriet Ross,
    274–277

O

O'Leary, Hazel Rollins,
    221–222
Olympics. *See* Athletes
Opera singers
  Anderson, Marian, 4–6
  Battle, Kathleen, 25–27
  Norman, Jessye, 217– 218
  Price, Mary Violet
    Leontyne, 227–229
  Verrett, Shirley, 282–283
Osborne, Estelle, 222–223

P

Painters
  Hunter, Clementine
    Clemence Rubin,
    140–142
  Ringgold, Faith, 233–234
  Thomas, Alma, 267–268
Parks, Rosa Louise McCauley,
    224–226
Performers
  Shange, Ntozake, 247–248
Philanthropists
  Malone, Annie Turnbo,
    192–193
  Mason, Biddy Bridget,
    196–197
  Walker, Madame C. J.,
    287–289
Photographers
  Simpson, Coreen, 250–251

Simpson, Lorna, 251–252

Weems, Carrie Mae, 301–303

Physicians
Cole, Rebecca J., 63
Dickens, Helen Octavia, 81–82
Elders, M. Joycelyn Jones, 93–94
Jemison, Mae Carol, 159–161
Lee, Rebecca, 183
Logan, Myra Adele, 187–188

Physicists
Jackson, Shirley Ann, 152–153

Pianists
Williams, Mary Lou, 312–314

Planned Parenthood Federation of America, 300–301

Plato, Ann, 226–227

Playwrights
Childress, Alice, 57–59
Hansberry, Lorraine, 121–122
Jordan, June, 165
Shange, Ntozake, 247–248

Poet laureates
Brooks, Gwendolyn Elizabeth (Illinois), 36–39
Dove, Rita (United States), 82–84
Lorde, Audre Geraldine (New York State), 188–189

Poets
Angelou, Maya, 7–8
Brooks, Gwendolyn Elizabeth, 36–39
Chase-Riboud, Barbara Dewayne, 54–56
Dove, Rita, 82–84

Giovanni, Yolanda Cornelia "Nikki," 107–108
Grimké, Angelina Weld, 113–114
Lorde, Audre Geraldine, 188–189
Plato, Ann, 226–227
Sanchez, Sonia, 243–244
Spencer, Anne (Scales, Annie Bethel), 257–258
Walker, Alice, 287
Walker, Margaret, 291–292
Wheatley, Phillis, 309–312

Political activists. *See also* Activists; Civil rights activists
Davis, Angela Yvonne, 75–76
Walker, Madame C. J., 287–289

Politicians. *See also* Activists; Civil rights activists
Baker, Ella J., and, 17
Belton, Sharon Sales, 27–28
Blackwell, Unita, 34–35
Burke, Yvonne Braithwaite, 43–44
Chisholm, Shirley, 59–60
Fauset, Crystal Dreda Bird, 95–96
Harris, Patricia Roberts, 126–128
Jordan, Barbara Charline, 161–163
Kelly, Sharon Pratt, 170–172
Lampkin, Daisy Elizabeth Adams, 181–183
Moseley-Braun, Carol, 209–212
Norton, Eleanor Holmes, 218–220
Waters, Maxine Moore, 298–300

Pop singers. *See* Singers
Portrait sculptors
Savage, Augusta Christine Fells, 244–247
Preachers
Jackson, Rebecca Cox, 151–152
Price, Mary Violet Leontyne, 227–229
Printmakers
Catlett, Elizabeth, 51
Professors. *See* College professors
Pulitzer Prize winners
Brooks, Gwendolyn Elizabeth, 38
Walker, Alice, 287

Q

Quilt artists
Hunter, Clementine Clemence Rubin, 140–142
Ringgold, Faith, 234

R

Raashad, Phylicia, 2
Radicals
Davis, Angela Yvonne, 75–76
Radio ministers
Horn, Rosa Artimus, 135–137
Rainey, Gertrude Pridgett "Ma," 230–231
Rape, Celia and, 53–54
Ray, Charlotte E., 231
Reformers. *See also* Activists
Jacobs, Harriet Ann, 153–155
Wells-Barnett, Ida Bell, 303–307

Religious leaders
    Harris, Barbara
        Clementine, 124–125
    Horn, Rosa Artimus,
        135–137
    Jackson, Rebecca Cox,
        151–152
    Remond, Sarah Parker,
        232–233
Representatives. *See*
    Congresswomen
Researchers. *See* Cancer
    researchers; Scientists
Rhythm and blues singers. *See
    also* Singers
    Franklin, Aretha Louise,
        99–100
    James, Etta, 156–157
Rights activists. *See* Activists;
    Civil rights activists
Ringgold, Faith, 233–234
Roberts, Patricia, 126–128
Rolle, Esther, 234–236
Roosevelt, Eleanor, 31
Roosevelt, Franklin D., Black
    Cabinet of, 34
Ross, Diana, 236–238
Rudolph, Wilma Glodean,
    238–240

S

Saar, Betye Irene, 241–243
Sanchez, Sonia, 243–244
Savage, Augusta Christine
    Fells, 244–247
Scales, Annie Bethel. *See*
    Spencer, Anne
SCEF. *See* Southern
    Conference
    Educational Fund
    (SCEF)
Schools. *See* Education; spe-
    cific schools

Science fiction writing
    Butler, Octavia Estelle,
        46–47
Scientists. *See also*
    Mathematicians
    Jackson, Shirley Ann,
        152–153
    Lloyd, Ruth Smith,
        186–187
    Wright, Jane Cooke, 321
    Young, Roger Arliner,
        322–323
SCLC. *See* Southern
    Christian Leadership
    Conference (SCLC)
Scruggs, Mary Elfrieda. *See*
    Williams, Mary Lou
Sculptors
    Catlett, Elizabeth, 51
    Chase-Riboud, Barbara
        Dewayne, 54–56
    Fuller, Meta Vaux Warrick,
        100–103
    Lewis, Edmonia, 183–186
    Ringgold, Faith, 233–234
    Savage, Augusta Christine
        Fells, 244–247
Senators
    Moseley-Braun, Carol,
        209–212
Sexual harassment, Hill,
    Anita, and, 131,
    132–133
Shange, Ntozake, 247–248
Short-story writers
    Butler, Octavia Estelle,
        46–47
    McMillan, Terry, 202–203
Simone, Nina (Waymon,
    Eunice Kathleen), 249
Simpson, Coreen, 250–251
Simpson, Lorna, 251–252
Singers
    Anderson, Marian, 4–6
    Bailey, Pearl, 13–14

Battle, Kathleen, 25–27
Carroll, Diahann, 48–49
Dandridge, Dorothy,
    72–74
Fitzgerald, Ella, 96–98
Flack, Roberta, 98–99
Franklin, Aretha Louise,
    99–100
Holiday, Billie, 134–135
Horne, Lena, 137–138
Houston, Whitney,
    138–140
Jackson, Janet, 147–149
Jackson, Mahalia, 149–151
James, Etta, 156–157
Kitt, Eartha Mae, 176–177
Knight, Gladys, 177–179
LaBelle, Patti, 180–181
McDaniel, Hattie,
    199–201
McRae, Carmen, 205–206
Norman, Jessye, 217–218
Price, Mary Violet
    Leontyne, 227–229
Rainey, Gertrude Pridgett
    "Ma," 230–231
Ross, Diana, 236–238
Simone, Nina (Waymon,
    Eunice Kathleen), 249
Smith, Bessie, 253–255
Smith, Mamie, 255–256
Tharpe, Sister Rosetta, 266
Thornton, Willie Mae "Big
    Mama," 269–270
Turner, Tina, 277–279
Vaughan, Sarah, 281–282
Verrett, Shirley, 282–283
Warwick, Dionne,
    292–293
Washington, Dinah (Jones,
    Ruth Lee), 293–294
Waters, Ethel, 296–298
Slaves and slavery. *See also*
    Abolitionists
    Celia, 53–54

Craft, Ellen, 67–69
Jacobs, Harriet Ann, and, 153–155
Keckley, Elizabeth, and, 169–170
Smith, Bessie, 253–255
Smith, Jane, 129
Smith, Mamie, 255–256
SNCC. *See* Student Nonviolent Coordinating Committee (SNCC)
Social reformers. *See also* Activists
Cole, Rebecca J., 63
Matthews, Victoria Earle (Smith), 197–199
Soul music. *See* Singers
Southern Christian Leadership Conference (SCLC)
Baker, Ella J., and, 16
Clark, Septima Poinsette, and, 62–73
Nash, Diane Bevel, and, 215
Parks, Rosa Louise McCauley, and, 226
Southern Conference Educational Fund (SCEF), Baker, Ella J., and, 16
Spencer, Anne (Scales, Annie Bethel), 257–258
Spingarn Medal, Jordan, Barbara Charline, and, 162
Spiritualists
Truth, Sojourner, 270–273
Sports. *See* Athletes
Standard American English (SAE), 145
Stereotypes, of "Mammy" character, 201

Stewart, Pearl, 258–259
Student Nonviolent Coordinating Committee (SNCC), 35
Baker, Ella J., and, 16–17
Hamer, Fannie Lou, and, 119–120
Nash, Diane Bevel, and, 35
Suffragists. *See* Women's rights activists
Supreme Court, Thomas, Clarence, and, 132–133
Supremes, 236, 237
Surgeons General
Elders, M. Joycelyn Jones, 93–94
Surgeons. *See also* Physicians
Logan, Myra Adele, 187–188
Swoopes, Sheryl, 259–261

T

Talk-show hosts
Winfrey, Oprah Gail, 318–320
Tanner family
Alexander, Sadie T. M., 1
Taylor, Susie Baker King, 262–263
Teachers. *See* Educators
Television
Allen, Debbie, 2–3
Angelou, Maya, and, 8
Carroll, Diahann, 49
Tennis players
Garrison, Zena, 104–105
Gibson, Althea, 105–107
Williams, Venus, 314–316
Terrell, Mary Eliza Church, 263–265

Tharpe, Sister Rosetta, 266
Theater
Childress, Alice, 57–59
Theater Owners Booking Association (TOBA), 253
Thomas, Alma, 267–268
Thomas, Clarence, 131, 132–133
Thomas, Debra J. "Debi," 268–269
Thornton, Willie Mae "Big Mama," 269–270
TOBA. *See* Theater Owners Booking Association (TOBA)
Townsend, Fannie Lou. *See* Hamer, Fannie Lou
Track and field
Ashford, Evelyn, 11–12
Griffith-Joyner, Florence Delorez, 111–113
Joyner-Kersee, Jacqueline, 165–167
Truth, Sojourner, 270–273
Tubman, Harriet Ross, 274–277
Turner, Tina, 277–279
Tyson, Cicely, 279–280

U

Underground Railroad, Tubman, Harriet Ross, and, 274–275
UNIA. *See* United Negro Improvement Association (UNIA)
United Nations
Anderson, Marian, and, 6
Bailey, Pearl, and, 14
United Negro Improvement Association (UNIA), 306

Universities and colleges
Bethune-Cookman
College, 32
Howard University, 51

V

Vaughan, Sarah, 281–282
Vernacular, Black English,
145
Verrett, Shirley, 282–283
Voting rights. *See also* Civil
rights activists
Guinier, Lani, and,
116–117

W

Walker, A'Lelia, 284–285,
288, 289
Walker, Alice, 285–287
Walker, Madame C. J.,
287–289
Walker, Maggie Lena,
289–291
Walker, Margaret, 291–292
Warwick, Dionne, 292–293
Washington, Dinah (Jones,
Ruth Lee), 293–294
Washington, Margaret
Murray, 294–295
Watergate scandal, Jordan,
Barbara Charline and,
162
Waters, Ethel, 296–298
Waters, Maxine Moore,
298–300
Wattleton, Faye, 300–301
Waymon, Eunice Kathleen.
See Simone, Nina
Weems, Carrie Mae,
301–303

Wells-Barnett, Ida Bell,
303–307
West, Dorothy, 307–308
Wheatley, Phyllis, 309–312
Williams, Mary Lou (Scruggs,
Mary Elfrieda), 312–314
Williams, Venus, 314–316
Wilson, Harriet E. Adams,
316–318
Winfrey, Oprah Gail, 318–320
WNBA. *See* Women's
National Basketball
Association (WNBA)
Women's club movement
Bethune, Mary McLeod,
and, 33
Height, Dorothy, and,
128–130
Washington, Margaret
Murray, and, 294–295
Women's National Basketball
Association (WNBA),
259, 261
Women's rights activists. *See
also* Activists
Harper, Frances Ellen
Watkins, 122–124
Height, Dorothy, 128–130
Terrell, Mary Eliza Church,
263–265
Truth, Sojourner, 270–273
Wells-Barnett, Ida Bell,
306
Wright, Jane Cooke, 321
Writers. *See also* Journalists;
Novelists; Poets
Angelou, Maya, 6–9
Bambara, Toni Cade,
20–21
Butler, Octavia Estelle,
46–47
Chideay, Farai, 56–57
Cooper, Anna Julia
Haywood, 65–67

Dunbar-Nelson, Alice,
84–86
Granville, Evelyn Boyd,
110–111
Grimké, Angelina Weld,
113–114
Grimké, Charlotte L.
Forten, 114–115
Harper, Frances Ellen
Watkins, 122–124
Hurston, Zora Neale,
142–146
Jacobs, Harriet Ann,
153–155
Jordan, June, 163–165
Kincaid, Jamaica,
172–173
Marshall, Paule, 193–196
Matthews, Victoria Earle
(Smith), 197–199
McMillan, Terry, 202–203
Morrison, Toni, 206–209
Naylor, Gloria, 215–216
Taylor, Susie Baker King,
262–263
Walker, Alice, 285–287
Walker, Margaret,
291–292
West, Dorothy, 307–308
Wilson, Harriet E. Adams,
316–318

Y

Young, Roger Arliner,
322–323

Z

Zoologists
Young, Roger Arliner,
322–323